THE BLOOMSBURY BOOK OF THE MIND

THE BLOOMSBURY BOOK OF THE MIND

Key writings on the mind from Plato and the Buddha through Shakespeare, Descartes and Freud to the latest discoveries of neuroscience

EDITED BY
STEPHEN WILSON

BLOOMSBURY

First published in Great Britain 2003

This paperback edition published 2004

Introductions, selection and arrangement copyright © Stephen Wilson 2003

For copyright purposes the acknowledgements pages constitute a
continuation of the copyright page.

Every reasonable effort has been made to trace all copyright holders of illustrative and
other copyright material reproduced in this book, but if any have been inadvertently
overlooked the publishers would be glad to hear from them.

The moral right of the author has been asserted

Bloomsbury Publishing Plc, 38 Soho Square, London W1D 3HB
A CIP catalogue record for this book is available from the British Library
ISBN 0 7475 6857 X

10 9 8 7 6 5 4 3 2 1

All paper used by Bloomsbury Publishing, including that in this book,
is a natural, recyclable product made from wood grown in sustainable,
well-managed forests. The manufacturing processes conform to the
environmental regulations of the country of origin.

Typeset by Palimpsest Book Production Limited,
Polmont, Stirlingshire
Printed in Great Britain by
Clays Ltd, St Ives plc

In memory of Anthony Storr (1920–2001),
who encouraged me to do this book.

Perhaps there is nothing in Nature more pleasing than the study of the human mind . . .

John Hunter (1728–1793)

CONTENTS

PREFACE

How can we speak of the action of the mind under any divisions, as of its knowledge, of its ethics, of its works, and so forth, since it melts will into perception, knowledge into act? Each becomes the other. Itself alone is. Its vision is not like the vision of the eye, but is union with the things known.

Ralph Waldo Emerson, 'Intellect', *Essays* (*1841*)

This book is about the human mind and is meant for the general reader. It is intended to be informative but not dogmatic. Anthologies should also give pleasure, so I have leavened the material by mixing different types of writing. There are poems and extracts from novels, essays, passages from diaries and medical case-histories as well as psychological theories, philosophy both ancient and modern and scientific reports. The main guideline I have followed is to include original source material for 'key ideas' which have become familiar – Descartes' 'Cogito', Pavlov on 'the conditioned reflex', Jung on 'the collective unconscious' or Freud on 'the Oedipus complex'. For the sake of readability I have sometimes ignored footnotes and references in these texts, translated a passage myself, or rendered an archaic excerpt into modern English. When an older version seemed more eloquent I have left it alone. Translations aside, all the secondary glosses are my own.

I have been attracted to some pieces of writing because they represent an early statement of something that still seems true, or that modern science has elaborated but not undermined. Others, both old and new, seem to me patently false, but I have included them because they represent a significant strand of opinion, or because they are charming, or because they speak to my sense of the bizarre. I have made no attempt to separate descriptions of 'normal' psychology from those of mental 'pathology', preferring to leave them side by side as phenomena of equal fascination. My professional background in psychiatry may have biased my choice in favour of the latter, but more often than not psychopathology is a kind of magnifying glass that shows the detail of normal functioning 'writ large'. I have partitioned most of the material into four chapters on mental faculties: perception; memory; emotion; and thought. The fifth chapter is devoted to the problem of consciousness and the perennial philosophical mind–body problem. Finally in Chapter 6, I deal with the 'self' including the unconscious mind, the problems of conflict and co-ordination, and the mental organization as a whole. However, as Ralph Waldo Emerson indicates, there is no way that the action of the mind can be adequately boxed. I am aware that much of the material could as well come under one heading as another, so I have tried to cross-reference wherever I thought this would be useful, using an asterisk where I have not given an exact page reference, to indicate that the person or idea referred to makes an appearance elsewhere in the book.

When I set out on this job, I supposed it easier than it turned out to be. Certainly there was no dearth of material, rather I was confronted with an embarrassment of choice. And every day, as it seemed, I came across more that offered itself for consideration, demanded to be digested and condensed, needed to be incorporated and organized. Although I have included work from people generally recognized to be major contributors, there is nothing encyclopaedic about this book. It is about as idiosyncratic as you could get. And I feel a responsibility to warn against attempting to swallow it whole. In offering it to the reader I am reminded of the words of Ecclesiastes and feel chastened – 'And furthermore, my son, be admonished: of making many books there is no end; and much study is a weariness of the flesh.'

INTRODUCTION

There is nothing we know better than our own mind, yet at the same time it remains obstinately resistant to scientific investigation. Advances in modern technology have allowed us increasing insight into the functioning of the human brain but the mind, by which we usually mean our subjective consciousness – the way it feels to be ourselves – appears to have no physical existence and therefore no spacial location. If we inspect the interior of our head we will not find it. During the 1990s, a period of time designated by the United States President and Congress as the 'Decade of the Brain', an enormous research effort was directed towards unlocking the secrets of cerebral functioning. Neuroscientists, psychologists, psychopharmacologists and clinicians co-operated in thousands of studies and a public campaign was set up to inform people about the benefits of brain research. Much new knowledge was accumulated concerning the way the brain reacts to environmental stimuli, transmits chemical messages across nerve junctions and processes information. With the help of modern scanning techniques we are no longer limited to a static 'anatomical' view of the brain, we can actually watch it at work, see which parts 'light up' when we act and when we think. For example, in the clinical field it has long been known that depressed patients admitted to hospital and treated with 'milieu therapy' and group psychotherapy may have a beneficial response that is indistinguishable from that associated with antidepressant drugs. We now know that there is a similar pattern of brain activity in both cases.[1]

Just how this brain activity is related to subjective experience remains a mystery. Brain scans send us information about the objective state of things rather like photographs which the

1 Helen Mayberg et al., *American Journal of Psychiatry* 159 (2002), 728–37.

Voyager space craft captures from distant planets. But pictures of 'inner space' cannot be obtained in the same way. For this we need to rely on old-fashioned communication, personal report, literature, art and music. In a sense we are all experts on the mind. We know what it means to think, feel, believe; to perceive, imagine, dream; to calculate, reason, plan; to intend and carry out actions. When we watch others, or search our own souls, we can come up with insights and explanations. We infer motives for behaviour that have an immediate appeal and ring true. Most of us are probably better at doing this than most professional psychologists. But nowadays philosophers of mind call this normal way of understanding ourselves 'folk psychology', and some hold that it is nothing but an illusion, a fairy-story we like to tell about ourselves which keeps us from a real understanding of our mental processes. Until the end of the nineteenth century it was all we had.

By the late 1800s, however, the remarkable success of physics and chemistry in understanding the natural world created a climate of optimism and a growing belief that the phenomena of the human mind could be explained by science. These phenomena included a range of extraordinary processes which had become the object of popular interest. Among them were the curious and sometimes intractable handicaps associated with *hysteria* – blindness, paralysis, fits. And odd psychological manifestations such as multiple personality, selective memory loss, and fugue states in which a person wanders off forgetting his or her own identity. The fact that all these conditions occurred in the absence of an obvious bodily cause, and in otherwise fully conscious individuals, suggested the operation of a hidden level of psychic function. When the famous French neurologist Jean-Martin Charcot demonstrated that hysterical signs of disease could be both induced and relieved by hypnotic suggestion, the existence of the unconscious mind seemed undeniable.

Thus modern psychology was born as an independent field of enquiry, divided from the outset into two approaches: 'experimental psychology' and 'depth psychology'. Both professed allegiance to the spirit of science, but whereas laboratories of experimental psychology sought to apply the methods of empirical observation to the apparently very private material of the mind, depth psychology (associated with the names of Sigmund Freud and his sometime associates Carl Gustav Jung and Alfred Adler) invented a very personal method, deriving its data from the prolonged study of individual cases in the intimate setting of the psychoanalytic consulting room.

Experimental psychology could be publicly verified and focused on calibration, measurement and the manipulation of psychological variables in strictly controlled settings. Depth psychology, through the interpretation of dreams, symbols, free associations and the relationship between analyst and patient, claimed to have found a way into the unconscious mind, though it was only visible to those who had been initiated into its procedures. The former was vulnerable to the accusation that what it investigated was so far removed from the context of everyday life that its findings were uninteresting and irrelevant – essentially trivial. The latter suffered from the shortcomings of esoteric procedures, unrepresentative samples, uncorroborated results and unfalsifiable hypotheses. Critics claimed that it 'explained everything and predicted nothing'.

Despite the anecdotal therapeutic successes to which psychoanalysis can point and the piecemeal accumulation of observational data resulting from experiment, it is probably true to say that psychology has not fulfilled its early promise. Experimental psychologists have singularly failed to produce laws that would predict human behaviour with the same degree of precision that physicists can predict the behaviour of atoms and molecules or biologists that of genes and chromosomes. Psychoanalysts, on the other hand, have cracked into a thousand therapeutic shards. They have failed to develop a coherent and generally accepted theory, and in many cases retreated into intuitionism, preferring to regard their activities as an inspirational art or craft.

There is always a good deal of suspicion concerning the results of internal enquiries. When an organization such as the police or the army sets the terms of an investigation into its own conduct, we are justifiably circumspect about the validity of its findings, and we must extend the same scepticism to our own attempts at self-knowledge. Perhaps the human mind is incapable of knowing itself in any objective way? None the less a programme of research has been going on since the beginning of history, and it is part of the purpose of this book to review how far we've got. That we have a long way to go is beyond doubt. The neuroscientist Michael Gazzaniga says, '. . . we are a light year or two away from truly understanding how the brain does its business . . .' But now more than ever, we are witnessing a rapprochement between the different disciplines concerned with mental phenomena. The twenty-first century may yet turn out to be the 'Century of the Mind'.

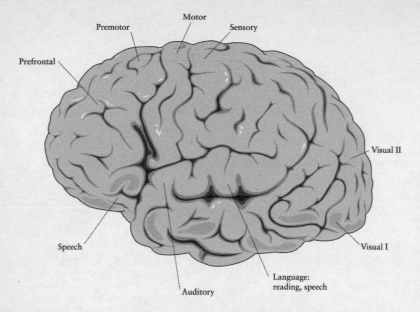

External view of the left cerebral hemisphere

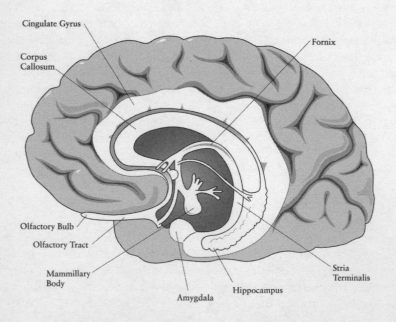

Diagram of the left cerebral hemisphere cut through from front to back

PERCEPTION

DO NOT ADJUST YOUR MIND:
REALITY IS AT FAULT

Graffito, men's toilet, Oxford Mental Health Service

As we go about our lives, we experience ourselves and the world in which we live in the form of mental representations or pictures in our minds. Broadly speaking we recognize two kinds, those which correspond with an immediately present external object and those which do not. Our normal perception through sight, sound, smell, taste, touch, balance and position, generates the first group. We owe these experiences to the effect of an external stimulus on our sense organs. The second kind of mental picture appears to originate spontaneously within ourselves and belongs to our imagination.

The distinction may seem obvious but most of us regularly get confused between the two and experience hallucinations of such intensity that we could swear they were real while they were happening. When these mistakes occur while we are asleep and we recognize them in our waking state, we say we have been dreaming. If the confusion persists we are suffering from a 'disorder of perception'. However, even when we are fully awake and functioning normally, we are not too difficult to fool. A series of well-known optical illusions demonstrates that what we see is not necessarily what is there. Identical parallel lines with flèches on the ends pointing in different directions appear to be different in length; a bright white square on a duller background each of whose corners appears to mask a quarter segment of a black disc is in fact a flat pattern with no foreground or background, no delineated square, no edges and no tonal difference in whiteness.

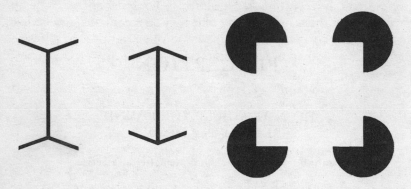

There is reality, says the graffito, and there is what goes on in our minds and they are different. If this discrepancy was a major problem, if our perceptions were totally out of kilter with the outside world, we would not get far. We would be bumping into lampposts all over the place. In fact our senses are generally reliable, it is only when they fail, and especially if we are unaware they are failing, that we get into trouble. People unfortunate enough to lose their protective sense of pain know this to their cost, and are continuously in danger of injuring themselves, as are patients on an operating table whose senses have been switched off by anaesthesia. But because we know our minds can be such skilled counterfeiters, the questions Descartes* so strikingly formulated, as to how active a part our internal processes play in shaping perception, how accurate a likeness of the external world we receive, and to what extent we can rely on it, distinguish internal from external, are never far away. They have informed philosophical debate for centuries, and in modern times stimulated scientific investigation.

At one end of the spectrum are those theories which see the mind as essentially passive – a 'tabula rasa' or blank slate, according to the seventeenth-century English philosopher John Locke*, on to which sense impressions inscribe their outlines. At the other end are those theories which see the mind as actively constructing perceptions out of its own bank of preconceived, remembered or possibly innate patterns, selecting and organizing from a variable input of more or less sensory data.

What we perceive is not a simple function of what gets written on our sense receptors. It depends to a large extent on the way we interpret the sensory input, which in turn depends upon what we are able to *conceive*. Furthermore our attention is selective and we are inclined to fill in the gaps with 'well-informed' guesses. For example, despite the fact that a 'blind spot' exists on our retina where the optic nerve leaves the eye (because there are no cells there to receive incoming light stimuli), our visual field appears uninterrupted. We do not see a hole in everything we look at. Conversely, we do routinely ignore certain light stimuli reaching the eye. We do not see objects in our visual fields which are irrelevant to our aims and expectations, as when we fail to find the butter in the fridge when it is under our nose, because it is not in the usual position. The magician's sleight of hand deceives us. Our contextual expectations and emotional state influence not only what we notice, but how we define it. A door creaking at night during the telling of a ghost-story, or the sudden flutter of wings sound different, louder, more threatening, than in daytime. And we are likely to construct a different story about its significance. Our sense organs register information from the outside world, our brains process it, and our minds perceive it. We do not see with our eyes, but with the whole of our mental apparatus. In order to perceive we must be able to conceive.

A number of advances in neuroscientific technique have enabled us to get a better idea of what parts of the brain are involved. Before the development of brain-imaging technology, most of our information came from the study of lesions, either experimentally or therapeutically induced, or occurring naturally as a result of injury and disease. If a given part of the brain was out of order and a very specific deficit in perception resulted, it could be inferred that that particular part of the brain was necessary (but not necessarily sufficient) for perception to occur. In this way, certain areas of the cortex of the brain were discovered to be required for vision, others for the experience of sound and so on.

Our ability to record electrical activity in a single brain cell, together with scanning techniques that show where there is increased bloodflow, or increased metabolic activity, for example glucose consumption, have led to a far more detailed picture. For example it is now thought that we become aware of the boundary between one object and another through the action of special 'edge detector' cells in the occipital lobe at the back of the brain. These cells respond to variations in the intensity of light falling upon the retina. Nerve impulses also travel from the retina to a large number of other brain areas which 'specialize' in receiving particular types of information. Some neurons are maximally responsive to line orientation, firing in response to particular angles, others sensitive to colour will respond to a particular wavelength, yet others respond to motion, correlating their activity with the velocity of the perceived object. There are interconnections between all these areas, but there is no single area which contains the whole picture. Moreover, it appears that imagining an object with one's eyes closed, say a Christmas pudding, results in activation of the same areas of the visual cortex as would be activated by seeing it with one's eyes open. It has been suggested that stored information from previous visual experience enhances the incoming sensory data to produce a well-defined picture.

Such theories, which privilege the contribution of past experience, point to the relatively scanty sense data we are prepared to accept as the basis for constructing a perception. We do not require a full sensory report on the characteristics of an object, nor do we have time to test every aspect before deciding what and where it is. Rather we seem to work on a probability basis; given a few sensory hints, we are inclined to believe that an object has certain properties and will behave in a particular way. If we see a foot swinging towards a small spherical object, we assume (and predict until proved otherwise) that the object is filled with air not lead. If we see a beefy athlete holding a small spherical object, we not only expect the opposite, we actually perceive the sphere as heavy.

But if all perceptions are 'fictions', or tentative hypotheses, which owe more to past experience than to incoming present stimuli, how are we to account for the very first ones? And how is past experience constructed, if not out of perceptions which have arisen in some more direct way? Questions such as these led psychologists Eleanor and James Gibson to propose a new 'ecological' theory of perception in the 1950s.[1] Dispensing with 'past experience' as the determining factor, the Gibsons proposed that from the very beginning our senses actively scanned the environment looking for sustained patterns of stimuli. They enabled us to navigate (on the whole) safely, because they sought and found arrays of stimuli which were indeed constantly conjoined, thus providing an accurate report on the outside world. It was the true and invariant nature of objects, faithfully investigated and differentiated by our sensory systems, rather than the fictional constructions generated by previous experience, they said, which shaped our developing relations with the world around us. We constantly probed, analysed and tested our world, we did not make it up on the basis of precarious past associations.

Turning now to those experiences which we readily admit are products of our imagination, there has, over the years, been an equally strong division of opinion as to how they should be valued. Genesis tells us that God brought about a flood because he saw that in man 'every imagination of the thoughts of his heart *was* only evil continually.'[2] And Plato, famously, would have banned certain poets from his State, precisely because they called into imaginative being emotions, opinions and situations of which he disapproved.[3] Imagination, he thought, was subversive. Yet others, typified by romantic poets such as Coleridge and Blake, have seen in human imagination the highest good, the most divine manifestation of our being. Certainly the source of both scientific and artistic creativity.

Where imagination is concerned, the question of good and bad is closely related to another issue, its 'truth-telling' function. Is it merely a species of lie? Or is it a purveyor of eternal truth?

---

1 For an up-to-date overview of this work see Eleanor Gibson and Anne Pick, *An Ecological Approach to Perceptual Learning and Development*, OUP, 2000.
2 See Chapter 7, verse 5.
3 See *Republic* III, 386–98.

If imagination is simply seen as a faulty kind of perception, it can do nothing but misguide us, and even if it is seen as an accurate reflector, it can do nothing but rearrange existing aspects of external reality – a relatively trivial function.[4] But the degree of correspondence between imaginary constructions and external reality is only one dimension. A second and more profound level involves the nature of the reports which imagination gives us on internal reality. When we become confused in the former case, we are outwardly disoriented and at risk; when our imagination deceives us in the latter case, we seem outwardly 'normal' but we are in danger of being untrue to ourselves, of betraying our deepest loves and embracing our most reviled values. On this view then, if we are to truly know ourselves, distinguishing between the inner and outer worlds is not enough. Once we have located an experience in the arena of our imagination, we are still left with the altogether more difficult task of evaluating its quality, its meaning, its degree of emotional integrity.

SENSATIONS AND IDEAS

The Internal Construction of Sensations

The name of Jean-Jacques Rousseau (1712–78) is not primarily associated with the philosophy of mind. He is more remembered for his critique of social institutions and optimistic faith in man's underlying nature – 'Man is born free', he famously declared in the opening chapter of the Social Contract, *'and everywhere he is in chains.' However, the following passage from* Emile, *a treatise on education, provides as good a statement as any of the rationale for an 'active' theory of perception.*

Rousseau's mother died shortly after his birth in Geneva, Switzerland, and his father, a watchmaker, left for France during his childhood. He was brought up by relatives of his parents and had no formal education. In his youth he was apprenticed to an engraver, but at the age of fifteen parted from his master and adopted a peripatetic lifestyle. Despite his apparent concern with

4 But see George Henry Lewes, pp. 21–4.

*the well-being of children, he fathered five of his own with an
illiterate maid-servant, all of whom were committed to a
foundling hospital. Supported partly by his own efforts and partly
by the generosity of friends and patrons, he travelled widely in
Europe, taking on a series of teaching and clerical posts. At the
age of thirty-eight he won first prize in an essay competition run
by the Academy of Dijon, on the subject of 'Science and the
Arts'. Thereafter he published important contributions in the
fields of political philosophy, moral theology, music and drama.
He also wrote novels, carried out a prodigious correspondence,
and published a confessional autobiography.*

My sensations take place in myself, for they make me aware of
my own existence; but their cause is outside me, for they affect
me whether I have any reason for them or not, and they are
produced or destroyed independently of me. So I clearly perceive
that my sensation, which is within me, and its cause or its object
which is outside me, are different things.

Thus, not only do I exist, but other entities exist also, that is
to say, the objects of my sensations; and even if these objects are
merely ideas, still these ideas are not me.

But everything outside myself, everything which acts upon my
senses, I call matter, and all the particles of matter which I suppose
to be united in separate entities I call bodies. Thus all the disputes
of the idealists and the realists have no meaning for me; their
distinctions between the appearance and the reality of bodies are
wholly fanciful.

I am now as convinced of the existence of the universe as of
my own. I next consider the objects of my sensations, and I find
that I have the power of comparing them, so I perceive that I
am endowed with an active force of which I was not previously
aware.

To perceive is to feel; to compare is to judge; to judge and to
feel are not the same. Through sensation objects present themselves to me separately and singly as they are in nature; by
comparing them I rearrange them, I shift them so to speak, I
place one upon another to decide whether they are alike or

different, or more generally to find out their relations. To my mind, the distinctive faculty of an active or intelligent being is the power of understanding this word 'is'. I seek in vain in the merely sensitive entity that intelligent force which compares and judges; I can find no trace of it in its nature. This passive entity will be aware of each object separately, it will even be aware of the whole formed by the two together, but having no power to place them side by side it can never compare them, it can never form a judgement with regard to them.

To see two things at once is not to see their relations nor to judge of their differences; to perceive several objects, one beyond the other, is not to relate them. I may have at the same moment an idea of a big stick and a little stick without comparing them, without judging that one is less than the other, just as I can see my whole hand without counting my fingers. These comparative ideas, *greater, smaller*, together with number ideas of *one, two etc.*, are certainly not sensations, although my mind only produces them when my sensations occur.

We are told that a sensitive being distinguishes sensations from each other by the inherent differences in the sensations; this requires explanation. When the sensations are different, the sensitive being distinguishes them by their differences; when they are alike, he distinguishes them because he is aware of them one beyond the other. Otherwise, how could he distinguish between two equal objects simultaneously experienced? He would necessarily confound the two objects and take them for one object, especially under a system which professed that the representative sensations of space have no extension.

When we become aware of the two sensations to be compared, their impression is made, each object is perceived, both are perceived, but for all that their relation is not perceived. If the judgement of this relation were merely a sensation, and came to me solely from the object itself, my judgements would never be mistaken, for it is never untrue that I feel what I feel.

Why then am I mistaken as to the relation between these two sticks, especially when they are not parallel? Why, for example, do I say the small stick is a third of the large, when it is only a quarter? Why is the picture, which is the sensation, unlike its model which is the object? It is because I am active when I judge, because the operation of comparison is at fault; because my understanding, which judges of relations, mingles its errors with the truth of sensations, which only reveal to me things.

Add to this a consideration which will, I feel sure, appeal to you when you have thought about it: it is this – If we were purely passive in the use of our senses, there would be no communication between them; it would be impossible to know that the body we are touching and the thing we are looking at is the same. Either we should never perceive anything outside ourselves, or there would be for us five substances perceptible by the senses, whose identity we should have no means of perceiving.

This power of my mind which brings my sensations together and compares them may be called by any name; let it be called attention, meditation, reflection, or what you will; it is still true that it is in me and not in things, that it is I alone who produce it, though I only produce it when I receive an impression from things. Though I am compelled to feel or not to feel, I am free to examine more or less what I feel.

Jean-Jacques Rousseau, *Emile* (1792)

The Source of Ideas

There are no innate ideas. John Locke's celebrated seventeenth-century argument against the in-born presence of ideas became the foundation for the British empirical tradition of philosophy. Counter to the Platonic notion that we come into the world equipped with a built-in package of concepts, Locke claimed that all our ideas were derived from experience. However, this did not mean that all our ideas were derived from sense-data, for Locke recognized two sources of experience: sensation and reflection. The latter being derived internally, from introspective observation of the various activities going on in our minds. If the ideas themselves are not innate, the capacity to perform the operations which 'reflection' then translates into ideas, might still be held to be so. Some modern neuroscience propounds a model of the mind which depends on an interaction between innate potentials for setting up neural networks, and experience.[5] Ideas – conscious ideas, are seen to derive from a staged process in the brain, whereby a small proportion of the brain's multifarious information processing activity is somehow given the quality of 'awareness'.

Locke (1632–1704) was the first son of an anti-Royalist Somerset lawyer. He was educated at Westminster School and Christ Church, Oxford, where he took courses in logic, metaphysics and classical languages. Oxford at that time was under Puritan control, and perhaps unsurprisingly, Locke's first published work was a poem written for Oliver Cromwell.

Under the influence of the great scientist Robert Boyle, he developed an interest in experimentation and went on to train as a physician. At the age of thirty-six, he was elected Fellow of the Royal Society. In the following years he began work on his Essay Concerning Human Understanding, *which was not published until 1690 after William III (of Orange) had succeeded to the English throne. His* Two Treatises of Government *was also published in the same year, a key source for later liberal-democratic ideas. Locke had been involved in Whig politics which denied the divine right of Charles II to rule, and in 1683 had fled to Holland. On returning to England after the Glorious Revolution, he met and became a friend of Isaac Newton, with whom he corresponded for the rest of his life.*

2. Let us then suppose the mind to be, as we say, white paper void of all characters, without any *ideas*. How comes it to be furnished? Whence comes it by that vast store which the busy and boundless fancy of man has painted on it with an almost endless variety? Whence has it all the materials of reason and knowledge? To this I answer, in one word, from *experience*; in that all our knowledge is founded, and from that it ultimately derives itself. Our observation, employed either about *external sensible objects, or about the internal operations of our minds perceived and reflected upon by ourselves, is that which supplies our understandings with all the materials of thinking.* These two

5 See Gerald Edelman, pp. 272–7.

are the fountains of knowledge, from whence all the *ideas* we
have, or can naturally have, do spring.

3. First, *our senses*, conversant about particular sensible
objects, do *convey into the mind* several distinct *perceptions* of
things, according to those various ways wherein those objects do
affect them. And thus we come by those *ideas* we have of *yellow,
white, heat, cold, soft, hard, bitter, sweet*, and all those which
we call sensible qualities; which when I say the senses convey
into the mind, I mean, they from external objects convey into
the mind what produces there those *perceptions*. This great
source of most of the *ideas* we have, depending wholly upon
our senses, and derived by them to the understanding, I call
SENSATION.

4. Secondly, the other fountain from which experience
furnisheth the understanding with *ideas* is the *perception of the
operations of our own minds* within us, as it is employed about
the *ideas* it has got; which operations, when the soul comes to
reflect on and consider, do furnish the understanding with another
set of *ideas*, which could not be had from things without. And
such are *perception, thinking, doubting, believing, reasoning,
knowing, willing*, and all the different actings of our own minds;
which we, being conscious of and observing in ourselves, do from
these receive into our understandings as distinct *ideas* as we do
from bodies affecting our senses. This source of *ideas* every man
has wholly in himself; and though it be not sense, as having
nothing to do with external objects, yet it is very like it, and might
properly enough be called internal sense. But as I call the other
sensation, so I call this REFLECTION, the *ideas* it affords being
such only as the mind gets by reflecting on its own operations
within itself. By REFLECTION then, in the following part of this
discourse, I would be understood to mean that notice which the
mind takes of its own operations, and the manner of them, by
reason thereof there come to be *ideas* of these operations in the
understanding. These two, I say, viz. external material things as
the objects of SENSATION, and the operations of our own minds
within as the objects of REFLECTION, are to me the only originals from whence all our *ideas* take their beginnings. The term
operations here I use in a large sense, as comprehending not barely

the actions of the mind about its *ideas*, but some sort of passions arising sometimes from them, such as is the satisfaction or uneasiness arising from any thought.

John Locke, 'Of Ideas in General, and their Original', *An Essay Concerning Human Understanding* (1690)

Perceptions Are Unconscious Inferences

Hermann von Helmholtz's notion that there could be inferences without consciousness was rejected by many who came afterwards as an impossibility. Today, in the age of computer science and artificial intelligence, it seems perfectly acceptable. Born in Potsdam, Germany, in 1821, he was the son of a local secondary school teacher. He developed an early interest in physics, but lacking the means to attend university, he undertook training as a military surgeon, which was free. During his student days he became friends with Dubois-Reymond, Virchow and Brücke, all of whom were students of Physiology at the University of Berlin. Together they pledged themselves to abjure 'vitalism' and expound the principle that 'No other forces than common physical chemical ones are active within the organism.' The young Sigmund Freud was educated under the influence of these Helmholtzian ideas.

Helmholtz made important contributions in both physics and physiology. At the age of twenty-six he read a paper on the indestructibility of energy to the Physical Society of Berlin. In 1851 he invented the ophthalmoscope, an instrument for examining the interior of the eye. In 1855 he was appointed Professor of Anatomy and Physiology at Bonn and three years later moved to a chair of Physiology at Heidelberg. He worked on a wide range of problems including measuring the speed of nerve impulses, hearing and the physiology of vision. In 1870 he moved to Berlin, where he had been offered the chair in Physics.

Helmholtz visited the United States in 1893 but suffered a severe accident on the return journey when he fell down the ship's companionway, from which he never fully recovered. He died of a stroke the following year, at the age of seventy-three.

The psychic activities that lead us to infer that in front of us at a certain place there is a certain object of a certain character are generally not conscious activities, but unconscious ones. In their result they are equivalent to a *conclusion*, to the extent that the observed action on our senses enables us to form an idea as to the possible cause of this action; although, as a matter of fact, it is invariably simply the nervous stimulations that are perceived directly, that is, the actions, but never the external objects themselves. But what seems to differentiate them from a conclusion, in the ordinary sense of that word, is that a conclusion is an act of conscious thought. An astronomer, for example, comes to real conscious conclusions of this sort, when he computes the positions of the stars in space, their distances, etc., from the perspective images he has had of them at various times and as they are seen from different parts of the orbit of the earth. His conclusions are based on a conscious knowledge of the laws of optics. In the ordinary acts of vision this knowledge of optics is lacking. Still it may be permissible to speak of the psychic acts of ordinary perception as *unconscious conclusions*, thereby making a distinction of some sort between them and the common so-called conscious conclusions. And while it is true that there has been, and probably always will be, a measure of doubt as to the similarity of the psychic activity in the two cases, there can be no doubt as to the similarity between the results of such unconscious conclusions and those of conscious conclusions.

These unconscious conclusions derived from sensation are equivalent in their consequences to the so-called *conclusions from analogy*. Inasmuch as in an overwhelming majority of cases, whenever the parts of the retina in the outer corner of the eye are stimulated, it has been found to be due to external light coming into the eye from the direction of the bridge of the nose, the inference we make is that it is so in every new case whenever this part of the retina is stimulated [e.g. by pressure with a finger on the closed eyelid, ed.]; just as we assert that every single individual now living will die, because all previous experience has shown that all men who were formerly alive have died.

But, moreover, just because they are not free acts of conscious thought, these unconscious conclusions from analogy are irresistible, and the effect of them cannot be overcome by a better understanding of the real relations. It may be ever so clear how we get an idea of a luminous phenomenon in the field of vision when pressure is exerted on the eye; and yet we cannot get rid of the conviction that this appearance of light is actually there at the given place in the visual field; and we cannot seem to comprehend that there is a luminous phenomenon at the place where the retina is stimulated. It is the same way in the case of all the images that we see in optical instruments.

On the other hand, there are numerous illustrations of fixed and inevitable associations of ideas due to frequent repetition, even when they have no natural connexion, but are dependent merely on some conventional arrangement, as, for example, the connection between the written letters of a word and its sound and meaning. Still to many physiologists and psychologists the connexion between the sensation and the conception of the object usually appears to be so rigid and obligatory that they are not much disposed to admit that, to a considerable extent at least, it depends on acquired experience, that is, on psychic activity. On the contrary, they have endeavoured to find some mechanical mode of origin for this connexion through the agency of imaginary organic structures. With regard to this question, all those experiences are of much significance which show how the judgement of the senses may be modified by experience and by training derived under various circumstances, and may be adapted to the new conditions. Thus, persons may learn in some measure to utilize details of the sensation which otherwise would escape notice and not contribute to obtaining any idea of the object. On the other hand, too, this new habit may acquire such a hold that when the individual in question is back again in the old original normal state, he may be liable to illusions of the senses.

Facts like these show the widespread influence that experience, training and habit have on our perceptions. But how far their influence really does extend, it would perhaps be impossible to say precisely at present.

Hermann von Helmholtz, 'Concerning the Perceptions in General', *Physiological Optics* (1866)

THE BIRTH OF THE IMAGINATION

It has taken more than 200 years for science to catch up with Wordsworth, who saw the development of imagination as a product of the nurturing, loving relationship between mother and child. It is known that the human brain more than doubles in size during the first year of life. Its growth and organization during that time are now thought to be influenced by emotional factors. The right hemisphere, in particular, undergoes a growth spurt which coincides exactly with the period of early attachment studied by developmental psychology. Early experience of sounds and images, for example emotionally charged pictorial memories of loving and understanding, or threatening and humiliating faces, are thought to be processed and stored in it. In place of Wordsworth's description, or more charitably, in addition to it, we now have Professor Allan Schore's thesis,[6] to the effect that 'the early social environment, mediated by the primary caregiver, directly influences the final wiring of the circuits in the brain that are responsible for the future socioemotional development of the individual.'

William Wordsworth (1770–1850), and his friend, Samuel Taylor Coleridge, whom he met in 1795, were champions of the first wave of British Romantic poets. Romanticism was a pan-European reaction against Classical tradition, Enlightenment rationalism and political authoritarianism, all perceived to be threats to the full and free expression of man's individual nature. Contemporary distrust of science resonates with the Romantic imagination, but has its own dangers when it leads to a wholesale flight from reason, and the threat of anarchy. Romantic ideologies have also been harnessed to fascist political regimes in modern times, and prove to be no guarantee against tyranny.*

Wordsworth was born at Cockermouth in the English Lake District. He lost his mother when he was eight years old and his father, who was a lawyer, died five years later. He was educated at Hawkshead Grammar School and St John's College,

6 *Affect Regulation and the Origin of the Self: The Neurobiology of Emotional Development*, Lawrence Erlbaum Associates, Inc., Mahweh, NJ, 1994.

Cambridge. In 1791 he spent a year in France and had a love affair with Annette Vallon, daughter of a local surgeon at Blois. In 1802 he married Mary Hutchinson with whom he had five children. He already had a daughter from his previous liaison. Like many people, he was a passionate anti-Establishment idealist in his youth and a member of the Establishment in his old age, becoming Poet Laureate in 1843.

> Blessed the infant babe –
> For with my best conjectures I would trace
> The Progress of our being – blest the babe
> Nursed in his mother's arms, the babe who sleeps
> Upon his mother's breast, who, when his soul
> Claims manifest kindred with an earthly soul,
> Doth gather passion from his mother's eye.
> Such feelings pass into his torpid life
> Like an awakening breeze, and hence his mind,
> Even in the first trial of its power,
> Is prompt and watchful, eager to combine
> In one appearance all the elements
> And parts of the same object, else detached
> And loath to coalesce. Thus day by day,
> Subjected to the discipline of love,
> His organs and recipient faculties
> are quickened, are more vigorous; his mind spreads,
> Tenacious of the forms which it receives.
> In one beloved presence – nay and more,
> In that most apprehensive habitude
> and those sensations which have been derived
> From this beloved presence – there exists
> A virtue which irradiates and exalts
> All objects through all intercourse of sense.
> No outcast he, bewildered and depressed;
> Along his infant veins are interfused
> The gravitational and the filial bond
> Of nature that connect him with the world.
> Emphatically such a being lives,
> An inmate of this *active* universe.

From Nature largely he receives, nor so
Is satisfied, but largely gives again;
For feeling has to him imparted strength,
And – powerful in all sentiments of grief,
Of exultation, fear and joy – his mind,
Even as an agent of the one great mind,
Creates, creator and receiver both,
Working but in alliance with the works
Which it beholds. Such, verily, is the first
Poetic spirit of our human life –
By uniform control of after years
In most abated and suppressed, in some
Through every change of growth or of decay
Pre-eminent till death.

William Wordsworth, *The Prelude* (1799)

Our Fantasizing Mind

As soon as we form a mental image, it becomes not just a pale representation or cardboard cutout of the external world, it is ineluctably associated with a range of other thoughts and feelings, embedded in a network of meaning, incorporated into a story, perhaps the story of our life. It becomes, as Susanne Langer points out, a symbol, thereby acquiring a secondary significance which may eclipse its original referential function. Thus a sunny day is more closely associated with a sense of well-being than with a meteorological condition. As long as we know the difference between our story about the day and the objective weather conditions, we will not get burnt.

Langer was born in New York in 1895. She studied with the British mathematician and philosopher, Alfred North Whitehead, at Radcliffe College, Cambridge, Massachusetts, and received her Ph.D. from Harvard in 1926. In 1954 she became professor of philosophy at Connecticut College, New London. Her main contribution was a theory of art as an expression of human emotion in non-discursive symbols, able to go beyond the functions of ordinary language.

If language is born, indeed, from the profoundly symbolific character of the human mind, we may not be surprised to find that this mind tends to operate with symbols far below the level of speech. Previous studies have shown that even the subjective record of sense experience, the 'sense-image', is not a direct copy of actual experience, but has been 'projected', in the process of copying, into a new dimension, the more or less stabile form we call a *picture*. It has not the protean, mercurial elusiveness of real visual experience, but a unity and lasting identity that makes it an object of the mind's possession rather than a sensation. Furthermore it is not firmly and fixedly determined by the pattern of natural phenomena, as real sensations are, but is 'free', in the same manner as the little noises which a baby produces by impulse and at will. We can call up images and let them fill the virtual space of vision between us and real objects, or on the screen of the dark, and dismiss them again, without altering the course of practical events. They are our own product, yet not part of ourselves as our physical actions are; rather might we compare them with our uttered words (save that they remain entirely private), in that they are objects to us, things that may surprise, even frighten us, experiences that can be contemplated, not merely lived.

In short, images have all the characteristics of symbols. If they were weak sense-experiences, they would confuse the order of nature for us. Our salvation lies in that we do not normally take them for bona fide sensations, but attend to them only in their capacity of *meaning* things, being *images* of things – symbols whereby those things are conceived, remembered, considered, but not encountered.

The best guarantee of their essentially symbolic function is their tendency to become metaphorical. They are not only capable of connoting the things from which our sense-experience originally derived them, and perhaps, by the law of association, the context in which they were derived (as the sight of a bell may cause one to think of 'ding-dong' and also of dinner), but they also have an inalienable tendency to 'mean' things that have only a logical analogy to their primary meanings. The image of a rose symbolizes feminine beauty so readily that it is actually harder to associate roses with vegetables than with girls. Fire is a natural symbol of life and passion, though it is the one element in which nothing can actually live. Its mobility and flare, its heat and colour, make it an irresistible symbol of all that is living, feeling, and active. Images are, therefore, our readiest instruments for abstracting concepts from the tumbling stream of actual impressions. They make our primitive abstractions for us, they are our spontaneous embodiments of general ideas . . .

Susanne Langer, *Philosophy in a New Key* (1942)

The Life of the Mind

Samuel Taylor Coleridge (1772–1834), youngest son of the vicar of Ottery St Mary, Devon, was sent to Christ's Hospital School in 1782, following his father's untimely death. He went on to read classics at Jesus College, Cambridge, and was awarded the gold medal in the Browne Greek Prize competition at the end of his first year, but never took a degree. He impulsively left Cambridge to enlist in the King's Fifteenth Light Dragoons, under the name of Silas Tomkin Comberbache, from which he was discharged four months later on grounds of insanity. He may have been suffering from depression following his brother's suicide and other reverses in his life. Coleridge became an opium addict. In 1797 he met William Wordsworth and his sister Dorothy. Their passionate entanglement for the next fourteen years was a creative force in English Romanticism, but may have contributed to the breakdown of his marriage and driven him further into drug addiction.[7]

The imagination then I consider either as primary or secondary. The primary imagination I hold to be the living power and prime agent of all human perception, and as a repetition in the finite mind of the eternal act of creation in the infinite I AM. The secondary I consider as an echo of the former, coexisting with the conscious will, yet still as identical with the primary in the kind of its agency, and differing only in degree, and in the mode

7 See Stephen Weissman, *His Brother's Keeper: A Psychobiography of Samuel Taylor Coleridge*, International Universities Press, 1989.

of its operation. It dissolves, diffuses, dissipates, in order to re-create; or where this process is rendered impossible, yet still at all events it struggles to idealize and to unify. It is essentially vital, even as all objects (*as* objects) are essentially fixed and dead.

Fancy, on the contrary, has no other counters to play with but fixities and definites. The fancy is indeed no other than a mode of memory emancipated from the order of time and space; and blended with and modified by that empirical phenomenon of the will, which we express by the word choice. But equally with the ordinary memory it must receive all its materials ready made from the law of association.

Samuel Taylor Coleridge, *Biographia Literaria* (1815–17)

The Infinite Imagination

William Blake (1757–1827), visionary poet and engraver, was the third son of a London hosier. He never attended school but was apprenticed to an engraver and subsequently studied at the Royal Academy. He became deeply influenced by the Swedish philosopher and mystic, Emanuel Swedenborg, who saw the end of creation as a fusion of God with Man. Like Milton*, Blake regarded God as the personification of love, but unlike Milton he located its source within himself, where all truth was to be found.

His unique brand of individualism made him a subversive influence in an authoritarian society. In 1803 he was charged at Chichester with high treason, for having uttered seditious expressions about the King. However he was acquitted, and in the same year returned to London to commence work on his sixteen-year project, 'Jerusalem: The Emanation of the Giant Albion'. In it, he has the character Los say 'I must Create a System or be enslav'd by another Man's', which has been taken to be a motto for his own life.

At the time of his death, Blake was generally thought to have been insane. But in the wake of the industrial revolution his antipathy to a materialist view of man, his emphasis on the primacy of mind over matter, became increasingly attractive. Blake conceived his creative imagination as an instrument of God.

This world of Imagination is the world of Eternity; it is the divine bosom into which we shall all go after the death of the Vegetated body. This World of Imagination is Infinite & Eternal, whereas the world of Generation, or Vegetation, is Finite & Temporal. There Exist in that Eternal World the Permanent Realities of Every Thing which we see reflected in this Vegetable Glass of Nature. All Things are comprehended in their Eternal Forms in the divine body of the Saviour, the True Vine of Eternity, The Human Imagination.

William Blake, 'A Vision of the Last Judgment' (1810)

The Limits of Imagination

There is nothing mysterious about imagination, according to George Henry Lewes (1817–78); it is merely the power to select and recombine experiences, to create new objects out of old materials. It is, moreover, as much the province of scientists (philosophers) as of poets. But those people who lack imagination live in a restricted, isolated, one-dimensional world – they have 'sluggish' minds.

Lewes himself was a small, ugly, man with a far from sluggish mind. Son of a theatre director who died when he was seven, he was brought up by his mother and stepfather, a retired sea-captain. He became a successful journalist and first editor of the Fortnightly Review. *As well as plays, novels and dramatic criticism, he wrote a distinguished biography of Goethe and later in his life, contributed in the areas of science and philosophy. He was a typical Victorian polymath.*

His own achievements are shrouded in the public mind by his relationship with the English novelist George Eliot*, whom he first met in 1851, and his role in promoting her talent. His twenty-four-year 'marriage' with Eliot, whose pen-name has been said by some to be an acronym for 'to L I owe it', began in 1854.

Lewes was by that time estranged from his wife, Agnes, but unable to obtain a divorce, because he had condoned her adultery with his friend T.L. Hunt. Lewes undoubtedly had a profound intellectual influence on his partner as well as providing her with moral support. Despite the immense success which George Eliot enjoyed in her lifetime, Lewes always hid critical book reviews, for fear they would upset her.

Imagination is not the exclusive appanage of artists, but belongs in varying degrees to all men. It is simply the power of forming images. Supplying the energy of Sense where Sense cannot reach, it brings into distinctness the facts, obscure or occult, which are grouped round an object or an idea, but which are not actually present to Sense. Thus, at the aspect of a windmill, the mind forms images of many characteristic facts relating to it; and the kind of images will depend very much on the general disposition, or particular mood, of the mind affected by the object: the painter, the poet and the moralist will have different images suggested by the windmill or its symbol. There are indeed sluggish minds so incapable of self-evolved activity, and so dependent on the immediate suggestions of Sense, as to be almost destitute of the power of forming distinct images beyond the immediate circle of sensuous associations; and these are rightly named unimaginative minds; but in all minds of energetic activity, groups and clusters of images, many of them representing remote relations, spontaneously present themselves in conjunction with objects or their symbols. It should, however, be borne in mind that Imagination can only recall what Sense has previously impressed. No man imagines any detail of which he has not previously had direct or indirect experience. Objects as fictitious as mermaids and hippogriffs are made up from the gatherings of Sense. 'Made up from the gatherings of Sense' is a phrase which may seem to imply some peculiar plastic power such as is claimed exclusively for artists: a power not of simple recollection, but of recollection and recombination. Yet this power belongs also to philosophers. To combine the half of a woman with the half of a fish – to imagine the union as an existing organism – is not really a different process from that combining the experience of a chemical action with an electric action, and seeing that the two are one existing fact. When the poet hears the storm-cloud muttering, and sees the moonlight sleeping on the bank, he transfers his experience of human phenomena to the cloud and the moonlight: he personifies, draws Nature within the circle of emotion, and is called a poet. When the philosopher sees electricity in the stormcloud, and sees the sunlight stimulating vegetable growth, he transfers his experience of physical phenomena to these objects, and draws within the circle of Law phenomena which hitherto have been unclassified. Obviously the imagination has been as active in the one case as in the other; the *differentia* lying in the purposes of the two and in the general constitution of the two minds.

It has been noted that there is less strain on the imagination of the poet; but even his greater freedom is not altogether disengaged from the necessity of verification; his images must have at least subjective truth; if they do not accurately correspond with objective realities, they must correspond with our sense of congruity. No poet is allowed the licence of creating images inconsistent with our conceptions. If he said the moonlight *burnt* the bank, we should reject the image as untrue, inconsistent with our conceptions of moonlight; whereas the gentle repose of the moonlight on the bank readily associates itself with images of sleep.

The often mooted question, What is Imagination? thus receives a very clear and definite answer. It is the power of forming images; it reinstates, in a visible group, those objects which are invisible, either from absence or from imperfection of our senses. That is its generic character. Its specific character, which marks it off from Memory, and which is derived from the powers of selection and recombination, will be expounded further on. Here I only touch upon its chief characteristic, in order to disengage the term from that mysteriousness which writers have usually assigned to it, thereby rendering philosophic criticism impossible. Thus disengaged it may be used with more certainty in an attempt to estimate the imaginative power of various works. [. . .]

A work is imaginative in virtue of its power over our emotions; not in virtue of any rarity or surprisingness in the images themselves. A Madonna and Child by Fra Angelico is more powerful over our emotions than a Crucifixion by a vulgar artist; a beggar boy by Murillo is more imaginative than an Assumption by the same painter; but the Assumption by Titian displays far greater imagination than either. We must guard against the natural tendency to attribute to the artist what is entirely due to accidental conditions. A tropical scene, luxuriant with tangled overgrowth and impressive in the grandeur of its phenomena, may more decisively arrest our attention than an English landscape with its green cornlands and plenteous homesteads. But this superiority of interest is no proof of the artist's superior imagination; and by a spectator familiar with the tropics, greater interest may be felt in the English landscape, because its images may more forcibly arrest his attention by their novelty. And were this not so, were the inalienable impressiveness of tropical scenery always to give the poet who described it a superiority in effect, this would not prove the superiority of his imagination. For either he has been familiar with such scenes, and imagines them just as the other poet imagines his English landscape – by an effort of mental vision, calling up the absent objects; or he has merely read the descriptions of others, and from these makes up his picture. It is the same with his rival, who also recalls and recombines. Foolish critics often betray their ignorance by saying that a painter or a writer 'only copies what he has seen, or puts down what he has known'. They forget that no man imagines what he has not seen or known, and that it is in the selection of the characteristic details that the artistic power is manifest.

George Henry Lewes, 'Of Vision in Art', *The Principles of Success in Literature* (1865)

We Imagine What We Desire

Wishful thinking was famously elevated into a theory of dream-production when Freud* published his Interpretation of Dreams *in 1900. George Eliot (1819–80), thinker and novelist, anticipated his interest in the unconscious mind. 'There is a great deal of unmapped country within us', she wrote in her last novel,* Daniel

Deronda, *'which would have to be taken into account in any explanation of our gusts and storms.' Hailed by many as the greatest novel written in the English language,* Middlemarch, *like all her work, is replete with psychological insight. In the following passage she describes the not uncommon pleasure derived by people from imagining that they are an observer at their own funeral.*

We are all of us imaginative in some form or other, for images are the brood of desire; and poor old Featherstone, who laughed much at the way in which others cajoled themselves, did not escape the fellowship of illusion. In writing the programme for his burial he certainly did not make clear to himself that his pleasure in the little drama of which it formed a part was confined to anticipation. In chuckling over the vexations he could inflict by the rigid clutch of his dead hand, he inevitably mingled his consciousness with that livid stagnant presence, and so far as he was preoccupied with a future life, it was with one of gratification inside his coffin. Thus old Featherstone was imaginative, after his fashion.

George Eliot, *Middlemarch* (1871)

THE WORK OF THE IMAGINATION

Little People and the Creative Imagination

Like many composers, writers and artists, Robert Louis Stevenson experienced himself as a 'servant to his muse', a mere drudge, copying and organizing what was 'given' to him by his unconscious mind. In the following passage he describes the origin of his world-famous novella, The Strange Case of Dr Jekyll and Mr Hyde, *in a dream. In it Dr Jekyll hazards the guess that '. . . man will be ultimately known for a mere polity of multifarious, incongruous and independent denizens.'*

Although he is popularly thought of as a children's writer, Stevenson had a deep interest in psychological matters, and is by common agreement one of the greatest stylists in the English language. Like Freud, he contributed to the Proceedings of the Society for Psychical Research, the publication of an anti-materialist society, set up in late nineteenth-century Cambridge, which was dedicated to the scientific proof of life after death.

Stevenson (1850–94) was the only child of an Edinburgh civil engineer. His grandfather, Robert, was associated with the building of the Bell Rock lighthouse. His mother was chronically sick, possibly with tuberculosis, which he is thought to have inherited. Ill-health prevented him from following his father's career and instead he trained for the bar at Edinburgh University. However, he never practised as an advocate, preferring to pursue a literary career. He was always attracted to older women,[8] and in 1880 married Fanny Osbourne, an American divorcée ten years his senior and the mother of three children, one of whom had died in infancy.

Following his father's death in 1887, Stevenson spent much time roaming the world together with his wife, widowed mother and stepchildren, in search of a climate that would be sympathetic to his respiratory problems. Eventually, after crossing the Pacific in a chartered schooner riddled with dry rot, they reached Samoa, where he spent the last five years of his life.

And for the Little People, what shall I say they are just my Brownies, God bless them! who do one-half my work for me while I am fast asleep, and in all human likelihood, do the rest for me as well, when I am wide awake and fondly suppose I do it for myself. That part which is done while I am sleeping is the Brownies' part beyond contention; but that which is done when I am up and about is by no means necessarily mine, since all goes to show the Brownies have a hand in it even then. Here is a doubt that much concerns my conscience. For myself – what I call I, my conscious ego, the denizen of the pineal gland unless

8 See S. Wilson, 'Robert Louis Oedipus', in *The Cradle of Violence: Essays on Psychiatry, Psychoanalysis and Literature*, Jessica Kingsley, 1995.

he has changed his residence since Descartes, the man with the conscience and the variable bank account, the man with the hat and boots, and the privilege of voting and not carrying his candidate at the general elections – I am sometimes tempted to suppose he is no story teller at all, but a creature as matter of fact as any cheesemonger or any cheese, and a realist bemired up to the ears in actuality; so that, by that account, the whole of my published fiction should be the single-handed product of some Brownie, some Familiar, some unseen collaborator, whom I keep locked in a back garret, while I get all the praise and he but a share (which I cannot prevent him from getting) of the pudding. I am an excellent adviser, something like Molière's servant; I pull back and I cut down; and I dress the whole in the best words and sentences that I can find and make; I hold the pen, too; and I do the sitting at the table, which is about the worst of it; and when all is done, I make up the manuscript and pay for the registration; so that on the whole, I have some claim to share, though not so largely as I do, in the profits of our common enterprise.

I can but give an instance or so of what part is done sleeping and what part awake, and leave the reader to share what laurels there are, at his own nod, between myself and my collaborators; and to do this I will first take a book that a number of persons have been polite enough to read, *The Strange Case of Dr Jekyll and Mr Hyde*. I had long been trying to write a story on this subject, to find a body, a vehicle, for that strong sense of man's double being which must at times come in upon and overwhelm the mind of every thinking creature. I had even written one, *The Travelling Companion*, which was returned by an editor on the plea that it was a work of genius and indecent, and which I burned the other day on the ground that it was not a work of genius, and that *Jekyll* had supplanted it. Then came one of those financial fluctuations to which (with an elegant modesty) I have hitherto referred in the third person. For two days I went about racking my brains for a plot of any sort; and on the second night I dreamed the scene at the window, and a scene afterward split in two, in which Hyde, pursued for some crime, took the powder and underwent the change in the presence of his pursuers. All the rest was made awake, and consciously, although I think I can trace in much of it the manner of my Brownies. The meaning of the tale is therefore mine, and had long pre-existed in my garden of Adonis, and tried one body after another in vain; indeed I do most of the morality, worse luck! and my Brownies have not a rudiment of what we call conscience. All that was given me was the matter of three scenes and the central idea of a voluntary change becoming involuntary.

Robert Louis Stevenson, 'A Chapter on Dreams', *Across the Plains* (1892)

Imagination Is Integral to Perception

Immanuel Kant (1724–1804) was born and spent his whole life in Königsberg, Prussia, now in Lithuania, where he became professor of logic and metaphysics in 1770. His complex ideas, which he labelled 'transcendental idealism', were influenced by the rationalism of Descartes* and Leibnitz, and the empiricism of Locke*, Berkeley* and Hume*. They had a profound effect on future generations of philosophers. Kant concluded that some of the properties we attribute to objects are in fact due to the nature of our own capacities for observation, rather than the objects themselves. Imagination, he thought, performed a synthesizing function. It was the faculty which enabled us to place particular sensory impressions, say the sight of certain coloured spheres, into categories such as oranges or apples. And it was also responsible for enabling us to have a sense of continuity, to appreciate that different perceptual 'snapshots' referred to the same continuously existing object.

Psychologists have hitherto failed to realize that imagination is a necessary ingredient of perception itself. This is due partly to the fact that that faculty has been limited to reproduction, partly to the belief that the senses not only supply impressions but also combine them so as to generate images of objects. For that purpose something more than the mere receptivity of impressions is undoubtedly required, namely, a function for the synthesis of them.

Immanuel Kant, *Critique of Pure Reason* (1781)

Creativity, Imagination and Perception

Oliver Sacks (1933–), English neurologist and author, son of two physicians, was born in London and educated at Queens College, Oxford, where he obtained his medical degree. In the early 1960s he emigrated to the United States and in 1965 joined the staff of Albert Einstein College of Medicine in New York City, where he later became a professor of neurology. He continues to live and work in New York, and has become well known for his humane, respectful and compassionate descriptions of neurological case histories. His eight books have received numerous awards and been translated into twenty-two languages.

In the following passage, by looking at what we know goes on in the brain during the relatively simpler process of visual perception or ordinary 'seeing', Dr Sacks indicates how complex the 'neurology of imagination' is likely to be.

Now, we don't have any way at the moment of studying the neurology of imagination. I hope there will be a way in the next millennium. I hope you will find some ways here, in Canberra. But one can study some of the lower levels in the nervous system, and this may be very valuable if there are analogies between what goes on at lower levels of perception – visual perception, say – and imagination. In his *Berlin Diary*, Christopher Isherwood starts by saying, 'I am a camera', but I think the notion that we may have been given the visual world, as a whole, full of colour and movement and sense is very, very misleading.

We are not given the visual world as a whole; there are something like forty or fifty different systems in the brain that are involved in the analysis and recreation of a visual world. We may start with a little picture, a little photograph at the back of the retina, but that is only the source in the beginning of this enormous process of breakdown and reconstruction.

At lower levels, there are parts of the visual cortex (I'm going to use a bit of shorthand), that physiologists refer to as V_1, V_2, V_3, V_4. Now the lower V's, if I can use the phrase, are concerned with particular aspects of visual perception, for example, for the perception of colour or the perception of motion. And if something goes wrong in this tiny area of the cortex, then one of these visual elements can be knocked out completely.

I have written at length about an artist who suddenly became totally colour blind as a result of bilateral damage to the colour-processing areas, V_4, on each side. And not only did he lose the ability to perceive colour, he lost the ability to imagine colour. He lost the ability to remember colour, he lost the ability to dream in colour. It seems that the same areas, or similar areas of the brain, may be involved in perception and imagination and memory. And to some extent these all go together.

It is similar in a very rare condition called motion blindness. There has only been a single case of this reported, but the case has been very well studied. This is a woman in Germany, who, following a stroke, suddenly lost the ability to see movement. She would see people and cars and so forth perfectly well, until they moved, and then they would vanish and reappear as stills every few seconds. Very difficult for her to cross the road, very dangerous. Very difficult to be in a room of people, because their voices were continuous, but their faces were not. Very difficult to pour a cup of tea, because she would not see the tea flowing, just a motionless, frozen stream, a sort of glacier of fluid from the spout to the cup, and then, all of a sudden, a puddle. And with this, she has lost the ability to imagine or remember movement visually, although the imagining of *heard* or *felt* movements was unaffected.

So, these are peculiar syndromes in which particular elements are knocked out. More complex is a condition called visual agnosia, when you can see perfectly well but you don't know what you're seeing, you can make no sense of it.

This can sometimes happen as a result of brain damage. It happened with the patient I called 'the man who mistook his wife for a hat', as a result of disease affecting not the V's, but a higher level, the visual association areas of the brain. This man now found himself in an abstract world, sometimes a chaos, of colours, shapes, movements, to which he could attach no meaning. Thus visual recognition became almost impossible – hence the possibility of such a ludicrous mistake as mistaking one's wife for a hat or a fire hydrant for a child.

I have also seen and described a similar condition in a man I call Virgil, who was born blind, or virtually blind, and given sight at the age of fifty. It is sometimes imagined that if it were possible surgically to operate on the eyes and give someone vision, then they would instantly see. It doesn't happen quite this way.

Many of the questions we ask now neurologically were originally asked by philosophers. William Molyneux, the Irish philosopher, wrote to John Locke* in the seventeenth century, and posed this question: if a person born blind were able to recognize a globe or a cube by touch and was then given sight, could they recognize it by sight?

This was not an entirely academic question, because Molyneux's wife was born blind. Locke thought that the answer was no; Leibnitz thought that the answer was yes. Their debate was resolved in the 1720s, when the first clinical case of this kind was reported, of a 15-year-old boy who had congenital cataracts removed. But because he had never learned to see, this boy could make no sense of the world, even with 'normal' vision. And it was similar with Virgil, my patient. He 'saw' everything, but he could recognize nothing; nothing had meaning for him. People in this state may be able to draw perfectly accurately, they may be able to copy or reproduce, but they may not know what they are copying, or reproducing; they cannot form representations, either perceptually or in their imaginations. So here at this level we begin to see that perception involves the synthesis of many different elements, and from this synthesis, sense or meaning starts to emerge.

There is no little man, there is no homunculus in the brain looking at the world [see pp. 270 and 305], there are something like fifty visual systems, all contributing, all playing their own tune, all talking to one another, and their orchestration yields the apparently seamless visual world – my visual world, your visual world.

The fact that forty or fifty different systems at least are involved is not something you can know. All you know is that you see the world. To you it seems seamless; the mechanisms that are involved in this wonderful synthesis or integration are completely inaccessible to introspection.

As in the same way, you cannot know how you move your hand or how you form a sentence. None of the internal mechanisms of perception or action or language can be known to one, they are necessarily unconscious. And this if you want, is a first level of a sort of physiological unconscious which has to underline all of the things you do.

If you had to think, if you had to have conscious knowledge of how to wipe your nose, you could not do it. You can only do it because it is automatic.

But clearly a different form of unconsciousness is involved in creativity, and a much richer and stranger and more mysterious form of unconsciousness.

Oliver Sacks, Transcript of inaugural lecture, 'Creativity, Imagination and Perception', Centre for the Mind, Australian Academy of Science, Canberra (1998)

THE SENSE OF CONTINUITY

Incurable Doubt

How do we know that the table we ate breakfast off this morning is the same one we ate off yesterday? True, our perception of it today seems remarkably like that of yesterday, but Hume argues we have no grounds for believing our perception of the table to be continuous, let alone the table itself. Since the mind knows nothing other than its own perceptions, it has no way of knowing whether they are being generated by the same external object or a different one producing the apparently same result. We come to believe that our perception of an object is 'uninterrupted', because our imagination insists that it must be so, in the face of unequivocal and reasonable evidence to the contrary.

David Hume (1711–76) was a leading figure of the Scottish

Enlightenment. In addition to his philosophical writing, he wrote a History of Great Britain *and made contributions in the field of politics. He was a friend of the young Adam Smith and Jean-Jacques Rousseau*.

I begun this subject with premising that we ought to have implicit faith in our senses, and that this would be the conclusion I should draw from the whole of my reasoning. But to be ingenuous, I feel myself *at present* of a quite contrary sentiment, and am more inclined to repose no faith at all in my senses, or rather imagination, than to place in it such an implicit confidence. I cannot conceive how such trivial qualities of the fancy, conducted by such false suppositions, can ever lead to any solid and rational system. They are the coherence and constancy of our perceptions, which produce the opinion of their continued existence; though these qualities of perceptions have no perceivable connection with such an existence. The constancy of our perceptions has the most considerable effect, and yet is attended with the greatest difficulties. It is a gross illusion to suppose that our resembling perceptions are numerically the same; and it is this illusion which leads us into the opinion that these perceptions are uninterrupted, and are still existent, even when they are not present to the senses. This is the case with our popular system. And as to our philosophical one, it is liable to the same difficulties; and is, over and above, loaded with this absurdity, that it at once denies and establishes the vulgar supposition. Philosophers deny our resembling perceptions to be identically the same, and uninterrupted; and yet have so great a propensity to believe them such, that they arbitrarily invent a new set of perceptions, to which they attribute these qualities. I say, a new set of perceptions: for we may well suppose in general, but it is impossible for us distinctly to conceive, objects to be in their nature anything but exactly the same with perceptions. What then can we look for from this confusion of groundless and extraordinary opinions but error and falsehood? And how can we justify to ourselves any belief we repose in them?

This sceptical doubt, both with respect to reason and the senses, is a malady which can never be radically cured, but must return upon us every moment, however we may chase it away, and sometimes may seem entirely free from it. It is impossible, upon any system, to defend either our understanding or senses; and we but expose them further when we endeavour to justify them in that manner. As the sceptical doubt arises naturally from a profound and intense reflection on those subjects, it always increases the further we carry our reflections, whether in opposition or conformity to it. Carelessness and inattention alone can afford us any remedy. For this reason I rely entirely upon them; and take it for granted, whatever may be the reader's opinion at this present moment, that an hour hence he will be persuaded there is both an external and internal world.

David Hume, 'Of Scepticism with Regard to the Senses', *A Treatise of Human Nature* (1739)

THE ROLE OF STORED IMAGES

There Is No Such Thing as Immaculate Perception

Professors Stephen Kosslyn and Amy Sussman, of the Departments of Psychology in Harvard and Yale Universities respectively, have shown that imagery and perception share common mechanisms. They have used positron emission tomography (PET) to demonstrate that seeing an object with one's eyes open and imagining the same object with one's eyes closed, activate the same areas of the brain. Thus, imagining small objects activates parts of the brain normally concerned with more central input during vision; imagining larger objects activates areas of the brain normally concerned with more peripheral inputs during vision.

The ability of a computer to recognize an object can be enhanced by supplying it with a store of pre-programmed images, rather in the same way as a spell-checker infers the word you intended to write from an incomplete pattern of letters. The brain may process information in a similar way. Kosslyn and Sussman argue that remembered images, encoded and stored in the brain, are used to augment the incoming information from sense organs, in order to produce a better picture. In addition they suggest that stored images 'prime' the perceptual system when one expects to see a specific object, enhancing the visual representation but also making it more likely that a mistake will occur. Socrates held a similar view.[9]

We argue that mental imagery plays an integral role in perception, and that it may have evolved primarily for this purpose and later have been recruited into higher cognitive processes. In this sense, imagery is like one's nose. It did not evolve to hold up glasses, but once it was present, it could be used to do so. The idea that higher cognitive processes contribute to perception is not new; however, we have recently learned much about the neuroanatomy and neurophysiology of vision that allows us to develop old ideas in new directions.

We take as our starting point the finding that imagery and perception share common mechanisms. [. . .]

We register what we see. However, in many situations, the input activates multiple representations in memory. This may happen when relatively few distinguishing properties are visible, and hence the input places relatively few constraints on what the object must be. For example, if one cannot see the edges that indicate a pen's clip, it will be difficult to use the remaining edges to distinguish between a pen and pencil. This problem is even more difficult when one is trying to identify a specific member of a category, such as one's own pen rather than somebody else's.

To solve such problems, David Lowe implemented a computer vision system that incorporated a second phase processing. He found that when the stable properties of the input do not strongly implicate a particular object, it is useful to activate a stored 'model' of the best-matching shape. Such models are stored in his system's visual memory [which corresponds to the pattern activation subsystem found in the human brain by Kosslyn and his team, ed.]. When activated, the model generates an image of an object in the input array (which corresponds to the visual

9 See Plato, p. 72.

buffer, in our terms). In Lowe's system, this generated image is then compared to the input image itself; the generated image is adjusted in size and orientation until it makes the best possible match to the input image. If the match is good enough, then the object is recognized. If Lowe is correct, then the ability to generate images is an essential part of our ability to recognize objects.

This sort of image-matching process can also augment the input itself. Recurrent connections allow the states of units farther along in the processing sequence to provide feedback to earlier units. In models of neural networks, this feedback may actually fill in missing elements of the input, a process called vector completion. Imagery may play a similar role: The image provides information that will complete missing parts of the input.

Stephen Kosslyn and Amy Sussman, 'Roles of Imagery in Perception: Or, There Is No Such Thing as Immaculate Perception' (1995)

PHANTOMS, TRICKS, VISIONS AND HALLUCINATIONS

Small Animals in the Mind

Disturbances of perception are commonplace in medical practice. Among the organic causes, it is well known that fevers, various kinds of metabolic imbalance, migraine, epilepsy, chronic brain syndromes, cerebral tumours and syphilis can all give rise to hallucinations, frequently of a visual nature. In addition, intoxication with a range of drugs or the ingestion of specific 'hallucinogens' can have the same effect. But perhaps the most bizarre, frightening and dramatic perceptual disturbances are associated with sudden withdrawal from addiction to the commonest drug of all – alcohol.

The aptly named Delirium Tremens (Trembling Delirium), a potentially life-threatening condition, is characterized by profound confusion, insomnia, terror, tremulousness and agitation. A range of perceptual disturbances occur, most particularly visual hallucinations of small animals, often in lurid colours. They are frequently of Lilliputian dimensions and in constant movement, producing intense but unstable emotional reactions ranging from amusement to outright horror. One report describes a patient who enthusiastically followed and commented on a game of football for about half an hour, played by two teams of normal-coloured miniature elephants in a corner of his room.[10]

The following description given by the Newcastle physician Samuel Burton Pearson is one of the earliest in medical literature.

BRAIN-FEVER. At the earnest solicitation of several people who have been afflicted with this grievous malady, I offer this small treatise to the public. Multifarious and repugnant theories on the science of life still continue to agitate the medical world. Galen's writings, after the extinction of literature for several ages, were again revived, and produced innumerable controversies: – The acrimonious opposition of the Galenists and Arabians, and the complete overthrow of the latter, are well known to every reader. The chemists attacked the Galenists with fury, and they sustained a defeat. Different sects have originated from Stahl, Hoffman, Boerhaave, Cullen and Brown. A medical review will convince anyone how the faculty worry each other at the present day, about their different dogmas, with much injury to themselves and patients. For the above reasons I disavow all theory and briefly state the circumstances as they occurred to me at the patient's bedside. Out of 93 cases that have been treated by the principles here adopted, not one has fallen a victim to the disorder; but, when a contrary mode has been attempted, few have recovered, and those only whose constitutions were sufficiently vigorous to resist its ravages.

I have called it Brain-Fever, because it is universally known in Newcastle and its vicinity by that term. The same observation extends to putrid fever.

Cause. – Frequent and excessive intoxication.

Description. – It is preceded by tremors of the hands; restlessness; irregularity of thought; deficiency of memory; anxiety

10 William Lishman, *Organic Psychiatry*, Blackwell, 1987.

to be in company; dreadful nocturnal dreams, when the quantity of liquor through the day has been insufficient; much diminution of appetite, especially an aversion to animal food; violent vomiting in the morning; and excessive perspiration from trivial causes. The above symptoms increase; the pulse becomes small and rapid, the skin hot and dry; but soon a clammy sweat bedews the whole surface of the body; confusion of thought arises to such a height, that objects are seen of the most hideous forms, and in positions that it is physically impossible they can be situated; the patient generally sees flies or other insects, or pieces of money, which he anxiously desires to possess; and often occupies much time in conversations of negotiation, if he be a commercial man. Often, for many days and nights, he will continue without rest, notwithstanding every effort is made on the part of the physician to appease his mind, by variety of conversation, and variety of stimuli. He frequently jumps suddenly out of bed in pursuit of a phantom, and holds the most ineffable contempt for the practitioner, if he does not concur in his proceedings. He commonly retains the most pertinacious opinion that he is not in his own house, and that some of his dearest relations have sustained a serious injury. During the concourse of these symptoms, he often can answer medical questions properly for a short space of time, and then relapses into the raving state. [. . .]

Method of cure. – A full dose of opium should be immediately administered in a glass of wine, and repeated in smaller doses for several hours successively; the quantity of which should be regulated by the constitution of the patient, habit of intoxication, degree of the disease, and other concomitant circumstances. The patient, if he eagerly request it, may be allowed to walk from room to room, and the most consoling language should be used by his attendants – The debility of the system should be resisted by sherry gruel, cold wine, and porter and soup; which may be given in sufficient quantity, as the stomach, in this complaint, is very tenacious of what it receives. I never saw the bark, blistering, or affusion of cold water on the head, of any use. Every unnecessary restraint should be carefully avoided; therefore the strait-jacket, which is so universally employed, is the most injurious remedy that can be applied; for, by the perpetual efforts the patient uses to rid himself from confinement, he excites profuse sweating, debilitates the muscular fibre, and soon exhausts the vital principle. If the above mode of treatment be successful, or at least affords the unhappy sufferer a chance of recovery; the impoverishing the system by bleeding, strait-jacket, or abstinence from invigorating remedies and diet, must be extremely mischievous.

Samuel Burton Pearson, 'Brain-Fever' (1801)

A Man with Three Arms

It has been known for centuries that following amputation, many people experience vivid, often painful sensations, which appear to be coming from the missing part of their body. These bodily 'mirages' can arise within twenty-four hours of an operation and last for an indefinite period of time. They are sometimes triggered by touch. Recent reports have described similar phenomena after damage to nerves in the armpit, and following brain haemorrhage. The presence of a phantom penis with phantom erection was reported in 1999, after an operation in which the penis had been totally removed.[11]

Somatic sensations are known to be 'mapped', that is to say sensory experience correlates with cell activity in particular parts of the brain cortex. Areas in a small man-like figure or 'homunculus' made of brain cells located in the sensory cortex become active when corresponding parts of the body are stimulated. Clearly, if these areas can be activated in the absence of peripheral stimulation from the lost part, or through stimulation of a different body part (perhaps represented in an adjacent location on the brain map), some reorganization of nervous connections in the brain must have occurred. The study of 'phantom phenomena' yields information about the brain's capacity to 'remap', and suggests that rapid reorganization of nervous circuitry can occur. Evidence is accumulating that neuronal connections are not 'hard-wired' and

11 C.M. Fisher, 'Phantom Erection After Amputation of the Penis', in *Canadian Journal of Neurological Science* 26 (1999), 53–6.

fixed just after birth, but remain 'plastic' throughout life.

The following interview, where E stands for examiner and P for patient, is with a sixty-five-year-old man who had suffered a stroke causing a blood clot in the basal ganglia, on the right side of his brain. The second extract describes the occurrence of 'phantom breast'.

E You were telling me yesterday something different about your hands?

P Yes, I have a third one.

E A third one?

P Yes.

E Where is that?

P It is in the middle.

[At this point, the patient was asked to indicate the 'third limb' on the examiner's drawing of a man. His performance is shown in Figure 3.] The interview was then continued.

E Can you show the middle one to me?

P It's the dead one, it was taken off 20 years ago by Dr (X) . . . I'm a bit vague about this, they tried to tell me I never had it off . . . a phantom limb . . . they tried to tell me I never had it off . . . I did . . . I know that.

E Why did they take it off?

P They took it off because presumably it needed taking off . . . I don't know, he's the surgeon.

E What do you think was wrong with your hand?

P I think it was just a waste of time . . . it was doing nothing.

E So tell me now at the moment, how many hands do you have?

P Three.

E Three . . . Show me your right hand (raises right arm). Count the number of hands you have for me.

P (looking down and pointing) . . . One . . . two . . . three.

E How many actually work?

P Two.

Fig 3. The patient's drawing of his 'third arm' on the examiner's drawing of a man

E Two of them work? Where are the good working hands located?
P On the right side and the left side and the middle I suppose.
E So which one does not work?
P The one in the middle.
E How is the middle one attached to your body?
P It's not . . . it's attached but detached in the sense of it was taken off . . . I don't know. I really don't know. I'm in a muddle about this.
E It's quite confusing, isn't it?
P Yes, it is . . . I know that the right one is alright.
E Can you move the left one?
P Yes, I can, but not very much . . . I can't do very much with it.
E Where is the other hand that does not work?
P In the middle . . . (pointing with right hand).
E Does it fit under your clothes?
P No, it does not . . . no, it is not covered with any clothes.
E Does it get cold?
P Yes, it does get cold.
E Can you feel it?
P Yes, I do!
E So sometimes this third hand gets cold?
P Yes, it does.
E What do you think of a person having three hands?
P It's an odd situation! . . . I'm a bit vague about it I must say.
  After a short break the interview resumed.

E OK, now I want you to raise your right hand (P raises his right hand). Now raise your left hand (grasps his left hand with his right, and then raises it). Can you raise your middle hand?

P No, I can't . . . it's dead . . . it's not connected to me anymore.

E Whereabouts is it?

P It's tucked away down here! (Points to left side) . . . It's an artificial limb.

E Can you touch it?

P Yes, I can, I can find bits of it in the bed . . . it's in 7 pieces . . . I think.

E How many legs do you have?

P Three . . . no, only got two legs.

E But you said you have three arms.

P Yes, and this arm is an awful nuisance, keeps getting in the way.

E Can you shake hands with this other arm?

P No I can't.

E Could I touch it?

P Yes, you could.

E Could you show me where it is?

P No, I can't.

E Where has it gone now?

P It's obviously wasted away.

E Does it come back?

P Yes, it does. They tell me that it was never taken off . . . I don't believe that.

E Why do you think it's difficult to explain three arms?

P It's an unusual number . . . unusual . . . I don't know. I'm in a muddle about it, I really don't know what to call it . . . I think it has just been left there . . . there seems to be quite a lot of heat in it. It's quite warm . . . warmer than the other hand.

E Do you think the surgeons could do anything about it?

P I don't think they could do anything. I think they just left it there . . . it seemed tidier to do it.

E Could they take it off again?

P No, they could not . . . I don't know.

E What did they do to your arm?

P They took it off.

E So if they took it off, then you would presumably have only one arm left wouldn't you?

P That's right.

E But you claim to have three arms!

P Yes.

E So it would seem as if they have given you another one back . . . ?

P Yes . . . it's very confusing . . . I don't know what to do.

E I don't seem to have worked this out exactly . . . they took off your arm . . . and now you claim to have three arms . . . sounds confusing!

P Yes I think so . . . I'm getting a bit tired.

E Is there anything else you would like to mention?

P No, I don't think so, it's very confusing . . . I agree with you, it does not seem to help at all. I don't seem to be as clear on the subject as I should be.

Peter Halligan, John Marshall and Derick Wade, 'Three Arms: A Case Study of Supernumerary Phantom Limb After Right Hemisphere Stroke' (1993)

Electric Currents in the Breast Produced by Light Touch of the Ear

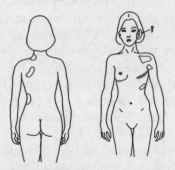

Fig 4. Schematic redrawing of SAEPS in patient 4. These areas were already present six days after the amputation and their border was stable across three different sessions performed at intervals of about three weeks. Localization in different regions of the breast was poor and sensations were mainly referred to the amputated nipple.

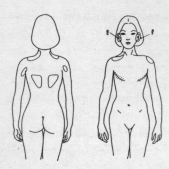
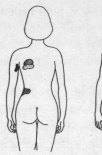

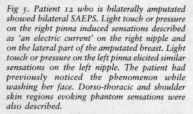
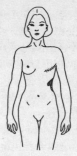

Fig 5. Patient 12 who is bilaterally amputated showed bilateral SAEPS. Light touch or pressure on the right pinna induced sensations described as 'an electric current' on the right nipple and on the lateral part of the amputated breast. Light touch or pressure on the left pinna elicited similar sensations on the left nipple. The patient had previously noticed the phenomenon while washing her face. Dorso-thoracic and shoulder skin regions evoking phantom sensations were also described.

Fig 6. Schematic redrawing of SAEPS in patient 16. In this patient a topographical remapping took place, probably due to the extensive resection. She was able to localize phantom sensations on the nipple (dotted area), on the areola (black area), on the entire breast (hatched area), and on the lower quadrants (plaid area). Also the quality of stimuli (pinpricks, pressure) referred to the phantom breast paralleled that of the actually delivered stimuli.

Fifteen patients [out of forty volunteers who had undergone mastectomy, ed.] reported phantom breast sensations . . . Phantom sensations were generally reported as swarming, burning, or itching arising from the amputated part (mainly from the nipple) [. . .] All women who felt phantom sensations at the time of testing, also showed skin areas which elicited sensations referred to the phantom breast [. . .] The quality of sensations induced on the phantom by the tactile stimuli usually reflected, at least roughly, the kind of stimulus delivered. Light touch was generally perceived in a similar way to pressure while pinpricks were reported as light electric stimuli [. . .] [In patient 12, ed.] light touch or pressure on the right pinna [earlobe, ed.] induced sensations described as 'an electric current' on the right nipple and on the lateral part of the amputated breast. Light touch or pressure on the left pinna elicited similar sensations on the left nipple. The patient had previously noticed the phenomenon while washing her face. Dorsothoracic [back and chest, ed.] and shoulder skin regions evoking phantom sensations were also described.

The present study provides the first description of the systematic elicitation of phantom sensations by means of somatic stimuli delivered to skin regions after breast amputation. Since these skin regions are represented in the somatosensory pathway near the amputated breast, they can be considered perceptual correlates of a clear neural remapping, thus indicating that neural connections are nothing but static even in the adult brain. The distribution of the above regions is basically explained on the basis of sensory Homunculus topography. Nevertheless, an interesting novel finding is the unexpectedly high anatomo-functional relation between pinna and nipple that could potentially give new clues to the understanding of referred sensations of pain.

Salvatore Aglioti, Feliciana Cortese and Cristina Franchini, 'Rapid Sensory Remapping in the Adult Human Brain as Inferred from Phantom Breast Perception' (1994)

Imagination Is Powerful

Michel de Montaigne (1533–92) was a Renaissance philosopher, generally credited with inventing the 'Essay' as a literary form, in which a number of 'trials' were made in order to test the author's response to different ideas and situations. In his youth he set out on a quest for objective truth, but after forty years concluded that it was not obtainable. In 1576, at the age of forty-two, he commissioned his famous medal with the inscription, 'Que sçais-je?' – What do I know? Counter to the received wisdom of Thomas Aquinas, which had dominated medieval philosophy and saw human reason as an expression of godliness – a pathway to absolute truth, Montaigne argued that it was a faulty tool leading to contradictory results. Disagreements among the experts throughout the ages, he thought, demonstrated clearly the hopelessness of achieving unimpeachable scientific knowledge. Man's mind was a distorting mirror and his imagination could easily play tricks.

Fortis imaginatio generat casum: A strong imagination creates its own reality, scholars say. I am one who is profoundly affected by the power of imagination. All men feel it to some extent, but some are overwhelmed. I am so deeply and irresistibly influenced that I do my best to avoid it. I wish I could be surrounded only by happy and contented men, for the sight of someone else's anguish makes me actually feel their pain, and I have often felt physical sensations belonging to another person. If someone can't stop coughing, I get a tickle in my own lungs and throat. I am more reluctant to visit sick people whom I know and care about, than those who have no special claim on my sympathy. When I observe an illness, I catch it and make it my own. I am not surprised that those who allow their imagination free rein suffer fevers and death. *Simon Thomas* was a great physician in his time. I remember being with him in Toulouse once, and visiting a rich old man who had respiratory problems. When the patient asked how he could be cured, Thomas told him that one of the best ways would be to spend time in my company. If he then concentrated on the liveliness and freshness of my face, and observed how I was bursting with youthful joy and vigour, it would somehow rub off on him. What he didn't say, was that my own health might simultaneously deteriorate.

Gallus Vibius tried so hard to understand the nature of insanity that he lost his own mind in the process and never recovered. He might rightly have claimed to have grown foolish through learning. There are some whose fear pre-empts the executioner's hand; and in one case when a man's blind-fold was removed so that friends could show him a last minute pardon, he was found stark dead upon the scaffold, slain by his own imagination. We sweat, we shiver, we turn white or go red as a result of our imagination, and lying in our bed we feel our bodies gripped by imaginary fear and anxiety, so much so that we are ready to die. And youth is often so overcome with passion, that even whilst asleep its sexual desires are satisfied in dreams.

> Ut quasi transactis saepe omnibus rebus profundant
>   Fluminis ingentes fluctus, vestenque cruentent.
>   (Lucretius iv 1027)
> As if all things were done, the mighty wave
>   Gushes forth and stains their garments.

Although there is nothing unusual in seeing horns grow during the night, on heads which had none at bedtime, nonetheless the case of Cippus, King of Italy is remarkable. During the day he had been watching a bull-fight, and all night long dreamed of having horns on his head. In the morning they were actually there, on his forehead, brought into being by power of imagination. Anger gave Croesus's son his voice, which nature had denied him [according to Herodotus, he regained the power of speech when he saw his father's life threatened, ed.]. And Antiochus became feverish in response to the imprint of Stratonica's beauty on his mind. [. . .]

[. . .] It is more than likely that belief in miracles, visions, magic spells and other extraordinary happenings stems mainly from the operation of the imagination, especially on the minds of common folk who are easily persuaded that they see what is not in fact there. I also think that those embarrassing difficulties which give rise to so much mirth in our society that nothing else is spoken of, are most probably produced by imaginary causes. For I know by experience, from someone who I can answer for as well as myself, and who could not possibly be thought weak or enchanted, who, after hearing a friend's account of an unexpected episode of impotence which caused much shame, was horrified to find the same droopy condition taking hold of himself. He was so tyrannized by the memory of this, that he took on a tendency to repeated sexual failure; but in due course developed a mental strategy to combat it. By confessing his difficulty in advance he relieved the conflict in his mind, diminished expectations, and felt less oppressed by the prospect of failure. At a time of his own choosing (his mind being unfocused and free and all parts of his body feeling quite normal), he tested his virility by arranging for it to be seized by the other party as if he were taken unawares: this resulted in a complete cure. Once a man has been capable in this way, he cannot afterwards become incapable again, unless there is an organic cause. The only exception concerns the situation where passionate desire is closely intermingled with profound respect, especially where the opportunity comes unexpectedly and requires an immediate response. There is no way of dealing with this problem; I know someone who found it helpful to approach sex with his body as it were half satisfied elsewhere, so that the heat of his passion was diminished and now that he is older finds himself more able by virtue of being less so. Another was also helped by a friend who assured him that he had an armoury of therapeutic spells, which would certainly be efficacious. It would not be amiss if I describe how this happened.

A Nobleman of very good family who was a close friend of mine was married to a beautiful lady whose ex-suitor was present at the marriage feast. This greatly disturbed his friends, especially the hostess, one of his elderly relatives, who confided her fears in me. I reassured her as best I could and told her she could rely on me. By chance, I had in my bag a small piece of gold with celestial figures engraved on it, used as a charm against the effects of the sun and a remedy for headaches when worn properly. It was fixed in the middle of the head and kept in place with a ribbon tied under the chin. An extraordinary idea, but very relevant to the subject under discussion. Jacques Pelletier [physician, mathematician and humanist, ed.] had given me this unusual gift while he was staying in my house, and I decided to put it to use. I told my friend he was at risk of encountering the same bad luck as other bridegrooms sometimes had, because there were those present who had ill will toward him. Nonetheless I advised him he need not fear going to bed since I would act as his friend. I promised that in case of need I would perform a miracle on his behalf, provided only that he kept the whole matter secret. He was merely to indicate to me around midnight when they brought in refreshments, if things were not going well. It happened that he was so troubled by thoughts of failure that at the appointed hour he made me the sign. I whispered in his ear that he should rise from his bed and under the guise of shooing us all from the room, take my night-shirt in jest and put it on himself (we were the same size). He was to keep it on until he had carried out all my instructions, which were that after we had gone he should leave the bed-chamber to make water, and whilst doing so perform certain gestures and repeat certain incantations three times over. On each repetition he was to tie the ribbon, which I gave him, around his waist and place the gold medallion attached to it just over his kidneys with the figures on it in a special position. Finally, after having secured the ribbon so that it could not be untied or accidentally lost, he was to return to the task in hand, not forgetting to take off my night-shirt and spread it over the bed so that it covered them both.

This nonsense is the essence of the matter, for we cannot but believe that strange rituals betoken secret powers. The more absurd they are, the more likely they are to command respect. To conclude, my magic charm proved more Venereal than Solar, more productive than preventative. It was an unusual impulse that caused me to do a thing so alien to my nature, for I am an enemy to all pretence and hate all forms of deception whether for profit or just for show – if the action is not wicked then the road to it is.

Michel de Montaigne, 'On the Force of Imagination', *Essays* (1580)

Sexual Images in Dreams

In religious thinking dreams may be holy or profane. They have often been supposed to have a spiritual capacity, whereby God's will is directly revealed to humankind. But dream-sleep is also seen as a condition which weakens spiritual control and promotes the unfettered expression of our darkest impulses. Plato saw 'reason' as the regulating factor, whose influence was diminished during sleep. For Freud* dreams were the 'Royal Road' to our Unconscious. They expressed (in a disguised form) the fulfilment of sexual wishes from infancy, held to be unacceptable to the conscious mind. However, it has been clear for more than 2,000 years that sexual wishes, whether infantile or adult, frequently receive direct expression in dreams without the need for any kind of cover-up. They are, as Wittgenstein* long ago remarked, 'as common as rain'.*

Franz Julius Delitzsch was a German Lutheran Old Testament scholar. Born in 1813, he became professor of theology at Rostock in 1846 and at Leipzig in 1867. He was learned in Hebrew and Rabbinical law, translated the New Testament into Hebrew and made vigorous efforts to convert the Jews.

But as soon as ever dreaming is combined with the sleep, the spirit suffers, from the side of the dark and fiery life of the soul withdrawn from its light – driven round by the flesh and self – a degradation towards the soul; and from the selfishness of the soul, its selfish impulses, its restlessness stimulated by selfishness, are formed in the heart all kinds of sinful images, of which the man is ashamed when he awakens, and on account of which remorse sometimes disturbs even the dreamer, especially those dreaming forms that proceed from the sexual impulse and its allurements, which will be all the more dominant and unchaste the less the man in his waking state strives, and is accustomed, to keep himself in strict discipline on this side of his natural disposition. The modern doctrine of the soul, indeed, regards these dreams as free from guilt; but Scripture decides otherwise, and even looks upon the involuntary emission of seed as a loathsome contamination, which makes him who suffers it unclean for the current day (Lev. xv. 16), and even banishes the warrior from the camp (Deut. xxiii. 10); for it is a disgrace of the spirit that it has lost its royalty, and should allow itself to be involuntarily driven round by the wheel of nature. Our own conscience confirms the judgement from which the institutions of the Torah proceed; and the whole of antiquity, from India to Egypt, is unanimous on this μαινειν την σαρκα [pollution of the flesh, ed.] of the dreamer (Jude ver. 5). These licentious dreams show just this, that the spirit has let go the reins; it attains to the perception of it in the veiling of the spirit that follows them. For so far as man in God has once more attained power over himself, the spirit of the sleeper sinks not into the flesh, but into God, from whom it originated: it communes with God, and finds itself with its senses in God, as in falling asleep, so also still in awakening (Isa. xxvi. 9; Ps. cxxxix. 18, comp. iii. 6, iv. 9).

Franz Julius Delitzsch, *A System of Biblical Psychology* (1861)

Certain of the unnecessary pleasures and appetites are deemed to be unlawful; every man appears to have them, only in some persons they are controlled by the laws and by reason, and the

better desires prevail over them, and either they are wholly
banished or are few and weak; while in the case of others they
are stronger, and there are more of them.

Which appetites do you mean?

I mean those which are awake when the reasoning and taming
and ruling power is asleep; the wild beast in our nature, gorged
with meat or drink, starts up and walks about naked, and surfeits
after his manner, and there is no conceivable folly or crime,
however shameless or unnatural – not excepting incest or parricide, or the eating of forbidden food – of which such a nature
may not be guilty.

That is most true, he said.

But when a man's pulse is healthy and temperate, and he goes
to sleep cool and rational, after having supped on a feast of
reason and speculation, and come to knowledge of himself, having
indulged appetites neither too much nor too little, but just enough
to lay them to sleep, and prevent them and their enjoyments and
pains from interfering with the higher principle – leaving that in
the solitude of pure abstraction, free to contemplate and aspire
to the knowledge of the unknown, whether in past, present, or
future: when, again, before going to sleep he has allayed the
passionate element, if he has a quarrel against anyone – I say,
when, after pacifying the two irrational principles, he rouses up
the third or rational element before he takes his rest, then, as
you know, he attains truth most nearly, and is least likely to be
sport of fanciful and lawless visions.

In that opinion I entirely agree.

In saying this I have been running into a digression; but the
point I desire to note is that in all of us, even in good men, there
is such a latent wild-beast nature, which peers out in sleep. Pray,
consider whether I am right, and you agree with me in this view.

Yes, I agree.

Plato, *The Republic*, Book IX, 571 (c.400 BCE)

THE APPREHENSION OF BEAUTY

Against Reality

Jean-Paul Sartre (1905–80) argues that the process of imbuing real objects with aesthetic qualities is an attempt to impose the qualities of the imaginary domain upon the outside world. People and places are not beautiful in themselves but beautiful because we see them as such. However, we are disturbed by the translation of qualities from inner to outer world. Imaginary objects, aesthetic objects, are elusive, like fading dreams, forever beyond our reach. When we transpose this attitude on to our relations with external objects it has a peculiar effect. We react indifferently to them, they lose their real status and become iconically distanced from us. They cannot be possessed and for this reason, according to Sartre, we cannot desire them. 'Great beauty in a woman', he says, 'kills the desire for her.'

Together with his long-time friend Simone de Beauvoir, Sartre played a leading part in the development of the Existentialist movement following the Second World War. It was a way of thinking that emphasized personal uniqueness, freedom of choice and individual moral responsibility. It valorized 'authentic' choices and excoriated any attempt to evade responsibility under the guise of social or biological determinism. Such special pleading was, for the Existentialists, nothing but self-deception and 'bad faith'. Philosopher, novelist, playwright, literary critic and left-wing political commentator, Sartre dominated the French intellectual scene during the 1950s and 1960s, and was awarded the Nobel prize for literature in 1964.

Aesthetic contemplation is an induced dream and the passing into the real is an actual waking up. We often speak of the 'deception' experienced on returning to reality. But this does not explain that this discomfort also exists, for instance, after having witnessed a realistic and cruel play, in which case reality should be experienced as comforting. This discomfort is simply that of the dreamer on awakening; an entranced consciousness, engulfed in the imaginary, is suddenly freed by the sudden ending of the play, of the symphony, and comes suddenly in contact with existence. Nothing more is needed to arouse the nauseating disgust that characterizes the consciousness of reality.

From these few observations we can already conclude that the real is never beautiful. Beauty is a value applicable only to the imaginary and which means the negation of the world in its essential structure. This is why it is stupid to confuse the moral with the aesthetic. The values of the Good presume being-in-the-world, they concern action in the real and are subject from the outset to the basic absurdity of existence. To say that we 'assume' an aesthetic attitude to life is to constantly confuse the real and the imaginary. It does happen, however, that we do assume the attitude of aesthetic contemplation towards real events or objects. But in such cases every one of us can feel in himself a sort of recoil in relation to the object contemplated which slips into nothingness so that, from this moment on, it is no longer *perceived*; it functions as an *analogue* of itself, that is, that an unreal image of what it is appears to us through its actual presence. This image can be purely and simply the object 'itself' neutralized, annihilated, as when I contemplate a beautiful woman or death at a bullfight; it can also be the imperfect and confused appearance of *what it could be* through what it is, as when the painter grasps the harmony of two colours as being greater, more vivid, *through* the real blots he finds on a wall. The object at once appears to be *in back of* itself, becomes *untouchable*, it is beyond our reach; and hence arises a sort of sad disinterest in it. It is in this sense that we may say that great beauty in a woman kills the desire for her. In fact we cannot at the same time place ourselves on the plane of the aesthetic when this unreal 'herself' which we admire appears and on the realistic plane of physical possession. To desire her we must forget she is beautiful, because desire is a plunge into the heart of existence, into what is most contingent and most absurd. Aesthetic contemplation of *real* objects is of the same structure as paramnesia [a disorder of memory in which scenes and events experienced for the first time are thought to have been 'remembered', ed.], in which the real object functions as an analogue of itself in the past. But in one of the cases there is a negating and in the other a placing a thing in the past. Paramnesia differs from the aesthetic attitude as memory differs from imagination.

Jean-Paul Sartre, *The Psychology of Imagination* (1948)

The Cultivation of Feelings

During the 'melancholy winter' of 1826–7 the empiricist philosopher and social reformer John Stuart Mill (1806–73) went through a crisis in his mental life. Everything that had previously afforded him pleasure now seemed devoid of interest, a source of nothing but indifference. A modern psychiatrist would probably have diagnosed him as suffering from 'clinical depression' and prescribed antidepressant medication. But Mill, who had been educated by his father to believe that pleasurable feelings were somehow bonded to experience through a process of association, attributed his depression to the severance of this bond, brought about by the habit of philosophical analysis! Asking himself whether he would be happy if all his objectives in life were realized, he came up with a resounding 'No'. It was borne in on him that something more than association was needed in order to infuse his perceptions with meaning which would resist dissolution by philosophical analysis – the function of imagination. Wordsworth's poetry had provided Mill with a profound insight into the workings of his own mind. However, it caused a rift with his friend and fellow member of the early Utilitarian Society, John Arthur Roebuck, who saw in it nothing but 'flowers and butterflies'.

What made Wordsworth's poems a medicine for my state of mind was that they expressed, not mere outward beauty, but states of feeling, and of thought coloured by feeling, under the excitement of beauty. They seemed to be the very culture of the feelings, which I was in quest of. In them I seemed to draw from a source of inward joy, of sympathetic and imaginative pleasure, which could be shared in by all human beings; which had no connexion with struggle or imperfection, but would be made richer by every improvement in the physical or social condition of mankind. From them I seemed to learn what would be the perennial sources of happiness, when all the greater evils of life shall have been removed. [. . .]

The English character, and English social circumstances, make it so seldom possible to derive happiness from the exercise of the sympathies, that it is not wonderful if they count for little in an Englishman's scheme of life. In most other countries the paramount importance of the sympathies as a constituent of individual happiness is an axiom, taken for granted rather than needing any formal statement; but most English thinkers almost seem to regard them as necessary evils, required for keeping men's actions benevolent and compassionate. Roebuck was, or appeared to be, this kind of Englishman. He saw little good in any cultivation of the feelings, and none at all in cultivating them through the imagination, which he thought was only cultivating illusions. It was in vain I urged on him that the imaginative emotion which an idea, when vividly conceived, excites in us, is not an illusion but a fact, as real as any of the other qualities of objects; and far from implying anything erroneous and delusive in our mental apprehension of the object, is quite consistent with the most accurate knowledge and most perfect practical recognition of all its physical and intellectual laws and relations. The intensest feeling of the beauty of a cloud lighted by the setting sun is no hindrance to my knowing that the cloud is vapour of water, subject to all the laws of vapours in a state of suspension; and I am just as likely to allow for, and act on, these physical laws whenever there is occasion to do so, as if I had been incapable of perceiving any distinction between beauty and ugliness.

John Stuart Mill, 'A Crisis in My Mental History', *Autobiography* (1873)

The Experience of Supreme Beauty

Aldous Huxley (1894–1963), grandson of T.H. Huxley and brother of the biologist, Sir Julian, is perhaps best known for his futuristic novel* Brave New World, *published in 1932. Educated* *at Eton and Balliol College, Oxford, where he read English, he afterwards became a writer and journalist, joining Lady Ottoline Morrell's circle of friends. He was a frequent visitor to her 'salon' at Garsington Manor during the First World War, together with D.H. Lawrence, John Middleton Murry, Virginia Woolf*, Bertrand Russell*, the Stracheys and other literary figures of the time.*

In 1937 he moved to California where he later experimented with mescalin, a drug derived from the peyote cactus, long known to Mexican Indians for its hallucinogenic properties, and used by them in religious ceremonies. He was struck by the heightened visual awareness produced, which went beyond any previously known perception, and was for him a transcendental revelation.

The images of the archetypal world are symbolic; but since we, as individuals, do not fabricate them, but find them 'out there' in the collective unconscious[12] they exhibit some at least of the characteristics of given reality and are coloured. The non-symbolic inhabitants of the mind's antipodes exist in their own right, and like the given facts of the external world are coloured. Indeed, they are far more intensely coloured then external data. This may be explained, at least in part, by the fact that our perceptions of the external world are habitually clouded by the verbal notions in terms of which we do our thinking. We are for ever attempting to convert things into signs for the most intelligible abstractions of our own invention. But in doing so, we rob these things of a great deal of their native thinghood.

At the antipodes of the mind, we are more or less completely free of language, outside the system of conceptual thought. Consequently our perception of visionary objects possesses all the freshness, all the naked intensity, of experiences which have never been verbalized, never assimilated to lifeless abstractions. Their colour (that hallmark of givenness) shines forth with a brilliance which seems to us praeternatural, because it is in fact entirely

12 See Carl Gustav Jung, pp. 342–8.

natural – entirely natural in the sense of being entirely unsophis-
ticated by language or the scientific, philosophical and utilitarian
notions, by means of which we ordinarily re-create the given world
in our own drearily human image.

Our linguistic habits lead us into error. For example, we are
apt to say, 'I imagine', when what we should have said is, 'The
curtain was lifted that I might see'. Spontaneous or induced,
visions are never our personal property. Memories belonging to
the ordinary self have no place in them. The things seen are
wholly unfamiliar. 'There is nor reference or resemblance', in Sir
William Herschel's phrase, 'to any objects recently seen or even
thought of.' When faces appear, they are never the faces of friends
or acquaintances. We are out of the Old World, and exploring
the antipodes.

For most of us most of the time, the world of everyday experience seems rather dim and drab. But for a few people often,
and for a fair number occasionally, some of the brightness of
visionary experience spills over, as it were, into common seeing,
and the everyday universe is transfigured. Though still recogniz-
ably itself, the Old World takes on the quality of the mind's
antipodes. Here is an entirely characteristic description of this
transfiguration of the everyday world [by the Irish poet A.E.
(George Russell) in his *Candle of Vision*, ed.].

'I was sitting on the seashore, half listening to a friend arguing
violently about something which merely bored me. Unconsciously to myself, I looked at a film of sand I had picked up
on my hand, when I suddenly saw the exquisite beauty of every
little grain of it; instead of being dull, I saw that each particle
was made up on a perfect geometrical pattern, with sharp angles,
from each of which a brilliant shaft of light was reflected, while
each tiny crystal shone like a rainbow . . . The rays crossed and
recrossed, making exquisite patterns of such beauty that they
left me breathless . . . Then, suddenly, my consciousness was
lighted up from within and I saw in a vivid way how the whole
universe was made up of particles of material which, no matter
how dull and lifeless they might seem, were nevertheless filled
with this intense beauty. For a second or two the whole world
appeared as a blaze of glory. When it died down, it left me with

something I have never forgotten and which constantly reminds me of the beauty locked up in every minute speck of material around us.' [. . .]

Aldous Huxley, *Heaven and Hell* (1956)

Shakespeare's Poetic Imagination

William Shakespeare (1564–1616), eldest son of John Shakespeare, a glovemaker, and Mary Arden, was born in Stratford-upon-Avon. At the age of eighteen he married Anne Hathaway, eight years his senior, and the following year a daughter, Susanna, was born. Two years later twins, Hamnet and Judith, were added to their family. He probably began writing for the stage in the late 1580s, but his plays were published by being performed, and many of them were not printed until after his death. Despite his poetic genius (which in the following extract he sees as akin to madness), and importance in world literature enduring over four centuries, there is a dearth of reliable information about his life.

> Lovers and madmen have such seething brains,
> Such shaping fantasies, that apprehend
> More than cool reason ever comprehends.
> The lunatic, the lover, and the poet
> Are of imagination all compact:
> One sees more devils than vast hell can hold;
> That is the madman: the lover, all as frantic,
> Sees Helen's beauty in a brow of Egypt:
> The poet's eye, in a fine frenzy rolling,
> Doth glance from heaven to earth, from earth to heaven,
> And, as imagination bodies forth
> The forms of things unknown, the poet's pen
> turns them to shapes, and gives to airy nothing
> A local habitation and a name.
> Such tricks hath strong imagination,
> That, if it would but apprehend some joy,
> It comprehends some bringer of that joy;

Or in the night, imagining some fear,
How easy is a bush supposed a bear?

William Shakespeare, *A Midsummer Night's Dream* (1594)

MEMORY

I had also, during many years, followed a golden rule, namely that whenever a published fact, a new observation or thought came across me, which was opposed to my general results, to make a memorandum of it without fail and at once; for I had found by experience that such facts and thoughts were far more apt to escape from the memory than favourable ones.

Charles Darwin, 'Autobiography', in *The Life and Letters of Charles Darwin* (1887)

Memory is about the past, but if it did nothing but provide us with a home movie of our lives, it would be merely recreational. It derives evolutionary importance because it helps us to learn from experience and to predict the future, to understand the nature of cause and effect and to adapt ourselves to prevailing conditions. The process begins early. It has recently been shown that unborn babies can be taught to recognize and remember that sounds and vibrations are 'harmless'. When unborn babies were first exposed to such stimuli an increase in foetal heart-rate and movements was observed. But after several repetitions the heart-rate and increased movements diminished. Twenty-four hours later the babies still failed to react. They appeared to have 'learnt' to ignore the acoustic stimuli.[1] Sadly however, it is well known that our ability to adapt tails off as we grow older, and this has

1 See Cathelijne F. van Heteren et al., 'Foetal Learning and Memory', *Lancet*, 356 (2000), 1169.

recently received experimental corroboration on a large sample of healthy people. There is a measurable and marked deterioration in our capacity to remember names, faces and appropriate reactions to situations, which falls away in a linear fashion from the age of forty-five.[2]

Success as a species suggests that memory, at least during the time taken to reproduce and rear a family, must be reasonably reliable. Yet just as philosophers and scientists have been bothered by issues concerning the accuracy of perception, so the truthfulness of memories has been called into question. The two processes are intimately linked, for if we are unsure to what degree immediate perception of the external world is shaped by internal factors, how much more does this apply to our experience of the past. Conjured as it is from within ourselves, brought into being as a copy, a reproduction from a distant original, we are bound to wonder at its trustworthiness.

This debate, particularly relevant to assessing the credibility of testimony in legal proceedings, has been given renewed urgency in recent times by the polarization of opinion about memories of childhood sexual abuse, 'recovered' or 'invented' during the course of psychotherapy. Such memories are not only versions of far-off events, but also lack continuity with the rest of a person's remembered life. If our normal experience is accompanied by an underlying sense of sequential order, by the availability in memory of a consistent history of our life, these recovered memories, by definition, interrupt that narrative. They appear as ugly intrusions in an apparently seamless story. Their existence raises as many questions about the process of forgetting, as it does about the act of remembering.

Do memories simply decay with the passage of time, and are they then lost for ever? Are they displaced by newly minted impressions? Are they 'repressed', as Freud[*] (and Darwin[*]) suggested, consigned to the unconscious mind because the conscious mind 'does not want to know', there to lie not dormant but perpetually threatening to our general well-being, wreaking

2 Keith Wesnes, personal communication, Cognitive Drug Research Ltd, Reading, England, 2001.

neurotic havoc with our lives until some therapeutic prince facilitates their reappearance? Or are traumatic memories (as Pierre Janet, Freud's younger contemporary, and Joseph Breuer, Freud's older mentor, thought), split off, dissociated from immediate consciousness, prevented from being worn away by the accretion of new associations, not because the conscious mind 'wants' to loose them, but because it does not possess the key to unlock them and so cannot do otherwise? Is it inherent in traumatic experiences to dissolve associative glue so that they become isolated and inaccessible, eclipsed by their very nature in some cut-off island of consciousness? Or perhaps more than likely, all of these things can happen.

Memory, in fact, is not a unitary category, it refers to a diverse group of mental phenomena – I can remember the meaning of the word 'father', I can recall my father's name and the telephone number of my first home, I can recognize him in a photograph, remember him teaching me how to ride a bicycle, remember the mixture of fear and exhilaration when he first let go of the saddle, and I can still remember how to cycle into town. All these represent different types of memory. Looked at from the cognitive point of view, what they have in common is the re-activation of previously stored information, and it turns out that they are mediated in different parts of the brain.

Explicit or declarative memory refers to the reactivation of conscious experiences from the past such as life-events (episodic or autobiographical) or learnt facts like the name of the Prime Minister (semantic). Implicit or non-declarative memory refers to unconsciously stored items and is further subdivided into priming (the preserved templates of sound or shape that facilitate recognition of objects from reduced cues), procedural (learnt skills and habits), and emotional (that is to say those aspects of an emotional experience that are unconsciously registered).

We can trace the 'life-history' of a package of sensory information being introduced into our memory system in the following manner. First there is 'iconic memory'. This refers to the peripheral after-effect of the stimulus on the end-organ; for example, the local changes induced in the retina of the eye during vision. It remains for less than a second, after which time the sensory receptor returns to its pre-stimulus state. If the sensation has not been 'moved on' during that time it will not be registered in the central system.

The next staging post is 'short-term' or 'working' memory. This system is located in the pre-frontal cortex and functions like a buffer in computing. It receives the incoming information and enables me to use it, combine it with pre-existing information called-up from 'long-term memory', and carry out various cognitive manipulations, reading, calculating, deciding, and so on. However, it only lasts for a period of minutes. I can only hold a limited amount of diverse information in my mind at the same time. If I want to remember the beginning of the sentence I am now writing and make it fit in with the end, it had better not be too long.

Finally there is 'long-term memory', where permanent storage occurs. Working memories will be further processed and encoded before being 'sent on' for storage in different parts of the brain, the particular site of storage depending upon the area of brain involved in the original experience. It would be wrong to gather from the above description that we know much about all this. We do not. Most of our knowledge comes from observing the specific deficits in memory that accompany damage to particular areas of the brain. Brain imaging is another source of evidence. For example it is thought that a part of the brain called the hippocampus is involved in storing spacial information. In some species of bird and small mammal it has been found to enlarge during seasons when the demand for navigational skills is greatest. And now there is evidence from MRI (magnetic resonance imaging) scans that London taxi drivers have larger hippocampi than normal folk, and they get bigger and bigger according to the number of years they have been driving![3] Similarly, evidence exists to show that areas of the brain representing the left-hand get progressively larger over the years in musicians who finger string instruments.[4] None the less 'Storage' really remains a

3 Eleanor Maguire et al., *Proceedings of the National Academy of Sciences of the USA*, March, 2000.
4 Thomas Elbert et al., *Science* 270 (1995).

metaphor for the unknown process that enables us to remember. How memories are encoded, whether or not they leave permanent physical traces or 'engrams' in the synaptic network, whether such traces are called into being by the act of retrieval, and how retrieval is accomplished are almost as much a mystery today as they were in Plato's time, when he compared the impress of events on memory to that of a ring on wax. But we do have some interesting hypotheses.

One of the most popular candidates for 'wax' in current neuroscientific thinking is the synaptic junction between nerves. This theory concerning the mechanism of memory at the cellular level invokes the phenomenon of 'long-term potentiation' or LTP, which has been widely studied in the aforementioned hippocampus. When the hippocampus is knocked out, new learning is impaired, it appears to play some role in all retrieval processes and so the behaviour of its neurons is particularly interesting. Suppose we have two neurons joined at a synapse, so that when an impulse travels down the first one and crosses the gap, the second becomes activated. What LTP refers to, is the enhanced responsiveness of the second neuron after high-frequency stimulation of the first. It has been shown that once LTP has been established, a relatively low level of stimulation of the first neuron will result in a high level of activity in the second, and this effect can last for several weeks. Conversely, LTD, 'long-term depression', has also been described, whereby the activity of a synapse is reduced in response to certain patterns of activity. It is not difficult to see why this physiological ability to turn the strength of synaptic connections up and down has suggested itself as a likely basis for the brain's enormous information-storing and processing capability.

However, there are difficulties with this idea. Memory lasts for months and years, not just days and weeks. If the physical 'files' in the brain are rapidly decaying or decaying at an uneven rate, as LTP does in networks of neurons, one would expect memory to be even more unstable than it is. Clearly we are far from knowing the whole story.

But however memory is physically represented, its nature and significance as an individual experience remain mysterious.

Those inwardly-directed people typified by romantic poets such as Coleridge* or writers like Hazlitt* and Proust*, who cherish the imagination over and above the mundane outside world, also tend to see something mystical, transcendental, in the transformation of present experience into the remembered past. For them, memories are not pale reflections of bygone experiences, they are heightened versions of reality, better indeed and more profoundly truthful, than the originals from which they are derived.

THE VALUE OF MEMORY

Memory as a Magnifying Glass

William Hazlitt (1778–1830), prolific journalist, writer and critic, was the son of a Unitarian minister. He was brought up in the village of Wem, near Shrewsbury. He took up literature under the influence of Coleridge*. His early career as a parliamentary reporter and political commentator was dictated by a keen sense of social responsibility. Like Coleridge he was an enthusiastic supporter of the French Revolution and of Napoleon. The following passage is abstracted from a posthumous publication.

Complaints are frequently made of the vanity and shortness of human life, when, if we examine its smallest details, they present a world by themselves. The most trifling objects, retraced with the eye of memory, assume the vividness, the delicacy, and importance of insects seen through a magnifying glass. There is no end of the brilliancy or the variety. The habitual feeling of the love of life may be compared to 'one entire and perfect chrysolite', which, if analysed, breaks into a thousand shining fragments. Ask the sum-total of the value of human life, and we are puzzled with the length of the account, and the multiplicity of items in it: take any one of them apart, and it is wonderful what matter for reflection will be found in it! As I write this, the *Letter-Bell* passes; it has a lively, pleasant sound with it, and not only fills the street with its importunate clamour, but rings clear through the length of many half-forgotten years. It strikes upon the ear, it vibrates to the brain, it wakes me from the dream of time, it flings me back upon my first entrance into life, the period of my first coming to town, when all around was strange, uncertain, adverse – a hubbub of confused noises, a chaos of shifting objects – and when this sound alone, startling me with the recollection of a letter I had to send to the friends I had lately left, brought me as it were to myself, made me feel that I had links still connecting me with the universe, and gave me hope and patience to persevere. At that loud-tinkling, interrupted sound, the long line of blue hills near the place where I was brought up waves in the horizon, a golden sunset hovers over them, the dwarf oaks rustle their red leaves in the evening breeze, and the road from Wem to Shrewsbury, by which I first set out on my journey through life, stares me in the face as plain, but, from time and change, not less visionary and mysterious than the pictures in the *Pilgrim's Progress*.

William Hazlitt, 'The Letter-Bell' (1839)

Proust's Madeleine

The mysterious nature of certain moments, as described by Marcel Proust, admits us into a world of remembered experience that transcends everyday reality. Proust (1871–1922), was the son of a French doctor and a beautiful Franco-Jewish woman named Jeanne Weil, who doted on him. He developed severe asthma at the age of nine, which plagued him for the rest of his life. Although he was a socialite in his youth, following the death of his parents within two years of each other he became a recluse. For the last sixteen years of his life, he scarcely left his room, which he had soundproofed with cork tiles.

It was during this period that he wrote A La Recherche du Temps Perdu, (*deadeningly translated into English as* Remembrance of Things Past), *a continuous novel which eventually appeared in eight volumes. His minute analysis of human sensibility and insight into the workings of the unconscious mind made it a masterpiece of modern literature.*

When I thought of what Bergotte had said to me: 'You are ill, but one cannot pity you for you have the joys of the mind', how mistaken he had been about me! How little joy there was in this sterile lucidity! Even if sometimes perhaps I had pleasures (not of the mind), I sacrificed them always to one woman after another; so that, had fate granted me another hundred years of life and sound health as well, it would merely have added a series of extensions to an already tedious existence, which there seemed to be no point in prolonging at all, still less for any great length of time. As for the 'joys of the intelligence', could I call by that name those cold observations which my clairvoyant eye or my power of accurate ratiocination made without any pleasure and which remained always unfertile?

But it is sometimes just at the moment when we think that everything is lost that the intimation arrives which may save us; one has knocked at all the doors which lead nowhere, and then one stumbles without knowing it on the only door through which one can enter – which one might have sought in vain for a hundred years – and it opens of its own accord. Revolving the gloomy thoughts which I have just recorded, I had entered the courtyard of the Guermantes mansion and in my absentminded state I had failed to see a car which was coming towards me; the chauffeur gave a shout and I just had time to step out of the way, but as I moved sharply backwards I tripped against the uneven paving-stones in front of the coach-house. And at the moment when, recovering my balance, I put my foot on a stone which was slightly lower than its neighbour, all my discouragement vanished and in its place was that same happiness which at various epochs of my life had been given to me by the sight of trees which I had thought that I recognized in the course of a drive near Balbec, by the sight of the twin steeples of Martinville, by the flavour of a madeleine dipped in tea, and by all those other sensations of which I have spoken and of which the last works of Vinteuil had seemed to me to combine the quintessential character. Just as, at the moment when I tasted the madeleine, all anxiety about the future, all intellectual doubts had disappeared, so now those that a few seconds ago had assailed me on the subject of the reality of my literary gifts, the reality even of literature, were removed as if by magic. I had followed no new train of reasoning, discovered no decisive argument, but the difficulties which had seemed insoluble a moment ago had lost all importance. The happiness which I had just felt was unquestionably the same as that which I had felt when I tasted the madeleine soaked in tea. But if on that occasion I had put off the task of searching for the profounder causes of my emotion, this time I was determined not to resign myself to a failure to understand them. The emotion was the same; the difference, purely material, lay in the images evoked: a profound azure intoxicated my eyes, impressions of coolness, of dazzling light, swirled round me and in my desire to seize them – as afraid to move as I had been on the earlier occasion when I had continued to savour the taste of the madeleine while I tried to draw into my consciousness whatever it was that it recalled to me – I continued, ignoring the evident amusement of the great crowd of chauffeurs, to stagger as I had staggered a few seconds ago, with one foot on the higher paving-stone and the other on the lower. Every time that I merely repeated this physical movement, I achieved nothing, but if I succeeded, forgetting the Guermantes party, in recapturing what I had felt when I first placed my feet on the ground in this way, again the dazzling and indistinct vision fluttered near me, as if to say: 'Seize me as I pass if you can, and try to solve the riddle of happiness which I set you.' And almost at once I recognized the vision: it was Venice, of which my efforts to describe it and the supposed snapshots taken by my memory had never told me anything, but which the sensation which I had once experienced as I stood upon two uneven stones in the baptistery of St Mark's had, recurring a moment ago, restored to me complete with all the other sensations linked on that day to that particular sensation, all of which had been waiting in their place – from which with imperious suddenness a chance happening had caused them to emerge – in the series of forgotten days. In the same way the taste of the little madeleine had recalled Combray to me. But why had the images of Combray and of Venice, at these two different moments, given me a joy which was like a certainty and which sufficed, without any other proof, to make death a matter of indifference to me?

Marcel Proust, *Remembrance of Things Past: Vol. III, Time Regained* (1927)

In Praise of Forgetfulness

Forgetting is not just a nuisance, it is an art to be cultivated. Most of us would like to forget unpleasant things, but Kierkegaard points out that the recollection of pleasant happenings also produces a kind of pain, an awareness of their irretrievable nature. So trying to eliminate all unpleasantness through suppression of all memory would, if successful, result in total oblivion. Moreover, unwanted memories have a habit of reappearing. Kierkegaard recommends a different procedure – talking. Writing thirteen years before Freud's birth, he proposes that talking about painful experiences can deprive them of their bitterness, their quality is transmuted through the act of remembering, so that they can then be more easily 'forgotten'.

Søren Kierkegaard (1813–55), was a Danish philosopher and religious writer. His struggle with a religious commitment, which was intermingled with ill-defined guilt, led him to break off his engagement to Regina Olsen, whom he loved. He explored the dilemma created by the opposition of faith and human love through a study of Abraham in his beautiful book, Fear and Trembling. *He attacked official Christianity, emphasizing the doctrine of 'subjective truth' to be found within the individual, and his work was an inspiration to existential theology. He was not above attacking his own books in anonymous reviews.*

To forget – all men wish to forget, and when something unpleasant happens, they always say: Oh, that one might forget! But forgetting is an art that must be practised beforehand. The ability to forget is conditioned upon the method of remembering, but this again depends upon the mode of experiencing reality. Whoever plunges into his experiences with the momentum of hope will remember in such wise that he is unable to forget. *Nil admirari* [to wonder at nothing, ed.] is therefore the real philosophy. No moment must be permitted so great a significance that it cannot be forgotten when convenient; each moment ought, however, to have so much significance that it can be recollected at will. Childhood, which is the age which remembers best, is at the same time most forgetful. The more poetically one remembers, the more easily one forgets; for remembering poetically is really only another expression for forgetting. In a poetic memory the experience has undergone a transformation, by which it has lost all its painful aspects. To remember in this manner one must be careful how one lives, how one enjoys. Enjoying an experience to its full intensity to the last minute will make it impossible either to remember or to forget. For there is then nothing to remember except a certain satiety, which one desires to forget, but which now comes back to plague the mind with an involuntary remembrance. Hence, when you begin to notice that a certain pleasure or experience is acquiring too strong a hold upon the mind, you stop a moment for the purpose of remembering. No other method can better create a distaste for continuing the experience too long. From the beginning one should keep the enjoyment under control, never spreading every sail to the wind in any resolve; one ought to devote oneself to pleasure with a certain suspicion, a certain wariness, if one desires to give the lie to the proverb which says that no one can have his cake and eat it too. The carrying of concealed weapons is usually forbidden, but no weapon is so dangerous as the art of remembering. It gives one a very peculiar feeling in the midst of one's enjoyment to look back upon it for the purpose of remembering it.

One who has perfected himself in the twin arts of remembering and forgetting is in a position to play at battledore and shuttle-cock with the whole of existence.

The extent of one's power to forget is the final measure of one's elasticity of spirit. If a man cannot forget he will never amount to much. Whether there be somewhere a Lethe gushing forth, I do not know; but this I know, that the art of forgetting can be developed. However, this art does not consist in permitting the impressions to vanish completely; forgetfulness is one thing, and the art of forgetting something quite different. It is easy to see that most people have a very meagre understanding of this art, for they ordinarily wish to forget only what is unpleasant, not what is pleasant. This betrays a complete one-sidedness. Forgetting is the true expression for an ideal process of assimilation by which the experience is reduced to a sounding-board for the soul's own music. Nature is great because it has forgotten that it was chaos; but this thought is subject to revival at any time. As a result of attempting to forget only what is unpleasant, most people have a conception of oblivion as an untameable force which drowns out the past. But forgetting is really a tranquil and quiet occupation, and one which should be exercised quite as much in connection with the pleasant as with the unpleasant. A pleasant experience has as past something unpleasant about it, by which it stirs a sense of privation; this unpleasantness is taken away by an act of forgetfulness. The unpleasant has a sting, as all admit. This, too, can be removed by the art of forgetting. But if one attempts to dismiss the unpleasant absolutely from mind, as many do who dabble in the art of forgetting, one soon learns how little that helps. In an unguarded moment it pays a surprise visit, and it is then invested with all the forcibleness of the unexpected. This is absolutely contrary to every orderly arrangement in a reasonable mind. No misfortune or difficulty is so devoid of affability, so deaf to all appeals, but that it may be flattered a little; even Cerberus accepted bribes of honey-cakes and it is not only the lassies who are beguiled. The art in dealing with such experiences consists in talking them over, thereby depriving them of their bitterness; not forgetting them absolutely, but forgetting them for the sake of remembering them. Even in the case of memories such that one might suppose an eternal oblivion to be the only safeguard, one need permit oneself only a little trickery, and the deception will succeed for the skilful. Forgetting is the shears with which you cut away what you cannot use, doing it under the supreme direction of memory. Forgetting and remembering are thus identical arts, and the artistic achievement of this identity is the Archimedean point from which one lifts the whole world. When we say that we *consign* something to oblivion, we suggest simultaneously that it is to be forgotten and yet also remembered.

Søren Kierkegaard, 'The Rotation Method', *Either/Or* (1843)

THE TRUSTWORTHINESS OF MEMORY

How False Memories and False Perceptions Can Arise

Plato* (c.428/7–c.348/7) *was an Athenian aristocrat. Little is known of his history, save for the close association with Socrates, who as an old man was sentenced to death for corrupting Athenian youth. Plato's account of Socrates' execution (by drinking hemlock) may be inaccurate, as may the other words he puts into Socrates' mouth as a rhetorical device. He wrote* Theaetetus *towards the end of his life. In it Socrates suggests that experiences (sensations, thoughts, etc.) may be imperfectly recorded in the mind, or that their record may become adulterated over a period of time. True recognition arises when the stored template or record is accurately matched with the pattern of stimuli that originally produced it.*[5] *Mismatch gives rise to false opinion and errors in perception.*

Lacking neuroanatomical knowledge, Plato does not speculate on the mechanism whereby mental records are established, he simply compares the process to the impress of a signet ring on a wax seal. In principle, however, modern neuroscientific notions of brain plasticity are not so different. We now envisage repeated stimuli deriving from external objects, being transformed by sense organs and conducted to the brain in the form of nerve impulses, where, in place of Plato's moulded wax, they set up an 'engram' conceived as an enduring pattern of connexions between different brain cells, a tendency for certain groups of neurons to fire at the same time. Such brain circuits can fire off spontaneously, in the absence of the original stimulus, thus producing a false perception.[6] *In order to render some parts less obscure, I have made minor editorial changes in the following passage.*

Soc.   I would have you imagine, then, that there exists in the
            mind of man a block of wax, which is of different sizes

5 For a modern version of this theory see S. Kosslyn and A. Sussman 1995. pp. 34–6.
6 See Joseph LeDoux, *The Emotional Brain* pp. 134–6.

in different men; harder, moister, and having more or less of purity in one than another, and in some of an intermediate quality.

Theaet.   I see.

Soc.   Let us say that this tablet is a gift of Memory, the mother of the Muses; and that when we wish to remember anything which we have seen, or heard, or thought in our own minds, we hold the wax to the perceptions and thoughts, and in that material receive the impression of them as from the seal of a ring; and that we remember and know what is imprinted as long as the image lasts; but when the image is effaced, or cannot be taken, then we forget and do not know.

Theaet.   Let us imagine that.

Soc.   Now, when a person has this knowledge, and is considering something which he sees or hears, may not false opinion arise in the following manner?

Theat.   In what manner?

Soc.   When he sometimes mistakes what he does not know for what he knows. We were wrong before in denying the possibility of this.

Theaet.   And how would you amend the former statement?

Soc.   I should begin by making a list of the impossible cases which must be excluded. No one can think one thing to be another when he does not perceive either of them, but has the memorial or seal of both of them in his mind; nor can any mistaking of one thing for another occur, when he only knows one, and does not know, and has no impression of the other; nor can he think that what he does not know is something else that he does not know, or that what he knows is what he does not know; nor that one thing which he perceives is some other thing which he perceives, or that a thing which he does not perceive is a thing which he perceives; or that one thing which he does not perceive is another thing which he does not perceive; or that a thing which he perceives is a thing which he does not perceive; nor again, can he think that one thing which he knows and perceives, and of which he has the impression coinciding with sense, is another thing which he knows and perceives, and of which he has the impression coinciding with sense; – this last case, if possible, is still more inconceivable than the others; nor can he think that a thing which he knows is any other thing which he knows and perceives, and of which he has the memorial coinciding with sense, nor so long as these agree, can he think that a thing which he perceives is another thing which he knows and perceives; or that a thing which he does not know and does not perceive, is the same as another thing which he does not know and does not perceive; or that a thing which he does not perceive is another thing which he does not know and does not perceive; or that a thing which he does not perceive is another thing which he does not know and does not perceive: – All these utterly and absolutely exclude the possibility of false opinion. The only cases, if any, which remain, are the following.

Theaet.   What are they? If you tell me, then I may perhaps understand you better; but at present I am unable to follow you.

Soc.   A person may think that some things which he knows and perceives, or which he perceives and does not know, are some other things which he knows; or that some things which he knows and perceives, are other things which he knows and perceives.

Theaet.   I understand you less than ever now.

Soc.   Hear me once more, then: – I, knowing Theodorus, and remembering in my own mind what sort of person he is, and also what sort of person Theaetetus is, at one time see them, and at another time do not see them, and sometimes I touch them, and at another time not, or at one time I may hear them or perceive them in some other way, and at another time not perceive them, but still I remember them, and know them in my own mind.

Theaet.   Very true.

Soc.   Then, first of all, I want you to understand that a man may or may not perceive that which he knows.

Theaet.	True.
Soc.	And oftentimes a man will not perceive that which he does not know, and oftentimes he will only perceive it.
Theaet.	That is true again.
Soc.	See whether you can follow me better now: Socrates can recognize Theodorus and Theaetetus, but he sees neither of them, nor does he perceive them in any other way; he cannot then by any possibility imagine in his own mind that Theaetetus is Theodorus. Am I not right?
Theaet.	You are quite right.
Soc.	Then that was the first case of which I spoke?
Theaet.	Yes.
Soc.	The second case was, that I, knowing one of you and not knowing the other, and perceiving neither, can never think that he whom I do not know is he whom I know.
Theaet.	True.
Soc.	In the third case, not knowing and not perceiving either of you, I cannot think that a person whom I do not know is someone else whom I do not know. I need not again go over the catalogue of excluded cases, in which I cannot form a false opinion about you and Theodorus, either because I know both or because I am in ignorance of both, or as knowing one and not knowing the other. And the same of perceiving: do you understand me?
Theaet.	I do.
Soc.	The only possibility of erroneous opinion is, when knowing you and Theodorus, and having the seal or impression of both of you in the wax block, but seeing you both imperfectly and at a distance, I try to assign the right impression of either of you to the right vision, and fit this into the proper mould: if I succeed in this, recognition will take place; but if I fail and transpose them, putting the shoe on to the wrong foot, that is to say, putting the vision of either of you on to the wrong seal, or seeing you as in a mirror, when the sight flows from right to left – then 'heterodoxy' and false opinion ensues.
Theaet.	Yes, Socrates, that is precisely the sort of thing.
Soc.	Or again, when I know both of you, and see as well as

know one and not the other, and knowledge does not accord with perception – that was a case which you did not understand just now?

Theaet. No, I did not.

Soc. I meant to say, that when a person knows and perceives one of you, and his knowledge accords with his perception, he will never think him to be some other person, whom he knows and perceives, and the knowledge of whom accords with his perception – we agreed to that?

Theaet. True.

Soc. But there was an omission of the further case, in which, as we say, false opinion may arise, when knowing both, or seeing, or having some other sensible perception of both, I fail in holding the seal over against the corresponding sensation; like a bad archer, I miss and fall wide of the mark – and this is called falsehood.

Theaet. Yes, truly.

Soc When, therefore, perception is present to one of the seals or impressions and not to the other, and the mind fits the seal of the absent perception on the one which is present, in any case of this sort the mind is deceived; in a word, if our view is sound, there can be no error or deception about things which a man does not know and has never perceived, but only in things which are known and perceived; in these alone opinion turns and twists about, and becomes alternately true and false – true when the seals and impressions of sense meet straight and opposite – false when they go awry and crooked.

Theaet. And is not that, Socrates, nobly said?

Soc. Wait a little, and you will be better able to judge; for to think truly is noble, but to be deceived is base.

Theaet. Assuredly.

Soc. The cause of this, as they say, is in the wax: – When the wax in the soul of any one is deep and abundant, and smooth and perfectly tempered, then the impressions which pass through the senses and sink into the [waxen] heart of the soul, as Homer says in a parable, meaning to indicate the likeness of the soul to wax (κηρ = heart, κηρος = wax); these, I say, being pure and clear, and having a sufficient depth of wax, are also lasting, and minds, such as these, easily learn and easily retain, and are not liable to confusion, but have true thoughts, for they have plenty of room, and having clear impressions of things, as we term them, quickly distribute them into their proper places on the block. And such men are called wise. Would you not agree to that?

Theaet. Entirely.

Soc. But when the heart of any one is shaggy – as the poet who knew everything says, or muddy and of impure wax, or very soft, or very hard, then there is a corresponding defect in the mind – the soft are good at learning, but apt to forget; and the hard are the reverse; the shaggy and rugged and gritty, or those who have an admixture of earth or dung in their composition, have the impressions indistinct, as also the hard, for there is no depth in them; and the soft too are indistinct, for their impressions are easily confused and effaced. Yet greater is the indistinctness when they are all jostled together in a little soul, which has no room. These are the sorts of natures which have false opinion; for when they see or hear or think of anything, they are slow in assigning the right objects to the right impressions – in their stupidity they confuse them, and are apt to see and hear and think amiss – and such men are said to be deceived in their knowledge of objects, and ignorant.

Theaet. No man, Socrates, can say anything truer than that.

Soc. Then now we may admit the existence of false opinion in us?

Theaet. Certainly.

Soc. And of true opinion also?

Theaet. Yes.

Soc. We have at length satisfactorily proven beyond a doubt there are these two sorts of opinion?

Theaet. Undoubtedly.

Plato, *Theaetetus* (c.340BCE)

Things Which We Only Partly Forget

Aurelius Augustine (354–430) was born in the Roman province of Numidia, North Africa. His father, a Roman functionary, was pagan, his mother was a devout Christian. Sent to Carthage at the age of sixteen with a view to becoming a lawyer, he decided after completing his studies in 373 to teach rhetoric instead. He simultaneously embraced Manicheanism, a popular heresy founded a century earlier by Manes, the Persian. Manichean thought emphasized the opposition between good and evil principles in both mind and matter, denied the virgin birth and Christ's crucifixion and was considered by Christians to be an offensive perversion of their religion. Later, Augustine believed himself to have been in error, and was baptized, giving up his worldly possessions and founding a monastery in his birthplace, the small town of Tagaste. In his early forties, he emerged from ascetic life to be consecrated a bishop.

Augustine believed the most certain knowledge to derive not from sense perception, but from introspective exploration of one's own self. He regarded man as a union of body and immortal soul. Man's mind was unitary but expressed itself through three faculties, reason, memory and will. In the following passage, Augustine seems to foreshadow the distinction between storage and retrieval of memory, which has grown important to modern cognitive psychologists.

How cometh it to pass, that when the *Memory* itself hath lost anything (as it hath when we forget it) we do yet endeavour to remember it? And where do we seek this, but in the *Memory* itself. And if, by accident, one thing be offered for another, we reject it, till that do at last occur, which was sought by us; and when it occurs, we say *This is it*; which yet we would not say, unless we knew it to be the same; neither would we acknowledge it. Without doubt then, we had forgotten it in some sort, yet we had not wholly forgotten it; but by that part of the thing which we remembered, we sought the other part which we remembered not. Because the *Memory* observeth that now it did not carry all that Notion up and down together, as it was wont; but halting, as it were, for lack of use, it desireth what was wanting may be added. As when a man well known to us (whose name we have yet forgotten), whether we see him with our eyes, or think of him otherwise, if we have a desire to recover his true *Name*, whatsoever other name doth occur; it is not knit to the rest of that conception, which we were wont to have, both concerning him and it is still rejected, till that name be brought wherein our *Mind* may entirely rest. And whence cometh this, but from the *Memory*? For when we are put in mind thereof, by any other body, we acknowledge that it is the same by virtue of *Memory*. And when we do not believe it as any new thing; but, that which was told us to be true, we approve by way of *remembrance*. Now if it had been utterly defaced out of the *Mind*, we could not have *remembered* it, although we had been admonished thereof. Nor can we be said entirely to have *forgotten* that, which we remember ourselves to have *forgotten*; For that which we have entirely *forgotten*, we cannot procure again to remember.

St Augustine, 'What It Is to Have Reminiscence', *Confessions* (397–8)

STATE-DEPENDENT MEMORY

The Influence of the Environment on Memory

Despite the generally deleterious effects of alcohol on memory, there is evidence to show that things learned in a drunken state are more accurately recollected when we are once again intoxicated (see Goodwin et al., 'Alcohol and Recall: State-Dependent Effects in Man', Science 163 (1969), 1358–60). Similarly information originally learned in one context, for example a particular room (see S.M. Smith, 'Environmental Context and Recognition Memory Reconsidered', Bulletin of the Psychonomic Society 23 (1985), 173–6), appears to be more easily recalled when we are back in the same situation. An odd experiment investigated whether this would hold true when tasks were carried out underwater and on dry land!

Sixteen volunteer amateur divers were tested (eleven men and five women).

Testing took place at an open water site. For safety reasons, subjects were randomly assigned a partner, with whom all tests were undertaken. In each condition of a repeated-measures design, subjects viewed a sixteen-word list for 3 min. and were instructed to remember as many words as possible. Subjects in environment D (Dry) sat in a diving boat prior to the dive, with their masks tipped back and breathing tubes removed. In environment W (Wet) they dived to 20m, taking the word lists with them. An experimenter controlled the timing. Given the time taken to change environments and to help prevent primary memory effects, a 5-min. delay was interposed between learning and recognition in all conditions. To help control the effects of disruption, conditions that involved no change of environment also required the subjects to perform simple arithmetic calculations on formica slates, which were obtained by diving to 20m (DD) or ascending to the surface (WW). In conditions DW and WD the arithmetic was performed underwater.

The order of testing conditions was randomized for each pair, as was the assignment of lists. The lists and conditions were equally represented in each test session, and no subject performed more than one test within 24 hr. The recognition test allowed the subjects 5 min. to circle as many of the original list as possible from a list of 100 words (that included the originals, randomly positioned). To prevent rereading of the test lists, subjects were instructed to erase the lists at the end of the 3-min. learning period. Only 16 choices were allowed in the recognition test.

Four hundred one-syllable, four- and five-letter English nouns were randomly selected from the *Concise Oxford English Dictionary*. They were randomly assigned to one of four A4-sized formica slates, on which they were printed in upper case (100 per slate in a 10x10 matrix). Sixteen words were randomly selected from each list to form a test list and printed with the same lettering on the reverse side of the slate in insoluble black ink. Subjects wore breathing apparatus and diving equipment according to personal preference. The slates and their attached pencils were tied to the diver's weight-belts.

The weather produced calm-water conditions at the surface. In the W conditions subjects sat in clear but cool (14 degree C) water, surrounded by rocks and seaweed. Tests were undertaken in the early part of the working day. However, to help ensure that the subjects performed the experiment in a similar physical state, the DW and DD conditions were undertaken shortly after a working dive.

Summary of Results:
Environmental context produced small but statistically reliable effects on recognition memory. Words learnt underwater were best recalled there and vice versa.

Paul Emmerson, 'Effects of Environmental Context on Recognition Memory in an Unusual Environment', *Perceptual and Motor Skills* (1986)

THE LOCATION OF MEMORY

Where Memories Live

In contrast to psychoanalytic thinking, which postulates an unconscious mind filled with dynamically active 'unconscious ideas', Eweld Hering, Professor of Physiology, University of Prague (1880), argues that unconscious memories exist, but solely in physiological form. On this view, our unconscious 'inner life' is subjectively inaccessible and can only be described in materialistic terms.[7]

On examining more closely, we see plainly that memory is a faculty not only of our conscious states, but also, and much more so, of our unconscious ones. I was conscious of this or that yesterday, and am again conscious of it today. Where has it been meanwhile? It does not remain continuously within my

7 See also Hugo Munsterberg on the subconscious mind, p. 325.

consciousness, nevertheless it returns after having quitted it. Our ideas tread for a moment upon the stage of consciousness, and then go back again behind the scenes, to make way for others in their place. As the player is only a king when he is on the stage, so they too exist as ideas so long only as they are recognized. How do they live when they are off the stage? For we know that they are living somewhere; give them their cue and they reappear immediately. They do not exist continuously as ideas; what is continuous is the special disposition of nerve substance in virtue of which this substance gives out today the same sound which it gave yesterday if it is rightly struck. Countless reproductions of organic processes of our brain connect themselves orderly together, so that one acts as a stimulus to the next, but a phenomenon of consciousness is not necessarily attached to every link in the chain. From this it arises that a series of ideas may appear to disregard the order that would be observed in purely material processes of brain substance unaccompanied by consciousness; but on the other hand it becomes possible for a long chain of recollections to have its due development without each link in the chain being necessarily perceived by ourselves. One may emerge from the bosom of our unconscious thoughts without fully entering upon the stage of conscious perception; another dies away in unconsciousness, leaving no successor to take its place. Between the 'me' of today and the 'me' of yesterday lie night and sleep, abysses of unconsciousness; nor is there any bridge but memory with which to span them. Who can hope after this to disentangle the infinite intricacy of our inner life? For we can only follow its threads so far as they have strayed over within the bounds of consciousness. We might as well hope to familiarize ourselves with the world of forms that teem within the bosom of the sea by observing the few that now and again come to the surface and soon return to the deep.

The bond of union, therefore, which connects the individual phenomena of our consciousness lies in our unconscious world; and as we know nothing of this but what investigation into the laws of matter teach us – as, in fact, for purely experimental purposes, 'matter' and the 'unconscious' must be one and the same thing – so the physiologist has a full right to denote memory as, in the wider sense of the word, a function of brain substance, whose results, it is true, fall, as regards one part of them, into the domain of consciousness, while another and not less essential part escapes unperceived as purely material processes.

Eweld Hering, *On Memory* (1880)

BRAIN DAMAGE AND MEMORY

Loss of Recent Memory Following Hippocampal Lesions

In September 1953, William Beecher Scoville carried out an experimental operation on a young man (H.M.), suffering from intractable epilepsy. Parts of the temporal lobe of the brain, especially the hippocampus, hippocampal gyrus and uncus, were thought likely to be triggering seizures, and were therefore removed. There was a marked improvement in the patient's condition during the first year after operation, but an unexpected deficit in his memory became apparent. The nature of his difficulties suggested that the parts of the brain which had been removed were responsible for the memory of recent experience. This was confirmed by subsequent observation of other cases, however since no memory loss occurred when only the uncus and amygdala were removed, it was concluded that the hippocampus was critically concerned in the retention of new memories.

After operation this young man could no longer recognize the hospital staff nor find his way to the bathroom, and he seemed to recall nothing of the day-to-day events of his hospital life. There was also a partial retrograde amnesia, inasmuch as he did not remember the death of a favourite uncle three years previously, nor anything of the period in hospital, yet could recall some trivial events that had occurred just before his admission to the hospital. His early memories were apparently vivid and intact.

This patient's memory defect has persisted without improvement to the present time, and numerous illustrations of its severity could be given. Ten months ago the family moved from their old house to a new one a few blocks away on the same street; he still has not learned the new address, though remembering the old one perfectly, nor can he be trusted to find his way home alone. Moreover, he does not know where objects in continual use are kept; for example, his mother still has to tell him where to find the lawn mower, even though he may have been using it only the day before. She also states that he will do the same jigsaw puzzles day after day without showing any practice effect and that he will read the same magazines over and over again without finding their contents familiar. This patient has even eaten luncheon in front of one of us (B.M.) without being able to name, a mere half-hour later, a single item of food he had eaten; in fact, he could not remember having eaten luncheon at all. Yet to a casual observer this man seems like a relatively normal individual, since his understanding and reasoning are undiminished [. . .]

Psychological Examination. – This was performed on April 26, 1955. The memory defect was immediately apparent. The patient gave the date as March, 1953, and his age as 27 [actually 29, ed.]. Just before coming into the examining room he had been talking to Dr Karl Pribram, yet he had no recollection of this at all and denied that anyone had spoken to him. In conversation, he reverted constantly to boyhood events and seemed scarcely to realize that he had had an operation.

On formal testing the contrast between his good general intelligence and his defective memory was most striking [. . .] An extensive test battery failed to reveal any deficits in perception, abstract thinking, or reasoning ability, and his motivation remained excellent throughout [. . .]

In summary, this patient appears to have a complete loss of memory for events subsequent to bilateral medial temporal-lobe resection 19 months before, together with a partial retrograde amnesia for the three years leading up to his operation; but early memories are seemingly normal and there is no impairment of personality or general intelligence.

William Beecher Scoville and Brenda Milner, 'Loss of Recent Memory After Bilateral Hippocampal Lesions' (1957)

Korsakoff's Psychosis

Sergei Sergeievich Korsakoff (1853–1900) was an outstanding Russian clinician, who authored a standard textbook of psychiatry before his untimely death at the age of thirty-seven. He is most famous for having described the peculiar mental disorder which now bears his name. The memory defects he observed, often seen in association with alcoholism but also in a range of other conditions, are thought to derive from damage to the deep midline structures of the brain, the third ventricle, aqueduct and posterior hypothalamus.

Summing up the observations of many cases of this disease, one may conclude that in some of them the predominant features are increased irritability and agitation, with relatively good preservation of consciousness; in other cases, on the contrary, confusion predominates, either apathetic or associated with excitement; and finally, in a third group, a characteristic disturbance of memory – a peculiar form of amnesia – stands in the foreground [. . .]

Together with the confusion, nearly always a profound disorder of memory is observed, although at times the disorder of memory occurs in pure form. In such instances the disorder of memory manifests itself in an extraordinarily peculiar amnesia, in which the memory of recent events, those which just happened, is chiefly disturbed, whereas the remote past is remembered fairly well. Mostly the amnesia of this particular type develops after prodromal agitation with confusion. This excitement may last several days and then the patient again becomes calm and his consciousness clears; he appears to be in a better possession of his faculties, he receives information correctly, and yet his memory remains deeply affected. This reveals itself primarily in that the patient constantly asks the same questions and repeats the same stories. At first, during conversation with such a patient, it is difficult to note the presence of psychic disorder; the patient gives the impression of a person in complete possession of his faculties; he reasons about everything perfectly well, draws correct deductions from given premises, makes witty remarks, plays chess or a game of cards, in a word, comports himself as a mentally sound person. Only after a long conversation with the patient, one may note that at times he utterly confuses events and that he remembers absolutely nothing of what goes on around him: he does not remember whether he had his dinner, whether he was out of bed. On occasion the patient forgets what happened to him just an instant ago: you came in, conversed with him, and stepped out for one minute; then you come in again and the patient has absolutely no recollection that you had already been with him. Patients of this type may read the same page over and again sometimes for hours, because they are absolutely unable to remember what they have read. In conversation they may repeat the same thing 20 times, remaining wholly unaware that they are repeating the same thing in absolutely stereotyped expressions. It often happens that the patient is unable to remember those persons whom he met only during the illness, for example, his attending physician or nurse, so that each time he sees them, even though seeing them constantly, he swears he sees them for the first time.

With all this, the remarkable fact is that, forgetting all events which have just occurred, the patients usually remember quite accurately the past events which occurred long before the illness. What is forgotten usually proves to be everything that has happened during the illness and a short time before the beginning of the illness. Such is the case in the more typical instances of the disease; in others, even the memory of remote events may also be disturbed.

It must be noted that in general, depending on the degree of the illness, that is, the depth of the affection, the amnestic manifestations vary. In milder degrees for example, there may be no complete abrogation of the memory of recent events, only the facts are remembered vaguely, unclearly. In some cases the facts themselves are remembered, but not the time when they occurred. In other cases the forgetfulness affects chiefly the patient's own thought processes, and as a result they do not remember what they have said, and so they constantly repeat the same question. At times, all facts are remembered, yet to recover traces of these facts in their memory, to recall the forgotten, the patients need specially favourable conditions. Inversely, in very severe cases the amnesia is much more profound; here, not only memory of recent events is lost, but also that of the long past. In such cases it most frequently happens that present events disappear from the patient's memory instantly, and instead, some events of decades ago are recollected – as a result the patients confuse old recollections with the present impressions. Thus, they may believe themselves to be in the setting (or circumstances) in which they were some 30 years ago, and mistake persons who are around them now for people who were around them at that time but who are now perhaps even dead. In still more severe forms of amnesia, the memory of facts is completely lost, even the memory of words; the patient forgets his own name and instead of words utters broken sounds. In severe forms of amnesia the confusion of consciousness is greater, and in the extremely severe cases a state of complete unconsciousness may occur.

In this disease the amnesia is not stationary; it may wax and wane. These fluctuations in its degree depend sometimes on individual circumstances such as the effort of attention, the degree of distress, and so forth. The memory often improves, yet with fatigue it again becomes worse. But of course, most frequently the intensity of the amnesia depends on the general course of the disease and on the depth of the affection, so that if the disease progresses toward improvement the amnesia diminishes and may entirely disappear; if the disease grows worse, however, the amnesia becomes deeper and the signs of profound confusion are added to the symptoms of amnesia.

In regard to the confusion, it must be noted that in this form of amnesia a slight degree of confusion is frequently present. This confusion does not involve that which the patient perceives at the present moment but affects only the recollection of the past events. Thus, when asked to tell how he has been spending his time, the patient would very frequently relate a story altogether different from that which actually occurred, for example, he would tell that yesterday he took a ride in town, whereas in fact he has been in bed for two months, or he would tell of conversations which have never occurred, and so forth. On occasion, such patients invent some fiction and constantly repeat it, so that a peculiar delirium develops, rooted in false recollections (pseudo-reminiscences).

Such are the more characteristic traits of the psychic disorder observed in patients suffering this disease. As I have said, along with the psychic symptoms, there exist symptoms of multiple degenerative neuritis in the form of paralyses of the lower and sometimes of the upper extremities. Yet it must be particularly noted that symptoms of multiple neuritis are far from being obvious in all cases. There occur instances in which there exist only a hint of these symptoms in the form of slight pains in the legs and unsteadiness of gait. Even the patellar reflexes do not always disappear; sometimes they may even be increased or remain unchanged. Yet, on careful examination some signs of neuritis will always be found, and this will help to establish the diagnosis of the psychic affection.

Sergei Korsakoff, 'Psychic Disorder in Conjunction with Multiple Neuritis' (1889)

MEMORY AND MADNESS

Motivated Forgetting Is the Root of Madness

Arthur Schopenhauer (1788–1860), son of a wealthy merchant, was born in Danzig (now Gdansk in Poland) and destined by his parents for a career in commerce. However, in 1807, two years after his father's death, probably by suicide, he abandoned his training as a merchant and began to prepare himself for an academic career. In 1819, he was appointed to a lectureship at Berlin University, but his lectures were poorly attended. His major work, 'The World as Will and Idea', completed in 1818, builds on Kant's* division of the world into phenomenal aspects (the way we apprehend things) and noumenal aspects (the things in

*themselves, that can never be known). Applying this to the notion
of 'self', Schopenhauer sees the Will as the noumenal aspect underlying our phenomenal perception of ourselves.*

*Schopenhauer's philosophy is famous for its pessimism, for the
Will is seen, not only as creating an illusory world but also as
fostering egoism, manifest in the selfish drive to perpetuate life.
Man's duty, therefore, is to overcome the 'will to live', to embrace
ascetism and chastity, and in so doing achieve a true form of
altruism by merging his identity into the universe of all beings.
However unpalatable this may be, Schopenhauer's analysis of
self-deception is compelling, and influenced the development of
Freud's ideas concerning dynamic repression in the unconscious
mind. In the following extract, he highlights the difficulties
involved in 'facing unpleasant truths', the painful process of
acknowledgment, and the tendency to obscure them with wishful
phantasies – a psychological strategy that taken to its logical
conclusion, must lead to madness.*

The health of the mind properly consists in perfect recollection.
Of course this is not to be understood as meaning that our
memory preserves everything. For the past course of our life
shrinks up in time, as the path of the wanderer looking back
shrinks up in space: sometimes it is difficult for us to distinguish
the particular years; the days have for the most part become
unrecognizable. Really, however, only the exactly similar events,
recurring an innumerable number of times, so that their images,
as it were, conceal each other, ought so to run together in the
memory that they are individually unrecognizable; on the other
hand, every event in any way peculiar or significant we must be
able to find again in memory, if the intellect is normal, vigorous
and quite healthy. In the text [para. 36 of first edition, *The World
as Will and Idea*, ed.] I have explained *madness* as the *broken
thread* of this memory, which still runs on regularly, although in
constantly decreasing fullness and distinctness. The following
considerations may serve to confirm this.

The memory of a healthy man affords a certainty as to an event
he has witnessed, which is regarded as just as firm and sure as

his present apprehension of things; therefore, if sworn to by him, this event is thereby established in a court of law. On the other hand, the mere suspicion of madness will at once weaken the testimony of a witness. Here, then, lies the criterion between the healthy mind and insanity. Whenever I doubt whether an event which I remember really took place, I throw upon myself the suspicion of madness: unless it is that I am uncertain whether it was not a mere dream. If another doubts the reality of an event, related by me as an eye witness, without mistrusting my honesty, then he regards me as insane. Whoever comes at last, through constantly recounting an event which originally was fabricated by him, to believe in it himself is, in this one point, really insane. We may ascribe to an insane person flashes of wit, single clever thoughts, even correct judgements, but his testimony as to past events no man will consider valid. In the *Lalita-vistara*, well known to be the history of Buddha Sakya-Muni, it is related that at the moment of his birth all the sick became well, all the blind saw, all the deaf heard, and all mad people 'recovered their memory'. This last is mentioned in two passages.[8]

My own experience of many years has led me to the opinion that madness occurs proportionally most frequently among actors. But what a misuse they make of their memory! Daily they have to learn a new part or refresh an old one; but these parts are entirely without connection, nay, are in contradiction and contrast with each other, and every evening the actor strives to forget himself entirely and be some quite different person. This kind of thing paves the way for madness.

The exposition of the origin of madness given in the text will become more comprehensible if it is remembered how unwillingly we think of things which powerfully injure our interests, wound our pride, or interfere with our wishes; with what difficulty do we determine to lay such things before our own intellect for careful and serious investigation; how easily, on the other hand, we unconsciously break away or sneak off from them again; how, on the contrary, agreeable events come into our

8 *Rgya Tcher Rol Pa, Hist. de Bouddha Chakya Mouni*, trad. du Tibétain, P. Foucaux, 1848, pp. 91 et 99.

minds of their own accord, and, if driven away, constantly creep in again, so that we dwell on them for hours together. In that resistance of the will to allowing what is contrary to it to come under the examination of the intellect lies the place at which madness can break in upon the mind. Each new adverse event must be assimilated by the intellect, *i.e.* it must receive a place in the system of the truths connected with our will and its interests, whatever it may have to displace that is more satisfactory. Whenever this has taken place, it already pains us much less; but this operation itself is often very painful, and also, in general, only takes place slowly and with resistance. However, the health of the mind can only continue so long as this is in each case properly carried out. If, on the contrary, in some particular case, the resistance and struggles of the will against the apprehension of some knowledge reaches such a degree that that operation is not performed in its integrity, then certain events or circumstances become for the intellect completely suppressed, because the will cannot endure the sight of them, and then, for the sake of the necessary connection, the gaps that thus arise are filled up at pleasure; thus madness appears. For the intellect has given up its nature to please the will: the man now imagines what does not exist. Yet the madness which has thus arisen is now the lethe of unendurable suffering; it was the last remedy of harassed nature, i.e. of the will.

Arthur Schopenhauer, 'On Madness' (1844)

LEARNING

Man Is a Learning Machine

Ivan Pavlov (1849–1936) was born in Ryazan, Russia, and educated there in a religious school. He entered St Petersburg University in 1870 where he studied natural history, specializing in animal physiology. In 1884 he went to Germany as a postdoctoral physiologist. He spent many years researching into the processes of digestion, was appointed professor at the St

Petersburg Institute of Experimental Medicine, and in 1904 received the Nobel prize for this work. But he is most famous for his investigations into what became known as the conditioned reflex, a term first coined in 1901.

The phenomenon of conditioning, the ability of an animal to shape its behaviour in response to new associative links, clearly has survival value. It enables the animal to learn (sometimes erroneously) that A causes B. In addition to Pavlov's 'Classical' observations, Skinner* showed that an animal placed in a box would spontaneously learn to press a lever in order to obtain food. This kind of reward-seeking behaviour, the basis of which had of course been known to trainers for years, was given the name 'Operant Conditioning'. Early behaviourist psychology made conditioning the cornerstone of its theory of learning, and much experimental work was devoted to exploring its vicissitudes. However, its role in human learning, which makes use of complex symbolic links and cognitive processing, may be a limited one.

Let us make two simple experiments which will always succeed. Some mild solution of any acid is poured into the mouth of a dog. It will cause the usual defence reaction of the animal: by active movements of the mouth the dog ejects the solution and at the same time saliva begins flowing copiously into the mouth cavity (and later escaping), thus diluting the acid which has been introduced and washing it away. Now the other experiment. Let us repeatedly apply to the dog any external agent, for instance, a definite sound, just before introducing into its mouth the same solution. What happens? It will then suffice merely to repeat the sound and the same reaction will be produced, the same movements of the mouth, the same flow of saliva. Both the facts are equally accurate and constant; and to both the same physiological term 'reflex' should be applied. Both will disappear if the motor nerves of the muscles of the mouth and the secretory nerves of the salivary glands (i.e. the efferent conductors) are cut, if the afferent conductors from the mucous membrane of the mouth and from the ear are severed, or lastly, if the central stations for conducting the nerve current, i.e., the moving process of nervous excitation from afferent to efferent conductors are destroyed. In the case of the first reflex this will be the medulla oblongata, in the second – the cerebral hemispheres.

In view of these facts the most severely critical mind will fail to offer an argument against this physiological conclusion. But at the same time the difference between the two reflexes is likewise apparent. In the first place, they have different central stations, as has just been mentioned. Secondly, as may be clearly seen from the above experiments, the first reflex was produced without any preparation, without any condition, while the second was obtained by virtue of a special procedure. What was the meaning of it? In the first case the nerve current was transmitted from one group of conductors to another directly, without any peculiar procedure. In the second – some preliminary was necessary to effect the transmission. It is most natural to suppose that matters stand as follows: in the case of the first reflex a direct road for the transmission of the nerve current was existing, while in the second it was necessary to form previously a way along which the nerve current might pass. The idea had long before originated in nervous physiology and found expression in the German word '*Bahnung*'. In this way the nervous system is found to possess two different central apparatuses: one of direct conduction of nerve current, and, secondly, an apparatus for its switching on and off.

It would have been strange to stand amazed when faced by the conclusion. Indeed, on our planet, the nervous system is an inexpressibly complex and delicate instrument for relations and connexions between the numerous parts of a living organism and between the organism, as a most complex system, and the infinite number of outward factors which may influence it. If, at present, the switching on and off of an electric current has become a most common technical device in our daily usage, surely there is no reason to argue against the realization of the same principle in the most wonderful instrument that we are now discussing.

[. . .]

Man is of course a system – roughly speaking, a machine – like every other system in nature subject to the unescapable and uniform laws of all nature; but the human system, in the horizon of our contemporary scientific view, is unique in being most highly self-regulatory. Among the products of man's hands, we are already familiar with machines which regulate themselves in various ways. From this standpoint the method of investigating the system of man is precisely the same as that of any other system; decomposition into parts, study of the significance of each part, study of the connexions of the parts, study of the relations with the environment, and finally the interpretation on this basis of its general workings and administration, if this be within the capacity of man. But our system is self-regulatory in the highest degree – self-maintaining, repairing, readjusting, and even improving. The chief, strongest, and ever-present impression received from the study of the higher nervous activity by our method is the extreme plasticity of this activity, its immense possibilities: nothing remains stationary, unyielding; and everything could always be attained, all could be changed for the better, were only the appropriate conditions realized.

The system or machine – and man with his host of ideals, aspirations, and achievements – what a terrifying, discordant juxtaposition this seems at first glance. But is it really so? For according to the view of evolution, is not man at the summit of nature, the supreme personification of the resources of a nature which is without limit, the realization of its powerful but still unknown laws? Is not this sufficient to maintain the dignity of man, to fill him with highest satisfaction? And there still remains in life all that is also embraced in the idea of freedom of will with its personal, social, and civic responsibility; for me there remains this possibility, and hence also the obligation for me to know myself and, constantly using this information, to maintain myself at the utmost height of my capabilities. Are not the social and civic duties and requirements, situations which present themselves to my system, and which must lead to appropriate reactions that will promote the integrity and perfection of the system?

Ivan Petrovitch Pavlov, *Lectures on Conditioned Reflexes* ('The Conditioned Reflex', 1935, 'Reply of a Physiologist to Psychologists', 1932)

3

EMOTION

> But cruel are the times, when we are traitors
> And do not know ourselves, when we hold rumour
> From what we fear, yet know not what we fear,
> But float upon a wild and violent sea
> Each way and move . . .

William Shakespeare, *Macbeth* (1606), Act 4,
Scene 2, ll. 18–23

Feelings, gut-feelings, heartfelt feelings, make us more aware than ever of the connection between mind and body. We recognize them as strong influences shaping our behaviour, frequently capable of overriding reason and judgement, which seem more distanced from bodily processes. The very word 'emotion' connotes movement and turbulence, yet feelings and emotions are also clearly mental in nature. We all know what they are, but they are almost impossible to define. Emotions can give rise to specific desires but is desire itself an emotion? Are some emotions more primitive than others? Are some primary, like colours, which when mixed give rise to others? Some, like love, sympathy or remorse are generally considered more worthwhile, others like anger, pride or envy are 'deadly sins'. Are we always conscious of our emotions? We may be overwhelmed yet unable to put a name to what we are feeling. If emotions are part of our mental furniture, at least we can try to say what they are not – they are not usually itemized together with beliefs, theories, ideas, mere sensations, thoughts and calculations or with actions.

We speak of strong or weak emotions, higher and lower emotions, superficial and deep ones, highly strung, finely tuned, flat or blunted emotions, but perhaps their most salient characteristic is the ability to possess us, to take us over in such a way that we feel out of control. Emotions, then, challenge our sense of autonomy, impel our behaviour, make us feel driven rather than driving. We tend to suffer emotions passively, hence the cognate 'passion', and in some jurisdictions the 'crime passionel', which diminishes our level of criminal responsibility. Little wonder that over the years philosophers have spent so much time working out ways to deal with these disruptive elements and regain control over our lives.

Paradoxically, however, the inability to experience a full range of emotion is generally regarded as an unwanted condition, a symptom of mental disorder – depressive illness, schizophrenia or perhaps psychopathy. So it would seem that, despite its disturbing functions, we value emotion. Life is difficult with emotions and impoverished without them.

A number of theories concerning the nature of emotion have been put forward. There are too many to describe here in detail, I therefore simply indicate some of the different levels of analysis that have been employed, which tend to coincide with the way that the field of psychology is itself divided. Looking at the individual and working our way upwards, so to speak, one can begin by focusing on the bodily changes so obviously associated with emotional experience. Next, the observable behaviour or dispositions to behave – clearly our emotions would have no effect on others or the world around us, if they remained internal happenings with no external manifestations. We can move on to consider the role of cognitive processing, intentional strategies of the will and then the phenomenological level – descriptions of emotional experience. We can broaden our view to take in the influence of social context, and from an even more distant perspective we can consider the evolutionary significance for our species. The Oxford psychologist Edmund Rolls[1] has suggested that emotions are

1 Edmund T. Rolls, *The Brain and Emotion*, Oxford: Oxford University Press, 1999.

'states elicited by rewards and punishments', including changes in brain biochemistry such as dopamine function. They form a natural reward system which motivates and shapes our behaviour, allowing a greater flexibility of response than do learned reflexes or innate predispositions. The principle of scientific parsimony (some might say the intellectual extravagance of theoreticians) demands that a theory organize as many of the known facts as it possibly can, in other words try to explain the diversity of observed phenomena by reference to a single overarching idea. This gives rise to generalizations of the 'All emotions are nothing but . . .' type, often defended by their adherents with militant ferocity. They challenge us to disconfirm them with contradictory evidence, or demonstrations of their incoherence. However, even if we are unable to achieve a general theoretical integration, each theory remains useful if it helps us to understand a particular aspect of the problem.

One important counterintuitive theory was put forward by William James[*] at the end of the nineteenth century. Rather than the common-sense view that feelings give rise to bodily states – 'I tremble because I am frightened', he suggested that 'I am frightened because I tremble', that the mental component of emotion was secondary to the visceral reaction. This idea implied some kind of direct response of the body, unmodified by higher perceptual processes, to outward events. The bodily change, he said, *was* the emotion.

But James's theory runs into a number of difficulties. Apart from the question as to whether direct 'visceral perception' exists (Cannon[2] observed in the 1920s that emotional behaviour occurred even when the viscera were isolated from the central nervous system), there is the telling objection that points to the wide variety of experiences that can be associated with a single bodily condition. By observing my body closely, I cannot discern exactly what emotion I am feeling. My gross physiological state does not, in fact, correlate obviously in a one-to-one way with specific feelings. I may gasp for joy, with outrage, or be breathless with surprise. I

2 W.B. Cannon, *Bodily Changes in Pain, Hunger, Fear and Rage*, Harper Torchbooks, 1963.

may wet myself with fear or laughter. My skin may be damp with apprehension or with guilt or both, and I may cry with all sorts of contradictory feelings – happiness, sadness, shame, relief, pain, impenitent self-hatred, and so on. Moreover there is well-known experimental evidence to the effect that subjects injected with adrenaline (a hormone that causes an increase in cardiac and respiratory rates, raised blood pressure, dilated pupils, peripheral vasoconstriction – bodily responses that have been understood to be a preparation for 'fight or flight') experienced next to no emotion if they were told beforehand what to expect. If they were not forewarned, they did experience emotion, but its nature was dependent on the surrounding atmosphere. Subjects interpreted their bodily function as anger when placed in a room with an angry stooge, and euphoria when put together with a happy one.[3] These results strongly suggested that emotion was dependent on generalized physiological *arousal*, but that the specific quality of the felt experience was given by other factors, by expectation and social experience.

Finally, the discovery that emotions cannot exist without the sub-cortical 'limbic' system of the brain puts paid to the Jamesian idea that there are no brain centres subserving this function. If physiological changes within our limbic system are the key determinants of our emotional states, then they must be more than mere perceptions of peripheral bodily changes, could even exist in the absence of such changes. So can we ditch James's theory? Not entirely, for there is some modern evidence to show that deliberate adoption of facial expressions, the cold-blooded stretching of facial muscles, can actually *produce* changes in our autonomic nervous system normally associated with the experience of emotion.[4] And a fine-grain analysis of these changes shows that some emotions can indeed be differentiated from others on a physiological basis. For example, although heart rate increases in both anger, fear and happiness, the extent of increase is much

3 Stanley Schacter and Jerome Singer, 'Cognitive, Social and Physiological Determinants of Emotional States', *Psychological Review* 69 (1962), 379–99.
4 P. Ekman et al., 'Autonomic Nervous System Activity Distinguishes Among Emotions', *Science* 221 (1983), 1208–10.

greater in the two negative emotions, which can be distinguished from one another by changes in skin temperature – raised in anger, lowered in fear. Interestingly, in the same experiment the deliberate 'reliving in imagination' of emotional experiences produced similar, but less clear-cut results. Not surprisingly, if we hold to the identity theory of mind and body, it proves impossible to make experience invariably antecedent or consequent to bodily change. It just may be that central limbic activity in the brain and peripheral autonomic activity in our bodily organs and the subjective experience of what we feel are not arranged in a sequential causal hierarchy but are simply part and parcel of the same emotional event.

Moving to the cognitive perspective, we can regard emotions as conveyors of information about the outside world. Our emotional *reaction* to an object may tell us something about the properties of that object or its likely behaviour. Emotions may be a type of perception. If so, they have a remarkably direct effect on our behaviour (and on other sensory perceptions), more akin to a reflex, perhaps, than a measured response, and as with other types of perception their accuracy may be questioned. Despite this, it is reasonable to assume that emotions have, or at least at some time had, survival value. Darwin* makes the case for regarding the facial expressions associated with emotion as vestigial actions, at one time useful in our evolutionary development. We now know that such expressions act as important social signals, often processed 'non-consciously' in the brain. For example, the amygdala may react to a fearful facial expression presented too quickly to be consciously perceived. But if emotional behaviour was originally under genetic control modified by environmental selection, and therefore automatic, it can no longer be regarded as a purely involuntary occurrence. Athletes and soldiers 'psych themselves up' in order to achieve a better performance, tennis players grunt when they serve, opera singers 'warm up' their voices with mental as well as physical exercises, in the hope that the autonomic changes thus induced will increase the body's physical capacity. And it seems that emotions play an important selective role in directing our attention towards relevant happenings, focusing our efforts, registering our memories, organizing our lives.

Nowadays, in the face of machine intelligence, emotions are beginning to achieve a better press. Computers can carry out many of the functions previously attributed to human reason, so we look to emotions to distinguish ourselves, to prove that we are more than just machines. If by doing so we risk being tainted by association with wild beasts, it now seems a risk worth taking. In order to raise ourselves above their level, we no longer seek to abolish emotion, rather to refine it, celebrate it, harness it to our higher purposes. Just as the nineteenth-century Romantics reacted against a narrow scientism, so, despite advances in neuroscientific exploration, we are now experiencing a renewed championing of the emotional mind.

THE NATURE OF EMOTION

Emotional Intelligence

Daniel Goleman argues that scientific views of human intelligence, since the creation of the first Stanford – Binet IQ tests, have been far too narrow. Not only have the psychologist's tests of intellectual ability failed to measure aspects of character such as impulse control, persistence, zeal, motivation and social sensitivity, but they also fail to correlate with success in life – with rewarding relationships and accomplishment at work.

Goleman believes impaired 'Emotional Intelligence', written into our brain circuitry following traumatic experience,[5] can be overwritten through better child-rearing practices, and emotional education. This can occur spontaneously over a period of time or be achieved through the medium of psychotherapy. Play in childhood, and art in the adult world, also provide arenas in which emotional intelligence can be developed.

Goleman is a science journalist and writer who was educated at Harvard University, where he received his Ph.D. He covers the behavioural and brain sciences for the New York Times *and was formerly senior editor at* Psychology Today.

5 See Joseph LeDoux, pp. 134–6.

During the middle decades of this century academic psychology was dominated by behaviourists in the mould of B. F. Skinner*, who felt that only behaviour that could be seen objectively, from the outside, could be studied with scientific accuracy. The behaviourists ruled all inner life, including emotions, out-of-bounds for science.

Then, with the coming in the late 1960s of the 'cognitive revolution', the focus of psychological science turned to how the mind registers and stores information, and the nature of intelligence, but emotions were still off-limits. Conventional wisdom among cognitive scientists held that intelligence entails a cold, hard-nosed processing of fact. It is hyperrational, rather like *Star Trek*'s Mr Spock, the archetype of dry information bytes unmuddied by feeling, embodying the idea that emotions have no place in intelligence and only muddle our picture of mental life.

The cognitive scientists who embraced this view have been seduced by the computer as the operative model of the mind, forgetting that, in reality, the brain's wetware is awash in a messy, pulsating puddle of neurochemicals, nothing like the sanitized, orderly silicon that has spawned the guiding metaphor for mind. The predominant models among cognitive scientists of how the mind processes information have lacked an acknowledgement that rationality is guided by – and can be swamped by – feeling. The cognitive model is, in this regard, an impoverished view of the mind, one that fails to explain the Sturm and Drang of feelings that brings flavour to the intellect. In order to persist in this view, cognitive scientists themselves have had to ignore the relevance for their models of mind of their personal hopes and fears, their marital squabbles and professional jealousies – the wash of feeling that gives life its flavour and its urgencies, and which in every moment biases exactly how (and how well or poorly) information is processed.

The lopsided scientific vision of an emotionally flat mental life – which has guided the last eighty years of research on intelligence – is gradually changing as psychology has begun to recognize the essential role of feeling in thinking. Rather like the Spockish character Data in *Star Trek: The Next Generation*, psychology is coming to appreciate the power and virtues of emotions in mental life, as well as their dangers. After all, as Data sees (to his own dismay, could he feel dismay), his cool logic fails to bring the right *human* solution. Our humanity is most evident in our feelings; Data seeks to feel, knowing that something essential is missing. He wants friendship, loyalty; like the Tin Man in *The Wizard of Oz*, he lacks a heart. Lacking the lyrical sense that feeling brings, Data can play music or write poetry with technical virtuosity, but not feel its passion. The lesson of Data's yearning for yearning itself is that the higher values of the human heart – faith, hope, devotion, love – are missing entirely from the coldly cognitive view. Emotions enrich; a model of mind that leaves them out is impoverished.

Daniel Goleman, 'Spock Vs. Data: When Cognition Is Not Enough', *Emotional Intelligence* (1995)

The James–Lange Theory

If we regard ourselves as mind-bodies, psycho-somatic entities, emotions more than any of our experiences seem to be compounded of the visceral and the cerebral. We can scarcely feel, without feeling in our bodies. When we respond to life-events with excitement or depression or fear or grief, there are obvious bodily changes that we undergo. Our heartbeat may alter, our skin go dry or wet, our hair stand on end, our muscles tense, our stomach cramp, our breathing quicken, our bowels empty or refuse to empty, and so on. These changes had traditionally been conceived as following on our perception, our mental recognition, of the provoking cause. But towards the end of the nineteenth century the American psychologist William James and the Danish physician C. G. Lange independently put forward a theory (the James–Lange theory) which turned this sequence on its head. Bodily changes did not follow from our emotional states, they said, rather our bodies reacted first and our emotional experience was nothing but the awareness of that reaction. We did not cry because we felt sad, rather crying was an immediate reaction to loss, and we felt sad because we were crying – the crying was the sadness . . .

William James (1842–1910) was born in New York, the eldest of five children. His brother, Henry, later to become a novelist, was fourteen months his junior. He had an unconventional education under the supervision of his wealthy father, who travelled the world together with his family, meeting famous thinkers, discussing ideas and hiring a series of tutors for his children. Under his father's influence William delayed settling on a career. He trained first as a painter, then as a scientist, before switching to the study of medicine and qualifying as a doctor in 1869. Even then he was unsure. Three years later he accepted a teaching post at Harvard University where he began a career in physiology. His unconfinable interests led him into philosophy and psychology. In 1878 he married a Boston schoolteacher, and together they went on to have five children. At the same time he contracted to write a book, Principles of Psychology, *which took him twelve years to complete. Its publication established his reputation as one of the greatest psychologists of his time.*

Our natural way of thinking about these coarser emotions is that the mental perception of some fact excites the mental affection called emotion, and that this latter state of mind gives rise to the bodily expression. My theory, on the contrary, is that *the bodily changes follow directly the perception of the exciting fact, and that our feeling of the same changes as they occur IS the emotion*. Common-sense says, we lose our fortune, are sorry and weep; we meet a bear, are frightened and run; we are insulted by a rival, are angry and strike. The hypothesis here to be defended says that this order of sequence is incorrect, that the one mental state is not immediately induced by the other, that the bodily manifestations must first be interposed between, and that the more rational statement is that we feel sorry because we cry, angry because we strike, afraid because we tremble, and not that we cry, strike, or tremble, because we are sorry, angry, or fearful, as the case may be. Without the bodily states following on the perception, the latter would be purely cognitive in form, pale, colourless, destitute of emotional warmth. We might then see the bear, and judge it best to run, receive the insult and deem it right to strike, but we should not actually *feel* afraid or angry.

Stated in this crude way, the hypothesis is pretty sure to meet with immediate disbelief. And yet neither many nor far-fetched considerations are required to mitigate its paradoxical character, and possibly to produce conviction of its truth.

To begin with, no reader of the last two chapters will be inclined to doubt the fact that *objects do excite bodily changes* by a pre-organized mechanism, or the farther fact that *the changes are so indefinitely numerous and subtle that the entire organism may be called a sounding-board*, which every change of consciousness, however slight, may make reverberate. The various permutations and combinations of which these organic activities are susceptible makes it abstractly possible that no shade of emotion, however slight, should be without a bodily reverberation as unique, when taken in its totality, as is the mental mood itself. The immense number of parts modified in each emotion is what makes it so difficult for us to reproduce in cold blood the total and integral expression of any one of them. We may catch the trick with the voluntary muscles, but fail with the skin, glands, heart and other viscera. Just as an artificially imitated sneeze lacks something of the reality, so the attempt to imitate an emotion in the absence of its normal instigating cause is apt to be rather 'hollow'.

The next thing to be noticed is this, that *every one of the bodily changes, whatsoever it be, is FELT, acutely or obscurely the moment it occurs*. If the reader has never paid attention to this matter, he will be both interested and astonished to learn how many different bodily feelings he can detect in himself as characteristic of his various emotional moods. It would be perhaps too much to expect him to arrest the tide of any strong gust of passion for the sake of any such curious analysis as this, but he can observe more tranquil states, and that may be assumed here to be true of the greater which is shown to be true of the less. Our whole cubic capacity is sensibly alive, and each morsel of it contributes its pulsations of feeling, dim or sharp, pleasant, painful or dubious, to that sense of personality that every one of us unfailingly carries with him. It is surprising what little items give accent to these complexes of sensibility. When worried by any slight trouble, one may find that the focus of one's bodily consciousness is the contraction, often quite inconsiderable, of the eyes and brows. When momentarily embarrassed, it is something in the pharynx that compels either a swallow, a clearing of the throat, or a slight cough; and so on for as many more instances as might be named. Our concern here being with the general view rather than with the details, I will not linger to discuss these, but, assuming the point admitted that every change that occurs must be felt, I will pass on.

I now proceed to urge the vital point of my whole theory, which is this: *If we fancy some strong emotion, and then try to abstract from our consciousness of it all the feelings of its bodily symptoms, we find we have nothing left behind,* no 'mind-stuff' out of which the emotion can be constituted, and that a cold and neutral state of intellectual perception is all that remains. It is true that, although most people when asked say that their introspection verifies this statement, some persist in saying theirs does not. Many cannot be made to understand the question. When you beg them to imagine away every feeling of laughter and of tendency to laugh from their consciousness of the ludicrousness of an object, and then to tell you what the feeling of its ludicrousness would be like, whether it be anything more than the perception that the object belongs to the class 'funny', they persist in replying that the thing proposed is a physical impossibility, and that they always *must* laugh if they see a funny object. Of course the task proposed is not the practical one of seeing a ludicrous object and annihilating one's tendency to laugh. It is the purely speculative one of subtracting certain elements of feeling from an emotional state supposed to exist in its fulness, and saying what the residual elements are. I cannot help thinking that all who rightly apprehend this problem will agree with the proposition above laid down. What kind of an emotion of fear would be left if the feeling neither of quickened heart-beats nor of shallow breathing, neither of trembling lips nor of weakened limbs, neither of goose flesh nor of visceral stirrings, were present, it is quite impossible for me to think. Can one fancy the state of rage and picture no ebullition in the chest, no flushing of the face, no dilation of the nostrils, no clenching of the teeth, no impulse to vigorous action, but in their stead limp muscles, calm breathing, and a placid face? The present writer, for one, certainly cannot. The rage is as completely evaporated as the sensation of its so-called manifestations, and the only thing that can possibly be supposed to take its place is some cold-blooded and dispassionate judicial sentence, confined entirely to the intellectual realm, to the effect that a certain person or persons merit chastisement for their sins. In like manner of grief: what would it be without its tears, its sobs, its suffocation of the heart, its pang in the breast-bone? A feelingless cognition that certain circumstances are deplorable, and nothing more. Every passion in turn tells the same story. A purely disembodied human emotion is a nonentity. I do not say that it is a contradiction in the nature of things, or that pure spirits are necessarily condemned to cold intellectual lives; but I say that for *us*, emotion dissociated from all bodily feeling is inconceivable. The more closely I scrutinize my states, the more persuaded I become that whatever moods, affections, and passions I have are in very truth constituted by, and made up of, those bodily changes which we ordinarily call their expression or consequence; and the more it seems to me that if I were to become corporeally anaesthetic, I should be excluded from the life of the affections, harsh and tender alike, and drag out an existence of merely cognitive or intellectual form. Such an existence, although it seems to have been the ideal of ancient sages, is too apathetic to be keenly sought after by those born after the revival of the worship of sensibility, a few generations ago.

Let not this view be called materialistic. It is neither more or less materialistic than any other view which says that our emotions are conditioned by nervous processes. No reader of this book is likely to rebel against such a saying so long as it is expressed in general terms; and if any one still finds materialism in the thesis now defended, that must be because of the special processes invoked. They are *sensational* processes, processes due to inward currents set up by physical happenings. Such processes have, it is true, always been regarded by the platonizers in psychology as having something peculiarly base about them. But our emotions must always be *inwardly* what they are, whatever be the physiological ground of their apparition. If they are deep, pure, worthy, spiritual facts on any conceivable theory of their physiological source, they remain no less deep, pure, spiritual, and worthy of regard on this present sensational theory. They carry their own inner measure of worth with them; and it is just as logical to use the present theory of emotions for proving that sensational processes need not be vile and material, as to use their vileness and materiality as a proof that such a theory cannot be true.

If such a theory is true, then each emotion is the resultant of a sum of elements, and each element is caused by a physiological process of a sort already well known. The elements are all organic changes, and each of them is the reflex effect of the exciting object. Definite questions now immediately arise – questions very different from those which were the only possible ones without this view. Those were the questions of classification: 'Which are the proper genera of emotion, and which the species under each?' or of description: 'By what expression is each emotion characterized?' The questions now are *causal*: 'Just what changes does that object excite?' and 'How come they to excite these particular changes and not others? We step from a superficial to a deep order of inquiry. Classification and description are the lowest stage of science. They sink into the background the moment questions of genesis are formulated, and remain important only in so far as they facilitate our answering these. Now the moment the genesis of an emotion is accounted for, as the arousal by an object of a lot of reflex acts which are forthwith felt, *we immediately see why there is no limit to the number of possible different emotions which may exist, and why the emotions of different individuals may vary indefinitely*, both as to their constitution and as to objects which call them forth. For there is nothing sacramental or eternally fixed in reflex action. Any sort of reflex effect is possible, and reflexes actually vary indefinitely, as we know.

We have all seen men dumb, instead of talkative, with joy; we have seen fright drive the blood into the head of its victim, instead of making him pale; we have seen grief run restlessly about lamenting, instead of sitting bowed down and mute; etc., etc., and this naturally enough, for one and the same cause can work differently on different men's blood vessels (since these do not always react alike), whilst moreover the impulse on its way through the brain to the vaso-motor centre is differently influenced by different earlier impressions in the form of recollections or associations of ideas.[6]

In short, *any classification of the emotions is seen to be as true and as 'natural' as any other*, if it only serves some purpose; and such a question as 'What is the "real" or "typical" expression of anger, or fear?' is seen to have no objective meaning at all. Instead of it we now have the question as to how any given 'expression' of anger or fear may have come to exist; and that is a real question of physiological mechanics on the one hand, and of history on the other, which (like all real questions) is in essence answerable, although the answer may be hard to find.

William James, 'The Emotions', *Principles of Psychology*, Vol. 2 (1890)

Desire Dispassionately Defined

Bertrand Russell (1872–1970) was a British aristocrat (3rd Earl Russell), philosopher, prolific writer and fellow of Trinity College, Cambridge. He was a controversial figure in politics and education, imprisoned for pacifism in 1918 and later for his activities in campaigning against nuclear arms. In 1940 he was prevented from teaching at the College of the City of New York because of his views. He was an atheist who believed that religion caused much harm in the world.

Orphaned as an infant, Russell was brought up by his grandmother and educated privately. His lasting contributions to the field of philosophy are generally agreed to be in the areas of logic and mathematics. Despite (or perhaps partly because of) his

6 C. Lange, *Über Gemüthsbewegungen*, trans. by H. Kurella, Leipzig, 1887.

unconventional morality, and social and political non-conformism,
he was awarded the Nobel prize for literature in 1950.

A mental occurrence of any kind – sensation, image, belief, or
emotion – may be a cause of a series of actions, continuing,
unless interrupted, until some more or less definite state of affairs
is realized. Such a series of actions we call a 'behaviour cycle'.
The degree of definiteness may vary greatly: hunger requires only
food in general, whereas the sight of a particular piece of food
raises a desire which requires the eating of that piece of food.
The property of causing such a cycle of occurrences is called
'discomfort'; the property of the mental occurrences in which
the cycle ends is called 'pleasure'. The actions constituting the
cycle must not be purely mechanical, i.e. they must be bodily
movements in whose causation the special properties of nervous
tissue are involved. The cycle ends in a condition of quiescence,
or of such action as tends only to preserve the *status quo*. The
state of affairs in which this condition of quiescence is achieved
is called the 'purpose' of the cycle, and the initial mental occurrence involving discomfort is called a 'desire' for the state of
affairs that brings quiescence. A desire is called 'conscious' when
it is accompanied by a true belief as to the state of affairs that
will bring quiescence; otherwise it is called 'unconscious'. All
primitive desire is unconscious, and in human beings beliefs as
to the purposes of desires are often mistaken. These mistaken
beliefs generate secondary desires, which cause various interesting complications in the psychology of human desire, without
fundamentally altering the character which it shares with animal
desire.

Bertrand Russell, 'Desire and Feeling', *The Analysis of Mind* (1921)

Instincts and Passions

Feelings which are intimately linked with our bodily function
have tended to be seen as more primitive, more animal-like, than
reason. In Western history there is a long tradition of separating

*reason from the expression of emotion. Its manifest association
with physical change has been perceived as a threat to the stability
of our daily lives. As a result emotion has been relegated to the
province of women, children, 'orientals' and animals, all of whom
have been considered potentially dangerous.*

*But passions, Erich Fromm suggests, are not just transforma-
tions of physiological needs. We are at our most human when
we are passionately involved in life, either for good or ill.
Ratiocination can be carried out by machines. Therefore we
achieve our distinctive humanity by virtue of our capacity to feel
which is master of our reason rather than its servant. It arises
as a manifestation of our individual search for meaning in life.*

*Erich Fromm (1900–80) was born in Germany and after
receiving a Ph.D. from the University of Heidelberg, trained in
psychoanalysis at the Berlin Institute, where he first met Karen
Horney, an early critic of Freud's ideas concerning female
psychology. They were later to become lovers. He soon broke
ranks with orthodox Freudian thinking, taking issue with Freud's
emphasis on biological drives and consequent neglect of social
factors. In 1933 he left Nazi Germany for the United States,
where his heretical views drew him towards Horney and brought
both of them into conflict with other analysts. He was appointed
Professor of Psychoanalysis at the National Autonomous
University of Mexico in 1951, and in 1962 returned to the United
States after being appointed Professor of Psychiatry at New York
University.*

The contemporary climate of thought encourages the axiom that
a motive can be intense only when it serves an organic need –
i.e., that only instincts have intense motivating power. If one
discards this mechanistic, reductionist viewpoint and starts from
a holistic premise, one begins to realize that man's drives must
be seen in terms of their function for the life process of the whole
organism. Their intensity is not due to specific physiological
needs, but to the need of the whole organism to survive – to
grow both physically and mentally.

These passions do not become powerful only *after* the more

elementary ones have been satisfied. They are at the very root of human existence, and not a kind of luxury which we can afford after the normal, 'lower' needs have been satisfied. People have committed suicide because of their failure to realize their passions for love, power, fame, revenge. Cases of suicide because of a lack of sexual satisfaction are virtually non-existent. These non-instinctual passions excite man, fire him on, make life worth living; as von Holbach, the philosopher of the French Enlightenment, once said: '*Un homme sans passions et désirs cesserait d'être un homme.*' ('A man without passions or desires would cease to be a man.') (P.H.D. d'Holbach, 1822.) They are so intense precisely because man would not be man without them.[†]

The human passions transform man from a mere thing into a hero, into a being that in spite of tremendous handicaps tries to make sense of life. He wants to be his own creator, to transform his state of being unfinished into one with some goal and some purpose, allowing him to achieve some degree of integration. Man's passions are not banal psychological complexes that can be adequately explained as caused by childhood traumata. They can be understood only if one goes beyond the realm of reductionist psychology and recognizes them for what they are: *man's attempt to make sense out of life and to experience the optimum of intensity and strength he can (or believes he can) achieve under the given circumstances*. They are his religion, his cult, his ritual, which he has to hide (even from himself) in so far as they are disapproved of by his group. To be sure, by bribery and blackmail,

---

[†] This statement by Holbach is of course to be understood in the context of the philosophical thinking of his time. Buddhist or Spinozist philosophy has an entirely different concept of passions; from their standpoint Holbach's description would be empirically true for the majority of people, but Holbach's position is exactly the opposite of what they consider to be the goal of human development. In order to appreciate the difference I refer to the distinction between 'irrational passions', such as ambition and greed, and 'rational passion', such as love and care for all sentient beings (which will be discussed later on). What is relevant in the text, however, is not this difference, but the idea that life concerned mainly with its own maintenance is inhuman. When I speak in the text of 'passions' I refer to all energy-charged impulses as distinct from those which have their origin in the need for the physiological maintenance of the body. Love and no-greed are, I believe, the highest form of manifestation of human energy.

i.e. by skilful conditioning, he can be persuaded to relinquish his 'religion' and to be converted to the general cult of the no-self, the automaton. But this psychic cure deprives him of the best he has, of being a man and not a thing.

The truth is that all human passions, both the 'good' and the 'evil', can be understood only as a person's attempt to make sense of his life. Change is possible only if he is able to 'convert himself' to a new way of making sense of life by mobilizing his life-furthering passions and thus experiencing a superior sense of vitality and integration to the one he had before. Unless this happens he can be domesticated, but he cannot be cured. But even though the life-furthering passions are conducive to a greater sense of strength, joy, integration and vitality than destructive-ness and cruelty, the latter are as much an answer to the problem of human existence as the former. Even the most sadistic and destructive man is human, as human as the saint. He can be called a warped and sick man who has failed to achieve a better answer to the challenge of having been born human, and this is true; he can also be called a man who took the wrong way in search of his salvation.[†]

These considerations by no means imply, however, that destruc-tiveness and cruelty are not vicious; they only imply that vice is human. They are indeed destructive of life, of body and spirit, destructive not only of the victim but of the destroyer himself. They constitute a paradox: they express *life turning against itself in the striving to make sense of it*. They are the only true perver-sion. Understanding them does not mean condoning them. But unless we understand them, we have no way to recognize how they may be reduced, and what factors tend to increase them.

Such understanding is of particular importance today, when sensitivity toward destructiveness-cruelty is rapidly diminishing, and necrophilia, the attraction to what is dead, decaying, lifeless and purely mechanical, is increasing throughout our cybernetic industrial society. The spirit of necrophilia was expressed first in

---

[†]'Salvation' comes from the Latin root *sal*, 'salt' (in Spanish *salud*, 'health'). The meaning stems from the fact that salt protects meat from decomposition; 'salva-tion' is the protection of man from decomposition (to protect his health and well-being). In this sense each man needs 'salvation' (in a nontheological sense).

literary form by F.T. Marinetti in his *Futurist Manifesto* of 1909. The same tendency can be seen in much of the art and literature of the last decades that exhibits a particular fascination with all that is decayed, unalive, destructive, and mechanical. The Falangist motto, 'Long live death', threatens to become the secret principle of a society in which the conquest of nature by machine constitutes the very meaning of progress, and where the living person becomes an appendix to the machine.

Erich Fromm, *The Anatomy of Human Destructiveness* (1973)

LOVE

Falling in Love[7]

This simple accident of falling in love is as beneficial as it is astonishing. It arrests the petrifying influence of years, disproves cold-blooded and cynical conclusions, and awakens dormant sensibilities. Hitherto the man had found it a good policy to disbelieve the existence of any enjoyment which was out of his reach; and thus he turned his back upon the strong sunny parts of nature, and accustomed himself to look exclusively on what was common and dull. He accepted a prose ideal, let himself go blind of many sympathies by disuse; and if he were young and witty, or beautiful, wilfully forwent these advantages. He joined himself to the following of what, in the old mythology of love, was prettily called *nonchaloir*; and in an odd mixture of feelings, a fling of self-respect, a preference for selfish liberty, and a great dash of that fear with which honest people regard serious interests, kept himself back from the straightforward course of life among certain selected activities. And now, all of a sudden, he is unhorsed, like St Paul, from his infidel affection. His heart, which has been ticking accurate seconds for the last year, gives a bound and begins to beat high and irregularly in his breast. It seems as if he had never heard or felt or seen until that moment; and by the report of his memory, he must have lived his past life

7 For a biographical note on R.L. Stevenson see p. 25.

between sleep and waking, or with the preoccupied attention of a brown study. He is practically incommoded by the generosity of his feelings, smiles much when he is alone, and develops a habit of looking rather blankly upon the moon and stars. But it is not at all within the province of a prose essayist to give a picture of this hyperbolical frame of mind; and the thing has been done already, and that to admiration. In 'Adelaide' [Beethoven song, ed.] in Tennyson's *Maud*, and in some of Heine's songs, you get the absolute expression of this midsummer spirit. Romeo and Juliet were very much in love; although they tell me some German critics are of a different opinion, probably the same who would have us think Mercutio a dull fellow. Poor Antony was in love, and no mistake. That lay figure Marius, in *Les Misérables*, is also a genuine case in his own way and worth observation. A good many of George Sand's people are thoroughly in love, and so are a good many of George Meredith's. Altogether, there is plenty to read on the subject. If the root of the matter be in him, and if he has the requisite chords to set in vibration, a young man may occasionally enter, with the key of art, into that land of Beulah which is upon the borders of Heaven and within sight of the City of Love. There let him sit awhile to hatch delightful hopes and perilous illusions.

Robert Louis Stevenson, 'On Falling in Love', *Virginibus Puerisque* (1881)

Love Is a Property of the Lover, Not the Beloved

George Granville, Baron Lansdowne (1667–1735) was an English poet and playwright of whom Dr Johnson had little good to say in his Lives of the English Poets, *but a handful of whose aphoristic lyrics, including this one on love, continue to hold their own.*

> Love is begot by fancy, bred
>   By ignorance, by expectation fed,
> Destroyed by knowledge, and, at best,
>   Lost in the moment 'tis possessed.

George Granville, Baron Lansdowne, 'Love' (eighteenth century)

The Dangers of Unregulated Emotion

Francis Bacon, Earl Verulam, Viscount St Albans (1561–1626),
was born in London, educated at Trinity College, Cambridge,
admitted to Gray's Inn as a barrister in 1582, and elected to
Parliament in 1584. He became a protégé of Elizabeth's favourite,
Essex, but ten years later played a large part in securing his
conviction as a rebel. His own public life came to an end in 1621
after admitting taking bribes as a judge. His writing covered a
range of philosophical subjects including a treatise on scientific
method published in his Novum Organum *of 1620. The following*
extract is from his Essays.

It is a strange Thing, to note the Excesse of this Passion; And
how it braves, the Nature, and value of things; by this, that the
Speaking in a perpetuall *Hyperbole*, is comely in nothing, but in
Love. Neither is it merely in the Phrase; For whereas it hath beene
well said, that the Arch-flatterer, with whom all the petty Flatterers
have Intelligence, is a Mans Selfe; Certainly, the *Lover* is more.
For there was never Proud Man, thought so absurdly well of
himself, as the *Lover* doth of the person *loved*: And therefore, it
was well said; *That it is impossible to love, and to be wise*. Neither
doth this weaknesse appear to others onely, and not to the Party
Loved; But to the *Loved*, most of all: except the *Love* be reciproque. For, it is a true Rule, that *Love* is ever rewarded, either
with the Reciproque, or with an inward, and secret Contempt.
By how much the more, Men ought to beware of this passion,
which loseth not only other things, but it selfe. As for the other
losses, the Poets Relation, doth well figure them; That he preferred
Helena, quitted the Gifts of *Iuno*, and *Pallas*. For whosoever
esteemeth too much Amorous Affection, quitteth both *Riches*, and
Wisdome. This Passion, hath his Floud, in the very times of
Weaknesse; which are, great *Prosperitie*; and great *Adversitie*;
though this latter hath beene lesse observed. Both which times
kindle *Love*, and make it more fervent, and therefore shew it to
be the Childe of Folly. They doe best, who, if they cannot but
admit *Love*, yet make it keepe Quarter: And sever it wholly, from

their serious Affaires, and actions of life: For if it checke once with Businesse, it troubleth Mens Fortunes, and maketh men, that they can, no wayes be true, to their owne Ends. I know not how, but Martiall men, are given to *Love*: I thinke it is, but as they are given to *Wine*; For *Perils*, commonly aske, to be paid in *Pleasures*. There is in Mans Nature, a secret Inclination, and Motion, towards *love* of others; which, if it be not spent, upon some one, or a few, doth naturally spread it selfe, towards many; and maketh men become Humane, and Charitable; As is seene sometime in Friars. Nuptiall *love* maketh Mankinde; Friendly *love* perfecteth it; but Wanton *love* Corrupteth, and Imbaseth it.

Francis Bacon, 'Of Love', *Essays* (1596)

Can Love Cure Madness?

Love has itself been likened to a form of madness, but is it in fact a medicine for madness? Kay Redfield Jamison (1946–) is uniquely placed to answer the question. Daughter of an Air Force officer, she was brought up in Washington, DC and in Los Angeles. She originally trained as a clinical psychologist at UCLA and went on to study zoology and neurophysiology at the University of St Andrews. She is now a Professor of Psychiatry at the Johns Hopkins University School of Medicine, and a leading authority on manic depression. She loves, is loved and has been mad. The following extract is from her autobiographical memoir.

No amount of love can cure madness or unblacken one's darkest moods. Love can help, it can make the pain more tolerable, but, always, one is beholden to medication that may or may not always work and may or may not be bearable. Madness, on the other hand, most certainly can, and often does kill love through its mistrustfulness, unrelenting pessimism, discontents, erratic behaviour, and, especially, through its savage moods. The sadder, sleepier, slower and less volatile depressions are more intuitively understood and more easily taken in stride. A quiet melancholy is neither threatening nor beyond ordinary comprehension; an angry, violent, vexatious despair is both. Experience and love have, over much time, taught both of us a great deal about dealing with manic-depressive illness; I occasionally laugh and tell him that his imperturbability is worth 300 milligrams of lithium a day to me, and it is probably true.

Sometimes, in the midst of one of my dreadful, destructive upheavals of mood, I feel Richard's quietness nearby and am reminded of Byron's wonderful description of the rainbow that sits 'Like Hope upon a death-bed' on the verge of a wild, rushing cataract; yet, 'while all around is torn/ By the distracted waters', the rainbow stays serene:

> Resembling, mid the torture of the scene,
> Love watching Madness with unalterable mien.

But if love is not the cure, it certainly can act as a very strong medicine. As John Donne has written, it is not so pure and abstract as one might once have thought and wished, but it does endure, and it does grow.

Kay Redfield Jamison, *An Unquiet Mind* (1995)

MELANCHOLY AND DEPRESSION

Savouring Sadness

In line with the Romantic valuation of all aspects of our unique subjectivity, John Keats* celebrates the negative emotion of melancholy. Emotion, the voice in the poem proposes, even if painful, should be fully experienced, not blotted out with drugs.

The Keats family seems to have been doomed. John Keats (1795–1821) lost his father, the manager of a livery stables, in childhood, and his mother died of tuberculosis when he was fourteen years old. He was the oldest of a family of two other brothers, George and Tom, and a sister, Fanny. But Tom died in 1818, and Keats himself succumbed to tuberculosis three years later. During his short life he trained in medicine and was licensed as an apothecary in 1816; however he gave up clinical practice almost immediately, in favour of poetry. Following the death of his brother in 1818, Keats had moved into a house in Hampstead owned by his friend, Charles Armitage Brown, where he met and fell in love with Fanny Brawne. Although his health was already declining, the ensuing period saw the production of his greatest work.

I

No, no! go not to Lethe, neither twist
    Wolf's-bane, tight-rooted, for its poisonous wine;
Nor suffer thy pale forehead to be kiss'd
    By nightshade, ruby grape of Proserpine
Make not your rosary of yew-berries,
    Nor let the beetle or the death-moth be
        Your mournful Psyche, nor the downy owl
A partner in your sorrow's mysteries;
    For shade to shade will come too drowsily,
        And drown the wakeful anguish of the soul.

II

But when the melancholy fit shall fall
    Sudden from heaven like a weeping cloud,
That fosters the droop-headed flowers all,
    And hides the green hill in an April shroud;
Then glut thy sorrow on a morning rose,
    Or on the rainbow of the salt sand-wave,
        Or on the wealth of globed peonies;
Or if thy mistress some rich anger shows,
    Emprison her soft hand, and let her rave,
        And feed deep, deep upon her peerless eyes.

III

She dwells with Beauty – Beauty that must die;
    And Joy, whose hand is ever at his lips

Bidding adieu; and aching Pleasure nigh,
   Turning to poison while the bee-mouth sips:
Ay, in the very temple of Delight
   Veil'd Melancholy has her sovran shrine,
      Though seen of none save him whose strenuous tongue
   Can burst Joy's grape against his palate fine;
His soul shall taste the sadness of her might,
      And be among her cloudy trophies hung

John Keats, 'Ode on Melancholy' (1820)

Mood and the Mono-Amine Hypothesis

There are many millions of nerve cells in the brain and an even larger number of connections between them. Transmission of impulses from one nerve cell to another within this complex network is brought about by secretion of chemicals into the neuronal junction, known as a synapse. The chemicals produced at the ending of the first cell act by uniting with proteins at 'receptor' sites on the ending of the cell receiving the stimulus – the post-synaptic membrane. This causes it to become more or less permeable to different ions, and thus to become either excited or inhibited. The process is modulated by transferring these chemicals out of the synapse and back into the original cell. Recreational drugs such as cocaine and amphetamine are widely used for their mood-elevating effect and are known to increase levels of the neurotransmitter dopamine. Ecstasy increases the release of both dopamine and serotonin, the latter now thought to play a part in creating increased sociability. For at least half a century, evidence has been accumulating that particular neurotransmitters called 'mono-amines' (serotonin and nor-adrenaline), play a part in the regulation of mood. Nerve cells producing serotonin arise in the brain-stem and fan out widely throughout the brain and spinal cord.

In the 1950s, reserpine, a drug isolated from the root of an Indian plant, Rauwolfia serpentina, and used in the treatment of high blood pressure, was reported to make some patients depressed and suicidal. This drug was known to lower brain amines. Another drug, iproniazid, used in the treatment of tuberculosis and known to increase brain amines (by interfering with the oxidation mechanism by which they are normally destroyed), produced euphoria and elation as a side-effect. Following these observations, drugs aimed at raising the amount of mono-amine in the brain were designed, and found to be helpful in alleviating depressive illness, though by no means all patients responded. Two groups of drugs have been synthesized: those which act like iproniazid, known as mono-amine oxidase inhibitors, and those which interfere with the removal of transmitter substances from the synapse, known as tricyclics or re-uptake inhibitors. Whereas older drugs simultaneously inhibited the re-uptake of both noradrenaline and serotonin, modern antidepressants can selectively interfere with the re-uptake of just one or the other neurotransmitter and thus produce fewer side-effects.

Despite indirect evidence produced by the widespread use of antidepressants, the biochemical nature of depressive illness has remained poorly understood, and until recently there has been little to show that lowered mono-amine levels could actually be the cause. For example, although depressed patients undergoing treatment with antidepressant drugs which increase the level of a particular mono-amine do become vulnerable to relapse when levels of that chemical are artificially reduced, experimenters have been unable to induce depression in normal subjects using the same procedures.

The research extracted below was carried out in the University Department of Psychiatry, Littlemore Hospital, Oxford, England, under the leadership of Professor Philip Cowen. It is important because it demonstrates that in some people vulnerable to depression but not actually depressed, a relapse can be experimentally induced, switched on and off quite rapidly, through direct manipulation of their diet so as to reduce and then increase the amount of mono-amine they are able to produce.

The body needs tryptophan (an essential amino acid normally present in the diet) in order to synthesize the mono-amine neurotransmitter serotonin. It also needs tryptophan for the production *of other proteins. Levels of tryptophan circulating in the blood can be dramatically reduced using an experimental procedure which involves feeding a person a mixture of amino acids from which tryptophan has been omitted. This mixture stimulates protein synthesis in the liver, but since the mixture contains no tryptophan, the body has to use its own stores in order to supply the necessary amino acid. As a result, circulating plasma levels become rapidly depleted and levels of serotonin in the brain are decreased.*

Methods
We studied 15 women who had suffered recurrent episodes of major depression but had recovered and were no longer on drug treatment. Patients received two amino acid mixtures in a double-blind crossover design. [An experimental design where each patient receives first one mixture and at least a week later the other. But neither experimenters nor patients are aware which mixture is being administered, ed.] One of the mixtures was nutritionally balanced and contained tryptophan and the other was identical except it contained no tryptophan. Participants were scored on the Hamilton rating scale for depression (HAM-D) before and 7 hours after drinking each mixture. They also completed hourly self-rated measures of mood during this period. Blood samples were also taken at baseline and after 7 hours for measurement of plasma tryptophan.

Findings
The tryptophan-free mixture produced a 75% reduction in plasma tryptophan concentration. After drinking the tryptophan-free mixture, ten of the 15 women experienced temporary but clinically significant depressive symptoms [. . .] No changes in mood were seen after taking the nutritionally balanced mixture . . .

A feature of particular interest was that the participants who had full relapses of symptoms described a reappearance of some of the depressive thoughts they had experienced when previously depressed. One of these participants whose previous episodes of clinical depression were associated with the loss of important friendships had, while depressed, been preoccupied with fears that she would never be able to sustain a relationship. She had not had such fears since then. She had been fully recovered and had not taken any medication for over a year. About 2 hours after drinking the tryptophan-free mixture she experienced a sudden onset of sadness, despair and uncontrollable crying. She feared that a current important relationship would end. She recognized that she was depressed but still considered that her fears were appropriate. The evening of the test day she started to feel better and the next day was fully recovered. She said that her fears about her current relationship had been unfounded and she now saw them as unrealistic.

K.A. Smith, C.G. Fairburn and P.J. Cowen, 'Relapse of Depression After Rapid Depletion of Tryptophan' (1997)

The Powers of Perforated St John's Wort

The use of St John's Wort as a treatment against demonic possession was known to the ancients, and described by Hippocrates, Pliny and Galen. In recent times standardized extracts of the plant have been tested in the treatment of depression using modern methods of trial design and statistical analysis (see Helmut Woelk for the Remotiv/Imipramine Study Group, 'Comparison of St John's Wort and Imipramine for Treating Depression: Randomised Controlled Trial', British Medical Journal 321 (2000), 536–9). In cases of mild to moderate depression, St John's Wort has been found to be therapeutically equivalent to the antidepressant drug imipramine, and to be better tolerated. Its mode of action remains uncertain.

PERFORATED ST JOHN'S WORT
Hypericum perforatum
Class POLYADELPHIA. Order POLYANDRIA. Nat. Ord.
HYPERICINEAE – ST JOHN'S WORT TRIBE

The English name of this bright yellow flower reminds us of the practices with which it was once connected. It was one of the

flowers gathered by our forefathers to be thrown into the bonfires
which were kindled in London on the Eve of St. John. It was
formerly worn in Scotland to preserve the wearer against witches
and enchantments; and in several continental countries the superstition lingers yet, that it is a charm against thunder and lightning, and the machinations of evil spirits. In many parts of France
and Germany, the peasantry still gather its golden blooms with
much ceremony on St. John's Day, and hang them up in their
windows and doorways to avert evil. Alfred Lear Huxford has
alluded to a somewhat similar practice –

> So then about her brow
> They bound Hypericum, whose potent leaves
> Have sovereign power o'er all the sullen fits
> And cheerless fancies that besiege the mind;
> Banishing ever, to their native night,
> Dark thoughts, and causing to spring up within
> The heart distress'd, a glow of gladdening hope,
> And rainbow visions of kind destiny.

The old name of this flower, Balm of the Warrior's Wound, is
now almost forgotten; but in the olden time, physicians and poets
alike celebrated its properties; and some medical writers deemed
it so efficacious an internal remedy for hypochondriacal disorders, that they fancifully termed it *Fuga Daemonum*.

A. Pratt, *Wild Flowers* (1853)

The Deleterious Effects of Unrequited Love

*Thomas Willis (1621–75) was born in the Wiltshire village of
Great Bedwyn where his father was steward to Sir Walter Smith.
He spent his boyhood in Oxford, and at the age of sixteen,
matriculated into the University of Oxford as a servitor (a position for bright lads of humble circumstances, who received education in return for providing domestic services). During his student
days he enlisted as a Royalist soldier in the Civil War, and after*

*the Restoration was rewarded by appointment to the Sedleian
chair of natural philosophy. In 1666 he moved to London, where
he practised medicine until his death.*

His Cerebri Anatome *was published in 1664, describing the
anatomy of the brain, and most famously the ring of arteries
around its base, still known as the circle of Willis. Accurate
anatomical observations were intermingled with a physiology
predicated on the circulation of 'Animal Spirits', by which Willis
meant chemical substances or fluids generated in the brain from
arterial blood, and flowing into the nerves. He distinguished two
souls, a rational one unique to man, and a corporeal one shared
with other animals. It is evident from the following passage that
he believed in the psychosomatic genesis of bodily symptoms,
just as much as the bodily influence upon the mind.*

Concerning the power of Love, saying nothing here of some most
noble Lord, or Heroic actions (which appear chiefly on the stage
of the *Theatre*, and on that of human life) it is a most common
observation, that if anyone being taken with the aspect and
conversation of any Woman, begins to desire her and to grow
mad for her inwardly, and for his most devoted affection has
nothing but loss and contempt allotted him, unless he be very
much supported by a firm reason, or is averted as it were by
other cross affections, there is great danger lest he falls into
Melancholy, Stupidity, or Love-Madness; with which passion, if
by chance he be distemper'd, he forthwith seems transformed
from himself, as it were into an animated statue, he thinks on,
nor speaks of anything but his Love; he endeavours to get into
her favour, with the danger of both the loss of his Life and
Fortune; in the meantime, he not only neglects the care of his
household affairs, or of the public, yea his own health, but
becoming desperate of his desires, he oftentimes lays violent hands
on himself. But if he be content to live, yet growing lean, or with-
ering away both in Soul and Body, he almost puts off man; for
the right use of reason being lost, omitting food and sleep, and
the necessary offices of Nature, he sets himself wholly to sighing
and groaning, and gets a mournful habit and carriage of body.

If we should inquire into the reason of this Distemper, it easily appears, that the Corporeal Soul of Man being obnoxious to violent affections, when it is wholly carried into the object most dear unto itself, viz. the beloved Woman, and cannot obtain and embrace her, there is nothing besides that can quiet or delight it; yea being refractory, it grows wholly deaf to the Rational Soul, and hears not its dictates, but carrying only tragical notions to the Imagination, darkens the sight of the intellect. Further, forasmuch as the *Pracordia* (the more plentiful afflux of the Spirits being denied to them) do slacken of their motions, the blood heaped up in the bosoms of the heart, and apt to stand still, stirs up a great weight and oppression, and for that reason, sighs and groans; in the mean time the face, and the outward members grow pale and languish, for that the affluence of the Blood and Spirits is withdrawn: Hence in our *Idiom* or Speech, the Heart of despairing Lovers is said to be broken, to wit, because this Muscle is not lively enough actuated by the animal Spirit, and so is shaken weakly and slowly, and doth not amply enough cast forward the blood with vigour, into all parts. Indeed in Love, the Corporeal Soul intimately embracing the *Idea* of its most grateful object, endeavours all it can to be joined, and fully united to the same; emitting toward her, the roots of the affections, with which it is most strictly enfolded, seems from thence to draw its chiefest life and growth; so that the body being neglected, when as it inclines it self wholly towards the thing beloved, if by chance being broken off from this union, it suffer a divorce, like a plant taken out of its natural soil, for that it does not receive any more, or assimilate food convenient for itself, it soon withers: Hence the Animal Spirits leaving their accustomed offices, and wonted tracts of expansion, do not actuate or irradiate either the Brain or the *Pracordia*, nor the nervous *Appendix*, after their due manner: wherefore, not only for the present an untrimmed, and a delirious disposition of mind, with a mournful habit of body, are excited; but from thence the vitiated Blood, and the Spirits, having gotten an acetous nature, an habitual *Melancholy* is introduced.

Such an inordination of the Animal Function as Mad-Love hath, about the acquisition of its object, the same or very like hath *Jealousy*, about the retention of the same, being gotten; so always (as well in the fruition as in the desire) *Res est solliciti plena timoris Amor: Love is ever full of careful fear*. This Soul, if it be not secure of its most dear prey, it presently grows hot, and pours forth darkness and clouds upon its own serenity: then afterwards being infected by a *Choleric* tincture, it receives every object, as if it were imbued with a yellow colour: for indeed, as the ferment of the stomach being too much indued with a sourness, perverts all things that is put into it, into its nature; so *Jealousy* being once arisen, changes all accidents and circumstances, into the food of its poison, and when the sensitive Soul, being as it were bowed inward in this passion, becomes not conform to its Body, for that reason the Economy of the Functions both Animal, Vital, and vegetative being depraved, *Jealousy* makes one rave, and to wither away.

Thomas Willis, 'Of Melancholy' (1672)

The Depths of Depression

Gerard Manley Hopkins (1844–89), poet, priest and classical scholar, was born in Stratford, Essex. The son of Anglican parents, he was educated at Highgate School and Balliol College, Oxford, and converted to Roman Catholicism in 1866. Two years later he decided to become a Jesuit. After ordination he worked as a priest but became convinced that he was a failure, and in 1884 took a chair in Greek and Latin at University College, Dublin. He died prematurely of typhoid fever. His poetry, largely unappreciated during his lifetime, was published by his friend Robert Bridges at the end of the First World War.

Hopkins was subject to melancholy all his life, but probably reached his lowest ebb in 1885. 'When I am at the worst', he wrote to Alexander Baillie, 'though my judgement is never affected, my state is much like madness.'

No worst, there is none. Pitched past pitch of grief,
More pangs will, schooled at forepangs, wilder wring.
Comforter, where, where is your comforting?

Mary, mother of us, where is your relief?
My cries heave, herds-long; huddle in a main, a chief-
woe, world-sorrow; on an age-old anvil wince and sing –
Then lull, then leave off. Fury had shrieked 'No ling-
ering! Let me be fell: force I must be brief'.
O the mind, mind has mountains; cliffs of fall
Frightful, sheer, no-man-fathomed. Hold them cheap
May who ne'er hung there. Nor does long our small
Durance deal with that steep or deep. Here! creep,
Wretch, under a comfort serves in a whirlwind: all
Life death does end and each day dies with sleep.

Gerard Manley Hopkins, Untitled early poem (c.1885)

Self-Torment

*More than any other writer, Franz Kafka is associated with
the alienation characteristic of modernism. The adjective
'Kafkaesque' has achieved widespread currency, meaning night-
marish or bewilderingly oppressive. Although he died in the
1920s, his work seems uncannily descriptive of the Nazi totali-
taian state which was to arise in Germany. Kafka (1883–1924)
was born in Prague to German-speaking Jewish parents. His three
novels, letters and diaries were published after his death, by his
friend Max Brod. They clearly indicate that his fictional world
mirrored the horrors of his own, at times desperate, mental state.
Kafka's personal desperation has become a symbol for the plight
of modern man.*

7 February Complete standstill. Unending torments.
At a certain point in self-knowledge, when other circumstances
favouring self-security are present, it will invariably follow that
you find yourself execrable. Every moral standard – however
opinions may differ on it – will seem too high. You will see that
you are nothing but a rat's nest of miserable dissimulations. The
most trifling of your acts will not be untainted by these dissimulations. These dissimulated intentions are so squalid that in the
course of your self-scrutiny you will not want to ponder them

closely but will instead be content to gaze at them from afar. These intentions aren't all compounded merely of selfishness, selfishness seems in comparison an ideal of the good and beautiful. The filth you will find exists for its own sake; you will recognize that you came dripping into the world with this burden and will depart unrecognizable again – or only too recognizable – because of it. This filth is the nethermost depth you will find; at the nethermost depth there will be not lava, no, but filth. It is the nethermost and the uppermost, and even the doubts self-scrutiny begets will soon grow weak and self-complacent as the wallowing of a pig in muck.

17 October
I don't believe people exist whose inner plight resembles mine; still, it is possible for me to imagine such people – but that the secret raven forever flaps about their heads as it does about mine, even to imagine that is impossible.

It is astounding how I have systematically destroyed myself in the course of the years, it was like a slowly widening breach in a dam, a purposeful action. The spirit that brought it about must now be celebrating triumphs; why doesn't it let me take part in them? But perhaps it hasn't yet achieved its purpose and can therefore think of nothing else.

Franz Kafka, *Diaries* (entries for 1915, 1921)

John Clare (1793–1864) was the son of an agricultural labourer. A poet of place and nature, he published several successful volumes in the 1820s and 1830s, but at the age of thirty-nine he left the cottage he had grown up in and moved to a new home, which seems to have unbalanced him. In 1837 he was admitted to an asylum in Essex from which he absconded in 1841, walking home to Northampton to be reunited with his first love, Mary, to whom he believed himself to be married. He spent the rest of his life in Northampton General Asylum. By the time of his death his work had fallen out of favour. This poem was written in the Northampton Asylum and published posthumously.

I am: yet what I am none cares or knows;
 My friends forsake me like a memory lost;
I am the self-consumer of my woes,
 They rise and vanish in oblivious host,
Like shades in love and death's oblivion lost;
And yet I am, and live with shadows tost

Into the nothingness of scorn and noise,
 Into the living sea of waking dreams,
Where there is neither sense of life nor joys,
 But the vast shipwreck of my life's esteems;
And e'en the dearest – that I loved the best –
Are strange – nay, rather, stranger than the rest.

I long for scenes where man has never trod;
 A place where woman never smiled or wept;
There to abide with my Creator, God,
 And sleep as I in childhood sweetly slept:
Untroubling and untroubled where I lie,
The grass below – above the vaulted sky.

John Clare, 'I Am' (1865)

ANGER

Collective Anger

Coleridge[8] rounds on his critics. People who lack an inner source of passion, he says, make up for it by gathering together in crowds. The anger of a howling claque is nothing but a cover for the absence of feeling and judgement in its individual members.

I have often thought, that it would be neither uninstructive nor unamusing to analyse, and bring forward into distinct consciousness, that complex feeling, with which readers in general take part against the author, in favour of the critic; and the readiness with

8 For a biographical note on S. T. Coleridge see p. 19.

which they apply to all poets the old sarcasm of Horace upon the scribblers of his time: 'Genus irritabile vatum [the irritable race of poets, ed.]'. A debility and dimness of the imaginative power, and a consequent necessity of reliance on the immediate impressions of the senses, do, we well know, render the mind liable to superstition and fanaticism. Having a deficient portion of internal and proper warmth, minds of this class seek in the crowd *circum fans* [around the temples, ed.] for a warmth in common, which they do not possess singly. Cold and phlegmatic in their own nature, like damp hay, they heat and inflame by coacervation; or like bees they become restless and irritable through the increased temperature of collected multitudes. Hence the German word for fanaticism (such at least was its original import) is derived from the swarming of bees, namely, *Schwärmen, Schwärmerey*. The passion being in inverse proportion to the insight, *that* the more vivid, as *this* the less distinct; anger is the inevitable consequence. The absence of all foundation within their own minds for that, which they yet believe both true and indispensable for their safety and happiness, cannot but produce an uneasy state of feeling, an involuntary sense of fear from which nature has no means of rescuing herself but by anger. Experience informs us that the first defence of weak minds is to recriminate.

Samuel Taylor Coleridge, *Biographia Literaria* (1815–17)

How to Rid Yourself of Anger

Galen (129–c.210) was born in Pergamum, a provincial city of the Roman Empire, situated on what is now the western coast of Turkey. Under the influence of a divine signal, his father encouraged him in the study of medicine (and philosophy). Galen, partially following Hippocrates, codified the ancient theory which stated that matter consisted of four fundamental qualities: hot, cold, wet and dry. These were said to manifest themselves in the basic constituents of the universe: earth, air, fire and water; and in the bodily humours: blood, phlegm, yellow and black bile. Galen's work influenced (and inhibited) the course of science for generations, becoming medieval dogma and spreading through

Europe and Arabia to the Far East. But his wisdom concerning the management of 'affections of the soul', which should be understood to mean 'disturbed mental states', has a modern ring.

Anger is nothing less than a madness, as may be seen from the actions of men in the grip of it. They strike out, kick, tear their clothes, and perform every act in an agitated manner, to the point where – as stated earlier – they even lose their temper with doors, stones, or keys, which they rattle, bite or kick.

You may argue that the above actions are those of people who actually are mad, while your own actions are those of a temperate person. Now, I would agree that the error of those who strike servants with their own hands is less than that of the biters and kickers of stones, doors and keys; yet it is my conviction that any act of ferocity perpetrated against a human being is a function of some kind of madness, albeit a mild one – or that of an animal that is wild and devoid of reason. For is not the power of reason the characteristic that marks out the human from the other animals? If you wish to remove this and gratify the spirit of anger, your life is the life of an animal, not a human. It should not be thought that human moderation consists merely in refraining from kicking, biting or stabbing those around us. One who only succeeds in that may avoid the epithet 'savage'; but he could hardly be called a moderate individual. His state, in fact, will be midway between savagery and moderation. (Are you going to be content with such a graduation from savagery, without any ambition to become a decent, upright individual? Is it not a preferable aim to avoid a continued state, not only of savagery, but also of imbecility and irrationality?) Moderation will be achieved when you are no longer a slave to anger, but perform every action by reference to the considerations which govern your judgement when made outside the influence of the affection.

How, then, can this come about? By awarding yourself the greatest esteem of which it is possible to conceive. When all other men are in the grip of anger, to remain free from that passion is to demonstrate one's superiority over the whole of humankind. It may, however, be that you wish to enjoy the reputation of superiority, but not the reality. This is just the same as though one were to desire to be sick in fact, but to be thought healthy. For is not anger a sickness of the soul? Or do you deny the sense of the ancients, who gave the name of 'affections of the soul' to these five: grief, rage, anger, desire, and fear?

The following appears to me much the best course of action for one who would rid himself as far as possible of the above affections. First, on rising in the morning one should pose oneself this question, before embarking on the day's tasks: is it better to live a constant slave to the affections, or to employ reason on every occasion? The man who wishes to become upright and good must, secondly, call to himself one who will make clear to him everything that he does wrong. One must, further, keep constantly in mind, every day and every hour of the day, the desirability of counting oneself amongst the good and the upright, and the impossibility of achieving this aim without the presence of that person who will make clear one's errors; one should, indeed, regard this revealer of one's every false step as his saviour, as the greatest of his friends. It is also important, even if you sometimes think his criticisms unjust, to preserve your calm, in the first place because it is quite likely that he has a clearer perception than you of each of your errors (as, reciprocally, you would have of his); it is also the case that even a false criticism will urge you towards a finer examination of your own actions.

Galen, 'The Affections and Errors of the Soul' [?193–c.210]

Anger is certainly a kinde of Basenesse: As it appeares well, in the Weaknesse of those Subjects, in whom it reignes: Children, Women, Old Folkes, Sicke Folkes. Only Men must beware, that they carry their *Anger*, rather with Scorne, then with Feare: so that they may seeme rather, to be above the Iniury, then below it: which is a Thing easily done, if a Man will give Law to himselfe in it.

For the Second Point; The *Causes* and *Motives* of *Anger*, are chiefly three. First, to be too *Sensible* of *Hurt*: For no Man is *Angry*, that *Feeles* not himselfe Hurt: And therefore Tender and Delicate persons, must needs be oft *Angry*: They have so many

Things to trouble them; which more Robust Natures have little Sense of. The next is, the Apprehension and Construction, of the Iniury offred, to be, in the Circumstances thereof, full of *Contempt*. For *Contempt* is that which putteth an Edge upon *Anger*, as much, or more, then the hurt it selfe. And therefore, when Men are Ingenious, in picking out Circumstances of *Contempt*, they doe kindle their *Anger* much. Lastly, Opinion of the Touch of Mans *Reputation*, doth multiply and sharpen *Anger*. Wherein the Remedy is, that a Man should have, as *Consalvo* was wont to say, *telam Honoris crassiorem* [a watertight reputation; lit. 'more tightly-woven web of honour', ed.]. But in all Refrainings of *anger*, it is the best Remedy to win Time; And to make Mans selfe beleeve, that the Opportunity of his Revenge is not yet come: But that he foresees a Time for it; And so to still Himselfe in the meane Time, and reserve it.

To containe *Anger* from *Mischiefe*, though it take hold of a Man, there be two Things, whereof you must have speciall Caution. The one, of extreme *Bitternesse of Words*; Especially, if they be Aculeate, and Proper: For *Communia Maledicta* are nothing so much: And againe, that in *Anger*, a Man reveale no Secrets: For that makes him not fit for Society. The other, that you doe not *peremptorily break off*, in any Businesse, do not *Act* any thing, that is not Revocable.

For *Raising* and *Appeasing Anger* in Another; It is done chiefly, by *Choosing of Times*, when men are frowardest and worst disposed, to incense them. Againe, by gathering (as was touched before) all that you finde out, to aggravate the *Contempt*. And the two *Remedies* are by the *Contraries*. The Former, to take good Times, when first to relate to a Man, an *Angry* Businesse: For the first Impression is much; And the other is, to sever, as much as may be, the Construction of the Iniury, from the point of *Contempt*: Imputing it, to Misunderstanding, Feare, Passion, or what you will.

Francis Bacon, 'Of Anger', *Essays* (1596)[9]

9 For a biographical note on Francis Bacon see p. 115.

FEAR

Once Established, Fear May Be Unconsciously Preserved in the Brain's Circuitry

Professor Joseph LeDoux and co-workers at Cornell University Medical College found that rats could be made to fear a sound (originally associated with a brief electric shock to the foot), even when part of the brain necessary for hearing (the auditory cortex) had been destroyed. However, blocking certain lower pathways in the midbrain and thalamus, which carried sound information to the auditory cortex, did prevent fear conditioning from taking place. It therefore appeared that the brain could respond emotionally to a fearful sound without actually 'hearing' it. The auditory information passed, unheard, via the subcortical areas to somewhere in the lower part of the brain where it was linked to the reactions normally associated with fear. By selectively destroying each of these places and seeing whether a fear reaction was prevented, LeDoux and colleagues discovered that the linkage was effected in the amygdala.

Fear conditioning has been shown in many different types of animal – from the lowly marine snail to small mammals, cats, dogs, primates and man. The 'emotional learning' that is involved in the creation of fear conditioning seems to happen at an unconscious level. Parts of the brain known to be required for conscious learning, such as the hippocampus, are not required. The neural basis of emotion in man is no doubt more complex than that in a rat; however, LeDoux's experiments are highly suggestive.

In the following passage, LeDoux describes how a circuit of brain cells in the amygdala mediating the fear response is established, and how this linkage is sustained in a kind of 'unconscious emotional memory', even when the original stimulus is no longer associated with fear. Sometimes the newly established circuit fires quite spontaneously. This could account for the tendency of some people to 'overreact' to apparently minor threats.

I recently had a scientific 'ah ha' experience, one of those rare, wonderful moments when a new set of findings from the lab suddenly makes you see something puzzling in a new, crystal clear way. The studies involved recordings of electrical activity of the amygdala before and after fear conditioning [in the rat, ed.] . . . We found dramatic increases in electrical responses elicited by the tone CS [conditional stimulus, ed.] after conditioning, and these increases were reversed by extinction. However, because we were recording from multiple individual neurons at the same time, we were also able to look at the activity relationship between the cells. Conditioning increased the functional interactions between neurons so that the likelihood that two cells would fire at the same time dramatically increased. These interactions were seen both in the response to the stimulus and in the spontaneous firing of the cells when nothing in particular was going on. What was most interesting was that in some of the cells, these functional interactions were not reversed by extinction. Conditioning appears to have created what Donald Hebb called 'cell assemblies', and some of these seemed resistant to extinction. Although the tone was no longer causing the cells to fire (they had extinguished), the functional interactions between the cells, as seen in their spontaneous firings, remained. It is as if these functional couplings are holding the memory even at a time when the external triggers of the memory (for example, phobic stimuli) are no longer effective in activating the memory and its associated behaviours (for example, phobic responses). Although highly speculative at this point, the observations suggest clues as to how memories can live in the brain at a time when they are not accessible by external stimuli. All that it would take to reactivate those memories would be a change in the strength of the input to the cell assembly. This may be something that stress can accomplish.

Unconscious fear memories established through the amygdala appear to be indelibly burned into the brain. They are probably with us for life. This is often very useful, especially in a stable, unchanging world, since we don't have to learn about the same kinds of dangers over and over again. But the downside is that sometimes the things that are imprinted in the amygdala's circuits are maladaptive. In these instances, we pay dearly for the incredible efficiencies of the fear system.

Joseph LeDoux, *The Emotional Brain* (1998)

Fear of Death

Philosophers have devoted much effort to proving that fear of death is irrational. Since the certainty of death is constant but the fear of death seems to vary according to other factors, including its perceived nearness in time, can the emotion be rational? Epicurus (341–270BCE), counsels against the folly of fearing non-existence, for where there is non-existence there can be no experience of loss.

Epicurus developed a following on the east Aegean coast, moving to Athens to found a school around 307BCE. His philosophy was essentially materialist. The human soul was no exception to his rule that all perceptible qualities resulted from the geometry and arrangement of atomic particles. The atomic arrangement decomposed with the body, therefore there could be no hereafter. However, during life, Epicurus taught, our primal good was ensured by maintaining the superiority of mental over physical pleasure. The pain of frustration could and should be eliminated by restricting desire to a few simple and easily gratified areas. In this way a sense of well-being could be permanently maintained. But this still left the problem of anticipating death, which he deals with in the following passage.

III. TRUE it is, indeed, and too true, that men generally abhor Death, sometimes because they look upon it as the Greatest of Pains, sometimes because they apprehend it as the cessation of all their enjoiments, or privation of all things that are dear to them in life; but in both these Respects, altogether without cause: since this thing *Not-to-live*, or *Not-to-be*, ought to be no occasion of Terror; because when once we come to that, we shall have no faculty left whereby to know, that Not-to-live hath any thing of Evil in it.

IV. HEREUPON we may conclude that those are great Fools

who abhor to think, that after Death their Bodies should be torn by wild beasts, burned in the flame of the funeral pile, devoured by worms, &c. for, they do not consider, that then they shall not be, and so not feel, nor complain, that they are torn, burned, devoured by corruption or worms. And that those are Greater Fools, who take it grievously, that they shall no longer enjoy the conversation of their Wives, Children, Friends, no longer do them good offices, nor afford them their assistance; for these do not consider, that then they shall have no longer Relation to, nor Desire of Wife, Children, Friends, or anything else.

V. WE said, that *Death* (accounted the King of Terrors, and most horrid of all Evils) *doth nothing concern us, because*, while we are, Death is not; and when Death is, we are not; so that he, who profoundly considers the matter, will soon conclude that Death doth concern neither the Living, nor the Dead; not the living, because it yet touches them not, not the Dead, because they are not.

VI. AND, as the assurance of this, that Death nothing concerns us, doth exempt us from the greatest of Terrors, so also doth it make us to enjoy life to the most advantage of pleasure, not be adding thereunto anything of uncertain Time, but by Detracting all desire of Immortality. For, in life there can be nothing Evil to him, who doth perfectly understand, that there can be nothing of Evil in the privation of life.

VII. AGAIN, He cannot be excused of Folly, who saith, that He fears Death, not because of any trouble or Anguish that it can bring, when it comes; but because of the perpetual Grief, and Horror, wherewith it afflicts the mind, till it comes, or while it is expected: foreasmuch as that, which can bring no trouble or anguish with it when it comes, ought not to make us sad before it comes. Certainly, if there be anything of Incommodity, or Fear in the business of Death, it is the fault of him that is Dying, not of Death it self: nor is there any trouble in Death, more than there is after it, and it is no less folly to fear Death, than to fear old Age, since as old Age follows close upon the heels of youth, so doth Death upon the heels of old Age.

Epicurus, *Morals* (c.300BCE)

PHOBIA

A Light-Hearted Inventory of Phobias

Benjamin Rush (1745–1813), often thought of as the father of American psychiatry, was educated at Edinburgh and Princeton, Philadelphia. He became a professor of chemistry and a great social reformer, establishing the first free clinics in the United States. He fought for free schooling, prison reforms and the abolition of slavery. Despite his generally liberal attitudes he was a man of his time and subscribed to the currently popular 'disease theory of negritude' which saw black skin as a dermatological disorder. He was one of the signatories to the American Declaration of Independence and served as treasurer to the US Mint from 1797 to 1813.

I shall define Phobia to be 'a fear of an imaginary evil, or an undue fear of a real one'. The following species appear to belong to it.

1. The CAT PHOBIA. It will be unnecessary to mention instances of the prevalence of this distemper . . . 2. The RAT PHOBIA is a more common disease than the first species that has been mentioned: It is peculiar, in some measure, to the female sex . . . 3. The INSECT PHOBIA. This disease is peculiar to the female sex. A spider – a flea – or a musqueto, alighting upon a lady's neck, has often produced an hysterical fit . . . 4. The ODOUR PHOBIA is a very frequent disease with all classes of people . . . 5. The DIRT PHOBIA. This disease is peculiar to certain ladies . . . They make every body miserable around them with their excessive cleanliness: the whole of their lives is one continued warfare with dirt . . . 6. The RUM PHOBIA. This disease is a very *rare* distemper . . . If it were possible to communicate this distemper as we do small-pox, by inoculation, what immense revenue would be derived from it by physicians . . . 7. The WATER PHOBIA. This species includes not the dread of swallowing, but of *crossing* water. I have known some people, who sweat with terror in crossing an ordinary ferry . . . 8. The SOLO PHOBIA; by which I mean

the dread of solitude . . . 9. The POWER PHOBIA. This distemper belongs to certain demagogues. Persons afflicted with it, consider power as an evil – they abhor even the sight of an officer of government . . . 10. The FACTION PHOBIA. This disease is peculiar to persons of an opposite character to those who are afraid of power . . . 11. The WANT PHOBIA. This disease is confined chiefly to old people . . . 12. The DOCTOR PHOBIA. This distemper is often complicated with other diseases. It arises, in some instances, from the dread of taking physic, or of submitting to the remedies of bleeding and blistering. In some instances I have known it occasioned by a desire sick people feel of deceiving themselves, by being kept in ignorance of the danger of their disorders . . . 13. The BLOOD PHOBIA. There is a native dread of the sight of blood in every human creature, implanted probably for the wise purpose of preventing our injuring or destroying ourselves, or others . . . 14. The THUNDER PHOBIA. This species is common to all ages, and to both sexes: I have seen it produce the most distressing appearances and emotions upon many people . . . 15. The HOME PHOBIA. This disease belongs to all those men who prefer the tavern, to domestic society . . . 16. The CHURCH PHOBIA. This disease has become epidemic in the city of Philadelphia . . . 17. The GHOST PHOBIA. This distemper is most common among servants and children . . . 18. The DEATH PHOBIA. The fear of death is natural to man – but there are degrees of it which constitute a *disease*.

Benjamin Rush, 'Medical Inquiries and Observations upon the Diseases of the Mind' (1812)

HATE

The Need to Be Hated

D.W. Winnicott (1896–1971) was a physician and paediatrician, who worked for forty years at the Paddington Green Children's Hospital, London. He trained as a psychoanalyst and went on to become President of the British Psychoanalytical Society. His clinical practice gradually changed from physical medicine to child psychiatry and child psychoanalysis. As well as contributing to the professional literature on psychoanalysis, he wrote and broadcast widely on the subject of child care. Winnicott's insights, though sometimes shocking, strike many people as revealingly true.

Now I want to add that in certain stages of certain analyses the analyst's hate is actually sought by the patient, and what is then needed is hate that is objective. If the patient seeks objective or justified hate he must be able to reach it, else he cannot feel he can reach objective love.

It is perhaps relevant here to cite the case of the child of the broken home, or the child without parents. Such a child spends his time unconsciously looking for his parents. It is notoriously inadequate to take such a child into one's home and to love him. What happens is that after a while a child so adopted gains hope, and then he starts to test out the environment he has found, and to seek proof of his guardian's ability to hate objectively. It seems that he can believe in being loved only after reaching being hated.

During the second world war a boy of nine came to a hostel for evacuated children, sent from London not because of bombs but because of truancy. I hoped to give him some treatment during his stay in the hostel, but his symptom won and he ran away as he had always done from everywhere since the age of six when he first ran away from home. However, I had established contact with him in one interview in which I could see and interpret through a drawing of his that in running away he was unconsciously saving the inside of his home and preserving his mother from assault, as well as trying to get away from his own inner world which was full of persecutors.

I was not very surprised when he turned up in the police station very near my home. This was one of the few police stations that did not know him intimately. My wife very generously took him in and kept him for three months, three months of hell. He was the most loveable and most maddening of children, often stark staring mad. But fortunately we knew what to expect. We dealt with the first phase by giving him complete freedom and a shilling whenever he went out. He had only to ring up and we fetched him from whatever police station had taken charge of him.

Soon the expected change-over occurred, the truancy symptom turned round, and the boy started dramatizing the assault on the inside. It was really a whole-time job for the two of us together, and when I was out the worst episodes took place.

Interpretation had to be made at any minute of day or night, and often the only solution in a crisis was to make the correct interpretation, as if the boy were in analysis. It was the correct interpretation that he valued above everything.

The important thing for the purpose of this paper is the way in which the evolution of the boy's personality engendered hate in me, and what I did about it.

Did I hit him? The answer is no, I never hit. But I should have had to have done so if I had not known all about my hate and if I had not let him know about it too. At crises I would take him by bodily strength, and without anger or blame, and put him outside the front door, whatever the weather or the time of day or night. There was a special bell he could ring, and he knew if he rang it he would be readmitted and no word said about the past. He used this bell as soon as he had recovered from an attack.

The important thing is that each time, just as I put him outside the door, I told him something; I said that what had happened had made me hate him. This was easy because it was so true.

I think these words were important from the point of view of his progress, but they were mainly important in enabling me to tolerate the situation without letting out, without losing my temper and every now and again murdering him.

This boy's full story cannot be told here. He went to an Approved School. His deeply rooted relation to us has remained one of the few stable things in his life. This episode from ordinary life can be used to illustrate the general topic of hate justified in the present; this is to be distinguished from hate that is only justified in another setting but which is tapped by some action of a patient (child).

A Mother's Love and Hate

Out of all the complexity of the problem of hate and its roots I want to rescue one thing, because I believe it has importance for the analyst of psychotic patients. I suggest that the mother hates the baby before the baby can know his mother hates him.

Before developing this theme I want to refer to Freud's remarks. In *Instincts and Their Vicissitudes* (1915) (where he says so much that is original and illuminating about hate), Freud says: 'we might at a pinch say of an instinct that it "loves" the objects after which it strives for purposes of satisfaction, but to say that it "hates" an object strikes us as odd, so we become aware that the attitudes of love and hate cannot be said to characterize the relation of instincts to their objects, but are reserved for the relations of the ego as a whole to objects . . .' This I feel is true and important. Does this not mean that the personality must be integrated before an infant can be said to hate? However early integration may be achieved – perhaps integration occurs earliest at the height of excitement or rage – there is a theoretical earlier stage in which whatever the infant does that hurts is not done in hate. I have used the word 'ruthless love' in describing this stage. Is this acceptable? As the infant becomes able to feel a whole person, so does the word hate develop meaning as a description of a certain group of his feelings.

The mother, however, hates her infant from the word go. I believe Freud thought it possible that a mother may under certain circumstances have only love for her baby boy; but we may doubt this. We know about a mother's love and we appreciate its reality and power. Let me give some reasons why a mother hates her baby, even a boy.

A. The baby is not her own (mental) conception.
B. The baby is not the one of childhood play, father's child, brother's child, etc.
C. The baby is not magically produced.
D. The baby is a danger to her body in pregnancy and at birth.
E. The baby is an interference with her private life, a challenge to preoccupation.

F. To a greater or lesser extent a mother feels that her own mother demands a baby, so that her baby is produced to placate her mother.

G. The baby hurts her nipples even by suckling, which is at first a chewing activity.

H. He is ruthless, treats her as scum, an unpaid servant, a slave.

I. She has to love him, excretions and all, at any rate at the beginning, till he has doubts about himself.

J. He tries to hurt her, periodically bites her, all in love.

K. He shows disillusionment about her.

L. His excited love is cupboard love, so that having got what he wants he throws her away like orange peel.

M. The baby at first must dominate, he must be protected from coincidences, life must unfold at the baby's rate and all this needs his mother's continuous and detailed study. For instance, she must not be anxious when holding him, etc.

N. At first he does not know at all what she does or what she sacrifices for him. Especially he cannot allow for her hate.

O. He is suspicious, refuses her good food, and makes her doubt herself, but eats well with his aunt.

P. After an awful morning with him she goes out, and he smiles at a stranger, who says: 'Isn't he sweet!'

Q. If she fails him at the start she knows he will pay her out for ever.

R. He excites her but frustrates – she mustn't eat him or trade in sex with him.

I think that in the analysis of psychotics and in the ultimate stages of the analysis, even of a normal person, the analyst must find himself in a position comparable to that of a mother of a new-born baby. When deeply regressed the patient cannot identify with the analyst or appreciate his point of view any more than the foetus or newly born infant can sympathize with the mother.

A mother has to be able to tolerate hating her baby without doing anything about it. She cannot express it to him. If, for fear of what she may do, she cannot hate appropriately when hurt by her child she must fall back on masochism, and I think it is this which gives rise to the false theory of a natural masochism in women. The most remarkable thing about a mother is her ability to be hurt so much by her baby and to hate so much without paying the child out, and her ability to wait for rewards that may or may not come at a later date. Perhaps she is helped by some of the nursery rhymes she sings, which her baby enjoys but fortunately does not understand?

> Rockabye Baby, on the tree top,
> When the wind blows, the cradle will rock,
> When the bough breaks the cradle will fall,
> Down will come baby, cradle and all.

I think of a mother (or father) playing with a small infant; the infant enjoying the play and not knowing that the parent is expressing hate in the words, perhaps in birth symbolism. This is not a sentimental rhyme. Sentimentality is useless for parents, as it contains a denial of hate, and sentimentality in a mother is no good at all from the infant's point of view.

It seems to me doubtful whether a human as he develops is capable of tolerating the extent of his own hate in a sentimental environment. He needs hate to hate.

If this is true, a psychotic patient in analysis cannot be expected to tolerate his hate of the analyst unless the analyst can hate him.

D.W. Winnicott, 'Hate in the Counter-Transference' (1949)

The Stink of Hatred

Adrian Stokes (1902–72), art critic, painter and poet, was also a founder member of the Imago Group – a gathering of thinkers which met from 1954 until his death to present papers and discuss the general application of psychoanalytic ideas. Although drawn from various fields, all members of the group had personal experience of psychoanalysis. This is apparent in Stokes' analysis of the amplification of hatred by virtue of 'projection', that is the act of imbuing the other person with hateful parts of oneself, which are then seen in him and hated all the more.

Stokes was born in Bayswater, London and died in Church

Row, Hampstead. Author of more than twenty critical books, he was hailed as one of the most original and creative writers on art in his generation.

The modern cliché to express hate, namely, to hate someone's guts, appears to be tautological. We tend already to dislike everyone's guts. The point of this expression is the bringing together of a specific hate and the dirty inside of the body. The expression means: I think of such-and-such person in terms of their guts only, which are of course aggressive and hateful, I see him as a drain, that is to say, I hate him. He stinks, and the stinking is unfathomable, irredeemable: it goes on and on, ends only in death and after utter dissolution. My hate, then, ceases only after his death, after I have killed him, when the bad thing in him ceases to be. But why do I hate him so? He has done this and that, his character is of such kind. But surely my hating him contributes to the volume of his capacity for stinking. It is my hate that stinks in him, and I have put into him my own capacity to stink as an addition to his own. He stinks doubly.

In most of us there exists the propensity to equate hatefulness with what stinks, especially if we are taken unawares, I have said. The wafting into a gathering, I have reminded you, of a sudden and strong bad smell may be a cause to all of acute embarrassment. So far as there can be no pretence to disregard it, the appropriate expression will be one of severity combined with a disclaiming look. We are reminded of what is hateful in ourselves and others, of powers permeating occasions that disown them. The lid lies off and the rotten rots the good as the stale decomposing and rancid processes in the garbage bin act upon what was once good food. Love integrates, hate decomposes. They have the same prime objects or part-objects, the human body and its products. The conjunction, before all else, qualifies the human situation.

Adrian Stokes, 'Strong Smells and Polite Society' (1973)

DISGUST

The Expression of Disgust

Charles Darwin (1809–92) was born at Shrewsbury, son of Robert, and grandson of Erasmus, both distinguished physicians. He too studied medicine, but gave it up in order to attend Christ's College, Cambridge, with a view to entering the Church. However, under the influence of botanist Professor J.S. Henslow he decided to become a naturalist. On graduating in 1831 he joined the survey ship HMS Beagle *in its five-year exploration of South America, New Zealand and the Galápagos Islands. During the voyage he developed the suspicion that species were not separately created but must have evolved. His reading of Thomas Malthus'* Essay on Population *led him to the insight that evolution proceeds by natural selection. Just as breeders produced new hybrids by artificial selection of desired characteristics, so, Darwin suggested, nature ensured the survival of plants and animals that were best suited to their environment. However, he did not entirely give up the parallel Lamarckian theory, that accounted for evolution through characteristics acquired by habitual use, and somehow passed down the generations.*

Darwin understood that similarities in behaviour united the members of a species, as much as did coincidence of bodily form. Moreover, like a human baby's grasp reflex, they could persist in a vestigial state long after they had outlived their original function. According to Darwin, the muscular activity involved in expressing emotion was once used for another biological purpose from which it had become severed. In the same way that organs such as the appendix linked humans with lower animals, so did the gestures and facial contortions associated with the communication of emotion.

The term 'disgust', in its simplest sense, means something offensive to the taste. It is curious how readily this feeling is excited by anything unusual in the appearance, odour, or nature of our food. In Tierra del Fuego a native touched with his finger some cold preserved meat which I was eating at our bivouac, and plainly showed utter disgust at its softness; whilst I felt utter disgust at my food being touched by a naked savage, though his hands did not appear dirty. A smear of soup on a man's beard looks disgusting, though there is of course nothing disgusting in the soup itself. I presume that this follows from the strong association in our minds between the sight of food, however circumstanced, and the idea of eating it.

As the sensation of disgust primarily arises in connection with the act of eating or tasting, it is natural that its expression should consist chiefly in movements round the mouth. But as disgust also causes annoyance, it is generally accompanied by a frown, and often by gestures as if to push away or to guard oneself against the offensive object. In the two photographs [Figure 7] Mr Rejlander has simulated this expression with some success. With respect to the face, moderate disgust is exhibited in various ways; by the mouth being widely opened, as if to let an offensive morsel drop out; by spitting; by blowing out of the protruded lips; or by a sound as of clearing the throat. Such guttural sounds are written *ach* or *ugh*; and their utterance is sometimes accompanied by a shudder, the arms being pressed close to the sides and the shoulders raised in the same manner as when horror is experienced. Extreme disgust is expressed by movements round the mouth identical with those preparatory to the act of vomiting. The mouth is opened widely, with the upper lip strongly retracted, which wrinkles the sides of the nose, and with the lower lip protruded and everted as much as possible. This latter movement requires the contraction of the muscles which draw downwards the corners of the mouth.

It is remarkable how readily and instantly retching or actual vomiting is induced in some persons by the mere idea of having partaken of any unusual food, as of an animal which is not commonly eaten; although there is nothing in such food to cause the stomach to reject it. When vomiting results, as a reflex action, from some real cause – as from too rich food, or tainted meat, or from an emetic – it does not ensue immediately, but generally after a considerable interval of time. Therefore, to account for retching or vomiting being so quickly and easily excited by a

Fig. 7
The expression of disgust 'simulated with some success,'
Darwin wrote, by his photographer, Mr Reijander.

mere idea, the suspicion arises that our progenitors must formerly
have had the power (like that possessed by some ruminants and
some other animals) of voluntarily rejecting food which disagreed
with them, or which they thought would disagree with them; and
now, though this power has been lost, as far as the will is
concerned, it is called into involuntary action, through the force
of a formerly well-established habit, whenever the mind revolts
at the idea of having partaken of any kind of food, or at anything
disgusting. This suspicion receives support from the fact, of which
I am assured by Mr Sutton, that the monkeys in the Zoological
Gardens often vomit whilst in perfect health, which looks as if
the act were voluntary. We can see that as man is able to communicate by language to his children and others, the knowledge of
the kinds of food to be avoided, he would have little occasion

to use the faculty of voluntary rejection; so that this power would tend to be lost through disuse.

As the sense of smell is so intimately connected with that of taste, it is not surprising that an excessively bad odour should excite retching or vomiting in some persons, quite as readily as the thought of revolting food does; and that, as a further consequence, a moderately offensive odour should cause the various expressive movements of disgust. The tendency to retch from a fetid odour is immediately strengthened in a curious manner by some degree of habit, though soon lost by longer familiarity with the cause of offence and by voluntary restraint. For instance, I wished to clean the skeleton of a bird, which had not been sufficiently macerated, and the smell made my servant and myself (we not having had much experience in such work) retch so violently, that we were compelled to desist. During the previous days I had examined some other skeletons, which smelt slightly; yet the odour did not in the least affect me, but, subsequently for several days, whenever I handled these same skeletons, they made me retch.

From the answers received from my correspondents it appears that the various movements, which have now been described as expressing contempt and disgust, prevail throughout a large part of the world. Dr Rothrock, for instance, answers with a decided affirmative with respect to certain Indian tribes of North America. Crantz says that when a Greenlander denies anything with contempt or horror he turns up his nose, and gives a slight sound through it. Mr Scott has sent me a graphic description of the face of a young Hindoo at the sight of castor-oil, which he was compelled occasionally to take. Mr Scott has also seen the same expression on the faces of high-caste natives who have approached close to some defiling object. Mr Bridges says that the Fuegians 'express contempt by shooting out the lips and hissing through them, and by turning up the nose'. The tendency either to snort through the nose, or to make a noise expressed by *ugh* or *ach*, is noticed by several of my correspondents.

Spitting seems an almost universal sign of contempt or disgust; and spitting obviously represents the rejection of anything offensive from the mouth. Shakespeare makes the Duke of Norfolk

say, 'I spit at him – call him a slanderous coward and a villain.'
So, again, Falstaff says, 'Tell thee what, Hal, – if I tell thee a lie,
spit in my face.' Leichhardt remarks that the Australians 'interrupted their speeches by spitting, and uttering a noise like pooh!
pooh! apparently expressive of their disgust.' And Captain Burton
speaks of certain negroes 'spitting with disgust upon the ground'.
Captain Speedy informs me that this is likewise the case with
Abyssinians. Mr Geach says that with the Malays of Malacca
the expression of disgust 'answers to spitting from the mouth';
and with the Fuegians, according to Mr Bridges 'to spit at one
is the highest mark of contempt'.

I never saw disgust more plainly expressed than on the face
of one of my infants at the age of five months, when, for the
first time, some cold water, and again a month afterwards, when
a piece of ripe cherry was put into his mouth. This was shown
by the lips and whole mouth assuming a shape which allowed
the contents to run or fall quickly out; the tongue being likewise protruded. These movements were accompanied by a little
shudder. It was all the more comical, as I doubt whether the
child felt real disgust – the eyes and forehead expressing much
surprise and consideration. The protrusion of the tongue in
letting a nasty object fall out of the mouth, may explain how it
is that lolling out the tongue universally serves as a sign of
contempt and hatred.

We have now seen that scorn, disdain, contempt and disgust
are expressed in many different ways, by movements of the
features and by various gestures; and that these are the same
throughout the world. They all consist of actions representing
the rejection or exclusion of some real object which we dislike
or abhor, but which does not excite in us certain other strong
emotions, such as rage or terror; and through force of habit and
association similar actions are performed, whenever any analogous sensation arises in our minds.

Charles Darwin, *The Expression of the Emotions in Man and Animals* (1872)

GRIEF AND SORROW

The Nature of Sorrow

Grief and sorrow cannot be assuaged like other passions, because their object no longer exists. They are defined precisely by being responses to absence and irretrievable loss. One way to escape them might be to take pre-emptive action by refusing to become attached to any body or thing, but Dr Johnson does not recommend this. If grief is inevitable, keeping busy is his preferred nostrum, and with the passage of time it will diminish.

Samuel Johnson (1709–84), was the son of a Lichfield bookseller. He attended grammar school and Pembroke College, Oxford, leaving without a degree. After a period of time as an unsuccessful schoolmaster, he turned to writing as a career. In 1735 he married a widow, Mrs Elizabeth Porter, and two years later they moved to London, where Johnson entered the service of Edward Cave, founder of The Gentleman's Magazine. At the age of thirty-eight he began work on his Dictionary, *which took nine years to complete, by which time he had lost his wife. Johnson was no stranger to melancholy, having suffered periodic bouts in his youth. The publication of the* Dictionary *established his literary reputation and his conversational virtuosity was passed down to future generations by his friend and biographer, James Boswell.*

Of the passions with which the mind of man is agitated it may be observed that they naturally hasten towards their own extinction by inciting and quickening the attainment of their objects. Thus fear urges our flight, and desire animates our progress; and if there are some which perhaps may be indulged till they outgrow the good appropriated to their satisfaction, as it is frequently observed of avarice and ambition, yet their immediate tendency is to some means of happiness really existing and generally within the prospect. The miser always imagines that there is a certain sum that will fill his heart to the brim; and every ambitious man, like King Pyrrhus, has an acquisition in his thoughts that is to terminate his labours, after which he shall pass the rest of his life in ease or gaiety, in repose or devotion.

Sorrow is perhaps the only affection of the breast that can be excepted from this general remark, and it therefore deserves the particular attention of those who have assumed the arduous province of preserving the balance of the mental constitution. The other passions are diseases indeed, but they necessarily direct us to their proper cure. A man once feels pain, and knows the medicine, to which he is carried with greater haste as the evil which requires it is more excruciating, and cures himself by unerring instinct as the wounded stags of Crete are related by Aelian to have recourse to vulnerary herbs. But for sorrow there is no remedy provided by nature. It is often occasioned by accidents irreparable, and dwells upon objects that have lost or changed their existence. It requires what it cannot hope, that the laws of the universe should be repealed, that the dead should return, or the past should be recalled.

Sorrow is not that regret for negligence or error which may animate us to future care or activity, or that repentance of crimes for which, however irrevocable, our Creator has promised to accept it as atonement. The pain which arises from these causes has very salutary effects, and is every hour extenuating itself by the reparation of those miscarriages that produce it. Sorrow is properly that state of mind in which our desires are fixed upon the past without looking forward to the future, an incessant wish that something were otherwise than it has been, a tormenting and harassing want of some enjoyment or possession which we have lost and which no endeavours can possibly regain. Into such anguish many have sunk upon some sudden diminution of their fortune, an unexpected blast of their reputation, or the loss of children or of friends. They have suffered all sensibility of pleasure to be destroyed by a single blow, have given up for ever the hopes of substituting any other object in the room of that which they lament, resigned their lives to gloom and despondency, and worn themselves out in unavailing misery.

Yet so much is this passion the natural consequence of tenderness and endearment, that, however painful and however useless, it is justly reproachful not to feel it on some occasions. And so widely and constantly has it always prevailed, that the laws of some nations and the customs of others have limited a time for the external appearances of grief caused by the dissolution of close alliances and the breach of domestic union.

It seems determined by the general suffrage of mankind that sorrow is to a certain point laudable, as the offspring of love, or at least pardonable as the effect of weakness; but that it ought not to be suffered to increase by indulgence, but must give way after a stated time to social duties and common avocations of life. It is at first unavoidable, and therefore must be allowed, whether with or without choice. It may afterwards be admitted as a decent and affectionate testimony of kindness and esteem. Something will be extorted by nature, and something may be given to the world. But all beyond the bursts of passion or the forms of solemnity is not only useless, but culpable; for we have no right to sacrifice to the vain longings of affection that time which Providence allows us for the task of our station.

Yet it too often happens that sorrow, thus lawfully entering, gains such a firm possession of the mind, that it is not afterwards to be ejected. The mournful ideas, first violently impressed and afterwards willingly received, so much engross the attention as to predominate in every thought, to darken gaiety, and perplex ratiocination. An habitual sadness seizes upon the soul, and the faculties are chained to a single object which can never be contemplated but with hopeless uneasiness.

From this state of dejection it is very difficult to rise to cheerfulness and alacrity, and therefore many who have laid down rules of intellectual health think preservatives easier than remedies, and teach us not to trust ourselves with favourite enjoyments, not to indulge the luxury of fondness, but to keep our minds always suspended in such indifference that we may change the objects about us without emotion.

An exact compliance with this rule might, perhaps, contribute to tranquillity, but surely it would never produce happiness. He that regards none so much as to be afraid of losing them must live for ever without the gentle pleasures of sympathy and confidence. He must feel no melting fondness, no warmth of benevolence, nor any of those honest joys which nature annexes to the power of pleasing. And, as no man can justly claim more tenderness than he pays, he must forfeit his share in that officious and watchful kindness which love only can dictate, and those lenient endearments by which love only can soften life. He may justly be overlooked and neglected by such as have more warmth in their heart; for who would be the friend of him whom, with whatever assiduity he may be courted and with whatever services obliged, his principles will not suffer to make equal returns, and who when you have exhausted all the instances of goodwill, can only be prevailed on not to be an enemy?

An attempt to preserve life in a state of neutrality and indifference is unreasonable and vain. If by excluding joy we could shut out grief, the scheme would deserve very serious attention. But since, however we may debar ourselves from happiness, misery will find its way at many inlets, and the assaults of pain will force our regard, though we may withhold it from the invitations of pleasure, we may surely endeavour to raise life above the middle point of apathy at one time, since it will necessarily sink below it at another.

But though it cannot be reasonable not to gain happiness for fear of losing it, yet it must be confessed that in proportion to the pleasure of possession will be for some time our sorrow for the loss. It is therefore the province of the moralist to inquire whether such pains may not quickly give way to mitigation. Some have thought that the most certain way to clear the heart from its embarrassment is to drag it by force into scenes of merriment. Others imagine that such a transition is too violent, and recommend rather to soothe it into tranquillity by making it acquainted with miseries more dreadful and afflictive, and diverting to the calamities of others the regard which we are inclined to fix too closely upon our own misfortunes.

It may be doubted whether either of those remedies will be sufficiently powerful. The efficacy of mirth is not always easy to try, and the indulgence of melancholy may be suspected to be one of those medicines which will destroy if it happens not to cure.

The safe and general antidote against sorrow is employment. It is commonly observed that among soldiers and seamen, though there is much kindness there is little grief. They see their friend fall without any of that lamentation which is indulged in security and idleness, because they have no leisure to spare from the care of themselves. And whoever shall keep his thoughts busy will find himself equally unaffected with irretrievable losses.

Time is observed generally to wear out sorrow, and its effects might doubtless be accelerated by quickening the succession and enlarging the variety of objects.

> Si tempore longo
> Leniri poterit luctus, tu sperne morari
> Qui sapiet sibi tempus erit.

GROTIUS

> Tis long ere time can mitigate your grief;
> To wisdom fly, she quickly brings relief.

F. LEWIS

Sorrow is a kind of rust of the soul, which every new idea contributes in its passage to scour away. It is the putrefaction of stagnant life, and is remedied by exercise and motion.

Samuel Johnson, 'Means of Regulating Sorrow' (1750–2)

THE EMOTIONS OF CHILDREN

Discovering the Oedipus Complex

Before Freud, the emotional life of children was a subject for mothers, nursemaids and romantic poets, not for serious scientific study. Indeed it was, and sometimes still is suggested that infants are too young to have deep emotions. Passionate love and over-bearing jealousy are the stuff of adult relationships, it is argued, not the quotidian of the nursery. Revisionist Freud scholars think the 'Oedipus Complex' a myth, rather than the Oedipus myth a psychological reality.

Freud's controversial 'discovery' changed the direction of psychoanalysis. Before 1897, his theories about the cause of neurosis centred on the experience of infantile sexual abuse. Afterwards, he believed the incidence of such abuse too small to be a sufficient cause for the amount of neurotic disorder in the general population. Instead he focused on the unconscious sexual fantasy life of the infant, which he took to entail a ubiquitous conflict between love and jealousy of the parents. The way this conflict was resolved, Freud thought, determined the future character and mental health of an individual.

One (not very good) reason he had for supposing the Oedipus Complex to be universal, was that he discovered its manifestations in himself. Yet there is little doubt nowadays that what anthropologists refer to as the 'motivational disposition to nuclear family incest', is a pan-human phenomenon.

Sigmund Freud, founder of psychoanalysis, was the son of Jacob, an impecunious Jewish wool merchant twenty years older than his third wife Amalia Nathansohn. He was born above a blacksmith's forge in 1856 in Freiberg, N. Moravia, now part of the Czech Republic. His family moved to Vienna in 1860 where he grew up and qualified in medicine twenty-one years later. He took an early interest in the work done by the French neurologist Jean-Martin Charcot on hypnotism and hysteria. In 1895 together with a physician colleague, Joseph Breuer, he published Studies on Hysteria, *a series of case studies illustrating his thesis that hysterical symptoms were caused by unconscious conflict. In 1900 he published the most famous of his twenty-four volumes – The Interpretation of Dreams, suggesting that these too could be understood as the end result of an unconscious conflict between primitive sexual wishes and censorious mental activity. He invented a system of treatment for mental problems, based on prolonged daily contact between physician and patient and analysis of the unconscious content of the therapeutic relationship that developed. In 1938 he fled Nazi Vienna and came to London where he died the following year. By that time his name had become a landmark in cultural history, marking the transition from nineteenth-century order to the modern and postmodern world.*

Being totally honest with oneself is a good exercise. A single idea of general value dawned on me. I have found, in my own case too, [the phenomenon of] being in love with my mother and jealous of my father, and I now consider it a universal event in early childhood, even if not so early as in children who have been made hysterical. (Similar to the invention of parentage [family romance] in paranoia – heroes, founders of religion.) If this is so, we can understand the gripping power of *Oedipus Rex*, in spite of all the objections that reason raises against the presupposition of fate; and we can understand why the later 'drama of fate' was bound to fail so miserably. Our feelings rise against any arbitrary individual compulsion, such as is presupposed in *Die Ahnfrau*[10] and the like; but the Greek legend seizes upon a compulsion which everyone recognizes because he senses its existence within himself. Everyone in the audience was once a budding Oedipus in fantasy and each recoils in horror from the dream fulfilment here transplanted into reality, with the full quantity of repression which separates his infantile state from his present one.

Fleetingly the thought passed through my mind that the same thing might be at the bottom of *Hamlet* as well. I am not thinking of Shakespeare's conscious intention, but believe, rather, that a real event stimulated the poet to his representation, in that his unconscious understood the unconscious of his hero. How does Hamlet the hysteric justify his words, 'Thus conscience does make cowards of us all'? How does he explain his irresolution in avenging his father by the murder of his uncle – the same man who sends his courtiers to their death without a scruple and who is positively precipitate in murdering Laertes [sic]: [Polonius]? How better than through the torment he suffers from the obscure memory that he himself had contemplated the same deed against his father out of passion for his mother, and – 'use every man after his desert, and who should scape whipping?' His conscience is his unconscious sense of guilt. And is not his sexual alienation in his conversation with Ophelia typically hysterical? And, finally his transferral of the deed from his own father to Ophelia's? And does he not in the end, in the same

10 F. Grillparzer's play (1817), concerning brother–sister incest and parricide.

marvellous way as my hysterical patients, bring down punishment on himself by suffering the same fate as his father of being poisoned by the same rival?

Sigmund Freud, Letter to Wilhelm Fliess (1897)

What It Is Like to Be a Baby?

The philosopher Thomas Nagel tells us that 'only a bat knows what it feels like to be a bat', but the psychoanalyst Melanie Klein* thinks she knows what it feels like to be a baby. Since none of us have been bats and we have all been babies, there is, perhaps, more chance that we can come to understand the latter.*

Klein (1882–1960) was born in Vienna, the youngest of four children. Her father was twenty-four years older than her mother, his second wife. He was an unsuccessful Jewish doctor, forced by circumstances into a combination of dental practice and acting as medical officer to a vaudeville company. Klein married in 1903 and over the next eleven years gave birth to a daughter (with whom she was later to fall out) and two sons. She separated from her husband in 1924. At the age of thirty-four, she had read Freud's paper On Dreams *and fallen in love with psychoanalysis, entering treatment with Sandor Ferenczi in Budapest and later Karl Abraham in Berlin. She was encouraged to apply the psychoanalytic method to children, and pioneered the development of play-therapy as a window into the child's unconscious mind, an equivalent to adult free-association.*

In 1926 she moved to London and was elected a member of the British Psychoanalytical Society in the following year. The insights she gained from children's play led her to formulate a series of conceptual innovations to Freud's model of the mind. These ideas, especially her notion of 'unconscious phantasy'[11] and reformulation of the 'Oedipus complex'[12] brought her into conflict with more orthodox analysts. Eventually they developed into an orthodoxy of their own. Klein saw infantile life as an emotionally intense struggle between love and hate, creative growth and

11 See pp. 336–9
12 See pp. 155–8

*destructiveness. She studied the psychological strategies used for
dealing with it, and believed the same processes were recapitu-
lated in the unconscious mind of the adult.*

The baby's first object of love and hate – his mother – is both
desired and hated with all the intensity and strength that is characteristic of the early urges of the baby. In the very beginning he
loves his mother at the time that she is satisfying his needs for
nourishment, alleviating his feelings of hunger, and giving him
the sensual pleasure which he experiences when his mouth is
stimulated by sucking at her breast. This gratification is an essential part of the child's sexuality, and is indeed its initial expression. But when the baby is hungry and his desires are not gratified,
or when he is feeling bodily pain or discomfort, then the whole
situation suddenly alters. Hatred and aggressive feelings are
aroused and he becomes dominated by the impulses to destroy
the very person who is the object of all his desires and who in
his mind is linked up with everything he experiences – good and
bad alike. In the baby hatred and aggressive feelings give rise,
moreover, as Joan Riviere has shown in detail[13], to most painful
states, such as choking, breathlessness and other sensations of
the kind, which are felt to be destructive to his own body; thus
aggression, unhappiness and fears are again increased.

The immediate and primary means by which relief is afforded
to a baby from these painful states of hunger, hate, tension and
fear is the satisfaction of his desires by his mother. The temporary
feeling of security which is gained by receiving gratification greatly
enhances the gratification itself; and thus a feeling of security becomes
an important component of the satisfaction whenever a person
receives love. This applies to the baby as well as to the adult, to
the more simple forms of love and to its most elaborate manifestations. Because our mother first satisfied all our self-preservative
needs and sensual desires and gave us security, the part she plays
in our minds is a lasting one, although the various ways in which
this influence is effected and the forms it takes may not be at all

13 J. Riviere, 'Hate, Guilt and Aggression', in *Love, Hate and Reparation*, ed.
   Melanie Klein, Hogarth Press, 1937.

obvious in later life. For instance, a woman may apparently have estranged herself from her mother, yet still unconsciously seek some of the features of her early relation to her in her relation to her husband or to a man she loves. The very important part which the father plays in the child's emotional life also influences all later love relations, and all other human associations. But the baby's early relation to him, in so far as he is felt as a gratifying, friendly and protective figure, is partly modelled on the one to the mother.

The baby, to whom his mother is primarily only an object which satisfies all his desires – a good breast, as it were – soon begins to respond to these gratifications and to her care by developing feelings of love towards her as a person. But this first love is already disturbed at its roots by destructive impulses. Love and hate are struggling together in the baby's mind; and this struggle to a certain extent persists through life and is liable to become a source of danger in human relationships.

The baby's impulses and feelings are accompanied by a kind of mental activity which I take to be the most primitive one: that is phantasy-building, or more colloquially, imaginative thinking. For instance, the baby who feels a craving for his mother's breast when it is not there, may imagine it to be there, *i.e.* he may imagine the satisfaction which he derives from it. Such primitive phantasying is the earliest form of the capacity which later develops into the more elaborate workings of the imagination.

The early phantasies which go along with the baby's feelings are of various kinds. In the one just mentioned he imagines the gratification which he lacks. Pleasant phantasies, however, also accompany actual satisfactions; and destructive phantasies go along with frustration and the feelings of hatred which this arouses. When a baby feels frustrated at the breast, in his phantasies he attacks this breast; but if he is being gratified by the breast, he loves it and has phantasies of a pleasant kind in relation to it. In his aggressive phantasies he wishes to bite up and to tear up his mother and her breasts, and to destroy her also in other ways.

A most important feature of these destructive phantasies, which are tantamount to death-wishes, is that the baby feels that what he desires in his phantasies has really taken place; that is to say he feels that he *has really destroyed* the object of his destructive

impulses, and is going on destroying it: this has extremely important consequences for the development of his mind. The baby
finds support against these fears in omnipotent phantasies of a
restoring kind: that too has extremely important consequences
for his development. If the baby has, in his aggressive phantasies,
injured his mother by biting and tearing her up, he may soon
build up phantasies that he is putting the bits together again and
repairing her. This, however, does not quite do away with his
fears of having destroyed the object which, as we know, is the
one whom he loves and needs most, and on whom he is entirely
dependent. In my view, these basic conflicts profoundly influence
the course and the force of the emotional lives of grown-up individuals.

Melanie Klein, *Love, Guilt and Reparation* (1937) [References omitted, ed.]

From The Ballad of Reading Gaol

*Oscar Wilde's humane identification with a murderer touches a
universal chord. Wilde (1854–1900), playwright, poet and story-
writer, was born in Dublin, son of Sir William Wilde, an Irish
surgeon, and Jane Francesca Elgee. Both parents were prodigious
writers. He studied classics at Trinity College, Dublin, and went on
to Magdalen College, Oxford, where he won the Newdigate Prize
for poetry. In 1884 he married, and his wife gave birth to two sons
in rapid succession. Although fond of his children, any attraction
he had felt for his wife seemed extinguished by her prolonged state
of pregnancy, which disgusted him. He increasingly sought the
company of young men. His mastery of the witty epigram brought
success on the London stage; however, his relationship with Lord
Alfred Douglas, son of the Marquess of Queensberry, led in 1895
to imprisonment for homosexual offences, which inspired* The
Ballad of Reading Gaol. *Shunned by most of his friends when he
came out of prison, Wilde lived the life of an exile in Paris, where
two years later he died in obscurity.*

*The following extract seems to bear out Melanie Klein's notion
of a universal and profound human tendency to attack loved
objects, to bite the breast that feeds us.*

I never saw a man who looked
   With such a wistful eye
Upon that little tent of blue
   Which prisoners call the sky,
And at every drifting cloud that went
   With sails of silver by.

I walked, with other souls in pain,
   Within another ring,
And was wondering if the man had done
   A great or little thing,
When a voice behind me whispered low,
   'That fellow's got to swing.'

Dear Christ! the very prison walls
   Suddenly seemed to reel,
And the sky above my head became
   Like a casque of scorching steel;
And, though I was a soul in pain,
   My pain I could not feel.

I only knew what hunted thought
   Quickened his step, and why
He looked upon the garish day
   With such a wistful eye;
The man had killed the thing he loved,
   And so he had to die.

Yet each man kills the thing he loves,
   By each let this be heard,
Some do it with a bitter look,
   Some with a flattering word,
The coward does it with a kiss,
   The brave man with a sword!

Oscar Wilde, *The Ballad of Reading Gaol* (1898)

BRAIN DAMAGE AND EMOTION

A Hole in the Head

In the US in September 1848 a young man named Phineas Gage survived a freak accident. He was the foreman in a team of excavation workers blasting rock for the construction of a road. Having drilled a hole, he was busy packing in explosive with a pointed 'tamping iron'. The iron measured a maximum of one and a quarter inches in diameter and three feet seven inches in length. Diverted by a call from one of his men, he turned his head and accidentally let go the iron, which fell on the rock and caused a spark. The powder ignited and shot the heavy iron rod right through his face and head and landed on the ground several yards away.

Extensive damage was done to the left side of Gage's brain; however, the psychological consequences so precisely described by John Harlow are now known to be most often associated with malfunction of the frontal lobes in particular. Typically in such conditions, personality changes are more evident than alterations in general cognitive ability. Slowness and lack of initiative are often accompanied by a generalized coarsening of the personality. There is disinhibition leading to social ineptness or frankly antisocial behaviour. Normal judgement is impaired and a person's demeanour may become fatuous or inappropriately euphoric.

Because damage to the frontal lobes of the brain seemed to produce a certain carefree state of mind without interfering drastically with other intellectual functions, psychosurgery, pioneered in the 1930s, sought to relieve intractable anxiety by deliberately interfering with their function. Early attempts produced an unacceptable number of negative effects, but modern developments incorporating very careful assessment of patients likely to benefit, and small finely placed lesions, have been more successful.

On the 25th (of November) he was taken, in a close carriage, a distance of thirty miles, to Lebanon N.H., where I saw him the succeeding week, and found him going on well. He continued to improve steadily, until on Jan. 1 1849, the opening on the top of his head was entirely closed, and the brain shut out from view, though every pulsation could be distinctly seen and felt. Gage passed the succeeding winter months in his own house and vicinity, improving in flesh and strength, and in the following April returned to Cavendish, bringing his 'iron' with him.

He visited me at that time, and presented something like the following appearances. General appearance good; stands quite erect, with his head inclined slightly towards the right side; his gait in walking is steady; his movements rapid and easily executed. The left side of his face is wider than the right side, the left malar bone being more prominent than its fellow. There is a linear cicatrix [scar, ed.] near the angle of the lower jaw, an inch in length. Ptosis [drooping, ed.] of the left eyelid; the globe considerably more prominent than its fellow, but not as large as when I last saw him. Can adduct and depress the globe [move inwards and downwards, ed.], but cannot move it in other directions; vision lost. A linear cicatrix, length two and one-half inches, from the nasal protuberance to the anterior edge of the raised fragment of the frontal bone, is quite unsightly. Upon the top of the head and covered with hair, is a large unequal depression and elevation – a quadrangular fragment of bone, which was entirely detached from the frontal, and extending low upon the forehead, being still raised and quite prominent. Behind this is a deep depression, two inches by one and one-half inches wide, beneath which the pulsations of the brain can be perceived. Partial paralysis of the left side of the face. His physical health is good, and I am inclined to say that he has recovered. Has no pain in the head, but says it has a queer feeling which he is not able to describe. Applied for his situation as a foreman, but is undecided whether to work or travel. His contractors, who regarded him as the most efficient and capable foreman in their employ previous to his injury, considered the change in his mind so marked that they could not give him his place again. The equilibrium or balance, so to speak, between his intellectual faculties and animal propensities, seems to have been destroyed. He is fitful, irreverent, indulging at times in the grossest profanity (which was not previously his custom), manifesting but little deference for his fellows, impatient of restraint or advice when it conflicts with his desires, at times pertinaciously obstinate, yet capricious and vacillating, devising many plans of future operation, which are no sooner arranged than they are abandoned in turn for others appearing more feasible. A child in his intellectual capacity and manifestations, he has the animal passions of a strong man. Previous to his injury, though untrained in the schools, he possessed a well-balanced mind, and was looked upon by those who knew him as a shrewd, smart business man, very energetic and persistent in executing all his plans of operation. In this regard his mind was radically changed, so decidedly that his friends and acquaintances said he was 'no longer Gage'.

His mother, a most excellent lady, now seventy years of age, informs me that Phineas was accustomed to entertain his little nephews and nieces with the most fabulous recitals of his wonderful feats and hair-breadth escapes, without any foundation except in his fancy. He conceived a great fondness for pets and souvenirs, especially for children, horses and dogs – only exceeded by his attachment for his tamping iron, which was his constant companion during the remainder of his life. He took to travelling, and visited Boston, most of the larger New England towns, and New York, remaining a while in the latter place at Barnum's with his iron. In 1851 he engaged with Mr Jonathan Currier, of Hanover, New Hampshire, to work in his livery stable. He remained there, without interruption from ill health, for nearly or quite a year and a half.

In August, 1852, nearly four years after his injury, he turned his back upon New England, never to return. He engaged with a man who was going to Chili, in South America, to establish a line of coaches at Valparaiso. He remained in Chili until July, 1860, nearly eight years, in the vicinity of Valparaiso and Santiago, occupied in caring for horses, and often driving a coach heavily laden and drawn by six horses. In 1859 and '60 his health began to fail, and in the beginning of the latter year he had a long illness, the precise nature of which, I have never been able to learn. Not recovering fully, he decided to try a change of climate, and in June, 1860, left Valparaiso for San Francisco, where his mother and sister resided. The former writes that 'he arrived in San Francisco on or about July 1st, in a feeble condition, having failed very much since he left New Hampshire. He suffered much from seasickness on his passage out from Boston to Chili. Had many ill turns while in Valparaiso, especially during the last year, and suffered much from hardship and exposure.'

After leaving South America I lost all trace of him, and had well nigh abandoned all expectation of ever hearing from him again. As good fortune would have it, however, in July, 1866, I was able to learn the address of his mother and very soon commenced a correspondence with her and her excellent son-in-law, D.D. Shattuck, Esq., a leading merchant in San Francisco. From them I learned that Gage was dead – that after he arrived in San Francisco his health improved, and being anxious to work, he engaged with a farmer at Santa Clara, but did not remain there long. In February, 1861, while sitting at dinner, he fell in a fit, and soon after had two or three fits in succession. He had no premonition of these attacks, or any subsequent ill feeling. 'Had been ploughing the day before he had the first attack; got better in a few days, and continued to work in *various places*'; 'could not do much, *changing often*, and always finding something which did not suit him in every place he tried.' On the 18th of May 1861, three days before his death he left Santa Clara and went home to his mother. At 5 o'clock, A.M. on the 20th, he had a severe convulsion. The family physician was called in, and bled him. The convulsions were repeated frequently during the succeeding day and night, and he expired at 10 P.M., May 21. 1861 – twelve years, six months and eight days after the date of his injury. These convulsions were unquestionably epileptic. It is regretted that an autopsy could not have been had, so that the precise condition of the encephalon at the time of his death might have been known. In consideration of this important omission, the mother and friends, waiving the claims of personal and private affection, with a magnanimity more than praiseworthy, at my request have cheerfully placed this skull (which I now show you) in my hands, for the benefit of science.

John Harlow, 'Recovery from the Passage of an Iron Bar Through the Head' (1868)

RISING ABOVE EMOTION

How to Conquer Emotion

Baruch Spinoza prescribes a series of mental exercises (which he claims are easy to do), designed to promote rational understanding of emotion and thus achieve freedom from its tyrannical control. Spinoza (1632–77) was born in Amsterdam of Jewish parents, who had fled persecution in Portugal. However in 1656 he was expelled from the Jewish community for heresy, and eighteen years later his Tractatus Theologico-Politicus *was banned by Christian theologians. His denial of a personal God, separate and distinct from man and nature, offended against religious orthodoxy. But Spinoza had his own pantheistic vision. His philosophy resolved the mind–body conundrum by regarding thoughts and physical events as different modes of the same basic substance – God, which infiltrated everything.*

An emotion, which is a passion, ceases to be a passion, as soon as we form a clear and distinct idea thereof
An emotion, therefore, becomes more under control, and the mind is less passive in respect to it, in proportion as it is more known to us.

Everyone has the power of clearly and distinctly understanding himself and his emotions, if not absolutely, at any rate in part, and consequently of bringing it about, that he should become less subject to them. To attain this result, therefore, we must chiefly direct our efforts to acquiring, as far as possible, a clear and distinct knowledge of every emotion, in order that the mind may thus, through emotion, be determined to think of those things which it clearly and distinctly perceives, and wherein it fully acquiesces: and thus that the emotion itself may be separated from the thought of an external cause, and may be associated with true thoughts; whence it will come to pass, not only that love, hatred, etc., will be destroyed, but also that the appetites or desires, which are wont to arise from such emotion, will become incapable of being excessive. Than this remedy for the emotions which consists in a true knowledge thereof, nothing more excellent, being within our power, can be devised.

The mind has greater power over the emotions and is less subject thereto, in so far as it understands all things are necessary
The more this knowledge, that things are necessary, is applied to particular things, which we conceive more distinctly and vividly, the greater is the power of the mind over the emotions, as experience also testifies. For we see, that the pain arising from the loss of any good is mitigated, as soon as the man who has lost it perceives that it could not by any means have been preserved. So also we see that no one pities an infant, because it cannot speak, walk or reason, or lastly, because it passes so many years, as it were, in unconsciousness. Whereas, if most people were born full-grown and only one here and there as an infant, everyone would pity the infants; because infancy would not then be looked on as a state natural and necessary, but as a fault or delinquency in Nature; and we may note several other instances of the same sort. The best we can do, so long as we do not possess a perfect knowledge of our emotions, is to frame a system of right conduct, or fixed practical precepts, to commit it to memory, and to apply it forthwith to the particular circumstances which now and again meet us in life, so that our imagination may become fully imbued therewith, and that it may be always ready to our hand.

For instance, we have laid down among the rules of life, that hatred should be overcome by love or high-mindedness, and not requited with hatred in return. Now, that this precept of reason may be always ready to our hand in time of need, we should often think over and reflect upon the wrongs generally committed by men, and in what manner and way they may be best warded off by high-mindedness: we shall thus associate the idea of wrong with the idea of this precept, which accordingly will always be ready for use when a wrong is done to us.

If we keep also in readiness the notion of our true advantage, and of the good which follows from mutual friendships, and common fellowships; further, if we remember that complete acquiescence is the result of the right way of life, and that men, no less than everything else, act by the necessity of their nature: in such case I say the wrong, or the hatred, which commonly arises therefrom, will engross a very small part of our imagination and will be easily overcome; or, if the anger which springs from grievous wrong be not overcome easily, it will nevertheless be overcome, though not without a spiritual conflict, far sooner than if we had not thus reflected on the subject beforehand.

We should, indeed, in the same way, reflect on courage as a means of overcoming fear; the ordinary dangers of life should frequently be brought to mind and imagined, together with the means whereby through readiness of resource and strength of mind we can avoid and overcome them.

But we must note, that in arranging our thoughts and conceptions we should always bear in mind that which is good in every individual thing, in order that we may always be determined to action by an emotion of pleasure. For instance, if a man sees that he is too keen in the pursuit of honour, let him think over its right use, the need for which it should be pursued, and the means whereby he may attain it. Let him not think of its misuse, and its emptiness, and the fickleness of mankind, and the like, whereof no man thinks except through a morbidness of disposition, with thoughts like these do the most ambitious most torment themselves, when they despair of gaining the distinctions they hanker after, and in thus giving vent to their anger would fain appear wise. Wherefore it is certain that those, who cry out the loudest against the misuse of honour and the vanity of the world, are those who most greedily covet it.

This is not peculiar to the ambitious, but is common to all who are ill used by fortune, and who are infirm in spirit. For a poor man also, who is miserly, will talk incessantly of the misuse of wealth and of the vices of the rich; whereby he merely torments himself, and shows the world that he is intolerant, not only of his own poverty, but also of other people's riches. So, again, those who have been ill received by a woman they love think of nothing but the inconstancy, treachery and other stock faults of the fair sex; all of which they consign to oblivion, directly they are again taken into favour by their sweet-heart. Thus he who would govern his emotions and appetite solely by the love of freedom strives, as far as he can, to gain a knowledge of the virtues and their causes, and to fill his spirit with the joy which arises from the true knowledge of them: he will in no wise desire to dwell on man's faults, or to carp at his fellows, or to revel in a false show of freedom. Whosoever will diligently observe and practise these precepts (which indeed are not difficult) will verily, in a short space of time, be able for the most part to direct his actions according to the commandments of reason.

Baruch Spinoza, 'Ethics' (1662–75)

4

THOUGHT

'I am inclined to think –', said I. 'I should do so,' Sherlock
Holmes remarked, impatiently.

Sir Arthur Conan Doyle, *The Valley of Fear* (1914)

If thoughts are the contents of the mind then thinking is what
we do with them. From the neuroscientific point of view it is a
matter of nerve cell activity; from the cognitive point of view it
is a matter of information processing; from the linguistic and
mathematical points of view it is a matter of expressing ideas
through systems of symbols, regulated by the rules of grammar
and logic. We also see thought as antecedent to action and as a
modulator of emotion and impulse. From a moral perspective we
judge the goodness and rightness of our thoughts and ensuing
behaviour.

Like other mental phenomena thought proves difficult to
define, and as with emotion it helps to approach the problem
by trying to establish what it is not. An automatic reflex is not
(by most people's standards) a thought, or an action produced
by a thought, because it lacks intention. When the doctor taps
your patella tendon in order to elicit a knee-jerk she does not
believe you mean to kick her, even if your foot should happen
to make contact during the examination. Moving up the ladder
of complexity, a set of instinctual responses to an environmental
stimulus is generally not considered to be a thought, Konrad
Lorenz's goslings are not 'thinking' when they swim along
behind their mother because they will equally well swim along

behind him or the first moving object that they see. Nor are bodily states generally regarded as thoughts although they may signal their presence. As Shakespeare's Moth remarks in *Love's Labour's Lost*: 'If she be made of white and red,/ Her faults will ne'er be known;/ For blushing cheeks by faults are bred,/ And fears by pale white shown.' However, changes in bodily function have also been taken to signify the absence of thought – a human skin rash or inflammation of the bowel is not a thought, but according to some psychosomatic theories, it may appear in place of one. Thought, it seems, is something extra, some intervening procedure which happens between stimulus and response, between impulse and action. But is it mere physiological activity, cognitive information processing or something more? We say we think things up, we experience ourselves playing with ideas, we make plans and nurse intentions. What does it mean for me to say that thoughts are mental or that mental activity is thought?

Another way of getting a handle on the problem is to look at the kind of things that go wrong when we say that we are *not* thinking normally. Both the quantity and quality of our thoughts may be affected. They may speed up as in mania, or slow down, as in depression, or as in both of these conditions our powers of concentration and focus may be reduced. We may feel plagued by repetitive unwanted thoughts or worn out by the effort of resisting their promptings as in obsessive-compulsive disorder. Sometimes, notably in schizophrenia, the associations between one thought and another seem to break down, so that they become muddled, vague and inconsequential or connected in unusual ways. If I try to think in the bizarre logic that characterizes the schizophrenic mode and ask myself the wisdom of the proverb: 'Every cloud has a silver lining', I might reply that the form of clouds is subject to continual change as is the number of silver coins that make up the small change in the lining of my pocket. Although this kind of process may be valued as a creative or poetic occurrence, more often than not it is accompanied by a general impoverishment of mental capacity.

We have reason to believe that some intellectual activity, for example linguistic or mathematical ability, is localized in particular parts of the brain. It may be preserved when other parts of the brain are out of action. However, diseases which spread diffusely across the brain produce a typical pattern of deficiency in thought, which suggests that most of the brain is required for optimal thinking to occur. A range of longstanding organic pathologies, including conditions such as dementia, cerebral tumours, infections, vascular disease, vitamin deficiencies, chemical and hormonal imbalance, epilepsy, drug intoxication and traumatic damage, can all give rise to a characteristic 'chronic brain syndrome'. Here, thought is typically banal, inflexible, slow and laboured. The ability to reason logically, hold more than one idea in mind at the same time and to address new problems is diminished, so that the same answer may be produced in response to a series of different questions. Abstract thinking is also typically impaired, so that the capacity to understand symbols is replaced by a literal-mindedness known as 'concrete thinking'. By contrast to the weird but creative schizophrenic response, an intelligent person suffering a chronic brain syndrome is likely to become bewildered when asked to interpret the cloud proverb. If he is willing to attempt an answer at all, he is likely to discourse on cloud colour and meteorology rather than hopefulness.

Most of the things we can do with thoughts depend on our ability to symbolize – that is to say represent one thing by another in our minds. There is a good deal of confusion over terminology in this area, but broadly speaking we can distinguish two different ways in which symbols are created – conventional and non-conventional. In the first category, sometimes known as 'signs', representations are linked to their referents by convention alone, they share nothing in common with what they represent, and their function is relatively uncontroversial. This includes musical, mathematical and logical notation and words.

In the second category, things are symbolized by virtue of some common property, shape, form, function or perhaps just proximity in space or time. It includes dreams, myths, folk stories, metaphors, all sorts of linguistic tropes and conceits and so on, and their interpretation is almost always controversial. Following Freud's view of dreams as disguises for forbidden wishes, the psychoanalyst Ernest Jones suggested that a small group of symbols, misleadingly designated 'true symbols', were created in our minds precisely in order to deceive ourselves as to their underlying meaning. That symbols can be employed as much to cover up troublesome thoughts and feelings as to express them is beyond doubt. In order to understand this one has only to consider the role of language in wartime propaganda, the euphemisms drawn from the process of washing and cleaning – 'flushing out', 'ethnic cleansing', etc., so frequently used to overcome moral resistance to the horrendously dirty work of killing, raping and torturing people. However, propaganda may be regarded as a perversion of the symbolizing process, which under normal circumstances serves a creative function.

Once we can think symbolically we can sort things into categories, compare and contrast them, and put them into order. We can perform mathematical and linguistic functions – add, subtract, multiply and divide, write poetry, plays and prose. We can attach 'value', recognize and attribute uniqueness to individual members of a class, so that unlike bees, we are able (but do not always choose) to experience and cherish each other as irreplaceable. We can reason, solve problems, plan and predict our own and other people's behaviour, modulate our emotions, understand the natural world, how things work and what people say. We can anticipate others' needs, express care and concern, we can comfort and console. And we can also lie.

Some idealist philosophers have argued that thought is all that there is, others, less extravagantly, that it is all that we can know, and Descartes* famously found thought (by which he meant consciousness) to be the guarantor of his existence. Our highly developed capacity to reason has often been taken as the distinguishing criterion that marks us out from other animals. On the other hand, materialists and behavioural psychologists have emphasized what we share in common with other species, regarding our sense of autonomy as an illusion and our behaviour as merely a complex pattern of determined responses to environmental stimuli.

Although we are doubtless driven by evolutionary forces, it does seem clear that there is an important distinction to be drawn between the rigidly patterned instinctual responses characteristic of, say, birds and bees, and the more variable responses which serve our own biological needs. Our instincts, inborn tendencies whatever they may be, find symbolic representation in our minds. They are translated into the psychological register where they become desires for particular things, intentional states potentially subject to modification by the thinking process. As Freud long ago pointed out, they undergo 'vicissitudes' before being satisfied, their strength and urgency may be modified, their aim and object may be changed, their gratification delayed or indirectly achieved by means of displacement on to some other object. In short, our capacity to adapt is enhanced by the flexibility of thought, its effect on shaping behaviour and its transmission between people and down the generations.

Thought might seem to be an unequivocal good, but we know that 'thinking too much' can also be a hindrance in the performance of many tasks. Much of the learning and training that goes into the acquisition of sensory-motor skills is aimed precisely at the elimination of thought, the creation of fast automatic responses which mimic the efficiency of instinctual activity. However while automatic patterns of instinctual response are useful in a relatively stable environment, they become counterproductive in the face of environmental change. Konrad Lorenz's geese will not succeed in propagating their genes by attempting to mate with him. But if they could think, they would realize that he had manipulated their environment, tricked them into mistaking him for one of their own kind, and they would then treat him with appropriate contempt!

The trouble with thinking is that it makes us uncomfortable, sometimes painfully so. It is not always a welcome activity and we have developed various ways of avoiding it. Psychoanalysis teaches us that not everything we do with our thoughts is 'thinking'. It appears that we have a repertoire of ways in which we can prevent thoughts from being born, stop them from being recognized, interfere with their effectiveness, rid ourselves of their unwanted consequences and generally render ourselves mindless. These regressive 'mental mechanisms', now commonly referred to as 'defences', are really types of 'anti-thinking'. In this view toleration of frustration necessarily precedes thought, so paraphrasing Descartes we might say: 'I bear mental pain, therefore I think.'

CONCEPTUAL THOUGHT

The Advantages and Disadvantages of Conceptual Thought

Lamarckism, the nineteenth-century theory postulating the inheritance of acquired characteristics, is no longer believed to have any biological foundation. However, our adaptation to a changing environment indicates a much faster mechanism at work than Darwinian selection could possibly provide. It is our capacity for conceptual thought – a mixed blessing, Konrad Lorenz argues – that speeded up evolution by giving us a way of passing knowledge down the generations.

Konrad Lorenz (1903–89) was born in Austria and trained initially as a physician before devoting himself to his first love – the study of animal behaviour. He was awarded a doctorate in zoology in 1933, and two years later described 'imprinting' – the process whereby certain animals, e.g. ducklings and goslings, learned to follow the first moving object they encountered. Thus the object of their attachment was not instinctively specified but required exposure to a particular stimulus during the first few hours of life. Once established, however, it was permanent and irreversible. Birds exposed at birth to a human, say Lorenz himself, would, even at maturity, court and attempt to mate with him.

Together with Karl von Frisch and Niko Tinbergen, Lorenz founded the field of ethology, the scientific study of animal behaviour, for which they were awarded the Nobel prize in 1973.

It is a curious paradox that the greatest gifts of man, the unique faculties of conceptual thought and verbal speech which have raised him to a level high above all other creatures and given him mastery over the globe, are not altogether blessings, or at least are blessings that have to be paid for very dearly indeed. All the great dangers threatening humanity with extinction are direct consequences of conceptual thought and verbal speech. They drove man out of the paradise in which he could follow his instincts with impunity and do or not do whatever he pleased. There is much truth in the parable of the tree of knowledge and its fruit, though I want to make an addition to it to make it fit into my own picture of Adam: that apple was thoroughly unripe! Knowledge springing from conceptual thought robbed man of the security provided by his well-adapted instincts long, long before it was sufficient to provide him with an equally safe adaptation. Man is, as Arnold Gehlen has so truly said, by nature a jeopardized creature.

Conceptual thought and speech changed all man's evolution by achieving something which is equivalent to the inheritance of acquired characters. We have forgotten that the verb inherit had a juridical connotation long before it acquired a biological one. When a man invents, let us say, bow and arrow, not only his progeny but his entire community will inherit the knowledge and the use of these tools and possess them just as surely as organs grow on the body. Nor is their loss any more likely than the rudimentation of an organ of equal survival value. Thus, within one or two generations a process of ecological adaptation can be achieved which, in normal phylogeny and without the interference of conceptual thought, would have taken a time of an altogether different, much greater order of magnitude. Small wonder indeed if the evolution of social instincts and, what is even more important, social inhibitions could not keep pace with the rapid development forced on human society by the growth of traditional culture, particularly material culture.

Obviously, instinctive behaviour mechanisms failed to cope with the new circumstances which culture unavoidably produced even at its very dawn. There is evidence that the first inventors of pebble tools, the African Australopithecines, promptly used their new weapon to kill not only game, but fellow-members of their species as well. Peking Man, the Prometheus who learned to preserve fire, used it to roast his brothers: beside the first traces of the regular use of fire lie the mutilated and roasted bones of

Sinanthropus pekinensis himself. One is tempted to believe that every gift bestowed on man by his power of conceptual thought has to be paid for with a dangerous evil as the direct consequence of it. Fortunately for us, this is not so. Besides the faculty of conceptual thought, another constituent characteristic of man played an important role in gaining a deeper understanding of his environment, and this is curiosity. Insatiable curiosity is the root of exploration and experimentation, and these activities, even in their most primitive form, imply a function akin to asking questions. Explorative experimentation is a sort of dialogue with surrounding nature. Asking a question and recording the answer lead to anticipating the latter, and, given conceptual thought, to the linking of cause and effect. From hence it is but a step to consciously foreseeing the consequences of one's actions. Thus, the same human faculties which supplied man with the tools and with power dangerous to himself, also gave him the means to prevent their misuse: rational responsibility.

Konrad Lorenz, 'Ecce Homo!', *On Aggression* (1963)

The Mathematical Brain

Brain diseases selectively impair our ability to do things. By carefully studying what can and can't be done we come to understand that different systems exist with the capacity to function independently. When we know exactly what part of the brain is out of order, it is sometimes possible to map the site of a particular function. Loss of language function is a relatively common occurrence, for example following a stroke, but it is frequently accompanied by loss of calculation ability. Sometimes loss of the ability to calculate occurs on its own. It has also become clear that, under certain circumstances, arithmetical abilities can be preserved in the absence of language.

In 1985, investigations carried out at the National Hospital for Neurology and Neurosurgery, London, clarified the preservation of arithmetical skills in a patient who had lost the ability to use language. He was a forty-six-year-old male joiner who, at the time of admission, could scarcely speak or understand a word.

His spontaneous speech was limited to a few stereotyped phrases such as 'I don't know' and idiosyncratic jargon utterances such as 'millionaire bub'. His wife said he had become increasingly fatuous. None the less he continued to care for himself and drive a car. He was thought to be suffering from a form of pre-senile dementia, affecting a large area of the left side of his brain, which when scanned, was markedly reduced in size.

The patient had no useful communication. His comprehension of spoken and written language was gravely impaired, and his propositional speech was reduced to a few repetitive and jargon utterances. In this context the observation of preserved calculation skills was particularly striking. Although his ability to read, repeat and to match a spoken number name to an arabic numeral was somewhat impaired, his ability to add and subtract even multidigit numbers was remarkably well preserved. His ability to perform multidigit addition requiring carrying was almost at ceiling. His ability to retrieve multiplication facts was not entirely intact but was at least partially preserved. It was of some interest that he demonstrated knowledge of the principle of multiplication in his solutions to the problems to which he was unable to retrieve the answer directly.

The present finding of selective preservation of calculation skills in the context of total language dissolution is the converse of the pattern of deficit observed in patients with selective impairment of calculation in the context of intact language skills. The evidence of double dissociation between language calculation processing skills demonstrates their potential functional independence. The notion that calculation skills are to any great extent parasitic on covert language processing appears no longer tenable. In line with this, Hermelin and O'Connor[1] report a case of an autistic boy with an apparently total developmental dysphasia. He was unable to speak or to understand spoken language. He was unable to obtain a score on the Peabody Picture Vocabulary test. Nevertheless, he

1 'Factors and Prime: A Specific Numerical Ability', *Psychological Medicine* 20 (1990), 163–9.

was able to write and read numerals, to add, subtract, multiply and divide large numbers and to generate and recognize factors and primes far more quickly than an adult with a mathematics degree. The clear implication of this case is that verbal abilities are not necessarily prerequisite for the development of even a high level of numerical skill. These two lines of evidence clearly demonstrate that calculation skills are not necessarily encompassed by the language processing system.

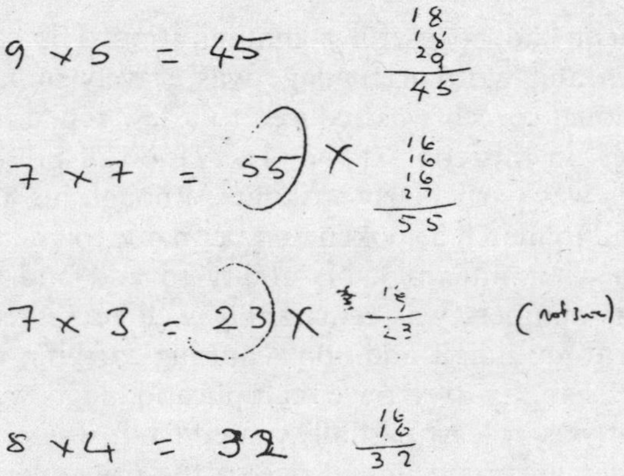

Fig 8. The patient's solutions of four simple multiplication problems

The present subject had a progressive atrophic condition and so his case cannot contribute significantly to the anatomical debate concerning the neural substrate of the components of numerical skills. The majority of selective calculation deficits in single-case studies have been associated with left parietal lesions, although other loci have also been implicated. However, the observation that in our patient the atrophy was maximal in the temporal lobe is perhaps of significance. We speculate that degenerative conditions that spare the left parietal lobe may also spare calculation skills.

M.N. Rossor, E.K. Warrington and L. Cipolotti, 'The Isolation of Calculation Skills' (1995)

Thinking and Linking

For Jung* thinking is essentially linking – a connecting process whereby mental 'presentations' are integrated in the form of concepts. He describes three ways in which this may happen. Active thinking in accordance with conscious rational principles; passive thinking in accordance with unconscious intuitive principles (which may or may not coincide with the former) and thinking that is driven by feeling, and has no logic of its own.

This I regard as one of the four basic psychological functions [the others being feeling, sensation and intuition, ed.]. Thinking is that psychological function which, in accordance with its own laws, brings given presentations into conceptual connection. It is an apperceptive activity and, as such, must be differentiated into *active* and *passive* thought-activity. Active thinking is an act of will, passive thinking an occurrence. In the former case, I submit the representation to a deliberate act of judgement; in the latter case, conceptual connections establish themselves, and judgements are formed which may even contradict my aim – they may lack all harmony with my conscious objective, hence also, for me, any feeling of direction, although by an act of active apperception I may subsequently come to a recognition of their directedness. Active thinking would correspond, therefore, with my idea of directed thinking. Passive thinking was inadequately characterized in my previous work as 'phantasying'. Today I would term it *intuitive thinking*.

To my mind, a simple stringing together of representations, such as is described by certain psychologists as *associative thinking*, is not thinking at all, but mere *presentation*. The term 'thinking' should, in my view, be confined to the linking up of representations by means of a concept, where in other words, an act of judgement prevails, whether such an act be the product of one's intention or not.

The faculty of directed thinking, I term *intellect*; the faculty of passive, or undirected thinking, I term *intellectual* intuition. Furthermore, I describe directed thinking or intellect as *rational* function, since it arranges the representations in accordance with the presuppositions of my conscious rational norm. Undirected thinking, or intellectual intuition, on the contrary is, in my opinion, an *irrational function, since it criticizes and arranges the representations according to norms that are unconscious to me and consequently not appreciated as reasonable. In certain cases, however, I may recognize subsequently that the intuitive act of judgement also corresponds with reason, although it has come about in a way that appears to me to be irrational.*

Thinking that is regulated by feeling, I do not regard as intuitive thinking, but as thought dependent upon feeling; it does not follow its own logical principle, but is subordinated to the principle of feeling. In such thinking the laws of logic are only ostensibly present; in reality they are suspended in favour of the aims of feeling.

Carl Gustav Jung, 'Soul (Anima) and Definitions', *Psychological Types* (1923)

ORIGINS OF THOUGHT

Intellect Is God Given

We receive our thoughts, we are bound by our thoughts, we do not control them, they control us. If we attempt to influence their course, impose our will on their development, our conscious logic on their intuitive order, Emerson says, we will fall into error. Born in Boston, Ralph Waldo Emerson (1803–82) was one of five brothers. He studied theology at Harvard and followed his father, a Unitarian minister who had died when Emerson was eight years old, into the church.

However, he underwent a crisis of faith shortly after the death of his first wife, and left Boston for Europe, where on a visit to England, he came under the influence of Coleridge*, Wordsworth* and Thomas Carlyle. On returning to America he remarried and settled in Concord, Massachusetts, pursuing a career as writer and lecturer. Like the English Lake poets, he embraced a quasi-mystical view of man and his place in nature, which he called Transcendentalism.

The growth of the intellect is spontaneous in every expansion. The mind that grows could not predict the times, the means, the mode of that spontaneity. God enters by a private door into every individual. Long prior to the age of reflection is the thinking of the mind. Out of darkness, it came insensibly into the marvellous light of to-day. In the period of infancy it accepted and disposed of all impressions from the surrounding creation after its own way. Whatever any mind doth or saith is after a law; and this native law remains over it after it has come to reflection and conscious thought. In the most worn pedantic, introverted self-tormentor's life, the greatest part is incalculable by him, unforeseen, unimaginable, and must be, until he can take himself up by his own ears. What am I? What has my will done to make me that I am? Nothing. I have been floated into this thought, this hour, this connection of events, by secret currents of might and mind, and my ingenuity and wilfulness have not thwarted, have not aided to an appreciable degree.

Our spontaneous action is always the best. You cannot, with your best deliberation and heed, come so close to any question as your spontaneous glance shall bring you, whilst you rise from your bed, or walk abroad in the morning after meditating the matter before sleep on the previous night. Our thinking is a pious reception. Our truth of thought is therefore vitiated as much by too violent direction given by our will, as by too great negligence. We do not determine what we will think. We only open our senses, clear away, as we can, all obstruction from the fact, and suffer the intellect to see. We have little control over our thoughts. We are the prisoners of ideas. They catch us up for moments into their heaven, and so fully engage us that we take no thought for the morrow, gaze like children, without an effort to make them our own. By and by we fall out of that rapture, bethink us where we have been, what we have seen, and repeat, as truly as we can, what we have beheld. As far as we can recall these ecstasies, we carry away in the ineffaceable memory the result, and all men and all the ages confirm it. It is called the Truth. But the moment we cease to report, and attempt to correct and contrive, it is not truth.

If we consider what persons have stimulated and profited us, we shall perceive the superiority of the spontaneous or intuitive principle over the arithmetical or logical. The first contains the second, but virtual and latent. We want, in every man, a long logic; we cannot pardon the absence of it, but it must not be spoken. Logic is the procession or proportionate unfolding of the intuition; but its virtue is as silent method; the moment it would appear as propositions, and have a separate value, it is worthless.

In every man's mind, some images, words, and facts remain, without effort on his part to imprint them, which others forget, and afterwards these illustrate to him important laws. All our progress is an unfolding, like the vegetable bud. You have first an instinct, then an opinion, then a knowledge, as the plant has root, bud, and fruit. Trust the instinct to the end, though you can render no reason. It is vain to hurry it. By trusting it to the end, it shall ripen into truth, and you shall know why you believe.

Ralph Waldo Emerson, 'Intellect', *Essays* (1841)

Thought Is a Property of Matter

Joseph Priestley argues, in the wake of Newtonian physics, that there can be no difficulty in attributing the quality of 'mentality' to matter. How much more so in the wake of modern quantum mechanics?

Priestley, physicist, chemist, political commentator and theologian, was born in Yorkshire in 1733. He is chiefly remembered for the discovery of oxygen, which he called 'dephlogisticated air'. He did not see any conflict between scientific materialism and belief in God, yet in his time he was reviled by many as an 'atheist'. His radical politics and sympathy with the French Revolution led to an arson attack on his house by a hostile mob.

He was elected a Fellow of the Royal Society in 1766 for his work on electricity. In 1794, following his sons who had left England the previous year, he emigrated to America. He died in Pennsylvania in 1804.

The principles of the Newtonian philosophy were no sooner known, than it was seen how few, in comparison, of the phenomena of nature, were owing to *solid matter*, and how much to *powers*, which were only supposed to accompany and surround the solid parts of matter. It has been asserted, and the assertion has never been disproved, that for anything we know to the contrary, all the solid matter in the solar system might be contained within a nutshell, there is so great a proportion of *void space* within the substance of the most solid bodies. Now when solidity had apparently so very little to do in the system, it is really a wonder that it did not occur to philosophers sooner, that perhaps there might be nothing for it to do at all, and that there might be no such thing in nature.

Since the only reason why the principle of thought, or sensation, has been imagined to be incompatible with matter, goes upon the supposition of the impenetrability being the essential property of it, and consequently that *solid extent* is the foundation of all the properties that it can possibly sustain, the whole argument for an immaterial thinking principle in man, on this new supposition, falls to the ground; matter, destitute of what has hitherto been called *solidity*, being no more incompatible with sensation and thought, than that substance, which, without knowing anything farther about it, we have been used to call *immaterial*.

[. . .]

It is true, that we have a very imperfect idea of what the *power of perception* is, and it may be as naturally impossible that we should have a clear idea of it, as that the eye should see itself. But this very ignorance ought to make us cautious in asserting with what other properties it may, or may not, exist. Nothing but a precise and definite knowledge of the nature of perception and thought can authorize any person to affirm, whether they not belong to an extended substance, which has also the properties of attraction and repulsion. Seeing, therefore, no sort of reason to imagine that these different properties are really *inconsistent*, any more than the different properties of *resistance* and *extension*, I am, of course, under the necessity of being guided by the *phenomena* in my conclusions concerning the proper seat of the powers of perception and thought. These phenomena I shall now briefly represent.

Had we formed a judgement concerning the necessary seat of thought, by the *circumstances that universally accompany it*, which is our rule in all other cases, we could not but have concluded, that in man it is a property of the *nervous system*, or rather of the *brain*. Because, as far as we can judge, the faculty of thinking, and a certain state of the brain, always accompany and correspond to one another; which is the very reason why we believe that any property is inherent in any substance whatever. There is no instance of any man retaining the faculty of thinking, when his brain was destroyed; and whenever that faculty is impeded, or injured, there is sufficient reason to believe that the brain is disordered in proportion; and therefore we are necessarily led to consider the latter as the seat of the former.

Moreover, as the faculty of thinking in general ripens, and comes to maturity with the body, it is also observed to decay with it; and if, in some cases, the mental faculties continue vigorous when the body in general is enfeebled, it is evidently because, in those particular cases, the *brain* is not much affected by the general cause of weakness. But, on the other hand, if the brain alone be affected, as by a blow on the head, by actual pressure within the skull, by sleep, or by inflammation, the mental faculties are universally affected in proportion.

Likewise, as the mind is affected in consequence of the affections of the body and brain, so the body is liable to be reciprocally affected by the affections of the mind, as is evident in the visible effects of all strong passions, hope or fear, love or anger, joy or sorrow, exultation or despair. These are certainly irrefragable arguments that it is probably no other than *one and the same thing* that is subject to these affections, and that they are necessarily dependent upon one another.

Joseph Priestley, *Disquisitions Relating to Matter and Spirit* (1777)

Birth of the Thinking Apparatus

Wilfred Bion (1897–1979) was born in India and came to England at the age of eight to receive his schooling. He was a tank commander in the First World War and was awarded the DSO and the Legion of Honour. He read history at Oxford before going on to qualify in medicine and ultimately become a psycho-analyst. Although he was President of the British Psychoanalytical Society from 1962 to 1965, he remained highly critical of the institutions of psychoanalysis. Arguably the most original psycho-analytic thinker of his time, Bion's work, considered by some to be frustratingly obscure, is challenging and controversial.

It is convenient to regard thinking as dependent on the successful outcome of two main mental developments. The first is the devel-opment of thoughts. They require an apparatus to cope with them. The second development therefore, is of this apparatus that I shall provisionally call thinking. I repeat – thinking has to be called into existence to cope with thoughts.

It will be noted that this differs from any theory of thought as a product of thinking, in that thinking is a development forced on the psyche by the pressure of thoughts and not the other way round. Psychopathological developments may be associated with either phase or both, that is they may be related to a breakdown in the development of thoughts, or a breakdown in the development of the apparatus for 'thinking' or dealing with thoughts, or both.

'Thoughts' may be classified, according to the nature of their developmental history, as preconceptions, conceptions or thoughts, and finally concepts; concepts are named and therefore fixed conceptions or thoughts. The conception is initiated by the conjunction of a pre-conception with a realization. The pre-conception may be regarded as the analogue in psycho-analysis of Kant's concept of 'empty thoughts'.

Psycho-analytically the theory that the infant has an inborn disposition corresponding to an expectation of a breast may be used to supply a model. When the pre-conception is brought into contact with a realization that approximates to it, the mental outcome is a conception. Put in another way, the pre-conception (the inborn expectation of a breast, the a priori knowledge of a breast, the 'empty thought') when the infant is brought into contact with the breast itself, mates with awareness of the realization and is synchronous with the development of a conception. This model will serve for the theory that every junction of a pre-conception with its realization produces a conception. Conceptions therefore will be expected to be constantly conjoined with an emotional experience of satisfaction.

I shall limit the term 'thought' to the mating of a pre-conception with a frustration. The model I propose is that of an infant whose expectation of a breast is mated with a realization of no breast available for satisfaction. This mating is experienced as a no-breast, or 'absent' breast inside. The next step depends on the infant's capacity for frustration: in particular it depends on whether the decision is to evade frustration or to modify it.

If the capacity for toleration of frustration is sufficient the 'no-breast' inside becomes a thought and an apparatus for 'thinking' it develops. This initiates the state, described by Freud in his *Two Principles of Mental Functioning*, in which dominance by the reality principle is synchronous with the development of an ability to think and so to bridge the gulf of frustration between the moment when a want is felt and the moment when action appropriate to satisfying the want culminates in its satisfaction. A capacity for tolerating frustration thus enables the psyche to develop thought as a means by which the frustration that is tolerated is itself made more tolerable.

If the capacity for toleration of frustration is inadequate, the bad internal 'no-breast', that a personality capable of maturity ultimately recognizes as a thought, confronts the psyche with the need to decide between evasion of frustration or of its modification.

Incapacity for tolerating frustration tips the scale in the direction of evasion of frustration [. . .] What should be a thought, a product of the juxtaposition of preconception and negative realization, becomes a bad object, indistinguishable from a thing-in-itself, fit only for evacuation. Consequently the development of an apparatus for thinking is disturbed [. . .] The model I propose for this development is a psyche that operates on the principle that evacuation of a bad breast is synonymous with obtaining sustenance from a good breast. The end result is that all thoughts are treated as if they were indistinguishable from bad internal objects; the appropriate machinery is felt to be, not an apparatus for thinking the thoughts, but an apparatus for ridding the psyche of accumulations of bad internal objects. The crux lies in the decision between modification or evasion of frustration.

Wilfred R. Bion, 'A Theory of Thinking' (1962)

The Hatred of Thought

'The mind is its own place', Milton says in Paradise Lost, 'and in itself/Can make a heaven of hell, a hell of heaven.' One primitive way of dealing with frustrations is to deny them, to turn hell into heaven by means of imaginary satisfaction – 'hallucinatory gratification'. This is clearly of limited value, for it has no external effect and although it temporarily assuages pain it does nothing to eliminate its original cause. By contrast, following Freud*, Klein* and Wilfred Bion*, the psychoanalyst Hanna Segal sees 'thought' as a more creative response to frustration, a way of working out how needs can be either satisfied or tolerated. However, because thought provides no immediate balm for pain, she suggests, we are inclined to turn away from it in hatred.

Segal (1918–) was born in Poland, where she grew up and underwent the first three years of her medical education, which was interrupted by the outbreak of war. She completed it in Paris and Edinburgh, qualifying as a doctor in 1943. Subsequently she trained as a psychoanalyst with the British Psychoanalytical Society, was analysed by Melanie Klein and became one of her co-workers. In 1977–8 she held the Freud Memorial Chair at University College, London.

Thinking first starts with, and then promotes, reality testing. It starts with the realization, 'This is not what is, it is what I made it to be in my mind.' But thinking also promotes reality testing in that omnipotent phantasy cannot be used for reality testing. Its very aim is to deny the reality of the experience. Thinking is not only an experimental action, as described by Freud, it is also an experimental hypothesis about the nature of things – a constant checking of what one phantasied against the evidence. Primitive thought starts at the preverbal level and is eventually encompassed in a word or phrase, 'Mummy – Daddy – Mummy gone.' A word or a sentence encompasses a complex experience.

Both the omnipotent phantasy-hallucination and thinking enable one to bear the gap between need and satisfaction: the absence and the need for a satisfying object. But while omnipotent phantasy denies the experience of need, thought, which admits the need, can be used to explore external and internal realities and deal with them. But because thought springs from and admits frustration, it can be attacked at its very inception.

This hatred of thought processes, deeply rooted in the unconscious, can be active throughout life. For example, I had a patient who was highly intelligent and articulate in some ways, but certain areas of his personality were functioning on a primitive level. He had psychosomatic symptoms – a gastric ulcer – and at times of tension, thinking was replaced by impulsive acting out. He had become aware in the course of his analysis of how he was obsessed with women's breasts. Toward the end of one session, he reported a dream in which a woman was giving the breast to a baby. The breasts were so close to the patient that he could fondle them. Then the woman went away, but she left the breast with the baby and the patient, who continued the sucking and the fondling. He added that the baby must also be himself, as it was so close to him. He started the next session with a great deal of irritation with himself. He said that he had plenty of important problems in his adult life which he wanted to talk about, but the moment he set eyes on the analyst he noticed she was wearing a white blouse and started thinking about her breasts and he said with exasperation, 'I am not obsessed with breasts, I am mad. I am obviously mad about breasts.' He then spoke about how he was always sucking something, like his toes and his thumb in childhood, and now sweets, chewing gum, cigarettes, anything just to have something in his mouth. As he was talking, he was getting more and more dreamy and remote. I drew his attention to this and reminded him of the dream in which he, the baby, sucked and fondled the breast while the woman went away. He interrupted me angrily, saying, 'Don't make me think. I don't want to think. I want to suck. I hate thoughts. When I have thoughts, it means I have nothing to suck.' My making the comment about his state of mind made him aware that what he was experiencing was a living through of the dream that he had possession of the breast, and made him aware of my presence. I was the woman with the white blouse, and there was a gap between us, necessitating speech for communication. The moment he became aware of that, he became aware that he was having thoughts, not a breast in his mouth, and he hated it. He hated the fact that he needed thinking to deal with this gap and with the problems he referred to at the beginning of the session, not the least of them being an impending analytic holiday.

The nascent thought conflicts with the illusion that the infant is merged with, or in possession of, an ideal breast. And disillusion must be tolerated for thought to develop. An element of this disillusion persists in sophisticated thought.

Hanna Segal, *Psychoanalysis and Freedom of Thought* (1977)

THE PHYSICAL EFFECTS OF THOUGHT

Paralysis Caused by an Idea

Paralysis resulting from psychological disturbance had been recognized for many years, but the following report in the British Medical Journal *by a nineteenth-century physician (cited by Charcot in his* Clinical Lectures, *1889) was one of the first attempts to systematically investigate the phenomenon. In the case described, a father and later his daughter both become paralysed following a reverse in the father's fortunes. The young woman is admitted to hospital and successfully treated with a mixture of attention, encouragement and apparently placebo procedures. It is noteworthy that no discussion of psychological factors antecedent to the father's paralysis occurs, which we are left to assume was organic in origin.*

The object of this paper is to show – 1. That some of the most serious disorders of the nervous system, such as paralysis, spasm, pain, and otherwise altered sensations, may depend upon a morbid condition of emotion, of idea and emotion, or of idea alone; 2. That such symptoms often exist for a long time, appearing as complicated diseases of the brain and spinal cord; 3. That they resist many different kinds of treatment, being alike unmoved by sedatives and irritants, by attention or neglect, but that they disappear entirely upon removal of the erroneous idea; 4. That they occur independently of anything that could be called either insanity of mind, hysteria, hypochondriasis, or malingering; 5. That they are often, but not constantly, associated with some bodily weakness or general debility; 6. That they sometimes associate themselves with distinct and definite diseases of the nervous centres, so that it becomes very important to know how much of a given case is due to organic lesion, and how much to morbid ideation; 7. That it is possible to make a diagnosis with regard to them in many instances; and 8. That the principles upon which their treatment should be conducted are simple, and their application marvellously successful.

1. Everyone is familiar with some of what may be termed the 'acute' effects of idea and emotion. It is well known that a man may be rendered instantaneously powerless or paralysed, rigid, stupefied, statuesque or unconscious by the sudden communication of startling intelligence. It is of daily occurrence, that pain is taken away by sudden fear; that some sensorial impressions are lost in the state of mental tension that accompanies intellectual effort; e.g. the child loses its toothache when it sits down in the dentist's chair; and the student does not hear the tick or the striking of his timepiece when he is busy at his work. It is familiar enough that the idea of pain constitutes much of what we denominate as pain, and that sometimes it makes up the whole of it, as it did, *e.g.* in the well known case of the butcher, who was agonized almost past endurance by the fact that a flesh-hook had caught itself, not in his skin, but only in his sleeve. Facts of the kind I have alluded to are at the very basis of our pathological interpretation of cases, but, at the same time, the 'chronic' effects of idea and emotion are often completely overlooked when they take the form of muscular and sensory disturbance. We recognize them at once when they show themselves in altered notions,

sentiments, or feelings, but we often fail to perceive their true nature when they appear as paralysis or pain. The following case will illustrate this kind of disturbance in its simplest form. A young lady who has seen better days, is admitted into hospital, paraplegic. She has become so gradually, and has lost flesh generally, and to a considerable extent. For two or three months, she has been quite unable to stand, even for a moment; now she lies in bed almost entirely. Her expression is anxious, but with some hopefulness. She thinks that, having come to the hospital – a great mental struggle for some who have, in former days, enjoyed every luxury at home – she may get better. These points are to be noticed in her case: that the paralysis is almost complete; the patient can just move the toes, or just raise either heel separately from the bed, while lying on her back; but there is no want of control over the sphincters, no local change of nutrition (*i.e.*, nutrition of the legs as compared with the arms), the cutaneous sensibility is perfect; reflex movements are difficult to arouse; the electric contractility and sensibility are perfect; there is no spasm, either tonic or clonic; there is no pain, either spontaneous or producible by movement of limb or pressure on the spinal column. There is no evidence of tubercular or other cachexia; there has been no blow; there has been no hysteria. It would be difficult to place this case among any of the well known categories of spinal disease, and I regarded it as ideal paralysis; her previous and subsequent history demonstrating the correctness of this view. The young lady's father, her only relation, was, a year and a half ago, reduced from affluence to poverty by one of those commercial accidents which produce effects of 'shock' as severe as, and often more permanent than, those of railway collision. He bore it bravely, and so did she; he, in his advancing years, went back into the work that he had long since renounced; she, in her youth, took upon herself duties and responsibilities that were, to her, entirely new. For a little time, all was well, and they did not grieve over their altered fortunes; but, now, the father became paralytic, suddenly, and the daughter nursed him tenderly, and so assiduously, that they soon came to be in the reality of want. The father was helpless, but not so ill that the daughter could not leave him; and so she worked hard as a daily governess, often walked where she used to ride, to save expense, and walked quickly to gain time and be the more at home. Thus, she lived and worked on for many dreary weeks, with paralysis constantly upon her mind, her brain overdone with thought and feeling, her limbs wearied with walking, and her heart tired out with the effort to look bright, and be so. Her limbs often ached, and a horror took hold of her, as the idea again and again crossed her mind, that she might become paralysed like her father; she tried to banish it, but it haunted her still, and, gradually, she had to give up walking, then to stop in the house, then in the room, and then in her bed. Her legs 'became heavier day by day', and she at last reached the state in which I found her when she was carried to the hospital.

She was told, and the nurses, and those about her, were all told, most confidently, that she would soon walk quite well; she was given some mild tonic medicine; faradization was applied to the muscles of the legs: be it remembered that the electric contractility was perfect, and that this was done merely to produce a mental impression. The back and limbs were well rubbed, and the patient was taken between two nurses – who acted as crutches – and made to walk up and down the ward for five minutes every four hours. On the day after treatment was commenced, she could stand with a little support; at the end of four or five days, she could walk fairly well; and, at the end of a fortnight, she was as strong and capable of exertion as she had ever been in her life.

J. Russell Reynolds, 'Remarks on Paralysis, and Other Disorders of Motion and Sensation, Dependent on Idea' (1869)

OBSESSION

Unwanted Thoughts

One of the strangest conditions to afflict the thinking process is obsessive-compulsive disorder (OCD). Although the full-blown syndrome is relatively rare, obsessive symptoms may be present in a range of other mental disorders, and obsessive personality traits are as common as boiled cabbage. The cause of the problem (or group of problems) is as yet unknown and it may turn out to be a combination of factors. Evidence to support various theories exists, which includes pointers to genetic predisposition, brain malfunction and psychological conflict. No treatment is generally effective and combinations of drug treatments with various types of psychotherapy are often employed in an attempt to alleviate the symptoms. In severe cases, where a person's life is crippled by intractable obsessions, modern psychosurgery has provided significant relief without producing unacceptable consequences.

Freud suggested that obsessional thoughts, for example those concerned with fear of contamination, were expressions of unacceptable (dirty) sexual desires relegated to the unconscious mind. The associated washing rituals and compulsions were employed as a counter-measure. Whatever the truth of this, his clinical description has enduring value.

Obsessional neurosis is shown in the patient's being occupied with thoughts in which he is in fact not interested, in his being aware of impulses in himself which appear very strange to him and in his being led to actions the performance of which give him no enjoyment, but which is quite impossible for him to omit. The thoughts (obsessions) may be senseless in themselves, or merely a matter of indifference to the subject; often they are completely silly, and invariably they are the starting-point of a strenuous mental activity, which exhausts the patient and to which he only surrenders himself most unwillingly. He is obliged against his will to brood and speculate as though it were a question of his most important vital problems. The impulses which the patient is aware of in himself may also make a childish and senseless impression; but as a rule they have a content of the most frightful kind, tempting him, for instance, to commit serious crimes, so that he not merely disavows them as alien to himself, but flies from them in horror and protects himself from carrying them out by prohibitions, renunciations and restrictions upon his freedom. At the same time, these impulses never – literally never – force their way through to performance; the outcome lies always in victory for the flight and the precautions. What the patient actually carries out – his so-called obsessional actions – are very harmless and certainly trivial things, for the most part repetitions or ceremonial elaborations of the activities of ordinary life. But these necessary activities (such as going to bed, washing, dressing or going for a walk) become extremely tedious and almost insoluble tasks. In different forms and cases of obsessional neurosis the pathological ideas, impulses and actions are not combined in equal proportions; it is the rule, rather, that one or other of these factors dominates the picture and gives its name to the illness, but the common element in all these forms is sufficiently unmistakable.

Certainly this is a crazy illness. The most extravagant psychiatric imagination would not, I think, have succeeded in constructing anything like it; and if one did not see it before one every day one would never bring oneself to believe in it. Do not suppose, however, that you will help the patient in the least by calling on him to take a new line, to cease to occupy himself with such foolish thoughts and to do something sensible instead of his childish pranks. He would like to do so himself, for he is completely clear in his head, shares your opinion of his obsessional symptoms and even puts it forward to you spontaneously. Only he cannot help himself. What is carried into action in an obsessional neurosis is sustained by an energy to which we probably know nothing comparable in normal mental life. There is only one thing he can do: he can make displacements, and exchanges, he can replace one foolish idea by another somewhat milder, he can proceed from one precaution or prohibition to another, instead of one ceremonial he can perform another. He can displace the obsession but not remove it. The ability to displace any symptom into something far removed from its original conformation is a main characteristic of his illness. Moreover it is a striking fact that in his condition the contradictions (polarities) with which mental life is interlaced emerge especially sharply differentiated. Alongside of obsessions with a positive and negative content, *doubt* makes itself felt in the intellectual field and little by little it begins to gnaw even at what is usually most certain.

The whole position ends up in an ever-increasing degree of inde-cision, loss of energy and restriction of freedom. At the same time, the obsessional neurotic starts off with a very energetic disposi-tion, he is often extraordinarily self-willed and as a rule he has intellectual gifts above the average. He has usually reached a satis-factorily high level of ethical development; he exhibits over-conscientiousness, and is more than ordinarily correct in his behaviour. You can imagine that no small amount of work is needed before one can make one's way any distance into this contradictory hotch-potch of character-traits and symptoms. And to begin with we aim at nothing whatever else than understanding a few of the symptoms and being able to interpret them. [. . .]

Sigmund Freud, 'General Theory of the Neuroses' (1917)

GOOD AND BAD THOUGHTS

What Are Good Thoughts?

John Bunyan (1628–88) was the son of a travelling tinker, educated in a local Bedfordshire school. Following service on the Parliamentary side during the Civil War he was discharged in 1647, and soon afterwards got married. In 1653 he converted to a Non-conformist church. Shortly after the Restoration in 1660, he was arrested for preaching without a licence, refused to give an undertaking not to repeat the offence, and was sent to jail, where he spent most of the next twelve years writing books. In 1672 he was released under the terms of Charles II's first Declaration of Indulgence and immediately took up duties as pastor of his Bedford church. Pilgrim's Progress *is the alle-gorical narrative of a single hero, Christian, setting out on a journey to save his soul. In the following passage Christian encounters 'Ignorance' and corrects his thinking.*

Ignor. What be good thoughts respecting ourselves?
Chr.   *Such as agree with the word of God.*

Ignor. When does our thoughts of our selves agree with the Word
        of God?

Chr.   *When we pass the same Judgement upon our selves which the
        Word passes. To explain myself: The Word of God saith of
        persons in a natural condition,* There is none Righteous, there
        is none that doth good (Rom. 3.). *It saith also,* That every
        imagination of the heart of man is only evil (Gen. 6.5.), and
        that continually. *And again,* The imagination of man's heart
        is evil from his Youth. *Now then, when we think thus of our
        selves, having sense thereof, then are our thoughts good ones,
        because according to the Word of God.*

Ignor. I will never believe that my heart is thus bad.

Chr   *Therefore thou never hadst one good thought concerning thy
        self in thy life . . .*

John Bunyan, *The Pilgrim's Progress* (1678)

THE THINKING ORGAN

Small Children Think with Their Mouths

*Jean Piaget (1896–1980) was born in Switzerland, studied
psychology and psychiatry in Germany and France, and returned
to Geneva in 1921 to become Director of Studies at the
Institut Jean-Jacques. Rousseau, and subsequently Professor of
Psychology. He followed a conversational method of inquiry,
presenting children of different ages with naive questions
regarding their experience, and thereby elucidating various stages
of cognitive development. His generalizations have been criti-
cized on the grounds that they are based on small samples, and
the age ranges with which he associates particular 'stages' should
not be interpreted too tightly. With regard to the child's notion
of 'thought', Piaget delineates three stages: the first, around the
age of six years, is characterized by locating the mouth as the
organ of thought. In the second, around the age of eight years,
lip service is paid to the head or brain as the originator of
thought, but thoughts themselves are often conceived as material in nature, consisting of sounds or substances such as air*

or blood, *having size and shape. In the third stage, around the age of eleven or twelve years, the notion of thought is generally more abstract.*

In the following extract, Piaget has used abbreviations for his subjects' names, and noted their ages in years and months.

MONT. (7;0)
You know what it means to think?
Yes.
Then think of your house. What do you think with?
The mouth.
Can you think with the mouth shut?
No.
With the eyes shut?
Yes.
Now shut your mouth and think of your house. Are you thinking?
Yes.
What did you think with?
The mouth.

KENN. (7;6)
What do you think with?
Inside my head.
Is the head empty or full?
Full.
If someone opened your head, would they see when you were thinking?
No, because they couldn't see.
If they could look inside your head without your dying, would they see your thought?
You can't hear it when you speak gently.
What do you think with?
The head.
With what part of the head?
The mouth.
What is inside the head? Is thought inside?
Yes, when you are thinking of something.
What is inside the head?
When you speak.

Can you think when your mouth is shut?
Yes, without speaking.
What do you think with when you don't speak?
The mouth.
What is there inside the head when you think?
Nothing.
Can you see thought?
No.
Could I hear it?
No.
Could I feel it if I put my finger there?
Yes.

TIE. (10;10)
Has thought got strength?
No, it has and then it hasn't.
Why hasn't it?
It depends on what you are thinking of.
When has it strength?
When you think of something strong.
If you think of this table, has it?
Yes.
If you think of the lake, has it?
No.
If you think of the wind, has it?
Yes.
(Tie has said a few minutes before that the water of the lake had
no strength '*because it was still*', that the wind had strength, '*because
it can blow down houses*', and that the table had, '*because things
can stand on it*'.)
Have words strength?
It depends on the word.
Which ones have got strength?
The word 'boxing' . . . *oh, no they haven't any strength* (laughing).
Why did you think they had at first?
I was wrong. I was thinking it was the word that hit.

Jean Piaget, *The Child's Conception of the World* (1929)

SCHIZOPHRENIA

Thought Control by a Machine

One of the most characteristic symptoms of schizophrenia is the subjective experience of 'thought control'. Psychotic mental illness of this type wreaks havoc with a person's sense of autonomy. Nowadays people suffering a schizophrenic episode are likely to experience themselves as being controlled by the television, but Victor Tausk's account of the 'influencing machine', written more than eighty years ago, gives a graphic description of the condition, which is still valid in all its essentials. The cause of schizophrenia remains unknown though much evidence has been collected on the role of genetic predisposition, brain pathology, psychological and social factors in determining its manifestation. Tausk's psychological interpretation of the 'influencing machine' as a projection of the patient's own body is compelling.

Victor Tausk (1879–1919) was a talented member of Freud's early circle, but he was also a troubled soul whose contribution to psychiatry was abruptly terminated. Born in Croatia, then a part of the Austro-Hungarian Empire, he attended the University of Vienna in 1897 where he studied law. At the age of twenty-six, following the failure of his marriage, he moved to Berlin, where he pursued a career in literature and journalism while his wife and two sons continued to live in Vienna. His love life followed an unsuccessful pattern with a series of women and he went through a period of depression. Subsequently he became interested in psychoanalysis and in 1908 returned to Vienna in order to study medicine and be close to Freud and his group. He qualified as a psychiatrist and gained wide clinical experience including work in the army during the First World War. After the war he returned to Vienna seeking to enter analysis with Freud but was disappointed to be referred to one of his junior colleagues, Helene Deutch, who was herself in analysis with Freud. He had a brief love affair with Freud's friend Lou Andreas-Salome (also renowned for her relationships with creative men such as Nietzsche and Rilke). Tausk's analysis with Deutch began to preoccupy her sessions with Freud and after a few months

Freud insisted that she call a halt to one or the other. She con-
tinued her own.

In the wake of the ending of his analysis, Tausk embarked on
a love affair with a former patient, Hilde Loewi, whom he deter-
mined to marry. He found himself unable to go through with it
and in the early hours of 3 July 1919, on the day he was due to
obtain a marriage licence, he shot himself dead.

The schizophrenic influencing machine is a machine of mystical
nature. The patients are able to give only vague hints of its
construction. It consists of boxes, cranks, levers, wheels, buttons,
wires, batteries, and the like. Patients endeavour to discover the
construction of the apparatus by means of their technical knowledge, and it appears that with the progressive popularization of
the sciences, all the forces known to technology are utilized to
explain the functioning of the apparatus. All the discoveries of
mankind, however, are regarded as inadequate to explain the
marvellous powers of this machine, by which the patients feel
themselves persecuted.

The main effects of the influencing machine are the following:

(1) It makes the patients see pictures. When this is the case,
the machine is generally a magic-lantern or cinematograph. The
pictures are seen on a single plane, on walls or window-panes,
and unlike typical visual hallucinations are not three-dimensional.

(2) It produces, as well as removes, thoughts and feelings by
means of waves or rays or mysterious forces which the patients'
knowledge of physics is inadequate to explain. In such cases, the
machine is often called a 'suggestion-apparatus'. Its construction
cannot be explained, but its function consists in the transmission
or 'draining off' of thoughts or feelings by one or several persecutors.

(3) It produces motor phenomena in the body, erections and
seminal emissions, that are intended to deprive the patient of his
male potency and weaken him. This is accomplished either by
means of suggestion or by air-currents, electricity, magnetism, or
X-rays.

(4) It creates sensations that in part cannot be described, because they are strange to the patient himself, and that in part are sensed as electrical, magnetic, or due to air-currents.

(5) It is also responsible for other occurrences in the patient's body, such as cutaneous eruptions, abscesses, and other pathological processes.

The machine serves to persecute the patient and is operated by enemies. To the best of my knowledge, the latter are exclusively of the male sex. They are predominantly physicians by whom the patient has been treated. The manipulation of the apparatus is likewise obscure, the patient rarely having a clear idea of its operation. Buttons are pushed, levers set in motion, cranks turned. The connection with the patient is often established by means of invisible wires leading into his bed, in which case the patient is influenced by the machine only when he is in bed. [. . .]

The case of Natalija A: Report

The patient is Miss Natalija A., thirty-one years old, formerly a student of philosophy. She has been completely deaf for a great number of years, due to an ulcer of the ear, and can make herself understood only by means of writing. She declares that for six and a half years she has been under the influence of an electrical machine made in Berlin, though this machine's use is prohibited by the police. It has the form of a human body, indeed, the patient's own form, though not in all details. Her mother, likewise the patient's male and female friends, are also under the influence of this machine or of similar machines. Of the latter she gives no explanation, describing only the apparatus to which she herself is subjected. She is certain that for men there is a masculine machine representing the masculine form and for women a female one. The trunk (torso) has the shape of a lid, resembling the lid of a coffin and is lined with silk or velvet. Regarding the limbs two significant explanations are given. At the first interview she described them as entirely natural parts of the body. A few weeks later these limbs were not placed on the coffin lid in their natural form, but were merely drawn on it in two dimensions, in the position they would occupy in the natural state of the body. She cannot see the head – she says she is not sure about it and she does not know whether the machine bears her own head. She has practically nothing to report about the head. The patient does not know definitely how this machine is to be handled, neither does she know how it is connected with her; but she vaguely thinks that it is by means of telepathy. The outstanding fact about the machine is that it is being manipulated by someone in a certain manner, and everything that occurs to it happens also to her. When someone strikes this machine, she feels the blow in the corresponding part of her body [see *Montaigne on Imagination*, ed.]. The ulcer (lupus) now present on her nose was first produced on the nose of the machine, and some time later the patient herself became afflicted with it. The inner parts of the machine consist of electric batteries, which are supposed to represent the internal organs of the human body. Those who handle the machine produce a slimy substance in her nose, disgusting smells, dreams, thoughts, feelings, and disturb her while she is thinking, reading or writing. At an earlier stage, sexual sensations were produced in her through manipulation of the genitalia of the machine; but now the machine no longer possesses any genitalia, though why or how they disappeared she cannot tell. Ever since the machine lost its genitalia, the patient has ceased to experience sexual sensations.

She became familiar with the apparatus, about which she had previously heard, through all kinds of occurrences, especially through conversations among people, that is, through auditory hallucinations. The man who utilizes the apparatus to persecute her, her rejected suitor, a college professor, is prompted by jealousy. Very soon after she had refused his courtship she felt that he was trying by means of suggestion to bring about a friendship between his sister-in-law, her mother, and herself, his obvious purpose being to use this influence to make her accept him. When, however, suggestion failed, he subjected her to the influence of the machine; not only she herself but also her mother, her physicians, her friends, all those who had her welfare at heart, came under the influence of this diabolic apparatus, with the result that the physicians submitted a mistaken diagnosis to her, the apparatus deluding them into diagnosing other ailments than those with which she was afflicted. She could no longer get along with her friends and relatives, arousing everyone's animosity, and feeling compelled to run away. It was impossible to obtain any further details from the patient. On her third visit she became inaccessible and only stated that the analyst, too, was under the influence of the apparatus, that he had become hostile to her, and that they could no longer understand each other.

Interpretation

This case provides a definite reason for believing that the influencing machine represents a stage in the development of a symptom which can also appear without this stage, as a delusion of reference. The patient clearly stated that her persecutor had recourse to the apparatus only when his attempt to influence her by suggestion failed. The fact that she seems to have previously heard about the machine is also enlightening. This vague recognition obviously awakened in the patient old familiar sensations that she had experienced before she was subjected to the apparatus; this is analogous to the well-known fact that persons in a state of infatuation have the feeling of having always known the beloved one – in reality they are merely rediscovering one of their old libidinal imagos. We shall hear later in how remote a past she had first experienced sensations similar to those caused by the influencing apparatus.

The peculiar construction of the machine substantiates our assumptions to a great extent, especially with regard to the significance of the machine as a projected symbol of the patient's genitalia. We may add that the apparatus represents not only the patient's genitalia but obviously, her whole person. It represents the projection of the patient's body on to the outer world. At least, the following results are unquestionably obtained from the patient's report: the apparatus is distinguished above all by its human form, easily recognized despite many non-human characteristics. In form it resembles the patient herself, and she senses all manipulations performed on the apparatus in the corresponding part of her own body and in the same manner all effects and changes undergone by the apparatus take place simultaneously in the patient's body, and *vice versa*. Thus, the apparatus loses its genitalia following the patient's loss of her genital sensations; it had possessed genitalia for as long as her genital sensations had lasted.

Applying the technique of dream interpretation to this case, it may be said that the patient's inability to provide any detailed description of the head of the apparatus, and especially her inability to decide whether it was her own head or not, proves conclusively that it is her own head. We know from analytic observations that the person not recognized in a dream is actually the dreamer himself. [. . .]

A further detail in the description of the apparatus – namely, that the lid is lined with silk or velvet – may substantiate this opinion. Women very frequently describe in such terms the feelings evoked by caressing their own skin. That the intestines appear in the form of batteries is only of slight significance here, although it will assume a profounder meaning later on. This superficial interpretation may be associated with the information given directly or indirectly to school-children to the effect that the viscera resemble a very complicated machine. In our case the tendency seems to be towards a verbal interpretation of this infantile conception. This conclusion regarding its ontogeny is arrived at with the help of the description given by the patient of her influencing apparatus.

At the very beginning the patient reported that the limbs of the apparatus appeared in their natural form and position. Several weeks later, she declared that her limbs were drawn on the lid. This is obviously a manifestation of the progressive distortion undergone by the apparatus, which, consequently, eventually loses all human characteristics and becomes a typical, unintelligible, influencing machine. First the genitalia, then the limbs are eliminated in this process. The patient, to be sure, is unable to report how the genitalia are removed. She states, however, that the limbs are removed in the following manner: they lose their three-dimensional human form and flatten to a two-dimensional plane. It would not have been surprising if after a lapse of several weeks, the patient had declared that the apparatus did not possess any limbs at all. Nor would it have been astonishing had she stated that the apparatus had never had any limbs. A failure to recall the developmental stages of the apparatus has obviously the same significance as that of forgetting the origin of dream pictures. It is not too bold a conclusion to draw that the coffin lid of the machine is a product of such successive distortions and that originally it had represented a human being – namely, the patient herself.

Psycho-analytic experience brings to light the causative factors in such distortion. Underlying every distortion of a psychic phenomenon there is a defence mechanism which has as its aim the protection of the conscious ego against the appearance or reappearance of undisguised fantasies. The patient obviously seeks not to recognize herself in the influencing machine and therefore in self-protection she divests it of all human features; in a word, the less human the appearance of the delusion, the less does she recognize herself in it. The origin of this rejection will be examined later.

When the influencing machine of Miss Natalija A. first came to my attention, it was in a special stage of development; I was fortunate, moreover, in observing the machine in the process of development as concerned the limbs, and also in obtaining specific information from the patient herself regarding the genitalia. I assume that this process will end with the production of the typical influencing apparatus known to clinical observation, but I cannot affirm that this apparatus will pass through all the stages of development to the very end. It is very possible that it will stop at a middle point, without proceeding further.

Victor Tausk, 'On the Origin of the "Influencing Machine" in Schizophrenia' (1919)

Against Thought

Schizophrenia involves a marked alteration in the quality of thought, yet, as Eugen Bleuler, the Swiss psychiatrist who coined the term, remarked: 'Even in the most severe cases, the majority of associations takes the usual pathways; because innumerable, nearly correct ideas and thought fragments are still produced.' What results is a state of mind that is eerily close to normal

thinking and at the same time clearly mad, a weird mixture of
sense and nonsense. Ideas are freed from their logical constraints
but they are not connected in a totally random fashion.
Contradictions happily sit together, trains of thought are derailed
but continue on their paralogistic way.

Schizophrenic thinking has something in common with the
language of dreams and the creative tropes employed in poetry,
yet it is invariably destructive to a person's well-being. Vaslav
Nijinsky (1890–1950), the Polish-Russian ballet dancer of
legendary fame, was at the height of his artistic powers when
struck by the condition. The following passage from his diary
was written in 1919, as he descended into insanity.

I will speak of Nietzsche and Darwin because they thought.
Darwin, like Nietzsche, was descended from apes. They imitate
those that they themselves have invented. They think they have
discovered America. By discovering America I mean that a
person says something that has already been said. Darwin was
not the first to have invented the ape. The ape is descended
from an ape, and that ape from God. God is descended from
God, and God from God. I have a good feeling because I understand everything I write. I am a man descended from God, not
from an ape. I am an ape if I do not feel. I am God if I feel. I
know that many people will admire my mind, and I will be
glad because my aim will be justified. I will dance in order to
earn money. I want to give my wife a fully furnished house.
She wants to have a little boy by me because she is afraid I will
die soon. She thinks I am mad, because she thinks a lot. I think
little and therefore understand everything that I feel. I am feeling
in the flesh and therefore not intellect in the flesh. I am the
flesh. I am feeling. I am God in the flesh and in feeling. I am
man and not God. I am simple. People must not think me. They
must feel me and understand me through feeling. Scholars will
ponder over me, and they will rack their brains needlessly,
because thinking will produce no results for them. They are
stupid. They are beasts. They are meat. They are death. I am
talking simply, but without any affectation. I am not an ape. I

am a man. The world has been created by God. Man has been created by God. It is not possible for men to understand God. God understands God. Man is God, and therefore understands God. I am God. I am a man. I am good and not a beast. I am an animal with reason. I have flesh. I am flesh. I am not descended from flesh. Flesh is created by God. I am God. I am God. I am God . . .

Vaslav Nijinsky, 'On Life', *The Diary of Vaslav Nijinsky* (1919)

DÉJÀ VU

Thoughts That Return

The Déjà Vu phenomenon, that nagging thought that something has happened before, is widely recognized. It also frequently occurs during epileptic activity in the brain's temporal lobe. How does it get into our minds? Oliver Wendell Holmes (1809–94) attempts an answer. Born in Cambridge, Massachusetts, he held the Chair of Anatomy and Physiology at Harvard University for thirty-five years and was an accomplished essayist, novelist and poet.

Just as we find a mathematical rule at the bottom of many of the bodily movements, just so thought may be supposed to have its regular cycles. Such or such a thought comes round periodically in its turn. Accidental suggestions, however, so far interfere with the regular cycles, that we may find them practically beyond our power of recognition. Take all this for what it is worth, but at any rate you will agree that there are certain particular thoughts that do not come up once a day, nor once a week, but that a year would hardly go round without your having them pass through your mind. Here is one which comes up at intervals in this way. Some one speaks of it, and there is an instant and eager smile of assent in the listener or listeners. Yes, indeed; they have often been struck by it.

All at once a conviction flashes through us that we have been

*in the same precise circumstances as at the present instant, once
or many times before.*

Oh dear, yes! – said one of the company, – everybody had had
that feeling.

The landlady didn't know anything about such notions; it was
an idea in folks' heads, she expected.

The schoolmistress said, in a hesitating sort of way, that she
knew the feeling well, and didn't like to experience it; it made
her think she was a ghost, sometimes.

The young fellow whom they call John, said he knew all about
it; he had just lighted a cheroot the other day, when a tremendous conviction all at once came over him that he had done just
that same thing ever so many times before. I looked severely at
him, and his countenance immediately fell – *on the side toward
me*; I cannot answer for the other, for he can wink and laugh
with either half of his face without the other half's knowing it.

– I have noticed – I went on to say – the following circumstances
connected with these sudden impressions. First, that the condition
which seems to be the duplicate of a former one is often very trivial
– one that might have presented itself a hundred times. Secondly,
that the impression is very evanescent, and that it is rarely, if ever,
recalled by any voluntary effort, at least after any time has elapsed.
Thirdly, that there is a disinclination to record the circumstances,
and a sense of incapacity to reproduce the state of mind in words.
Fourthly, I have often felt that the duplicate condition had not only
occurred once before, but that it was familiar and, as it seemed,
habitual. Lastly, I have had the same conviction in my dreams.

How do I account for it? – Why, there are several ways that I
can mention, and you may take your choice. The first is that which
the young lady hinted at: – that these flashes are sudden recollections of a previous existence. I don't believe that; for I remember
a poor student I used to know told me he had such a conviction
one day when he was blacking his boots, and I can't think he had
ever lived in another world where they use Day and Martin.

Some think that Dr Wigan's doctrine of the brain's being a
double organ, its hemispheres working together like the two eyes,
accounts for it. One of the hemispheres hangs fire, they suppose,
and the small interval between the perceptions of the nimble and

the sluggish half seems an indefinitely long period, and therefore the second perception appears to be the copy of another, ever so old. But even allowing the centre of perception to be double, I can see no good reason for supposing this indefinite lengthening of the time, nor any analogy that bears it out. It seems to me most likely that the coincidence of circumstances is very partial, but that we take this partial resemblance for identity, as we occasionally do resemblances of persons. A momentary posture of circumstances is so far like some preceding one that we accept it as exactly the same, just as we accost a stranger occasionally, mistaking him for a friend. The apparent similarity may be owing, perhaps, quite as much to the mental state at the time, as to the outward circumstances.

Oliver Wendell Holmes, *The Autocrat of the Breakfast-Table* (1857–8)

BEHAVIOURISM

Thinking as a Motor Activity

John Hughlings Jackson (1835–1911) was born in Yorkshire. His mother died when he was very young and he took his middle name from her family. He had little formal education and grew up into a shy man who attended York Medical School with about twelve other student-apprentices. He never held a university post but did become a member of staff at the National Hospital in Queen's Square, London, famous for the treatment of nervous disease, where he practised and conducted research. He published numerous papers and developed an international reputation as a founding father of modern neurology. He proposed that thinking was simply our most complex motor act. This hypothesis continues to inform the theorizing of some contemporary researchers.[2]

2 See I. Feinberg and M. Guazzelli, 'Schizophrenia – a Disorder of the Corollary Discharge Systems That Integrate the Motor Systems of Thought with the Sensory Systems of Consciousness', *British Journal of Psychiatry* 174 (1999), 196–204.

It is sometimes objected that we cannot 'understand' 'how energizing of nervous processes, representing *movements*, can give or share in giving us *ideas*'. This is a very naive objection. We cannot understand how any conceivable arrangement of any sort of matter can give us mental states of any kind. Is it more difficult to understand why we remember a word during energizing of cells and fibres because we believe those cells and fibres represent articulatory *movements*? I do not concern myself with mental states at all, except indirectly in seeking their anatomical substrata. I do not trouble myself about the mode of connection between mind and matter. It is enough to assume a parallelism. That along with excitations or discharges of nervous arrangements in the cerebrum, mental states occur, I, of course, admit; but how this is I do not enquire; indeed, so far as clinical medicine is concerned, I do not care. If anyone feels warranted in assuming that physical states in the highest nervous centres and mental states are one and the same thing, he is just as much bound as anyone else to seek the anatomical nature of the nervous arrangements in which the psychico-physical states occur. *To give a materialistic explanation of mental states is not to give an anatomical one*. For clinical purposes it matters nothing whether we believe (1) that conscious states are parallel with active states of nerve fibres and cells, the nature of the association being unknown, or (2) that mental states and nervous states are the very same thing, or (3) whether we believe that there is a soul acting through a mere mechanism. I wish to insist that to hold any one of these beliefs does not one whit justify us in omitting anatomy. Betwixt our morphology of the nervous system and our psychology there must be anatomy and physiology. Morphology has to do with cells and fibres or with masses of them. Anatomy has to do with sensori-motor processes.

[. . .]

If we *acquire* ideas of the primary or statical qualities of bodies by movements – if, when we 'really' see an object, movement [of the eye required to bring the sentient parts of the retina successively into contact with light coming from different parts of the object, ed.] is essential – must there not be an element of movement represented in those anatomical substrata during excitation or discharge of which we see the object 'ideally'? For when we 'think' of the object which is absent ('recollect' it, 'are conscious' of it, etc.) we necessarily see it ideally of some shape, as well as of some colour. The inference is irresistible that there must be a motor, as well as a sensory, element in the nervous arrangement in the 'organ of mind' which is faintly discharged when we 'think of' an object. This notion is to many unfamiliar. It seems unlikely to be true, but apparently only because it is novel. 'What can *movement* have to do with *ideas*? One is a physical process, the other a mental process.' But, I repeat, that it is only said that movement enters as an element, not into ideas, but into the anatomical substrata of ideas. I merely wish to discuss the nature of nervous arrangements which all people admit to be in a state of activity when we have ideas. I do not know, nor as a physician do I care, how it is that the physiological process of nascent or strong molecular changes in a nervous arrangement representing movement, or representing anything, is attended by any kind of psychical state. Clearly, however, it does not seem to those who deny, or perhaps I should say ignore, the motor element (efferent nerves and centres) a strange supposition that we obtain ideas of objects from energizing of our sensory (afferent) nerves and centres. We may infer that those who say nothing of the motor element believe that the anatomico-physiological process, which goes on whilst we have ideas of shape and size, is a sensory process merely. But we will speak of colour only. What I wish to point out is, that it is just as impossible to tell why we have the mental state, colour, during energizing of certain sensory nerves and centres, as it is to tell why we have ideas of shape during energizing of motor nerves and centres. It does not, at first glance, *seem so* difficult, because the word 'sensation' is often used in two senses. It is applied both to a physical state and to the mental state that occurs along with that physical state (see Mill's *Logic*, vol. ii, p. 43).

John Hughlings Jackson, 'On the Anatomical and Physiological Localization of Movements in the Brain' (1873)

The End of Autonomous Thought

Burrhus Frederic Skinner (1904–90) was the leading exponent of behaviourism in his generation. He was born in Pennsylvania and educated at Harvard University, where he went on to become Edgar Pierce Professor of Psychology. Counter to popular belief, psychologists in universities during most of the twentieth century have not considered themselves to be investigating 'the mind', for the simple reason that they regarded it as nothing more than the sum of a person's observable responses to his or her environment. Skinner is famous for inventing a 'box' into which an experimental animal could be put, in order to investigate its behaviour under carefully controlled circumstances.

'Mentalism', the doctrine that there exist special determinants of behaviour that are immaterial, accessible to an individual only through introspection (see John Eccles*), was considered by Skinner to be a dirty word, smacking of airy-fairy nonsense. In order to be scientific and acquire real knowledge, psychology had to address itself to observable behaviour alone, which was determined by environmental factors. A related strand of philosophical argument was devoted to demonstrating that psychological concepts could be analysed in purely behavioural terms (see Gilbert Ryle*).

Perhaps the last stronghold of autonomous man is that complex 'cognitive' activity called thinking. Because it is complex, it has yielded only slowly to explanation in terms of the contingencies of reinforcement. When we say that a person *discriminates* between red and orange, we imply that discrimination is a kind of mental act. The person himself does not seem to be doing anything; he responds in different ways to red and orange stimuli, but this is the result of discrimination rather than the act. Similarly, we say that a person *generalizes* – say, from his own limited experience to the world at large – but all we see is that he responds to the world at large as he has learned to respond to his own small world. We say that a person *forms a concept or an abstraction*, but all we see is that certain kinds of contingencies of reinforcement have brought a response under the control of a single property of a stimulus. We say that a person *recalls* or *remembers* what he has seen or heard, but all we see is that the present occasion evokes a response, possibly in weakened or altered form, acquired on another occasion. We say that a person *associates* one word with another, but all we observe is that one verbal stimulus evokes the response previously made to another. Rather than suppose that it is therefore autonomous man who discriminates, generalizes, forms concepts or abstractions, recalls or remembers, and associates, we can put matters in good order simply by noting that these terms do not refer to forms of behaviour.

A person may take explicit action, however, when he solves a problem. In putting a jig-saw puzzle together he may move the pieces around to improve his chances of finding a fit. In solving an equation he may transpose, clear fractions and extract roots to improve his chances of finding a form of the equation he has already learned how to solve, the creative artist may manipulate a medium until something of interest turns up. Much of this can be done covertly, and is then likely to be assigned to a different dimensional system, but it can always be done overtly, perhaps more slowly but also often more effectively, and with rare exceptions it must have been learned in overt form. The culture promotes thinking by constructing special contingencies. It teaches a person to make fine discriminations by making differential reinforcement more precise. It teaches techniques to be used in solving problems. It provides rules which make it unnecessary to be exposed to the contingencies from which the rules are derived, and it provides rules for finding rules.

Self-control, or self-management, is a special kind of problem solving which, like self-knowledge, raises all the issues associated with privacy [. . .] It is always the environment which builds the behaviour with which problems are solved, even when the problems are to be found in the private world inside the skin. None of this has been investigated in a very productive way, but the inadequacy of our analysis is no reason to fall back on a miracle-working mind. If our understanding of contingencies of reinforcement is not yet sufficient to explain all kinds of thinking, we must remember that the appeal to mind explains nothing at all.

In shifting control from autonomous man to the observable environment we do not leave an empty organism. A great deal goes on inside the skin, and physiology will eventually tell us more about it. It will explain why behaviour is indeed related to the antecedent events of which it can be shown to be a function. [. . .]

Autonomous man is a device used to explain what we cannot explain in any other way. He has been constructed from our ignorance, and as our understanding increases, the very stuff of which he is composed vanishes. Science does not dehumanize him, it dehomunculizes him, and it must do so if it is to prevent the abolition of the human species. To man *qua* man we readily say good riddance. Only by dispossessing him can we turn to the real causes of human behaviour. Only then can we turn from the inferred to the observed, from the miraculous to the natural, from the inaccessible to the manipulable.

It is often said that in doing so we must treat the man who survives as a mere animal. 'Animal' is a pejorative term, but only because 'man' has been made spuriously honorific. Krutch[3] has argued that whereas the traditional view supports Hamlet's exclamation, 'How like a god!', Pavlov, the behavioural scientist, emphasized 'How like a dog!' But that was a step forward. A god is the archetypal pattern of an explanatory fiction, of a miracle-working mind, of the metaphysical. Man is much more than a dog, but like a dog he is within the range of scientific analysis.

B.F. Skinner., 'What Is Man', *Beyond Freedom and Dignity* (1971)

The Irrelevance of Passive Thought

Frustration with the unreliability of findings based on subjective introspection led John Broadus Watson (1878–1958) to suggest that psychology dispense with all reference to consciousness. The inaccessibility of private experience to observation and measurement meant that it was not a suitable subject for scientific investigation. Psychology, he averred, should concern itself with observable actions, it should dispense with all reference to

3 Joseph Wood Krutch, 'Epitaph for an Age', *New York Times Magazine*, 30 June 1967.

consciousness, and freely admit that mental states were not the subject of its observations. Its goal was to examine human and animal behaviour and develop principles whereby this could be predicted and controlled.

Watson's famous 1913 lecture, 'Psychology as the Behaviourist Views It', undermined the foundations of psychology as it then was and became known as the 'behaviourist manifesto'. By the mid 1930s, his ideas had become the dominant paradigm for academic and research work in the field. It is not surprising, however, that behaviourist thinking, with its reductive insistence that what could not be measured either did not exist or was not important, made less impression in the clinical sphere.

Watson was brought up in poverty in South Carolina. He was educated at Furman University where he obtained an MA degree, enabling him to go on to the University of Chicago in 1900 and study animal behaviour. At the age of thirty he was offered a Full Professorship and moved to Johns Hopkins University, Baltimore, where he remained for the following twelve years. In 1920, however, he was forced to resign as a result of divorce proceedings in which one of his graduate students, later to become his second wife, was named as correspondent. He never returned to academic psychology.

In the passage extracted below, Watson makes the case for regarding all types of thought as species of action.

One reason why experimentation in this field is backward is due to the fact that the thoughts of those around us sooner or later eventuate in explicit bodily action – no one except possibly a certain type of schizophrenic remains for any length of time 'sicklied o'er with the pale cast of thought'. Even the philosopher occasionally breaks his implicit word chains and favours us with a morsel in the form of a spoken or written word. There is in general no practical need or even scientific need for recording thought, since, in the first place most of it in mankind is worthless from the standpoint of society. It merely keeps the individual under tension (equal action in flexor and extensor muscles plus the emotional drama) without freeing any overt action system, or consists of one train of reverie after another, day-dreaming, castle-building and the like. Any consistent series of thought processes which is of any social interest will, if sufficiently well integrated with other bodily action systems, take issue finally in overt action.

To get thought to issue in overt action is not left always to the person thinking. We arrange special situations to hasten or even force the process along. The cleverness of the lawyer is gauged by his ability to twist the subject's overt words in such a way as to show contradictions in statements. The lawyer uses the contra-dictions to 'prove' to the judge that the individual's thought or intent was bad or good as the case may be. The psycho-pathologists, by word-association methods, analysis of dreams or constant conversation with the patient, create a situation by which the barriers to external action are broken down and thought becomes expressed in overt words or other acts. In this way conflicts in implicit organization may be noted. Society as a whole is under constant endeavour to get the individual to materialize his thoughts in overt speech or in deeds. The methods and technic for bringing about a transition from thought to overt action have hardly been touched by conventional psychology. This is in part due to the fact that the laboratory is largely divorced from life. A clever lawyer, a newspaper man, diplomat or adventuress knows a good deal more about predicting thought in others and in devising methods for getting an issuance of thought into action than do most psychologists.

Now and then it would be advantageous to be able to record thought as we record speech. The psychopathologist would find it very helpful at times to get into the patient's thought stream espe-cially in those cases where each implicit process ordinarily leading to overt action in a normal individual under a given situation, merely arouses in the patient another implicit process with a conflicting explicit motor outcome. The patient, hence, remains without action. Again, in legal work the jury and the judge would find the recording of implicit processes invaluable especially where the possible guilt of the defendant is based upon circumstantial evidence. There is no known direct method of detecting whether an individual is lying, notwithstanding the many plethysmographic and associational studies made upon that topic. From the romantic point of view the lover would, of course, always like to be able to read his mistress' thoughts. In all of these cases, though, continued observation of the thinker and the bringing to bear of data that can be noted usually provide stimuli sufficient for the observer of the thinker to guide his own conduct or for society to take action.[†]

Forms of Thought

1 **Logical.** – Society has specified down to the minutest details how the individual may use words. Our conjugations, declensions and laws of syntax are examples of this fact. In argumentative work, oral or written, there are also definite moulds just as conventionalized as are the cases and tenses of the words themselves. The various propositions and syllogisms of logic are examples. Whether the individual actually thinks in syllogistic forms or in accordance with the laws of syntax is extremely doubtful. Probably if he has been brought up in a family where careful diction and logical presentation are insisted upon from the start his thoughts will take the same orderly form. If, on the other hand, he is brought up as most children are, logical forms and nice grammatical construction will be put on in thought if at all only when his environment changes; for example, when he begins to go out in society, to debate or to begin his legal training. There is no more necessity for an individual to think in logical form than there is for him to shave, bathe and dress according to a rigidly specified routine.

2 **Little Thought Work Is of the Routine Type.** – In most manual activity that is well organized we rarely go through any preliminary movements of a preparatory kind. The moment we take off

[†] If the implicit processes could be recorded, the world would have to be made over. Women as a rule are 'mysterious' to the male sex, and banking upon this many are at pains to build up a background of mystery and capriciousness. It has been a wonderful cloak for lack of organization. On the other hand, it works in most cases and keeps the man in hand long enough while he is attempting to solve the enigma, for acquaintanceship to ripen and for other factors to exert their potency. If such processes could be recorded the 'hard to understand' woman would lose her prestige. The pompous individual who hides behind a studious and severe exterior would also have to find some other way to cover up his short-comings. Even those who are real thinkers would shrink from having exposed to an unkind world the prevalence in their thoughts of things banned by society and the frequency with which the trivial affairs connected with the day's work intrude.

our coats and take a billiard cue in our hands our acts are controlled in accordance with the movements of the ball. A similar thing is possible with laryngeal activity. The teacher used to speaking to his elementary classes rarely organizes anything he has to say in advance. The moment he steps upon the platform speech is mere progression comparable to swimming or any other bodily work (routine). On the other hand, when we have to do some work with our hands which we have not done before we must proceed in part at least by the trial and error process. A similar thing happens when we are performing new acts with the implicit laryngeal mechanism. Before the final word phrasing representing the completion of the adjustment occurs ('conclusion') devious useless word acts are executed. This is constructive work.

3 **Constructive Work.** – In order to understand work of the constructive type let us take two constrasting situations, the one in constructive manual work, the other in constructive laryngeal work. I start to build a bridle path to the top of a hill with no special instruments and never having built a road before. If the grade is too steep I build my road around the side of the hill, taking advantage of various level places to approach the top; where the stones are too large or cannot easily be dislodged I build the road around them, finally coming out at the top. The process of constructing such a path requires manual labour almost wholly. It is a type of task that the most uneducated ditch digger can perform. Nevertheless, it is constructive work in the sense that a passable road is built which did not exist before. In the process, though, parts of many previously organized habit systems have been used momentarily in slightly new connections. Just so in simple thought work, for example, in a new and extremely simple proposition in geometry: it may be only the working out of a corollary or the production of a verse or a limerick. There is a similar trial and error use of the laryngeal organization until the adjustment is finally reached. The individual, of course, depends upon his past organization, but a new product is the outcome of his work. We can greatly complicate the complexity of our problem in manual labor, making it the construction of a new type of submarine. The amount of excess work done (actual manual work) and the number of false steps taken can be gathered

from the heap of discarded models which litters up the work-shop. Likewise, we can complicate our example of thought work. The number of false starts made, wrong tentative conclusions reached in working up a new system of philosophy or chemical theory cannot be directly observed by the beholder as in the case of the submarine invention, but it can be gathered from the length of time it takes the individual to finally put his thought conclusions into final form (issuance of thought into overt action).

4 Play and Emotional Forms of Thought Activity. – Under the influence of certain emotional states overt activity takes certain forms – whistling, dancing, singing, the playing of games and, best for present illustrative purposes, improvising on some musical instrument. In the latter example the performer is not under the sway of any particular, definite habit, that is, he is not playing any score ever played before. His fingers wander, as we say, idly over the keys. But his equipment and organization show at every moment and new combinations (a new product) are hit upon just as a new stroke is hit upon in tennis. A condition wholly analogous to this is found in thought in reverie. This is a form of play with the vocal equipment as improvised solo dancing is a form of play of the hand, arm, leg and trunk equipment. Solo dancing is not wholly manual play nor is reverie wholly verbal play. In contrasting these various types of thought activity with manual activity we have overemphasized the separation and distinction of the two. We can only insist once more that the separation is made for purely illustrative reasons.

John B. Watson, *Psychology from the Standpoint of a Behaviourist* (1919)

THE EXPERIENCE OF THINKING

Pure Thinking[4]

Hartley, looking out of my window, fixed his eyes steadily and for some time on the opposite prospect and said, 'Will yon mountains *always* be there?' I showed him the whole magnificent prospect in the looking-glass, and held it up, so that the whole was like a canopy or ceiling over his head, and he struggled to express himself concerning the difference between the thing and the image almost with convulsive effort. I never before saw such an abstract of *thinking* as a pure act of energy – of thinking as distinguished from thought.

Samuel Taylor Coleridge, *Notebooks* (17 March 1801)

The Falsification of Our Experience of Thinking

In a discussion of the significance of music, Anthony Storr draws attention to the way in which our conscious thoughts fail to correspond with what we know to be true. Music is inextricably associated with a sense of continuous movement, yet it consists of nothing but a sequence of notes. Our minds transpose what we hear, which is extended in time, into a spacial analogue. As Dr Storr puts it: 'Consciousness inevitably converts the diachronic into the synchronic'. Our experience of thinking is similarly transformed.

Anthony Storr (1920–2001) was born in London, son of the sub-dean of Westminster Abbey; he was the youngest of four children by ten years. Brought up in the seclusion of the Dean's Yard, he was a solitary child who found it difficult to socialize when sent away to boarding school at the age of eight. He went on to Winchester College, where he was bullied and miserable, and developed a passion for music which gave him solace.

In 1939 he attended Christ's College, Cambridge, where his moral tutor, C.P. Snow, encouraged him to study medicine with

a view to entering psychiatry. He qualified as a doctor in 1944
and during the course of a distinguished career as writer and
psychiatrist became a Fellow of the Royal College of Physicians,
Royal College of Psychiatrists and Royal Society of Literature,
and Emeritus Fellow of Green College, Oxford.

Our perception of a melody as something continuous is an illusion; but so is the stream of consciousness of which music is said
to be an analogue. The inner clocks of the body inform us when
it is time to eat, time to sleep, and so on, thus providing us with
a subliminal, intermittent awareness of time's passage: the inner
flow of life referred to earlier. Momentary discomforts make us
aware of digestive and excretory processes which for the most
part proceed without conscious awareness. But, just as consciousness of bodily processes is intermittent, so is consciousness of
mental processes. This is so clearly the case that I am not sure
whether it is legitimate to speak of being aware of a mental
process.

Although we may describe what goes on in our own minds as
continuous, the 'stream of consciousness', we cannot actually
perceive this. It is more like a stream of unconsciousness, with
elements we call conscious floating like occasional twigs on the
surface of the stream. When something occurs to us, a new
thought, a linking of perceptions, an idea, we take pains to isolate
it, to make it actual by putting it into words, writing it down,
stopping the 'flow' of mental activity for the time being as we
might reach out and grab one of the twigs floating past.

We like to describe the processes of thought as continuous,
as a 'train of thought' inexorably proceeding by logical steps to
a new conclusion. Yet what many thinkers describe is more like
floundering about in a slough of perplexity, a jumble of incoherence, relieved by occasional flashes of illumination when a
new pattern suddenly emerges. Ordered, coherent progression
of thought is a retrospective falsification of what actually
happens.

The interesting question is why we have this incorrigible
compulsion to order thoughts sequentially and retrospectively.

Our thoughts go to Birmingham by way of Beachy Head; but we feel compelled to look back on the journey as if it had been a simple, uninterrupted trip from London along the M40 motorway.

I believe that we have to falsify our experience of thinking if we are to chronicle our thoughts and remember them. We are compelled to make coherent patterns out of our mental processes if we are to retain them in consciousness. Chaos cannot be accurately recalled. Meaningful sentences are more easily recalled than nonsense syllables; and music, the great promoter of order, makes words and sentences still more easily remembered.

This creation of coherent patterns need not be the consequence of conscious deliberation. It is a mental activity which is proceeding in all of us with little intermission. We link things together, combine opposites, create new wholes out of data which were previously unconnected. J.G. Herder, the eighteenth-century philosopher whose observations on songs as repositories of tribal history were quoted earlier, is equally perceptive in this context.

That the creation of integrated wholes out of discrete data is the fundamental organizing activity of human nature, is a belief that is central to Herder's entire social and moral outlook; for him all creative activity, conscious and unconscious, generates, and is, in turn, determined by, its own unique *Gestalt*, whereby every individual and group strives to perceive, understand, act, create, live.[5]

What is it about human nature which compels this preoccupation with creating integrated wholes?

Anthony Storr, 'The Significance of Music', *Music and the Mind* (1992)

Do I Decide to Act?

Bernhard Schlink (1944–) is a professor of law at the University of Berlin and a novelist. In this passage he considers the relationship between thought and behaviour.

5 Isaiah Berlin, *Vico and Herder*, Hogarth Press, 1976, p. 216, p. 175 (note 1).

I think, I reach a conclusion, I turn the conclusion into a decision, and then I discover that acting on the decision is something else entirely, and that doing so may proceed from the decision, but then again it may not. Often enough in my life I have done things I had not decided to do. Something – whatever that may be – goes into action; 'it' goes to the woman I don't want to see any more, 'it' keeps on smoking although I have decided to give up, and then gives up smoking just when I've accepted the fact that I'm a smoker and always will be. I don't mean to say that thinking and reaching decisions have no influence on behaviour. But behaviour does not merely enact whatever has already been thought through and decided. It has its own sources, and is my behaviour, quite independently, just as my thoughts are my thoughts, and my decisions my decisions.

Bernhard Schlink, *The Reader* (1997)

Cogito Ergo Sum

Descartes[6] predicates our existence on thought. There is nothing else of which we can be sure. This, however, does not lead him to deny the reality of the external world. On the contrary, it leads him to seek some other way of assuring it. In fact, Descartes does discover what for him is another certainty – the existence of God. Once God exists outside ourselves, we are no longer dependent on our own transitory experience to guarantee the existence of the world.

Descartes was the third child born into a family of French landed gentry, whose ancestral estates lay in the Loire valley. His father was a lawyer. He was educated at a local Jesuit College in La Flèche, his birthplace, where he remained until the age of sixteen. As a young man he moved to Paris and trained in the law. Later, in order to 'see the world', he joined the army of Prince Maurice of Nassau in Holland. At the age of thirty-three he settled in that country in order to pursue his philosophical and mathematical work.

6 For a further note on Descartes see pp. 244–5.

I had long before remarked that, in relation to practice, it is sometimes necessary to adopt, as if above doubt, opinions which we discern to be highly uncertain, as has been already said; but as I then desired to give my attention solely to the search after truth, I thought that a procedure exactly the opposite was called for, and that I thought to reject as absolutely false all opinions in regard to which I could suppose the least ground for doubt, in order to ascertain whether after that there remained aught in my belief that was wholly indubitable. Accordingly, seeing that our senses sometimes deceive us, I was willing to suppose that there existed nothing really such as they presented to us; and because some men err in reasoning, and fall into paralogisms, even on the simplest matters of Geometry, I, convinced that I was as open to error as any other, rejected as false all the reasonings I had hitherto taken for demonstrations; and finally, when I considered that the very same thoughts (presentations) which we experience when awake may also be experienced when we are asleep, while there is at that time not one of them true, I supposed that all the objects (presentations) that had ever entered into my mind when awake, had in them no more truth than the illusions of my dreams. But immediately upon this I observed that, whilst I thus wished to think that all was false, it was absolutely necessary that I, who thus thought, should be somewhat; and as I observed that this truth, *I think, hence I am*, was so certain and of such evidence, that no ground of doubt, however extravagant, could be alleged by the Sceptics capable of shaking it, I concluded that I might, without scruple, accept it as the first principle of the Philosophy of which I was in search.

René Descartes, *Discourse on Method* (1637)

Nowhere Thoughts

It might be supposed that an empiricist view of mental contents would be linked with a materialist conception of the mind. If ideas derive exclusively from experience, from the registration of sensations stimulated by substantive objects (rather than any innately given structure), then the ideas themselves might be *thought of as somehow substantial. The Scottish philosopher, David Hume* (1711–76), however, shows that this is emphatically not the case. Although all our knowledge derives from experience, Hume argues, we have no direct access to its roots, we only know how things seem, not how they are. If this is so, if the link between the external world and our internal conception of it is uncertain, then all our attempts at investigation may tell us more about ourselves, more about the way our minds work than about the outside world. And our 'selves', Hume famously regarded as no more than 'a bundle of sensations'. Hume distinguished two types of effect left in the mind by experience – impressions and ideas, which roughly coincided with the difference between feeling and thinking. The former, including sensations, passions and emotions, were forcefully, vitally and immediately imprinted in the mind, whereas the latter were but pale images used in the process of thinking and reasoning. There were times, Hume said, when we found it difficult to distinguish one from the other – in sleep, fever or madness, and might mistake an idea of something for its original impression, but generally speaking we knew the difference well. Hume could not doubt the presence of these mental entities, yet he was equally sure that none of them could be located in space. Hence the conclusion that an object can exist and yet be nowhere (see Gilbert Ryle's example of a category error).*

There is one argument commonly employed for the immateriality of the soul, which seems to me remarkable. Whatever is extended [exists in space, ed.] consists of parts; and whatever consists of parts is divisible, if not in reality, at least in the imagination. But it is impossible anything divisible can be *conjoined* to a thought or perception, which is a being altogether inseparable and indivisible. For, supposing such a conjunction, would the indivisible thought exist on the left or on the right hand of this extended divisible body? On the surface or in the middle? On the back or foreside of it? If it be conjoined with the extension, it must exist somewhere within its dimensions. If it exist within its dimensions, it must either exist in one particular part;

and then that particular part is indivisible, and the perception is conjoined only with it, not with the extension: or if the thought exists in every part, it must also be extended, and separable, and divisible, as well as the body, which is utterly absurd and contradictory. For can anyone conceive a passion of a yard in length, a foot in breadth, and an inch in thickness? Thought therefore and extension are qualities wholly incompatible, and never can incorporate together into one subject.

This argument affects not the question concerning the *substance* of the soul, but only that concerning its *local conjunction* with matter; and therefore it may not be improper to consider in general what objects are, or are not susceptible of a local conjunction. This is a curious question, and may lead us to some discoveries of considerable moment.

The first notion of space and extension is derived solely from the senses of sight and feeling; nor is there anything, but what is coloured or tangible, that has parts disposed after such a manner as to convey that idea. When we diminish or increase a relish, it is not after the same manner that we diminish or increase any visible object; and when several sounds strike our hearing at once, custom and reflection alone make us form an idea of the degrees of the distance and contiguity of those bodies from which they are derived. Whatever marks the place of its existence, either must be extended, or must be a mathematical point, without parts or composition. What is extended must have a particular figure, as square, round, triangular; none of which will agree to a desire, or indeed to any impression or idea, except of these two senses above mentioned. Neither ought a desire, though indivisible, to be considered as a mathematical point. For in that case it would be possible, by the addition of others, to make two, three, four desires; and these disposed and situated in such a manner as to have a determinate length, breadth and thickness; which is evidently absurd.

It will not be surprising after this if I deliver a maxim, which is condemned by several metaphysicians, and is esteemed contrary to the most certain principles of human reason. This maxim is, *that an object may exist, and yet be nowhere*; and I assert that this is not only possible, but that the greatest part of beings do and must exist after this manner. An object may be said to be nowhere, when its parts are not so situated with respect to each other, as to form any figure or quantity; nor the whole with respect to other bodies so as to answer to our notions of contiguity or distance. Now this is evidently the case with all our perceptions and objects, except those of the sight and feeling. A moral reflection cannot be placed on the right or on the left hand of a passion; nor can a smell or sound be either of a circular or a square figure. These objects and perceptions, so far from requiring any particular place, are absolutely incompatible with it, and even the imagination cannot attribute it to them. And as to the absurdity of supposing them to be nowhere, we may consider that if the passions and sentiments appear to the perception to have any particular place, the idea of extension might be derived from them as well as from the sight and touch; contrary to what we have already established. If they *appear* not to have any particular place, they may possibly *exist* in the same manner; since whatever we conceive is possible.

David Hume, 'On the Immateriality of the Soul' (1739)

All in the Mind

George Berkeley (1685–1753), considered it a 'vulgar error' to suppose that anything other than thoughts existed. Since knowledge was immaterial, it seemed obvious that it could not be relied on to guarantee the existence of anything other than itself. The philosophico-scientific problem concerning the material world, still unresolved, is the question of how matter could possibly give rise to mind. Locke's* answer, that certain 'primary' qualities such as shape and solidity were inherent in external objects, but that others such as colours and tastes were not, seemed incoherent. Berkeley did not deny the 'reality' of objects such as houses or mountains, only their 'externality'. However, if such objects are to be deemed interior (and only seemingly exterior), one might ask why, under normal non-hallucinatory circumstances, they take so much effort to construct? Berkeley was born in Kilkenny, Ireland, of English parents. He was educated at Trinity College,

Dublin, and became Bishop of Cloyne in 1734. In the following passage, presented as a 'Platonic' dialogue between Hylas and Philonus, Berkeley proves his point.

Phil. But (to pass by all that hath been hitherto said, and reckon it for nothing, if you will have it so) I am content to put the whole on this issue. If you can conceive it possible for any mixture or combination of qualities, or any sensible object whatever, to exist without the mind, then I will grant it actually to be so.

Hyl. If it comes to that, the point will soon be decided. What more easy than to conceive a tree or house existing by itself, independent of, and unperceived by any mind whatsoever? I do at this present time conceive them existing after that manner.

Phil. How say you, Hylas, can you see a thing which is at the same time unseen?

Hyl. No, that were a contradiction.

Phil. Is it not a contradiction to talk of *conceiving* a thing which is *unconceived*?

Hyl. It is.

Phil. The tree or house therefore which you think of, is conceived by you.

Hyl. How should it be otherwise?

Phil. And what is conceived is surely in the mind.

Hyl. Without question, that which is conceived is in the mind.

Phil. How then came you to say, you conceived a house or tree existing independent and out of all minds whatsoever?

Hyl. That was, I own, an oversight; but stay, let me consider what led me into it – it is a pleasant mistake enough. As I was thinking of a tree in a solitary place, where no one was present to see it, methought that was to conceive a tree as existing unperceived or unthought of, not considering that I myself conceived it all the while. But now I plainly see, that all I can do is to frame ideas in my own mind. I may indeed conceive in my own thoughts the idea of a tree, or a house, or a mountain, but that is all. And this is far from proving, that I conceive them *existing out of the minds of all spirits*.

Phil. You acknowledge then that you cannot possibly conceive how
        any one corporeal sensible thing should exist otherwise than
        in a mind.
Hyl. I do.

George Berkeley, 'First Dialogue Between Hylas and Philonus' (1713)

How to Drive Yourself Mad – The Danger of Abstract Speculation

*Count Lev Nikolaevich Tolstoy (1828–1910) is numbered with
the greatest of Russian writers. He was born in Yasnya Polyana,
and published the first volume of an autobiographical trilogy*
Childhood *at the age of twenty-four. The following passage is
extracted from the second volume,* Boyhood, *which appeared two
years later. Tolstoy is perhaps most famous for his novels* War
and Peace *and* Anna Karenina. *His opposition to institutionalized authority, both church and state, led to the censorship of
his books and to excommunication by the Orthodox Church in
1901.*

But not one of these philosophical theories held me so much
as scepticism, which at one time brought me to the verge of
insanity. I fancied that besides myself nobody and nothing
existed in the universe, that objects were not real at all but
images which appeared when I directed my attention to them,
and that so soon as I stopped thinking of them these images
immediately vanished. In short, I came to the same conclusion
as Schelling, that objects do not exist but only my relation to
them exists. There were moments when I became so deranged
by this *idée fixe* that I would glance sharply round in some
opposite direction, hoping to catch unawares the void (the
néant) where I was not.

What a pitiful trivial spring of moral activity is the mind of
man!

My feeble intellect could not penetrate the impenetrable, and in
that back-breaking effort lost one after the other the convictions

which, for my life's happiness, I ought never to have dared disturb.

All this weary mental struggle yielded me nothing save an artful elasticity of mind which weakened my will-power, and a habit of perpetually dissecting and analysing, which destroyed spontaneity of feeling and clarity of reason.

Abstract speculations are generated in consequence of man's capacity by intuition to apprehend the state of his soul at a given moment, and transfer that apprehension to his memory. My fondness for abstract reasoning developed my conscious being to such an unnatural degree that frequently, thinking about the simplest things, I would fall into the vicious circle of analysis of my thoughts, entirely losing sight of the question that had occupied my mind at the outset, and thinking, instead, about what I was thinking about. Asking myself: 'Of what am I thinking?' I would answer: 'I think of what I am thinking. And now what am I thinking of? I think that I am thinking of what I am thinking of.' And so on. I was at my wits' end.

Leo Tolstoy, *Boyhood* (1854)

Mental Processes Are Queer

Ludwig Wittgenstein (1889–1951) was born in Vienna. He studied engineering before turning to philosophy which he read at Cambridge University in 1912, under the aegis of Bertrand Russell. He returned to Trinity College in 1929, later becoming Professor of Philosophy from 1939 to 1947. His fascination with the way in which language was related to both inner and outer reality, the nature of meaning, profoundly influenced the development of his subject in the English-speaking world. During his lifetime the only book to appear was the Tractatus Logico-Philosophicus, *in 1921. Many other writings were posthumously published.*

359. Could a machine think? – Could it be in pain? – Well, is the human body to be called such a machine? It surely comes as close as possible to being such a machine.

360. But a machine surely cannot think! – Is that an empirical statement? No. We only say of a human being and what is like one that it thinks. We also say it of dolls and no doubt of spirits too. Look at the word 'to think' as a tool.

361. The chair is thinking to itself: . . .

WHERE? In one of its parts? Or outside its body; in the air around it? Or not *anywhere* at all? But then what is the difference between this chair's saying something to itself and another one's doing so next to it? – But then how is it with man: where does *he* say things to himself? How does it come about that this question seems senseless; and that no specification of a place is necessary except just that this man is saying something to himself? Whereas the question *where* the chair talks to itself seems to demand an answer. – The reason is: we want to know *how* the chair is supposed to be like a human being; whether, for instance, the head is at the top of the back and so on.

What is it like to say something to oneself; what happens here? – How am I to explain it? Well, only as you might teach someone the meaning of the expression 'to say something to oneself'. And certainly we learn the meaning of that as children. – Only no one is going to say that the person who teaches it to us tells us 'what takes place'.

362. Rather it seems to us as though in this case the instructor *imparted* the meaning to the pupil – without telling him it directly; but in the end the pupil is brought to the point of giving himself the correct ostensive definition. And this is where our illusion is.

363. 'But when I imagine something, something certainly *happens*!' Well, something happens – and then I make a noise. What for? Presumably in order to tell what happens. – But how is *telling* done? When are we said to *tell* anything? – What is the language-game of telling?

I should like to say: you regard it much too much as a matter of course that one can tell anything to anyone. That is to say: we are so much accustomed to communication through language, in conversation, that it looks to us as if the whole point of communication lay in this: someone else grasps the sense of my words – which is something mental: he as it were takes it into his own mind. If he then does something further with it as well, that is no part of the immediate purpose of language.

One would like to say 'Telling brings it about that he *knows* that I am in pain; it produces this mental phenomenon; everything else is inessential to the telling.' As for what this queer phenomenon of knowledge is – there is time enough for that. Mental processes just are queer. (It is as if one said: 'The clock tells us the time. *What* time is, is not yet settled. And as for what one tells the time *for* – that doesn't come in here.')

Ludwig Wittgenstein, *Philosophical Investigations* (1945)

Mr Punch Is a Phallic Symbol

Ernest Jones (1879–1958) was the first born and only son of a colliery manager working in the Gower Peninsula of South Wales. He was educated at Swansea Grammar School and Llandovery College (where he claimed to have learnt the depths of cruelty and obscenity to which human beings can descend). He studied medicine at the University Colleges of South Wales and London, qualifying as a doctor at the age of twenty-one. His interest in the newly emerging field of psycho-analysis led him to participate in the organisation of the first Psycho-Analytical Congress, in Salzburg in 1908, during which he met Sigmund Freud* and Carl Gustav Jung*. Jones subsequently played a major part in the psycho-analytic movement, becoming President of the International Psycho-Analytical Association, Honorary President of the British Psycho-Analytical Society and Founder of the International Journal of Psycho-Analysis. He published numerous papers and books, and became Freud's biographer.

'True Symbolism', Jones suggested, was a primitive process whereby emotions associated with one idea, and incapable of being channelled (sublimated) into socially acceptable form, were unconsciously invested in another, apparently irrelevant idea. Jones believed that only a small number of fundamental ideas were symbolized in this way: the self, including body parts, immediate relatives, and the phenomena of birth, love and death. The

psychological function of such symbolism was not to enhance communication and heighten appreciation, but to limit and attenuate unruly emotion. Symbolization was therefore a mode of self-deception.

The conception of the male organ as a 'little man' is extremely widespread, and, by the process known to mythologists as 'decomposition', it often becomes personified and incorporated in an independent figure. A large number of dwarfs, gnomes, and goblins so common in folk-lore and legend are of this nature, their characteristic attributes being that they are deformed, ugly caricatures of men, wicked and even malign – yet sometimes willing to be friendly and to yield services under certain conditions, able to perform wonderful and magical feats, and winning their own way in spite of their obvious disadvantages. Sand's description of Punchinello is in these respects typical: *'Il a le coeur aussi sec que son bâton, c'est un egoiste dans tout l'acception du mot. Sous une apparente belle humeur, c'est un être feroce; il fait le mal pour le plaisir de la faire. Se souciant de la vie d'un homme comme de celle d'une puce, il aime et cherche des querelles . . . Il ne craint ni Dieu ni diable, lui qui a vu passer, sous son nez crochu et verruqueux, tant de société et de religions . . .* (speaking of his passion for women) *malgré ses bosses et sa figure peu faite seduire, il est si caustique, si persuasif, si entreprenant et si insolent, qu'il a des success.'* Nodier fittingly apostrophises him, *'O Polichinelle, simulacre anime de l'homme naturel abandonné a ses instincts.'* His physical characteristics well accord with this interpretation: the long hooked nose, long chin, projecting hump on his back, prominent stomach, and pointed cap.

Punchinello seems first to have made his appearance in England with the Restoration, but his history and that of similar figures is a world-wide one. In England he quickly became assimilated with, and took some of his features from, the English clown and Jack Pudding, just as in Germany he fused with Hanswurst. In eastern countries he is met with as Karagheus. The prototype of all modern polichinellos is the Neopolitan *polecenella*, who cannot be traced farther back than the Renaissance. It is highly probable, however, that he is a lineal descendant of the Maccus of the Roman atellanes (introduced in the sixth century), for the statue of Maccus in the Capponi Museum at Rome (found in 1727, but dating from Roman times) shows the closest resemblance to the modern figure.

The attribute of comicality attaching to such figures is of considerable interest in more than one direction. The idea of the male organ as a comic manikin, a 'funny little man', is a very common one, and is much more natural to women than to men. The source and meaning of this alone constitutes a problem which cannot be dealt with here, since it would lead us too far away into the nature of the comic in general. The idea itself is a subsection of phallic symbolism, concerning which the reader may be reminded of the following points: There are two broad classes of such symbols, the patriarchal symbols of the eagle, bull, etc., representing the father's power and rights, and the matriarchal symbols representing the revolutionary son. The latter are again divided into two sub-groups: those, such as the devil, the cock, the serpent, etc., which are tabooed and interdicted, and those, such as the goat, the ape, and the ass (the animal sacred to the worship of Priapus, with which the figure of Punchinello is constantly brought into association), which are condemned as ridiculous and comic.

I might add that there is a slight trace of the original revolutionary meaning of the matriarchal phallic symbol left in the pose of such comic figures – the most striking example of which was the medieval court jester – as critics who lash the conventions of society. There is a hint of this point in one of Bernard Shaw's prefaces; it runs: 'Every despot must have one disloyal subject to keep him sane . . . Democracy has now handed the sceptre of the despot to the sovereign people; but they, too, must have their confessor, whom they call Critic. Criticism is not only medicinally salutary: it has positive popular attractions in its cruelty, its gladiatorship, and the gratification given to envy by its attacks on the great, and to enthusiasm by its praises. It may say things which many would like to say, but dare not . . . Its iconoclasms, seditions, and blasphemies, if well turned, tickle those whom they shock; so that the Critic adds the privileges of the court jester to those of the confessor. Garrick, had he called Dr. Johnson Punch, would have spoken profoundly and wittily; whereas Dr. Johnson, in hurling that epithet at him, was but picking up the cheapest sneer an actor is subject to.'

Ernest Jones, *The Theory of Symbolism* (1916)

Unexpressed Thoughts

Jenny Teichman is a philosopher, elected to a College Fellowship at New Hall, Cambridge in 1968. She argues (counter to Gilbert Ryle, see p. 246) that mere descriptions of behaviour can never entail propositions about states of mind. If some thoughts are necessarily silent, unaccompanied by any outward manifestation, this is enough to discredit behaviourism.

What is essential to thought is not silence: however, the *possibility* of silence is enough to make a behaviourist reduction impossible. It is not essential to thinking that it should always in itself be silent but it is essential to the overall notion of thought that some thoughts are not expressed. In this *thinking* differs from *reading*.

It will probably be agreed that the idea of an unexpressed thought is not a contradiction in terms. Then is an unexpressed thought somehow unreal, like the novel I have not yet written? Obviously not. It is doubtful, perhaps, whether I ever could write that novel, and until I do, the novel, of course, does not exist, it really is unreal; but an unexpressed thought is not non-existent.

Everyone does have unexpressed thoughts. If people had to learn to stay silent about their thoughts, as they (perhaps) have to learn to read silently after learning to read aloud, the fact that everyone has unexpressed thoughts would be a sheer accident. But surely it is not a sheer accident. For first, if someone really did express every single thought he had, it would not be right to call him a man who had simply failed to acquire a certain skill, that of thinking silently. And second, it is not possible anyway for a person to express or describe every single thought and every single emotion and every single sensation that he has. At any one moment one may have 'passing through one's head' (as we say) many thoughts and feelings, so shortage of time prevents total expression. But third, shortage of time is not the only reason why it is impossible to express all one's thoughts and feelings. Many feeling-states are indescribable, or are again such that nothing hangs on how they are described. There isn't here a sharp boundary-line between having a thought and having a feeling, so that one can speak not only of vague feelings but also of vague thoughts. Finally, words and sentences can be numbered, for every linguistically competent person knows what counts as one word, what counts as one phrase, what counts as one sentence, etc., but there are no rules which tell us what counts as one thought, what counts as two thoughts, etc., nor could there be.

That there are and have to be such things as unexpressed thoughts is part of the concept of *thought*. This is *prima facie* consistent with dispositional accounts of the mind, but not with any form of behaviourism which insists that the 'cashings' of dispositions must be overt or in principle observable.

Jenny Teichman, *The Mind and the Soul* (1974)

5

CONSCIOUSNESS

Examine for a moment an ordinary mind on an ordinary day. The mind receives a myriad impressions – trivial, fantastic, evanescent, or engraved with the sharpness of steel. From all sides they come, an incessant shower of innumerable atoms; as they fall, as they shape themselves into the life of Monday or Tuesday, the accent falls differently from of old; the moment of importance came not here but there; so that, if a writer were a free man and not a slave, if he could write what he chose, not what he must, if he could base his work upon his own feeling and not upon convention, there would be no plot, no comedy, no tragedy, no love interest or catastrophe in the accepted style, and perhaps not a single button sewn on as the Bond Street tailors would have it. Life is not a series of gig lamps symmetrically arranged; life is a luminous halo, a semi-transparent envelope surrounding us from the beginning of consciousness to the end . . .

Virginia Woolf, 'Modern Fiction' (*1919*)

We apprehend ourselves in two distinct ways, through subjective experience which seems ethereal and as objects in the physical world, bodies consisting of cells, tissues and organs, space-occupying material. Just how these two modes of being can exist simultaneously, and in what way they are related to one another, is the mysterious mind–body problem which will not go away.

Much effort on the part of philosophers and psychologists has gone into this problem, usually directed towards showing that the two states – physical and mental – are only seemingly different. Clearly, if these two states could be satisfactorily 'reduced' to one, then the problem of their interaction across an apparently unbridgeable chasm would be solved. But attempts to effect a successful reduction have almost always foundered on the rock of reality – the reality of the difference between mind and matter, between experiential and non-experiential qualities.

What philosphers call 'eliminative idealism' seeks to comprehend the world and everything in it as essentially mental. On this view, what we normally take for granted – the physical existence of objects – is regarded as a kind of illusion. Things such as mountains and lakes, tables and chairs, animals and people, are not material substances existing in a world external to our own minds. They are simply ideas or sensations. They exist only in the eye of the beholder and depend for their continued existence on being beheld, if not by one individual then by another or by some eternal spirit which sustains them. A very brief summary of the argument of its most famous exponent, Bishop Berkeley, was presented in the previous chapter on 'Thought'. The passage extracted from Lev Tolstoy's *Boyhood*, describing the effect of embracing such a sceptical philosophy, should act as a kind of authorial 'health warning'.

Idealism is a difficult position to sustain but the reductions proposed by behaviourists and materialists are just as problematic. By the end of the nineteenth century, introspection, the descriptive method most suited to plumbing the depths of subjective experience and favoured by the romantics, had acquired a bad name. It was frustratingly individual, tantalizingly unreliable, and did not yield the kind of generalizations that science required. The parlous state of the mind's would-be scientific explorers prompted some to devise an ingenious rescue – the abolition of the object of their interest! If the mind so stubbornly resisted being known, could it be that investigators were barking up the wrong tree, perhaps the problem had been wrongly conceptualized? There was, said the 'behavioural psychologists' of yesteryear such as John Broadus Watson and B.F. Skinner, either no accessible mind or no conscious mind. There was, according to the Oxford philosopher Gilbert Ryle, no 'Ghost in the Machine' somehow separate from yet able to direct the works of our body, only the sum total of our 'dispositions' to carry out certain procedures.

An even more radical 'reduction' of the notion of consciousness, 'eliminative materialism', current among some modern philosophers, holds that mental terms are just a mistaken way of talking about things that will ultimately be completely and satisfactorily described in the language of material science. If there is no mind, there is nothing for psychology to know. Nothing, that is to say, save the possibly erroneous way things seem to us to be, the observable actions we carry out and, in the case of humans, the vicissitudes of neurological (carbon-based) material. And if there was and is no mind, then of course there can be no mind–body problem. It follows that what we call consciousness is not necessarily limited to our own species or even to living organisms. Computers and robots, after all, are disposed to carry out all sorts of actions, so on the materialist view artificial (silicon-based) intelligence and consciousness are, in principle, no more or less problematic than our own.

Mind might itself now be in danger of disappearing, held hostage to its own logic, in rather the same way that natural science eclipsed the divine spirit of previous centuries. But there is an important difference. Whereas the notion of 'spirit' refers to something which informs our experience, and leaves open the possibility that something else, some other material factor, might be held to do the same job, mind denotes nothing other than our experience. The difficulty, of course, which materialists face in seeking to scupper our traditional notion of consciousness, lies in the need to deny the reality of something that is defined precisely in terms of the way that it appears. It seems pointless to assert that consciousness is a mere 'appearance' when nothing more is being claimed. Nobody would be impressed by the claim that characters in a movie were not real, that they merely consisted of flickering images generated by shining light through celluloid. Consciousness simply *is* the way things seem. And if the puzzling data of consciousness, the gaps and paradoxes of our thought processes, lead us to infer the existence of unconscious mental activity as well, then that too is part of the way we experience ourselves, an expanded conception of mind. Much of the contents of this book concern different aspects of experience – thoughts, feelings, dreams, memories, phantasies, etc. These things happen and we are not easily persuaded that their subjective reality can be ignored.

What philosophers of mind call 'monism' – the doctrine that there is only one kind of stuff in the world which is either all physical or all mental, is therefore problematic. Part of the appeal of early Eastern philosophy, for example the Hindu Upanishads, is its apparent resolution of this problem by invoking some kind of deep underlying 'oneness' which is neither physical nor mental. Yet even in the example cited here from the Mandukya Upanishad we see a division of the self into 'four quarters' or 'states', a distinction drawn between consciousness of what is within and what is without.

What of the alternatives? Suppose thoughts to be substantially different from material or embodied things. Does the doctrine of 'dualism', most famously propounded by the seventeenth-century French philosopher and mathematician, René Descartes, fare any better? Descartes' dualism, which asserted that mind and matter were essentially different in constitution, different kinds of stuff existing in independent spheres of reality, immediately highlighted the problem of their inter-relatedness. How was it that immaterial thoughts and intentions, existing in some nowhere-land, could operate on material bodily organs to produce actions and movements in the external world? And conversely, how, for example, could mortification of the flesh produce the subjective and immaterial sensation of pain? As his interested and intelligent correspondent, Princess Elizabeth of Bohemia, remarked in a letter dated 21 May 1643, 'I must admit that it would be easier for me to attribute matter and extension to the soul, than to attribute to an immaterial being the capacity to move and be moved by a body.' Descartes had no convincing answer. His well-known view to the effect that mind–body interaction occurred in the pineal gland, merely provided the process with a local habitation. It did nothing to answer the question, how? It really got no further than traditional biblical psychology, which not only distinguished between mind and body but more often than not held them to be at war with one another.[1] Divine spirit was commonly understood to be opposed to the human body, with 'soul' somehow mediating between the two. If the authority of scripture was the only basis for believing this, Descartes' reasoned meditations produced precious little more. Religious faith leaps over the hurdles that reason erects, 'knows' things that reason doubts, reconciles us to the mysteries of the mind by defining its explanatory principles in supernatural terms. For those who find its categories meaningless or mistaken, Descartes' dualism offers no intellectual repose.

But there is another kind of dualism which does provide a potential resolution to the difficulty, albeit one based on the acceptance of ignorance. When we consider the difference between physical causality and mental intention we can acknowledge that we have two different and apparently irreconcilable stories. We can agree that each is logically distinct from and incapable of being 'reduced' to the other. Yet they may both be aspects or properties of the same basic substance. We have no problem in understanding that a single thing may be apprehended in multiple ways, that an electric current running through a wire can be seen as bright, felt as hot, and can generate a magnetic field. Hence our sense of consciousness (and unconsciousness), despite its own claim to categorical independence, is almost certainly generated by neuronal activity. Since we do not know how, we have to assume that it derives from an undiscovered and at present inconceivable property – not alien to the material world, just one of its diverse manifestations. Writers such as Joseph Priestley, G.J. Romanes, Thomas Huxley and in our own time, Galen Strawson, have championed this view. There seems nothing for it but to get on with the multitrack task of describing experience as best we can, looking closely at the accompanying physical changes and speculating on their mutual relations.

1 See Paul, Romans, 8, 22, 23.-'For I delight in the law of God after the inward man: But I see another law in my members, warring against the law of my mind, and bringing me into captivity to the law of sin which is in my members.'

THE MIND–BODY PROBLEM

Can the Mind Exist Without the Body?
Or Are They Indissolubly Linked?

Nowadays there are few who subscribe to the notion of an incorporeal mind guaranteed by the existence of God, as did the great mathematician and philosopher, René Descartes[2] (1596–1650). He must certainly take credit for bringing the subject of consciousness to the forefront of philosophical thinking, but the massive influence of his logic, dubbed by the writer Arthur Koestler 'the Cartesian catastrophe', has been blamed for holding back the progress of our understanding for centuries. Materialists point to the logical error in assuming that because he could conceive the mind to be separate from the body, it followed that it had to be so. But an even greater mistake, according to Koestler, was his identification of the mind with 'conscious thinking' alone, thus impoverishing psychology by limiting the scope of its inquiry.

Apparently, like many modern-day students, he had the habit of staying in bed until after midday. However, in Descartes' case, reflections carried out in this condition gave rise to a philosophical masterpiece – Meditations (1641). Although his independent thought ran counter to scholastic authority, Descartes strove unsuccessfully to present his ideas as consistent with the authority of the Church. Publication of his Method (1644) led to charges in Utrecht of atheism and madness. Legal proceedings against Descartes were instituted, only to be stopped when the French ambassador and the Prince of Orange intervened on his behalf.

His work became widely known throughout Europe and engaged the interest of Royalty. Among his many correspondents was Charles I's niece, Princess Elizabeth of Bohemia. In 1649 he travelled to Sweden at the invitation of Queen Christina, in order to tutor her in philosophy. It was an ill-fated move which involved adaptation to a cold climate and change in lifestyle. Descartes now had to rise at five in the morning in order to give the queen her lessons! It seems unlikely that this would have had fatal

2 But see Sir John Eccles pp. 291–3.

consequences; however, he succumbed to pneumonia and died the following February at the age of fifty-four.

It is sufficient that I am able clearly and distinctly to conceive one thing apart from another, in order to be certain that the one is different from the other, seeing they may at least be made to exist separately, by the omnipotence of God; and it matters not by what power this separation is made, in order to be compelled to judge them different; and, therefore, merely because I know with certitude that I exist, and because, in the meantime, I do not observe that aught necessarily belongs to my nature or essence beyond my being a thinking thing, I rightly conclude that my essence consists only in my being a thinking thing (or a substance whose whole essence or nature is merely thinking). And although I may, or rather, as I will shortly say, although I certainly do possess a body with which I am very closely conjoined; nevertheless, because, on the one hand, I have a clear and distinct idea of myself, in as far as I am only a thinking and unextended thing, and as, on the other hand, I possess a distinct idea of body, in as far as it is only an extended and unthinking thing, it is certain that I (that is, my mind, by which I am what I am), is entirely and truly distinct from my body, and may exist without it.

[. . .] within its space

Nature likewise teaches me by these sensations of pain, hunger, thirst, etc., that I am not only lodged in my body as a pilot in a vessel, but that I am besides so intimately conjoined, and as it were intermixed with it, that my mind and body compose a certain unity. For if this were not the case, I should not feel pain when my body is hurt, seeing I am merely a thinking thing, but should perceive the wound by the understanding alone, just as a pilot perceives by sight when any part of his vessel is damaged; and when my body has need of food or drink, I should have a clear knowledge of this, and not be made aware of it by the confused sensations of hunger and thirst: for, in truth, all these sensations of hunger, thirst, pain, etc., are nothing more than certain confused modes of thinking, arising from the union and apparent fusion of mind and body.

René Descartes, 'Of the Existence of Material Things, and of the Real Distinction Between the Mind and the Body of Man' (1641)

The Doctrine of 'The Ghost in the Machine'

In his book The Concept of Mind, *first published in 1949, Gilbert Ryle launched a brilliant attack on what he called 'the official theory' of mind, by which he meant the everyday dualistic notion of mind and body as two qualitatively different entities, one somehow contained within the other. Although such a view had been traditionally propagated by religion, Ryle reserved most of his scorn for Descartes, whom he blamed for misleading future generations of philosophers.*

Ryle set himself the task of exposing absurdities and mistaken ways of thinking embedded in our language. He wanted to see how far he could push the 'behaviourist'³ doctrine which claimed that psychological terms were fundamentally no more than descriptions of actual or possible behaviour. To think otherwise, he averred, was to commit a category error, to talk about one thing 'mind' – an abstraction, as if it belonged in the same category as another 'body' – a concrete reality. Ryle did not deny the existence of 'mental life', but he insisted that such a way of speaking was merely a kind of metaphorical shorthand for describing the organization of behaviour.

Gilbert Ryle (1900–76) was a student of Christ Church, and from 1945, Professor of Metaphysical Philosophy in the University of Oxford – institutions which he takes care to point out belong to different logical categories. He was a 'linguistic philosopher' and friend of Ludwig Wittgenstein*.

There is a doctrine about the nature and place of minds which is so prevalent among theorists and even among laymen that it deserves to be described as the official theory. Most philosophers, psychologists and religious teachers subscribe, with minor reservations, to its main articles and, although they admit certain

3 See B. F. Skinner (pp. 214–16) and J.B. Watson (pp. 216–21).

theoretical difficulties in it, they tend to assume that these can be overcome without serious modifications being made to the architecture of the theory. It will be argued here that the central principles of the doctrine are unsound and conflict with the whole body of what we know about minds when we are not speculating about them.

The official doctrine, which hails chiefly from Descartes, is something like this. With the doubtful exception of idiots and infants in arms every human being has both a body and a mind. Some would prefer to say that every human being is both a body and a mind. His body and his mind are ordinarily harnessed together, but after the death of the body his mind may continue to exist and function.

Human bodies are in space and are subject to the mechanical laws which govern all other bodies in space. Bodily processes and states can be inspected by external observers. So a man's bodily life is as much a public affair as are the lives of animals and reptiles and even the careers of trees, crystals and planets.

But minds are not in space, nor are their operations subject to mechanical laws. The workings of one mind are not witnessable by other observers; its career is private. Only I can take direct cognizance of the states and processes of my own mind. A person therefore lives through two collateral histories, one consisting of what happens in and to his body, the other consisting of what happens in and to his mind. The first is public, the second private. The events in the first history are events in the physical world, those in the second are events in the mental world.

It has been disputed whether a person does or can directly monitor all or only some of the episodes of his own private history; but, according to the official doctrine, of at least some of these episodes he has direct and unchallengeable cognizance. In consciousness, self-consciousness and introspection he is directly and authentically apprised of the present states and operations of his mind. He may have great or small uncertainties about concurrent and adjacent episodes in the physical world, but he can have none about at least part of what is momentarily occupying his mind.

It is customary to express this bifurcation of his two lives and of his two worlds by saying that the things and events which belong to the physical world, including his own body, are external, while the workings of his own mind are internal. This antithesis of outer and inner is of course meant to be construed as a metaphor, since minds, not being in space, could not be described as being spatially inside anything else, or as having things going on spatially inside themselves. But relapses from this good intention are common and theorists are found speculating how stimuli, the physical sources of which are yards or miles outside a person's skin, can generate mental responses inside his skull, or how decisions framed inside his cranium can set going movements of his extremities.

Even when 'inner' and 'outer' are construed as metaphors, the problem how a person's mind and body influence one another is notoriously charged with theoretical difficulties. What the mind wills, the legs, arms and the tongue execute; what affects the ear and the eye has something to do with what the mind perceives; grimaces and smiles betray the mind's moods and bodily castigations lead, it is hoped, to moral improvement. But the actual transactions between the episodes of the private history and those of the public history remain mysterious, since by definition they can belong to neither series. They could not be reported among the happenings described in a person's autobiography of his inner life, but nor could they be reported among those described in someone else's biography of that person's overt career. They can be inspected neither by introspection nor by laboratory experiment. They are theoretical shuttlecocks which are forever being bandied from the physiologist back to the psychologist back to the physiologist.

Underlying this partly metaphorical representation of the bifurcation of a person's two lives there is a seemingly more profound and philosophical assumption. It is assumed that there are two different kinds of existence, or status. What exists or happens may have the status of physical existence, or it may have the status of mental existence. Somewhat as the faces of coins are either heads or tails, or somewhat as living creatures are either male or female, so, it is supposed, some existing is physical existing, other existing is mental existing. It is a necessary feature of what has physical existence that it is in space and time; it is a necessary feature of what has mental existence that it is in time but not in space. What has physical existence is composed of matter, or else is a function of matter; what has mental existence consists of consciousness, or else is a function of consciousness.

There is thus a polar opposition between mind and matter, an opposition which is often brought out as follows. Material objects are situated in a common field, known as 'space', and what happens to one body in one part of space is mechanically connected with what happens to other bodies in other parts of space. But mental happenings occur in insulated fields, known as 'minds', and there is, apart maybe from telepathy, no direct causal connection between what happens in one mind and what happens in another. The mind is its own place and in his inner life each of us lives the life of a ghostly Robinson Crusoe. People can see, hear and jolt one another's bodies, but they are irremediably blind and deaf to the workings of one another's minds and inoperative upon them.

What sort of knowledge can be secured of the workings of the mind? On the one side, according to the official theory, a person has direct knowledge of the best imaginable kind of the workings of his own mind. Mental states and processes are (or are normally) conscious states and processes, and the consciousness which irradiates them can engender no illusions and leaves the door open for no doubts. A person's present thinkings, feelings and willings, his perceivings, rememberings and imaginings are intrinsically 'phosphorescent'; their existence and their nature are inevitably betrayed to their owner. The inner life is a stream of consciousness of such a sort that it would be absurd to suggest that the mind whose life is that stream might be unaware of what is passing down it.

True, the evidence adduced recently by Freud seems to show that there exist channels tributary to this stream, which run hidden from their owner. People are actuated by impulses the existence of which they vigorously disavow; some of their thoughts differ from the thoughts which they acknowledge; and some of the actions which they think they will to perform they do not really will. They are thoroughly gulled by some of their own hypocrisies and they successfully ignore facts about their mental lives which on the official theory ought to be patent to them. Holders of the official theory tend, however, to maintain that anyhow in normal circumstances a person must be directly and authentically seized of the present state and workings of his own mind.

Besides being currently supplied with these alleged immediate data of consciousness, a person is also generally supposed to be able to exercise from time to time a special kind of perception, or introspection. He can take a (non-optical) 'look' at what is passing in his mind. Not only can he view and scrutinize a flower through his sense of sight and listen to and discriminate the notes of a bell through his sense of hearing; he can also reflectively or introspectively watch, without any bodily organ of sense, the current episodes of his inner life. This self-observation is also commonly supposed to be immune from illusion, confusion or doubt. A mind's reports of its own affairs have a certainty superior to the best that is possessed by its reports of matters in the physical world. Sense-perceptions can, but consciousness and introspection cannot, be mistaken or confused.

On the other side, one person has no direct access of any sort to the events of the inner life of another. He cannot do better than make problematic inferences from the observed behaviour of the other person's body to the states of mind which, by analogy from his own conduct, he supposes to be signalized by that behaviour. Direct access to the workings of a mind is the privilege of that mind itself; in default of such privileged access, the workings of one mind are inevitably occult to everyone else. For the supposed arguments from bodily movements similar to their own to mental workings similar to their own would lack any possibility of observational corroboration. Not unnaturally, therefore, an adherent of the official theory finds it difficult to resist this consequence of his premises, that he has no good reason to believe that there do exist minds other than his own. Even if he prefers to believe that to other human bodies there are harnessed minds not unlike his own, he cannot claim to be able to discover their individual characteristics, or the particular things that they undergo and do. Absolute solitude is on this showing the ineluctable destiny of the soul. Only our bodies can meet . . .

(2) The Absurdity of the Official Doctrine

Such in outline is the official theory. I shall often speak of it, with deliberate abusiveness, as 'the dogma of the "Ghost in the Machine"'. I hope to prove that it is entirely false, and false not in detail but in principle. It is not merely an assemblage of particular mistakes. It is one big mistake and a mistake of a special kind. It is, namely, a category-mistake. It represents the facts of mental life as if they belonged to one logical type or category (or range of types or categories), when they actually belong to another. The dogma is therefore a philosopher's myth. In attempting to explode the myth I shall probably be taken to be denying well-known facts about the mental life of human beings, and my plea that I aim at doing nothing more than rectify the logic of mental-conduct concepts will probably be disallowed as mere subterfuge.

I must first indicate what is meant by the phrase 'Category-mistake'. This I do in a series of illustrations.

A foreigner visiting Oxford or Cambridge for the first time is shown a number of colleges, libraries, playing fields, museums, scientific departments, and administrative offices. He then asks 'But where is the University? I have seen where the members of the Colleges live, where the Registrar works, where the scientists experiment and the rest. But I have not yet seen the University in which reside and work the members of your University.' It has then to be explained to him that the University is not another collateral institution, some ulterior counterpart to the colleges, laboratories and offices which he has seen. The University is just the way in which all that he has already seen is organized. When they are seen and when their co-ordination is understood, the University has been seen. His mistake lay in his innocent assumption that it was correct to speak of Christ Church, the Bodleian Library, the Ashmolean Museum *and* the University, to speak, that is, as if 'the University' stood for an extra member of the class of which these other units are members. He was mistakenly allocating the University to the same category as that to which the other institutions belong [. . .]

Gilbert Ryle, 'Descartes' Myth' (1949)

Where Is Consciousness Located?

In 1976 Julian Jaynes put forward an original and controversial theory concerning the emergence of consciousness, particularly modern self-consciousness, in the human mind. Reviewing the literature of early Mediterranean civilisations, especially Mycenean writings such as Homer's Iliad, *he concluded that Homeric man did not have a conscious mind in the same sense as we know it. Instead, Jaynes suggested, the characters portrayed in the Trojan siege were like robots, pushed about by the gods. They heard 'voices' which gave them directions, and spoke through them. Their minds were more akin to the modern-day schizophrenic than to the supposedly 'normal'.*

Jaynes proposed that the 'gods' dwelt in one hemisphere of the brain, issuing instructions via the corpus callosum (connecting fibres) to the other hemisphere which then implemented them. He believed the breakdown of this division was accompanied by a sense of loss – loss of internal direction. That it occurred by a process of slow sociocultural erosion which dispersed 'bicameral societies' and promoted a sense of individual responsibility and subjective self-consciousness.

Born in Newton, Massachusetts, Professor Jaynes (1920–97) was the son of a clergyman. He was educated at Harvard College and McGill University and took his master's and doctorate degrees from Yale University. He taught at Princeton University from 1966 to 1990, where he was a professor of psychology and where he became interested in trying to study the origin of consciousness.

Everyone, or almost everyone, immediately replies, in my head. This is because we introspect, we seem to look inward on an inner space somewhere behind our eyes. But what on earth do we mean by 'look'? We even close our eyes sometimes to introspect even more clearly. Upon what? Its spatial character seems unquestionable. Moreover we seem to move or at least 'look' in different directions. And if we press ourselves too strongly to further characterize this space (apart from its imagined contents), we feel a vague irritation, as if there were something that did not want to be known, some quality which to question was somehow ungrateful, like rudeness in a friendly place.

We not only locate this space of consciousness inside our own heads. We also assume it is there in others'. In talking with a friend, maintaining periodic eye-to-eye contact (that remnant of our primate past when eye-to-eye contact was concerned in establishing tribal hierarchies), we are always assuming a space behind our companion's eyes into which we are talking, similar to the space we imagine inside our own heads where we are talking from.

And this is the very heartbeat of the matter. For we know perfectly well that there is no such space in anyone's head at all! There is nothing inside my head or yours except physiological tissue of one sort or another. And the fact that it is predominantly neurological tissue is irrelevant.

Now this thought takes a little thinking to get used to. It means that we are continually inventing these spaces in our own and other people's heads, knowing perfectly well that they don't exist anatomically; and the location of these 'spaces' is indeed quite arbitrary. The Aristotelian writings, for example, located consciousness or the abode of thought in and just above the heart, believing the brain to be a mere cooling organ since it was insensitive to touch or injury. And some readers will not have found this discussion valid since they locate their thinking selves somewhere in their upper chest. For most of us, however, the habit of locating consciousness in the head is so ingrained that it is difficult to think otherwise. But, actually, you could, as you remain where you are, just as well locate your consciousness around the corner in the next room against the wall near the floor, and do your thinking there as well as in your head. Not really just as well. For there are very good reasons why it is better to imagine your mind-space inside of you, reasons to do with volition and internal sensations, with the relationship of your body and your 'I' which will become apparent as we go on.

That there is no phenomenal necessity in locating consciousness in the brain is further reinforced by various abnormal instances in which consciousness seems to be outside the body. A friend who received a left frontal brain injury in the war regained consciousness in the corner of the ceiling of a hospital ward looking down euphorically at himself on the cot swathed in bandages. Those who have taken lysergic acid diethylamide commonly report similar out-of-body or exosomatic experiences, as they are called. Such occurrences do not demonstrate anything metaphysical whatever; simply that locating consciousness can be an arbitrary matter.

Let us not make a mistake. When I am conscious, I am always and definitely using certain parts of my brain inside my head. But so am I when riding a bicycle, and the bicycle riding does not go on inside my head. The cases are different of course, since bicycle riding has a definite geographical location, while consciousness does not. In reality, consciousness has no location whatever except as we imagine it has.

Julian Jaynes, *The Origin of Consciousness in the Breakdown of the Bicameral Mind* (1977)

THE SOUL

Mandukya Upanishad[4]

The Upanishads are a series of ancient philosophical and religious discourses belonging to the early Brahmans of India and written in Sanskrit. The word Upanishad may originally have referred to the sitting of a disciple before a master in some kind of mystical séance. In the later Upanishads, 'Brahma', the unitary world spirit, is identified with the self-consciousness of the individual thinker. The intuitive recognition of this was said to lead to the salvation of the soul.

In recent times dissatisfaction with scientific materialism and established religion in the West has led to widespread enthusiasm for ancient Hindu ideas, and attempts to reconcile them with modern knowledge.

4 Diacritics have been omitted for the purposes of this book.

1. Hari Om. This syllable 'Om' is this whole universe. And the interpretation thereof is this:

> What was and is and is yet to be –
>   All of it is Om;
> And whatever else the three times transcends, –
>   That too is Om.

2. For all this [world] is Brahman. This self has four quarters.

3. The waking state, conscious (*prajna*) of what is without, seven-limbed, with nineteen mouths, experiencing what is gross, common to all men (*vaisvanara*), is the first quarter.

4. The state of dream, conscious of what is within, seven-limbed, with nineteen mouths, is the second quarter.

5. When a man is asleep and desires nothing whatever, dreams no dream, that is deep sleep (*susupta*).

The state of deep sleep, unified, a very mass of wisdom (*prajnana*), composed of bliss, experiencing bliss, with thought as its mouth, wise (*prajna*), is the third quarter.

6. This is the Lord of all. This the omniscient. This is the Inner Controller: This is the source of all, for it is both the origin and the end of contingent beings.

7. Conscious (*prajna*) of neither within nor without, nor of both together, not a mass of wisdom (*prajna*), neither wise nor unwise, unseen, one with whom there is no commerce, impalpable, devoid of distinguishing mark, unthinkable, indescribable, its essence the firm conviction of the oneness of itself, bringing all development (*prapanca*) to an end, tranquil and mild, devoid of duality, such do they deem this fourth to be. That is the Self: that is what should be known.

8. [Now,] this is the Self in its relationship to syllables: it is Om. As to the letters, the quarters [enumerated above] are the letters; and the letters are the quarters – A, U, M.[5]

9. The waking state, common to all men, is A, the first letter, signifying *apti*, 'obtaining', or *adimattva*, 'what is in the beginning'.

---

5 *Om* analysed as A+U+M.

For he who knows this obtains all his desires and becomes the beginning.

10. The state of dream, composed of light, is U. the second letter, signifying *utkarsa*, 'exaltation', or *ubhayatva*, 'partaking of both'. He who knows this exalts the continuum of knowledge and becomes like [Brahman]. In his family there is none who does not know Brahman.

11. The state of deep sleep, the wise, is M, the third letter, signifying *miti*, 'building up' [or 'measuring'], or *apiti*, 'absorption'. He who knows this builds up [or measures] the whole universe in very deed and is absorbed [into it].

12. The fourth is beyond [all] letters: there can be no commerce with it; it brings [all] development to an end; it is mild and devoid of duality. Such is Om, the very Self indeed. He who knows this merges of his own accord (*atmana*) into the Self – yes, he who knows this.

'Mandukya Upanishad' (c.500BCE)

THE EFFECT OF THE BODY ON THE MIND

Epilepsy and Ecstasy

The dramatic and sometimes bizarre manifestations of epilepsy have been known since antiquity and often attributed to supernatural causes, spirit possession or divine retribution. However, as early as 400BCE, Hippocrates in his discourse On the Sacred Disease *put forward a naturalistic explanation, implicating malfunction of the brain in the production of epileptic fits. Measurements of electrical activity in the brain have shown us that during epileptic fits it is overactive. Epilepsy can occur spontaneously or be provoked by a brain lesion, metabolic problem or by sensory stimulation, for example flickering lights. A wide range of effects, usually of limited duration, is produced, according to the part of the brain affected. Although it is now clear that the majority of those subject to epilepsy suffer no mental dysfunction, those unusual experiences which are associated with over-activity of the brain, offer us useful insight into the workings of its different parts, as well as presenting a fascinating conceptual dilemma concerning the 'validity' of experience.*

Dostoyevsky (1821–81) was born in Moscow and was, in childhood, often overcome by groundless feelings of melancholy and dreamy death-like states. He left notes begging his family to postpone burial, should he appear dead. In his youth he studied engineering at St Petersburg and embraced socialism. As a result he was subjected to a mock execution by the Tsar and imprisoned in Siberia for four years, during which time he underwent a religious crisis, rejected his socialist beliefs and turned toward the Russian Orthodox Church. His literary output established a worldwide reputation for him as one of Russia's finest writers, but as he grew older his life was increasingly disturbed by epileptic fits, probably involving the temporal lobe of his brain. In the character of Prince Myshkin whose thoughts are described below, Dostoyevsky gives a vivid account, undoubtedly based on his own experience, of the altered state of consciousness preceding an epileptic fit.

He was thinking, incidentally, that there was a moment or two in his epileptic condition almost before the fit itself (if it occurred during his waking hours) when suddenly amid the sadness, spiritual darkness and depression, his brain seemed to catch fire at brief moments, and with an extraordinary momentum his vital forces were strained to the utmost all at once. His sensation of being alive and his awareness increased tenfold at those moments which flashed by like lightning. His mind and heart were flooded by a dazzling light. All his agitation, all his doubts and worries, seemed composed in a twinkling, culminating in a great calm, full of serene and harmonious joy and hope, full of understanding and the knowledge of the final cause. But those moments, those flashes of intuition, were merely the presentment of the last second (never more than a second) which preceded the actual fit. This second was, of course, unendurable. Reflecting about that moment afterwards, when he was well again, he often said to himself that all those gleams and flashes of the highest awareness and, hence, also of 'the highest mode of existence', were nothing but a disease, a departure from the normal condition, and, if so, it was not at all the highest mode of existence, but, on the contrary, must be considered to be the lowest. And yet he arrived at last at the paradoxical conclusion: 'What if it is a disease?' he decided at last. 'What does it matter that it is an abnormal tension, if the result, if the moment of sensation, remembered and analysed in a state of health, turns out to be harmony and beauty brought to their highest point of perfection, and gives a feeling, undivined and undreamt of till then, of completeness, proportion, reconciliation, and an ecstatic and prayerful fusion in the highest synthesis of life?' These vague expressions seemed to him very comprehensible, though rather weak. But that it really was 'beauty and prayer', that it really was 'the highest synthesis of life', he could not doubt, nor even admit the possibility of doubt. For it was not abnormal and fantastic visions he saw at that moment, as under the influence of hashish, opium, or spirits, which debased the reason and distorted the mind. He could reason sanely about it when the attack was over and he was well again. Those moments were merely an intense heightening of awareness – if this condition had to be expressed in one word – of awareness and at the same time of the most direct sensation of one's own existence to the most intense degree. If in that second – that is to say, at the last conscious moment before the fit – he had time to say to himself, consciously and clearly, 'Yes, I could give my whole life for this moment', then this moment by itself was, of course, worth the whole of life.

Fyodor Dostoyevsky, *The Idiot* (1868)

Appeasing the Body for the Mind's Sake

Samuel Beckett (1906–89) was born in Dublin, the second son of a quantity surveyor, from a well-to-do Protestant family. He was educated at Portora Royal School, Eniskillen, going on to Trinity College, Dublin, where he studied English and Modern

Languages. Two years after graduating he took up a teaching post in the Ecole Normale Supérieure in Paris, where he met and became lasting friends with James Joyce. During the 1930s he spent several years travelling in Europe, including a period in England when he underwent psychotherapy with Wilfred Bion, later to become a controversial figure in psychoanalysis. He eventually settled in France, producing a series of literary works of unparalleled bleakness. Characteristically they consisted of a lengthy and despairing monologue, mitigated only by the black humour of the protagonist. He seemed to have a direct line into the core of modern man's alienated being. In 1953 his play* En Attendant Godot *was first performed in Paris to wide acclaim. He was classified as a leading exponent of the 'Theatre of the Absurd' and his work had a profound influence on future generations of playwrights. In 1969, he was awarded the Nobel prize for literature.*

The sun shone, having no alternative, on the nothing new. Murphy sat out of it, as though he were free in a mew in West Brompton. Here for what might have been six months he had eaten, drunk, slept, and put his clothes on and off, in a medium-sized cage of north-western aspect. Soon he would have to make other arrangements, for the mew had been condemned. Soon he would have to buckle to and start eating, drinking, sleeping, and putting his clothes on and off, in quite alien surroundings.

He sat naked in his rocking-chair of undressed teak, guaranteed not to crack, warp, shrink, corrode, or creak at night. It was his own, it never left him. The corner in which he sat was curtained off from the sun, the poor old sun in the Virgin again for the billionth time. Seven scarves held him in position. Two fastened his shins to the rockers, one his thighs to the seat, two his breast and belly to the back, one his wrists to the strut behind. Only the most local movements were possible. Sweat poured off him, tightened the thongs. The breath was not perceptible. The eyes, cold and unwavering as a gull's, stared up at an iridescence splashed over the cornice moulding, shrinking and fading. Somewhere a cuckoo-clock, having struck between twenty and thirty, became the echo of a street-cry, which now entering the mew gave *Quid pro quo! Quid pro quo!* directly.

These were the sights and sounds that he did not like. They detained him in the world to which they belonged, but not he, as he fondly hoped. He wondered dimly what was breaking up his sunlight, what wares were being cried. Dimly, very dimly.

He sat in his chair in this way because it gave him pleasure! First it gave his body pleasure, it appeased his body. Then it set him free in his mind. For it was not until his body was appeased that he could come alive in his mind, as described in section six. And life in his mind gave him pleasure, such pleasure that pleasure was not the word.

Samuel Beckett, *Murphy* (1938)

THE EFFECT OF THE MIND ON THE BODY

A Rose by any Other Name?

Morton Prince (1854–1929), a Bostonian, was appointed Professor of Nervous Diseases at Tufts College Medical School in 1902 and later held the Chair of Abnormal and Dynamic Psychology at Harvard University. Prince antedated Pavlov in believing that ideas, sensations, emotions and volitions occurring together, tend by constant repetition to become so strongly associated, that the presence of one of them reproduces the others. He called this the 'psychological law of association of mental processes'.

I know of no more beautiful illustration of the association of a single *mental state with a pure physical* process than that furnished by a case of Dr Mackensie, of Baltimore. It was that of a lady who had been for years a terrible sufferer from rose cold, or hay fever. The disease became aggravated by the addition of asthmatic attacks which complicated the coryza. She had become so sensitive that the number of exciting causes of an attack was very large. She was so sensitive to roses that the mere presence of a rose in the same room was sufficient to induce an attack. Suspecting the nature of her trouble, Mackensie obtained an artificial rose of such exquisite workmanship that it presented a perfect counterfeit of the original. One day, when the lady came to his office, after assuring himself by careful examination that she was perfectly free from coryza, Mackensie produced the artificial rose from behind a screen where it had been concealed, and held it in front of her. Almost immediately a violent attack of coryza developed. Her eyes became suffused with tears, the conjunctivae injected, the puncta lachryma began to itch violently; her face became flushed, the nasal passages obstructed, her voice hoarse and nasal; she complained of a desire to sneeze and tickling and intense itching in the back of the throat and in the auditory meatus; there was also photophobia and secretion of fluid from the nasal passages; to this was added a feeling of oppression in the chest and a slight embarrassment of respiration. Examination showed the nostrils almost completely obstructed by swollen, reddened and irritable turbinated structures and filled with fluid. The mucous membrane of the throat was injected. At this point Mackensie stopped the experiment, thinking it had gone far enough, and the patient left the office with a severe attack of coryza.

The sequel is equally interesting. The true nature of the rose was shown to the patient, with the result that on her next visit she plunged her face into a real bunch of roses without ill effect.

I know nothing more instructive than this case. We have all the phenomena of inflammation, a series of apparently organic processes set into activity by the force of an associated idea. It would seem as if the physiological processes of secretion of tears, secretion of mucus, vasomotor action (causing injection of tissue), pain, etc., were united into an automatic mechanism, and the whole connected (associated), as with a spring with a higher visual centre, which when touched set off the whole mechanism. The principle here involved is an important one, and it will be well to bear it in mind when we come to consider other complex associations. It shows conclusively the possibility of an automatic nervous process of considerable complexity becoming established, and afterward excited anew as an independent neurosis by a purely physiological stimulus . . .

Morton Prince, 'Association Neuroses' (1891)

Impotence from Mental Causes[6]

John Hunter (1728–93), Member of the Surgeons' Corporation, FRS, surgeon to St George's Hospital, London and to George III, was also surgeon-general to the army. In the following passage he considers the mind's effect on the body.

Copulation is an act of the body, the spring of which is in the mind; but it is not volition; and according to the state of the mind so is the act performed. To perform this act well, the body should be in health, and the mind should be perfectly confident of the powers of the body; the mind should be in a state entirely disengaged from every thing else; it should have no difficulties, no fears, no apprehensions; not even an anxiety to perform the act well; for even this anxiety is a state of mind different from what should prevail; there should not be even a fear that the mind itself may find a difficulty at the time the act should be performed. Perhaps no function of the machine depends so much upon the state of the mind as this. The will, and reasoning faculty, have nothing to do with this power; they are only employed in the act, so far as voluntary parts are made use of; and if they ever interfere, which they sometimes do, it often produced another state of the mind which destroys that which is proper for the performance of the act; it produces a desire, a wish, a hope, which are all only diffidence and uncertainty, and create in the mind the idea of a possibility of the want of success, which destroys the proper state of mind, or necessary confidence. There is perhaps no act in which a man feels himself more interested, or is more anxious to perform well, his pride being engaged in

6 See also Montaigne, 'On the Force of Imagination', pp. 45–9.

some degree, which if within certain bounds would produce a degree of perfection in an act depending upon the will, or an act in voluntary parts; but when it produces a state of mind contrary to that state on which the perfection of the act depends, a failure must be the consequence. The body is not only rendered incapable of performing this act, by the mind being under the above influence, but also by the mind being perfectly confident of its power, but conscious of an impropriety in performing it; this in many cases producing a state of mind which shall take away all power. The state of a man's mind respecting his sister takes away all power. A conscientious man has been known to lose his powers on finding the woman he was going to be connected with unexpectedly a virgin [. . .]

From the above account of the necessity of having the mind independent, respecting the act, we must see that it may very often happen that the state of mind will be such as not to allow the animal to exert its natural powers; and every failure increases the evil. We must also see from this state of the case, that this act must be often interrupted; and the true cause of this interruption not being known, it will be laid to the charge of the body or want of powers. As these cases do not arise from real inability, they are to be carefully distinguished from such as do; and perhaps the only way to distinguish them is to examine into the state of mind respecting this act. So trifling often is the circumstance which shall produce this inability, depending on the mind, that the very desire to please shall have that effect, as in making the woman the sole object to be gratified. Cases of this kind, we see every day; one of which I shall relate as an illustration of this subject, and also of the method of cure. A gentleman told me, that he had lost his powers in this way. After above an hour's investigation of the case, I made out the following facts; that he had at unnecessary times strong erections, which showed that he had naturally this power; that the erections were accompanied with desire, which are all the natural powers wanted; but that there was still a defect somewhere, which I suppose to be from the mind. I inquired if all women were alike to him, his answer was no; some women he could have connection with as well as ever. This brought the defect, whatever it was, into a smaller compass; and it appeared that there was but one woman that produced this inability, and that it arose from a desire to perform the act with this woman well; which desire produced in the mind a doubt, or fear of the want of success, which was the cause of the inability of performing the act. As this arose entirely from the state of the mind, produced by a particular circumstance, the mind was to be applied to for the cure; and I told him that he might be cured, if he could perfectly rely on his own power of self-denial. When I explained what I meant, he told me that he could depend upon every act of his will, or resolution; I then told him, if he had a perfect confidence in himself in that respect, that he was to go to bed to this woman, but first promise to himself, that he would not have any connection with her, for six nights, let his inclinations and powers be what they would; which he engaged to do; and also to let me know the result. About a fortnight after he told me that this resolution had produced such a total alteration in the state of his mind, that the power soon took place, for instead of going to bed with the fear of inability, he went with fears that he should be possessed with too much desire, too much power, so as to become uneasy to him, which really happened; for he would have been happy to have shortened the time; and when he had once broke the spell, the mind and powers went on together; his mind never returning to its former state.

John Hunter, *Treatise on the Venereal Disease* (1786)

THE VALIDITY OF EXPERIENCE

We Cannot Conceive How a Physical Process Could Explain a Mental One

Physical processes are publicly observable. They can be seen from many points of view. But the facts of experience, Thomas Nagel famously argued, are accessible from only one point of view – that of the experiencing organism. There is something 'it is like'

*to be a bat, but only a bat knows what it is. And can one bat
know anything about the experience of another? Certainly we
will never discover the felt quality of events by studying their
physical properties.*

*Professor Thomas Nagel was born in 1937 and educated at
Cornell, Oxford and Harvard Universities. He currently holds
the Chair in Philosophy and Law at New York University.*

Conscious experience is a widespread phenomenon. It occurs at
many levels of animal life, though we cannot be sure of its presence in simpler organisms, and it is very difficult to say in general
what provides evidence of it. (Some extremists have been prepared
to deny it even of mammals other than man.) No doubt it occurs
in countless forms totally unimaginable to us, on other planets
in other solar systems throughout the universe. But no matter
how the form may vary, the fact that an organism has conscious
experience *at all* means, basically, that there is something it is
like to *be* that organism. There may be further implications about
the form of experience; there may even (though I doubt it) be
implications about the behaviour of the organism. But fundamentally an organism has conscious mental states if and only if
there is something it is like to *be* that organism – something it
is like *for* the organism.

I assume we all believe that bats have experience. After all,
they are mammals, and there is no more doubt that they have
experience than that mice or pigeons or whales have experience.
I have chosen bats instead of wasps or flounders because if one
travels too far down the phylogenetic tree, people gradually shed
their faith that there is experience there at all. Bats, although
more closely related to us than those other species, nevertheless
present a range of activity and a sensory apparatus so different
from ours that the problem I want to pose is exceptionally vivid
(though it certainly could be raised with other species). Even
without the benefit of philosophical reflection, anyone who has
spent some time in an enclosed space with an excited bat knows
what it is to encounter a fundamentally *alien* form of life.

I have said that the essence of the belief that bats have

experience is that there is something that it is like to be a bat.
Now we know that most bats (the microchiroptera, to be precise)
perceive the external world primarily by sonar, or echolocation,
detecting the reflections, from objects within range, of their own
rapid, subtly modulated, high-frequency shrieks. Their brains are
designed to correlate the outgoing impulses with the subsequent
echoes, and the information thus acquired enables bats to make
precise discriminations of distance, size, shape, motion, and
texture comparable to those we make by vision. But bat sonar,
though clearly a form of perception, is not similar in its operation to any sense that we possess, and there is no reason to
suppose that it is subjectively like anything we can experience or
imagine. This appears to create difficulties for the notion of what
it is like to be a bat. We must consider whether any method will
permit us to extrapolate to the inner life of the bat from our own
case,[†] and if not, what alternative methods there may be for
understanding the notion.

Our own experience provides the basic material for our imagination, whose range is therefore limited. It will not help to try
to imagine that one has webbing on one's arms, which enables
one to fly around at dusk and dawn catching insects in one's
mouth; that one has very poor vision, and perceives the
surrounding world by a system of reflected high-frequency sound
signals; and that one spends the day hanging upside down by
one's feet in an attic. Insofar as I can imagine this (which is not
very far), it tells me only what it would be like for *me* to behave
as a bat behaves. But that is not the question. I want to know
what it is like for a *bat* to be a bat. Yet if I try to imagine this,
I am restricted to the resources of my own mind, and those
resources are inadequate to the task. I cannot perform it either
by imagining additions to my present experience, or by imagining segments gradually subtracted from it, or by imagining some
combination of additions, subtractions, and modifications.

To the extent that I could look and behave like a wasp or a

[†] By 'our own case' I do not mean just 'my own case', but rather the mentalistic
ideas that we apply unproblematically to ourselves and other human beings.

bat without changing my fundamental structure, my experiences would not be anything like the experiences of those animals: On the other hand, it is doubtful that any meaning can be attached to the supposition that I should possess the internal neuro-physiological constitution of a bat. Even if I could by gradual degrees be transformed into a bat, nothing in my present consti-tution enables me to imagine what the experiences of such a future stage of myself thus metamorphosed would be like. The best evidence would come from the experiences of bats, if we only knew what they were like.

So if extrapolation from our own case is involved in the idea of what it is like to be a bat, the extrapolation must be incom-pletable. We cannot form more than a schematic conception of what it *is* like. For example, we may ascribe general *types* of experience on the basis of the animal's structure and behaviour. Thus we describe bat sonar as a form of three-dimensional forward perception; we believe that bats feel some version of pain, fear, hunger and lust, and that they have other, more familiar types of perception besides sonar. But we believe that these expe-riences also have in each case a specific subjective character, which it is beyond our ability to conceive. And if there is conscious life elsewhere in the universe, it is likely that some of it will not be describable even in the most general experiential terms available to us.† (The problem is not confined to exotic cases, however, for it exists between one person and another. The subjective char-acter of the experience of a person deaf and blind from birth is not accessible to me, for example, nor presumably is mine to him. This does not prevent us each believing that the other's expe-rience has such a subjective character.)

[. . .]

This bears directly on the mind–body problem. For if the facts of experience – facts about what it is like *for* the experiencing organism – are accessible only from one point of view, then it is a mystery how the true character of experiences could be revealed

---

† Therefore the analogical form of the English expression 'what it is *like*' is misleading. It does not mean 'what (in our experience) it *resembles*', but rather 'how it is for the subject himself'.

in the physical operation of that organism. The latter is the domain of objective facts *par excellence* – the kind that can be observed and understood from many points of view and by individuals with differing perceptual systems. There are no comparable imaginative obstacles to the acquisition of knowledge about bat neurophysiology by human scientists, and intelligent bats or Martians might learn more about the human brain than we ever will.

Thomas Nagel, 'What Is It Like to Be a Bat?', in *Mortal Questions* (1979)

THE IDENTITY THEORY OF MIND

Free Will Is an Aspect of Brain Activity

It is difficult to square our sense of free will with the notion that our decisions are 'caused', and therefore preceded by physical changes in the brain. It is equally difficult to understand how immaterial mental events, like intentions, could give rise to bodily changes. G.J. Romanes (1848–94), British biologist and friend of Darwin, gives an eloquent statement of the 'identity theory of mind' which appears to offer a way out of this dilemma. Mental and physical events are not considered to be separate (but correlated) happenings, as in the theory of 'psychophysical parallellism', rather they are seen as different aspects of the same basic phenomenon. One cannot occur without the other, but neither is antecedent, both are contingent. Despite this identity, the theory acknowledges that statements couched in the language of experience are logically distinct from, and cannot be reduced to, statements about neurophysiological processes.

Spiritualism being thus unsatisfactory, and materialism impossible, is there yet any third hypothesis in which we may hope to find intellectual rest? In my opinion there is. If we unite in a higher synthesis the elements both of spiritualism and of materialism, we obtain a product which satisfies every fact of feeling on the one hand, and of observation on the other. The manner in which this synthesis may be effected is perfectly simple. We have only to suppose that the antithesis between mind and motion – subject and object – is itself phenomenal or apparent: not absolute or real. We have only to suppose that the seeming duality is relative to our modes of apprehension; and, therefore, that any change taking place in the mind, and any corresponding change taking place in the brain, are really not two changes but one change. When a violin is played upon we hear a musical sound, and at the same time we see a vibration of the strings. Relatively to our consciousness, therefore, we have here two sets of changes, which appear to be very different in kind; yet we know that in an absolute sense they are one and the same: we know that the diversity in consciousness is created only by the difference in our modes of perceiving the same event – whether we see or whether we hear the vibration of the strings. Similarly, we may suppose that a vibration of nerve-strings and a process of thought are really one and the same event, which is dual or diverse only in relation to our modes of perceiving it.

The great advantage of this theory is that it supposes only one stream of causation, in which both mind and motion are simultaneously concerned. The theory, therefore, escapes all the difficulties and contradictions with which both spiritualism and materialism are beset. Thus, motion is supposed to be producing nothing but motion, mind-changes nothing but mind-changes: both producing both simultaneously, but neither could be what it is without the other, because without the other neither could be the cause which in fact it is. Impossible, therefore, is the supposition of the materialist that consciousness is adventitious, or that in the absence of mind changes of brain could be what they are; for it belongs to the very causation of these changes that they should have a mental side. The use of mind to animals is thus rendered apparent; for intelligent volition is thus shown to be a true cause of adjustive movement, in that the cerebration which it involves could not otherwise be possible: the causation would not otherwise be complete.

A simple illustration may serve at once to render this doctrine more easily intelligible, and to show that, if accepted, the doctrine, as it appears to me, terminates the otherwise interminable controversy on the freedom of the will.

In an Edison lamp the light which is emitted from the burner may be said indifferently to be caused by the number of vibrations per second going on in the carbon, or by the temperature of the carbon; for this rate of vibration could not take place in the carbon without constituting that degree of temperature which affects our eyes as luminous. Similarly a train of thought may be said indifferently to be caused by brain-action or by mind-action; for, *ex hypothesi*, the one could not take place without the other. Now, when we contemplate the phenomena of volition by themselves, it is as though we were contemplating the phenomena of light by themselves: volition is produced by mind in brain, just as light is produced by temperature in carbon. And just as we may correctly speak of light as the cause, say, of a photograph, so we may correctly speak of volition as the cause of bodily movement. That particular kind of physical activity which takes place in the carbon could not take place without the light which causes a photograph; and, similarly, that particular kind of physical activity which takes place in the brain could not take place without the volition which causes a bodily movement. So that volition is as truly a cause of bodily movement as is the physical activity of the brain; seeing that, in an absolute sense, the cause is one and the same. But if we once clearly perceive that what in a relative sense we know as volition is, in a similar sense, the cause of bodily movement, we terminate the question touching the freedom of the will. For this question in its last resort – and apart from the ambiguity which has been thrown around it by some of our metaphysicians – is merely the question whether the will is to be regarded as a cause of Nature. And the theory which we have now before us sanctions the doctrine that it may be so regarded, if only we remember that its causal activity depends upon its identity with the obverse aspect known as cerebration, without which identity in apparent duality neither volition nor cerebration could be the cause which in fact they are. It thus becomes a mere matter of phraseology whether we speak of the will determining, or being determined by, changes going on in the external world; just as it is but a matter of phraseology whether we speak of temperature determining, or being determined by, molecular vibration. All the requirements alike of the free-will and of the bond-will hypotheses are thus satisfied by a synthesis which comprises them both. On the one hand, it would be as impossible for an *un*conscious automaton to do the work or to perform the adjustments of a conscious agent, as it would be for an Edison lamp to give out light and cause a photograph when not heated by an electric current. On the other hand, it would be as impossible for the will to originate bodily movement without the occurrence of a strictly physical process of cerebration, as it would be for light to shine in an Edison lamp which had been deprived of its carbon-burner.

It may be said of this theory that it is highly speculative, not verifiable by any possible experiment, and therefore at best it is but a mere guess. All which is, no doubt, perfectly true, but, on the other hand, we must remember that this theory comes to us as the only one which is logically possible, and at the same time competent to satisfy the facts alike of the outer and of the inner world. It is a speculation in the sense of not being verifiable by experiment; but it has much more value than ordinarily attaches to an unverifiable speculation, in that there is really no alternative hypothesis to be considered: if we choose to call it a guess, we must at the same time remember it is a guess where it does not appear that any other is open. Once more to quote Hobbes, who, as we have seen, was himself a remarkable instance of what he here says: 'The best prophet naturally is the best guesser; and the best guesser, he that is most versed and studied in the matters he guesses at.' In this case, therefore, the best prophet is not the physiologist, whose guess ends in materialism; nor the purely mental philosopher, whose guess ends in spiritualism; but rather the man who, being 'versed and studied' in all the facts appertaining to both sides of the matter, ends in the only alternative guess which remains open. And if that most troublesome individual, the 'plain man' of Locke, should say it seems at least opposed to common sense to suppose that there is anything in a burning candle or a rolling billiard-ball substantially the same as mind, the answer is that if he could look into my brain at this moment he would see nothing there but motion of molecules, or motion of masses; and apart from the accident of my being able to tell him so, his 'common sense' could never have divined that these motions in my brain are concerned in the genesis of my spoken thoughts.

G.J. Romanes, 'Mind and Motion' (1885)

NEURAL DARWINISM

The Brain Is not a Computer

If the brain is conceptualized as a kind of computer, who programmes it? Who creates the rules which it follows in organizing our response to the environment? If there is some overarching executive telling the rest of the brain what to do, who tells the executive what instructions to give? And if the brain is like a computer, shouldn't the network of minute nervous connections in each one be more or less identical? Yet it is not.

Just as Darwinism explains the diversity of the natural order in terms of genetic selection rather than divine instruction, so Neural Darwinism explains the cerebral order in terms of neuronal-network selection driven by environmental stimuli, rather than supra-ordinate instruction. The beauty of both theories is that they dispense with the need to postulate an unknown and mysterious determining force. Gerald Edelman (1929–) proposes a Theory of Neuronal Group Selection (TNGS) which reduces to three basic tenets. No additional assumptions are required, he claims, in order to explain 'even so remarkable a property as consciousness'.

My understanding of Edelman's theory is that it hinges on the way connections between nerve cells are either strengthened or weakened in response to environmental stimuli, giving rise to particular patterns of brain activity. These patterns or maps then interact with each other, so that certain maps tend to fire simultaneously, giving rise to multidimensional perceptions. Consciousness arises when a 'value-category' map becomes linked to a group of others, say those concerned with the physiological co-ordination of movement, sound or vision. Everything therefore depends on how 'value-categories' come into being, and subsequently how 'semantic capability' arises. But these maps seem to be taken for granted in the theory. The process whereby patterns of neuronal firing generate value experiences, remains unexplained. Edelman's theory is at the level of neurological co-ordination and feedback in response to external and internal stimuli. It seems to be about what the philosopher David Chalmers called the 'easy' problems. It does not crack the 'hard' one.

Professor Edelman of Rockefeller University, New York, is a medical scientist and Nobel Laureate, honoured for his work on the chemical structure of antibodies in 1972.

I have already argued that the world is not a piece of tape and that the brain is not a computer. If we take such a position, we have to show how a behaving animal nevertheless adaptively matches its responses to unforseen novelty occurring in such a world. There is an additional set of reasons for assuming that recognition cannot be instructive. We have already seen that the individuality and structural diversity of brains even within one species is confounding to models that consider the brain to be a computer. Evidence from developmental studies suggests that the extraordinary anatomical diversity at the finest ramifications of neural networks is an unavoidable consequence of the embryological process. That degree of individual diversity cannot be tolerated in a computer system following instructions. But it is just what is needed in a selective system.

A potent additional reason for adopting a selective rather than an instructive viewpoint has to do with the homunculus. You will remember that the homunculus is the little man that one must postulate 'at the top of the mind', acting as an interpreter of signals and symbols in any instructive theory of mind. If information from the world is processed by rules in a computerlike brain, his existence seems to be obliged. But then another homunculus is required in *his* head and so on, in an infinite regress. Selectional systems, in which matching occurs *ex post facto* on an *already existing* diverse repertoire, need no special creations, no homunculi, and no such regress.

If we assume that brain functions are built according to a selectional process, we must be able to reconcile the structural and functional variability of the brain with the need to explain how it carries out categorization. To do so, we need a theory with a number of essential characteristics. It must be in accord with the facts of evolution and development; account for the adaptive nature of responses to novelty; show how the brain's functions are scaled to those of the body as the body changes with growth and experience; account for the existence and functions of maps in the brain – why they fluctuate, how multiple maps lead to integrated responses, and how they lead to generalizations of perceptual responses, even in the absence of language. Eventually, such a theory would also need to account for the emergence of language itself. And finally, such a theory must account for how the various forms of perceptual and conceptual categorization, of memory, and of consciousness arose during evolution. To be scientific, the theory must be based on the assumption that all cognition and all conscious experience rest solely on processes and orderings occurring in the physical world. The theory must therefore take care to explain how psychological processes are related to physiological ones.

The theory I have proposed to account for these matters is known as the theory of neuronal group selection (TNGS) . . . its basic tenets, however, are only three in number. No additional tenets are required to explain even so remarkable a property as consciousness. What *is* required to explain such a property, however, is the evolution of new kinds of morphology in both the body and the brain. So I will take up some features of these morphologies as we go along.

The three tenets of the TNGS are concerned with how the anatomy of the brain is first set up during development, how patterns of responses are then selected from this anatomy during experience, and how re-entry, a process of signalling between the resulting maps of the brain, gives rise to behaviourally important functions.

According to the first tenet, developmental selection, the dynamic primary processes of development [. . .] lead to the formation of the neuroanatomy characteristic of a given species. This anatomy obligatorily possesses enormous variation at its finest levels and ramifications [. . .] A population of variant groups of neurons in a given brain region, comprising neural networks arising by processes of somatic selection, is known as a *primary repertoire*. The genetic code does not provide a specific wiring diagram for this repertoire. Rather, it imposes a set of *constraints* on the selectional process [by specifying and regulating, through 'morphoregulatory molecules' the adhesion of cells, in a mechanical environment where they are moving and dying in unpredictable ways, ed.]. Even with such constraints, genetically identical individuals are unlikely to have identical wiring, for selection is epigenetic.

The second tenet of the TNGS provides another mechanism of selection that, in general, does not involve an alteration of the anatomical pattern. It assumes that, during behaviour, synaptic connections in the anatomy are selectively strengthened or weakened by specific biochemical processes. This mechanism, which underlies memory and a number of other functions, effectively 'carves out' a variety of functioning *circuits* (with strengthened synapses) from the anatomical network by selection. Such a set of variant functional circuits is called a *secondary repertoire*.

To some extent, the mechanisms leading to the formation of primary and secondary repertoires are intermixed. This is so because at certain times and places the formation of the primary repertoire depends on changing synaptic strengths, as in the activity-dependent matching of connections [e.g. the mapping of visual fields in a frog's brain in response to light stimulation, ed.].

The third tenet of the TNGS is concerned with how the selectional events described in the first two tenets act to connect psychology to physiology. It suggests how brain maps interact by a process called re-entry. This is perhaps the most important of all the proposals of the theory, for it underlies how the brain areas that emerge in evolution co-ordinate with each other to yield new functions.

To carry out such functions, primary and secondary repertoires must form maps. These maps are connected by massively parallel and reciprocal connections. The visual system of the monkey, for example, has over thirty different maps, each with a certain degree of functional segregation (for different orientation, colour, movement, and so forth), and linked to the others by parallel and reciprocal connections. Re-entrant signalling occurs along these connections. This means that as groups of neurons are selected in a map, other groups in re-entrantly connected but different maps may also be selected at the same time. Correlation and co-ordination of such selection events are achieved by re-entrant signalling and by strengthening of interconnections between the maps within a segment of time.

A fundamental premise of the TNGS is that the selective co-ordination of the complex patterns of interconnection between neuronal groups by re-entry is the basis of behaviour. Indeed, re-entry (combined with memory, which I discuss later) is the main basis for a bridge between physiology and psychology.

[. . .]

Primary consciousness is achieved by the re-entry of a value-category memory to current ongoing perceptual categorizations that are carried out simultaneously in many modalities. It links parallel stimuli in time and space (including those not necessarily causally connected) into a correlated scene. In an individual animal, the features of that scene achieve salience from that animal's past values and learning history. Primary consciousness is limited to the remembered present. It is necessary for the emergence of higher-order consciousness, and it continues to operate in animals capable of higher-order consciousness.

Higher-order consciousness arises with the evolutionary onset of semantic capabilities, and it flowers with the accession of language and symbolic reference. Linguistic capabilities require a new kind of memory for the production and audition of the co-articulated sounds that were made possible by the evolution of the supralaryngeal space. The speech areas mediating categorization and memory for language interact with the already evolved conceptual areas of the brain. Their proper function in a speech community connects phonology to semantics, using interactions with the conceptual areas of the brain to guide learning. This gives rise to syntax when these same conceptual centres categorize the ordering events occurring during speech acts. As a syntax begins to be built and a sufficiently large lexicon is learned, the conceptual centres of the brain treat the symbols and their references and the imagery they evoke as an 'independent' world to be further categorized. A conceptual explosion and ontological revolution – a world, not just an environment – are made possible by the interaction between conceptual and language centres.

By these means, concepts of self and of a past and a future emerge. Higher-order consciousness depends on building a self through affective intersubjective exchanges. These interactions – with parental figures, with grooming conspecifics, and with sexual partners – are of the same kind as those guiding semiotic exchange and language building. Affectively coloured exchanges through symbols initiate semantic bootstrapping. The result is a model of a world rather than an echoniche, along with models of the past, present and future. At the same time that higher-order consciousness frees us from the tyranny of the remembered present, however, primary consciousness coexists and interacts with the mechanisms of higher-order consciousness. Indeed, primary consciousness provides a strong driving force for higher-order processes. We live on several levels at once.

Gerald Edelman, *Bright Air, Brilliant Fire: On the Matter of the Mind* (1992)

CONSCIOUSNESS IS A DUBIOUS GIFT

Bearing the Burden of Consciousness

We are inclined to think that our 'consciousness' is higher than that of other animals. Most of the time we experience ourselves exercising choice, figuring out what we will do, feeling free to act one way or another.[7] On the other hand we assume that

7 But see Bernhard Schlink, *The Reader*, pp. 224–5.

animals, for the most part, respond automatically and instinctively to the stimuli they receive. Lacking a ready response to every situation we are forced into thoughtfulness and invention, but the price we pay for our higher consciousness, Carl Gustav Jung* (1875–1961) suggests, is the experience of uncertainty and fear, the constant need to make decisions based on inadequate evidence.

In order to overcome this we deny problems, or institute routines and mindless procedures for dealing with them. In a way, we try to avoid exercising our capacity for independent thought as much as possible, preferring to imitate instinct. When it comes to carrying out tasks such as driving a car or playing a musical instrument, the economy of effort involved in not having to re-learn the procedure every time, is advantageous. But personal and social relations founder when subjected to the same treatment. We like to be regarded as unique individuals, demanding that each encounter be experienced and confronted anew. Jung tells us, we have no option but to strive to develop a wider and higher consciousness, which alone can give us the certainty we crave.

It is the growth of consciousness which we must thank for the existence of problems; they are the dubious gift of civilization. It is just man's turning away from instinct – his opposing himself to instinct – that creates consciousness. Instinct is nature and seeks to perpetuate nature; while consciousness can only seek culture or its denial. Even when we turn back to nature, inspired by Rousseauesque longing, we 'cultivate' nature. As long as we are still submerged in nature we are unconscious, and we live in the security of instinct that knows no problems. Everything in us that still belongs to nature shrinks away from a problem; for its name is doubt, and wherever doubt holds sway, there is uncertainty and the possibility of divergent ways. And where several ways seem possible, there we have turned away from the certain guidance of instinct and handed over to fear. For consciousness is now called upon to do that which nature has always done for her children – namely, to give a certain, unquestionable and unequivocal decision. And here we are beset by an all-too-human fear that consciousness – our Promethean conquest – may in the end not be able to serve us in the place of nature.

Problems thus draw us into an orphaned and isolated state where we are abandoned by nature and are driven to consciousness. There is no other way open to us; we are forced to resort to decisions and solutions where we formerly trusted ourselves to natural happenings. Every problem, therefore, brings the possibility of a widening of consciousness – but also the necessity of saying goodbye to childlike unconsciousness and trust in nature. This necessity is a psychic fact of such importance that it constitutes one of the essential symbolic teachings of the Christian religion. It is the sacrifice of the merely natural man – of the unconscious, ingenuous being whose tragic career began with the eating of the apple in Paradise. The biblical fall of man presents the dawn of consciousness as a curse. And as a matter of fact it is in this light that we first look upon every problem that forces us to greater consciousness and separates us even further from the paradise of unconscious childhood. Every one of us gladly turns away from his problems; if possible, they must not be mentioned, or, better still, their existence denied. We wish to make our lives simple, certain and smooth – and for that reason problems are *tabu*. We choose to have certainties and no doubts – results and no experiments – without even seeing that certainties can arise only through doubt, and results through experiment. The artful denial of a problem will not produce conviction; on the contrary, a wider and higher consciousness is called for to give us the certainty and clarity we need.

Carl Gustav Jung, 'The Stages of Life and Basic Postulates of Analytical Psychology', *Modern Man in Search of a Soul* (1933)

MATERIALISM

Consciousness Is an Epiphenomenon

The idea that we consciously determine our actions is turned upside down by Thomas Huxley (1825–95). Rather than being its guiding force, Huxley suggests that consciousness is a relatively unimportant spectator of human activity – about as essential to our functioning as the whistle of a locomotive to the running of the train!

Born in London, Huxley was the seventh of eight children. His father taught mathematics at Ealing School, which the young boy attended for two years, before the family moved to Coventry. This was his only formal education. He was an auto-didact and won a scholarship to study medicine at Charing Cross Hospital, but never completed his degree. At the age of twenty-one he signed on as assistant surgeon to the HMS Rattlesnake, commissioned to chart the seas around Australia and New Guinea. During the voyage he collected specimens and undertook detailed studies of marine invertebrates, for which he was later elected Fellow of the Royal Society.

Following the publication of Darwin's Origin of Species he became an outspoken champion of the theory of evolution, as a result of which he acquired the nickname 'Darwin's Bulldog'. In June 1860, he engaged in a famous debate with Archbishop Samuel Wilberforce at the British Association meeting in Oxford. Wilberforce asked him whether he was descended from an ape on his grandmother's or grandfather's side, to which he is alleged to have replied, 'I would rather be the offspring of two apes than be a man and afraid to face the truth.'

It is experimentally demonstrable – any one who cares to run a pin into himself may perform a sufficient demonstration of the fact – that a mode of motion of the nervous system is the immediate antecedent of a state of consciousness. All but the adherents of 'Occasionalism', or of the doctrine of 'Pre-established Harmony' (if any such now exist), must admit that we have as much reason for regarding the mode of motion of the nervous system as the cause of the state of consciousness, as we have for regarding any event as the cause of another. How the one phenomenon causes the other we know, as much or as little, as in any other case of causation; but we have as much right to believe that the sensation is an effect of the molecular change, as we have to believe that motion is an effect of impact; and there is as much propriety in saying that the brain evolves sensation, as there is in saying that an iron rod, when hammered, evolves heat.

As I have endeavoured to show, we are justified in supposing that something analogous to what happens in ourselves takes place in the brutes, and that the affections of their sensory nerves give rise to molecular changes in the brain, which again give rise to, or evolve, the corresponding states of consciousness. Nor can there be any reasonable doubt that the emotions of brutes, and such ideas as they possess, are similarly dependent upon molecular brain changes. Each sensory impression leaves behind a record in the structure of the brain – an 'ideagenous' molecule, so to speak, which is competent, under certain conditions, to reproduce, in a fainter condition, the state of consciousness which corresponds with that sensory impression; and it is these 'ideagenous molecules' which are the physical basis of memory.

It may be assumed, then, that molecular changes in the brain are the causes of all the states of consciousness of brutes. Is there any evidence that these states of consciousness may, conversely, cause those molecular changes which give rise to muscular motion? I see no such evidence. The frog walks, hops, swims and goes through his gymnastic performances quite as well without consciousness, and consequently without volition, as with it; and, if a frog, in his natural state, possesses anything corresponding with what we call volition, there is no reason to think that it is anything but a concomitant of the molecular changes in the brain which form part of the series involved in the production of motion.

The consciousness of brutes would appear to be related to the mechanism of their body simply as a collateral product of its working, and to be as completely without any power of modifying that working as the steam-whistle which accompanies the work of a locomotive engine is without influence upon its machinery. Their volition, if they have any, is an emotion indicative of physical changes, not a cause of such changes.

This conception of the relations of states of consciousness with molecular changes in the brain – of *psychoses* with *neuroses*[8] – does not prevent us from ascribing free will to brutes. For an agent is free when there is nothing to prevent him from doing that which he desires to do. If a greyhound chases a hare, he is a free agent, because his action is in entire accordance with his strong desire to catch the hare; while so long as he is held back by the leash he is not free, being prevented by external force from following his inclination. And the ascription of freedom to the greyhound under the former circumstances is by no means inconsistent with the other aspect of the facts of the case – that he is a machine impelled to the chase, and caused, at the same time, to have the desire to catch the game by the impression which the rays of light proceeding from the hare make upon his eyes, and through them upon his brain.

Much ingenious argument has at various times been bestowed upon the question: How is it possible to imagine that volition, which is a state of consciousness, and, as such, has not the slightest community of nature with matter in motion, can act upon the moving matter of which the body is composed, as it is assumed to do in voluntary acts? But if, as is here suggested, the voluntary acts of brutes – or, in other words, the acts which they desire to perform – are as purely mechanical as the rest of their actions, and are simply accompanied by the state of consciousness called volition, the Inquiry, so far as they are concerned, becomes superfluous. Their volitions do not enter into the chain of causation of their actions at all.

---

8 In recent usage the terms 'psychoses' and 'neuroses' have been employed in an almost opposite sense – the former referring to severe mental disorders characterized by loss of touch with reality, hallucinations and delusions, often linked with an organic cause; the latter to a range of conditions involving mental conflict and distress. Due to the difficulty in defining them, both terms have gone out of fashion in psychiatric classification [ed.].

The hypothesis that brutes are conscious automata is perfectly consistent with any view that may be held respecting the often discussed and curious question whether they have souls or not; and, if they have souls, whether those souls are immortal or not. It is obviously harmonious with the most literal adherence to the text of Scripture concerning 'the beast that perisheth'; but it is not inconsistent with the amiable conviction ascribed by Pope to his 'untutored savage', that when he passes to the happy hunting-grounds in the sky, 'his faithful dog shall bear him company'. If the brutes have consciousness and no souls, then it is clear that, in them, consciousness is a direct function of material changes; while, if they possess immaterial subjects of consciousness, or souls, then, as consciousness is brought into existence only as the consequence of molecular motion of the brain, it follows that it is an indirect product of material changes. The soul stands related to the body as the bell of a clock to the works, and consciousness answers to the sound which the bell gives out when it is struck.

Thus far I have strictly confined myself to the problem with which I proposed to deal at starting – the automatism of brutes. The question is, I believe, a perfectly open one, and I feel happy in running no risk of either Papal or Presbyterian condemnation for the views which I have ventured to put forward. And there are so very few interesting questions which one is, at present, allowed to think out scientifically – to go as far as reason leads, and stop where evidence comes to an end – without speedily being deafened by the tattoo of 'the drum ecclesiastic' – that I have luxuriated in my rare freedom, and would now willingly bring this disquisition to an end if I could hope that other people would go no farther. Unfortunately, past experience debars me from entertaining any such hope, even if

> . . . that drum's discordant sound
> Parading round and round and round[9]

were not, at present, as audible to me as it was to the mild poet

9 Huxley's reference is to a poem 'The Drum' by the Quaker poet John Scott of Amwell (1731–83).

who ventured to express his hatred of drums in general, in that well-known couplet.

It will be said, that I mean that the conclusions deduced from the study of the brutes are applicable to man, and that the logical consequences of such application are fatalism, materialism, and atheism – whereupon the drums will beat the *pas de charge.*

One does not do battle with drummers; but I venture to offer a few remarks for the calm consideration of thoughtful persons, untrammelled by foregone conclusions, unpledged to shore-up tottering dogmas, and anxious only to know the true bearings of the case.

It is quite true that, to the best of my judgement, the argumentation which applies to brutes holds equally good of men; and, therefore, that all states of consciousness in us, as in them, are immediately caused by molecular changes of the brain-substance. It seems to me that in men, as in brutes, there is no proof that any state of consciousness is the cause of change in the motion of the matter of the organism. If these positions are well based, it follows that our mental conditions are simply the symbols in consciousness of the changes which takes place automatically in the organism; and that, to take an extreme illustration, the feeling we call volition is not the cause of a voluntary act, but the symbol of that state of the brain which is the immediate cause of that act. We are conscious automata, endowed with free will in the only intelligible sense of that much-abused term – inasmuch as in many respects we are able to do as we like – but none the less parts of the great series of causes and effects which, in unbroken continuity, composes that which is, and has been, and shall be – the sum of existence.

As to the logical consequences of this conviction of mine, I may be permitted to remark that logical consequences are the scarecrows of fools and the beacons of wise men. The only question which any wise man can ask himself, and which any honest man will ask himself, is whether a doctrine is true or false. Consequences will take care of themselves; at most their importance can only justify us in testing with extra care the reasoning process from which they result.

So that if the view I have taken did really and logically lead to fatalism, materialism, and atheism, I should profess myself a fatalist, materialist, and atheist; and I should look upon those who, while they believed in my honesty of purpose and intellectual competency, should raise a hue and cry against me, as people who by their own admission preferred lying to truth, and whose opinions therefore were unworthy of the smallest attention.

But, as I have endeavoured to explain on other occasions, I really have no claim to rank myself among fatalistic, materialistic or atheistic philosophers. Not among fatalists, for I take the conception of necessity to have a logical, and not a physical foundation; not among materialists, for I am utterly incapable of conceiving the existence of matter if there is no mind in which to picture that existence; not among atheists, for the problem of the ultimate cause of existence is one which seems to me to be hopelessly out of reach of my poor powers. Of all the senseless babble I have ever had occasion to read, the demonstrations of these philosophers who undertake to tell us all about the nature of God would be the worst, if they were not surpassed by the still greater absurdities of the philosophers who try to prove that there is no God.

Thomas Henry Huxley, 'On the Hypothesis That Animals Are Automate' (1874)

Mental States Can Be Explained in Terms of Material Mechanisms

Daniel Dennett is Distinguished Arts and Sciences Professor and Director of the Center for Cognitive Studies at Tufts University, Boston, Massachusetts. If I have understood him correctly, he embraces the curious view that even though we 'seem' to have conscious experiences, we are not actually having them.

Philosophers have adopted various names for the things in the beholder (or properties of the beholder) that have been supposed to provide a safe home for the colours and the rest of the properties that have been banished from the 'external' world by the

286 THE BOOK OF THE MIND

triumphs of physics: 'raw feels', 'sensa', 'phenomenal qualities', 'intrinsic properties of conscious experiences', 'the qualitative content of mental states', and, of course, 'qualia', the term I will use. There are subtle differences in how these terms have been defined, but I am going to ride roughshod over them. In the previous chapter I seemed to be denying that there are any such properties, and for once what seems so is so. I am denying that there are any such properties. But (here comes that theme again) I agree wholeheartedly that there seem to be qualia.

There seem to be qualia, because it really does seem as if science has shown that the colours can't be out there, and hence must be in here. Moreover, it seems that what is in here can't *just* be the judgements we make when things seem coloured to us. This reasoning is confused, however. What science has actually shown us is just that the light-reflecting properties of objects cause creatures to go into various discriminative states, scattered about in their brains, and underlying a host of innate dispositions and learned habits of varying complexity. And what are *their* properties? Here we can play Locke's card a second time. These discriminative states of observers' brains have various 'primary' properties (their mechanistic properties due to their connections, the excitation states of their elements, etc.), and in virtue of these primary properties, they have various secondary, merely dispositional properties. In human creatures with language, for instance, these discriminative states often eventually dispose the creatures to express verbal judgements alluding to the 'colour' of various things. When someone says 'I know the ring isn't really pink, but it sure seems pink', the first clause expresses a judgement about something in the world, and the second clause expresses a second-order judgement about a discriminative state about something in the world. The semantics of such statements makes it clear what colours supposedly are: reflective properties of the surfaces of objects, or of transparent volumes (the pink ice cube, the shaft of limelight). And that is just what they are in fact – though saying just *which* reflective properties they are is tricky.

Daniel Dennett, 'Qualia Disqualified', *Consciousness Explained* (1991)

Things May Not Be as They Seem. We May 'Seem to Have a Problem' Which We Don't Have!

In 2001 Professor Galen Strawson was appointed to a chair of philosophy at the University of Reading, Berkshire. He argues here that Descartes' biggest error was attempting to show that human consciousness was not a physical process. Granted that thoughts or sentiments seem to be constituted so differently from substances – from stones – Strawson argues that this is only a function of our ignorance. It is a problem of 'seeming' rather than a problem of 'being'. We need not seek to conflate personal consciousness with observable public behaviour (see Ryle*, Watson*, Skinner*), we need only acknowledge that our present understanding of the properties of matter is insufficient to explain its relation to mind.

The standard formulation of the 'mind–body problem' rests on a huge and wholly unjustified assumption (this assumption, in fact, is Descartes' deepest error). It is not content with the obvious truth that matter and consciousness *seem* to us to be utterly heterogeneous things. It slides onto the claim that matter and consciousness are *in fact* utterly heterogeneous things, in such a way that it is mysterious how one could ever be the basis or 'realization' of the other. It shifts from a harmless and true epistemological claim about how things seem to us to a mega-therial metaphysical claim about how things are in reality.

Why? Why indeed? The root cause of the mistake is the unsupported assumption that current physics – or indeed ordinary experience, in its own modest but compelling way – gives us a pretty good fix on the fundamental nature of matter, and shows it to be utterly qualitatively unlike consciousness. It is only relative to this assumption that the existence of consciousness in a material world seems in any way mystifying, for there is nothing particularly puzzling about consciousness as it is in itself. We know just what it is like – or at least what certain forms of it are like. Consider an experience of blue or giddiness. Consider it as it is in itself. You know what it is. So, if our best picture of matter makes it seem incomprehensible that matter should be the basis of (or simply be) conscious experience, all this shows in the inadequacy of our best picture of matter. Locke, Hume, Priestley, Kant and others were very clear about this, but few understand it today. Many now make Descartes' deepest error, in fact, with far less justification than him – while condemning him for his errors.

It is not in any way anti-scientific to claim that we do not have a good fix on the fundamental nature of matter. Current physics instructs us daily in how foolish it is to assume that we do (while providing a magnificent theoretical framework in which to express and exploit a great deal of information about the behaviour of matter). It is widely agreed that the current 'Standard Model' is unsatisfactory; the old quarrel between relativity theory and quantum mechanics remains unresolved; there is turmoil in general cosmology; and String Theory, after the 'second superstring revolution', is again pressing obscurely at the door.

The first problem of consciousness, then, the mind–body problem or qualia problem, is just a vivid proof of our ignorance of the nature of matter, and of the difficulty – seeming impossibility – of reconciling first-personal and impersonal data. There is no metaphysical mind–body problem, only an epistemological one.

Galen Strawson, 'Esprit de Core: A New Way of Viewing "the Movie-in-the-Brain"' (2000)

THE MYSTERY OF CONSCIOUSNESS

Spiritual Intelligence

It is one thing to propose, as Galen Strawson* does, that our present understanding of the properties of matter is insufficient to explain its relation to mind. It is quite another to boldly conclude that our sense of conscious meaning and value is produced by a particular wavelength of electrical activity in the brain, and then to extend this argument to suggest that all *matter* *possesses the quality of proto-consciousness. This animistic belief, common among primitive peoples, is given a curious twist by Danah Zohar, by combining it with ideas derived from quantum physics.*

Zohar rejects the notion that consciousness is a property specific to neural tissue on the grounds that it 'doesn't explain very much' and appears to emerge 'suddenly' with the advent of mammals. However the notion that new properties emerge 'suddenly' as a result of greater complexity of organization, both in the physical and biological worlds, does not seem at all difficult to understand. We do not say that hydrogen possesses the quality of 'proto-wetness', and that it would be odd to think that 'wetness' arises suddenly, when it combines with oxygen to give us water!

Zohar was an undergraduate at MIT, where she studied physics and philosophy. She went on to Harvard University, where she studied psychology and theology. She is a Visiting Fellow at Cranfield School of Management. Her co-author and husband, Ian Marshall, studied psychology and philosophy at Oxford University before taking a medical degree at London University. He is a psychiatrist and psychotherapist.

The notion that there is a third kind of thinking of which the brain is capable, and hence a third intelligence connected inherently to meaning, is radically new. It flies in the face of twentieth-century cognitive science, which sees mind essentially as a computation machine. There are no previous non-academic accounts of research data that backs up this book's claim for the existence of SQ [spiritual, intelligence, ed.]; indeed, there are no technical papers that combine all the relevant research. What, in plain words, are the wider implications of all this neurology and quantum physics? What can they tell us about the origins of SQ, about the extent of the transcendent dimension that it adds to our experience?

Experimental research presented here has shown that:

• there are 40 Hz oscillations across the whole brain

- these oscillations seem necessarily to be associated with the possibility of consciousness in the brain
- these oscillations 'bind' individual perceptual and cognitive events in the brain into a larger, more meaningful whole, and
- there may be a quantum dimension to the ion channel activity that generates the oscillations, as well as quantum coherence among the oscillations at multi-neurone level.

From all this I have concluded that the 40 Hz oscillations are the neural basis of SQ, a third intelligence that places our actions and experience in a larger context of meaning and value, thus rendering them more effective. Everything else discussed in this chapter boils down to two questions. Where does consciousness come from? And following on from that, where does meaning come from? Both are closely related to two further questions. Where do we conscious human beings belong in the universe? And how deep are our roots?

The first possible answer to where consciousness comes from is that it originates with brains, or at least with mammalian brains, all of which display 40 Hz oscillations. I reject this limited possibility, because it doesn't really explain very much. It says that consciousness just suddenly emerges with the mammals, as a new property of the universe.

The second possibility is that consciousness originates with brains because neurones possess proto-consciousness (pre-consciousness that in some combinations can become conscious). Here, I am assuming that the 40 Hz oscillations are the required factor for combining proto-conscious bits into consciousness. If this is the case, since neurones are single cells we human beings may be rooted in all other single-cell life on this planet. Our spiritual intelligence is rooted in life itself, and thus has biological and evolutionary origins, though life itself may still be just an accident in the universe, and thus without meaning or purpose beyond itself. I think this is possibly true, but unlikely. It presents the same problem as assuming that consciousness begins just with brains, only at a more primary celular level. *Why* should proto-consciousness begin just with neurones? Does it really have no roots in fundamental physics?

After considering all the main arguments, I have opted for the stronger view that proto-consciousness is a fundamental property of the material universe, just as mass, charge, spin and location are. Further, I have accepted the argument that everything possesses a degree of proto-consciousness but that only certain special structures, like brains, have what is needed to generate full-blown consciousness. In this case, we conscious human beings have our roots at the origin of the universe itself. Our spiritual intelligence grounds us in the wider cosmos, and life has purpose and meaning within the larger context of cosmic evolutionary processes.

Danah Zohar and Ian Marshall, *Spiritual Intelligence* (2000)

Consciousness Is a Mystery That Cannot Be Explained by Natural Science

Sir John Eccles (1903–97) argues against the materialist assumption that the mind is nothing but a property of the brain. He dismisses the notion that advances in science yielding a greater understanding of brain function will eventually prove this to be true, ironically calling it 'promisory materialism'. He proposes that there exists another immaterial world which interacts with the physical one, and suggests that the units of this mental world be called 'psychons'. Each psychon would represent a unitary conscious experience, somehow linked with a neurological unit so that in willed action the appropriate psychon momentarily increases the probability of the firing of selected neurons. Interaction among the psychons themselves accounts for the subjective sense of self and the inner world of our mind.

Eccles was an Australian neurophysiologist who won the Nobel prize for medicine in 1963. Born in Melbourne, he graduated in medicine in 1925, and took up a Victorian Rhodes Scholarship at Magdalen College, Oxford, in the same year, studying under Sir Charles Sherrington and later becoming his research assistant. He was awarded an Oxford D.Phil. in 1929, and for the next five years continued to work in Oxford on synaptic transmission. In 1937 he left England to become director of a research unit in Sydney and in 1944 went on to take a Chair in Physiology at the University of Otago in New Zealand. It was here that he first met the philosopher Karl Popper with whom he collaborated in developing ideas about the mind–body problem. He was elected a Fellow of the Royal Society in 1941. He was a rare brain scientist, who believed in the supernatural origin of mind.

If as conjectured the self-conscious mind is not a special part of World 1, that is of the physical and biological worlds, it is likely to have different fundamental properties. Though it is in liaison with special zones of the neocortex, it need not itself have the property of spacial extension. Apparently it integrates instantaneously what it reads out from diverse scattered elements of the active neocortex, largely of the dominant hemisphere, but probably also from the minor hemisphere of the normal brain. But the question: where is the self-conscious mind located? is unanswerable in principle. This can be appreciated when we consider some components of the self-conscious mind. It makes no sense to ask where are located the feelings of love or hate, or of joy or fear, or of such values of truth, goodness and beauty which apply to mental appraisals. These are experienced. Abstract concepts such as in mathematics have no location per se, but can be materialized, as it were, in specific examples or demonstrations. Similarly a location of the self-conscious mind appears when its actions become materialized in its interactions with the liaison brain.

[. . .]

My position is this. I believe that my personal uniqueness, that is my own experienced self-consciousness, is not accounted for by this emergent explanation [deriving from the brain, ed.] of the coming-to-be of my own self. It is the experienced uniqueness that is not so explained. Genetic uniqueness will not do. It can be asserted that I have my experienced uniqueness because my brain is built by the genetic instructions of a quite unique genetic code, my genome with its 30,000 or so genes (Dobzhansky, personal communication) strung along the immense double helix of the human DNA with its 3.5×10^9 nucleotide pairs. It has to be recognized that with 30,000 genes there is a chance of $10^{10,000}$ against that uniqueness being achieved. That is, if my uniqueness of self is tied to the genetic uniqueness that built my brain, then the odds against myself existing in my experienced uniqueness are $10^{10,000}$ against.

So I am constrained to believe that there is what we might call a supernatural origin of my unique selfhood or soul; and that gives rise of course to a whole new set of problems. How does my soul come to be in liaison with my brain that has an evolutionary origin? By this idea of a supernatural creation I escape from the incredible improbability that the uniqueness of my own self is genetically determined. There is no problem about the genetic uniqueness of my brain. It is the uniqueness of the experienced self that requires this hypothesis of an independent origin of the self or soul, which is then associated with a brain, that so becomes my brain. That is how the self comes to act as a self-conscious mind, working with the brain in all the ways that we have been discussing, receiving and giving to it and doing a marvellous integrating and driving and controlling job on the neural machinery of the brain.

There are deep problems of how this liaison self with brain comes to be and how it will cease to be. These are a new set of problems; but on the other hand I believe that these problems derive from a more realistic hypothesis than the one which could assume that my self is in a transcendent emergent relationship with my brain, and therefore in that explanation completely derived from a material structure in World 1.

John Eccles, *The Self and Its Brain*: 'Personal Uniqueness' (1977)

6

SELF

I love all men who *dive*. Any fish can swim near the surface,
but it takes a great whale to go down stairs five miles or more;
& if he don't attain the bottom, why, all the lead in Galena
can't fashion the plummet that will. I'm not talking of Mr
Emerson now – but of the whole corps of thought-divers, that
have been diving & coming up again with bloodshot eyes since
the world began.

Herman Melville, Letter to Evert A. Duyckinck (1849)

Individuality is something most people tend to take for granted.
The idea that there is some kind of unique, single, subjective 'I'
that I call my 'self' and that I can observe. Somehow, just as I
see my body by looking outwards I think I can see myself by
looking inwards, by means of introspection. Indeed self-
consciousness is one of the characteristics we have come to think
of as a distinguishing mark for our species. Yet the unity of 'self'
has often seemed problematic. L.L. Whyte puts it nicely when he
says:

The intuitive sense of a persisting experiencing self constitutes
a treacherous basis for an ordering of experience, because the
direct awareness of the human individual does not justify the
attribution to the self either of permanence, or of unchanging
identity, or of continuous awareness. Indeed the facts of
growth, ageing and death, and the transitory wandering character of awareness render this assumption of a permanent identical conscious subject most peculiar.[1]

1 L.L. Whyte, *The Unconscious before Freud*, Julian Freedman, London, 1979.

Perhaps the most peculiarly human quality of mind is not consciousness but conflict. It is the price we pay for our sense of freedom. We are often 'in two minds'. Cognitive conflict or 'dissonance' – contradictions between newly acquired facts and what we thought we knew, opinions which do not fit with other opinions that we simultaneously hold, or behaviour which seems to fly in the face of both, is indeed commonplace. The rational-scientific view would dictate that when this kind of conflict occurs we should alter our original views or change our behaviour. But there is reason to think we tend to avoid making such changes. Instead we conveniently adjust our cognitions.[2] In other words we have ways of ignoring information that disturbs us, of burying our heads in the sand. The same can be said for the regulation of feelings, and the resolution of moral and social dilemmas.

Turning away from reality seems pretty pointless in terms of survival, but the ability to suppress awareness of some things is useful. Concentrating our attention on a particular topic usually involves blotting out irrelevant sensory information. We are not quite like dolphins who manage to have one half of their brain asleep while the other is up and about, yet our minds do seem to have an amazing ability to 'dissociate', that is to be able to isolate one set of experiences from another. If it were merely a question of trying to organise and attend to (or disregard) a mass of incoming sense data so that we do not 'overload' the system, the task would be difficult enough. But we also have to live together without the help of inbuilt rigidly patterned social dispositions. And this involves us in another kind of struggle, in regulating the conflict between individual desire and social standards, in taming our egoism. Conscience, the means of accomplishing this, is often in confrontation with what we would like to do, and we have developed all sorts of ways of getting around it. It is famously 'soluble in alcohol'. In many people, however, as Stanley Milgram's experiments in the early 1970s sadly confirmed, it also dissolves under the influence of authority. Blind obedience to external authority, especially where its directions coincide with

2 See Leon Festinger, *A Theory of Cognitive Dissonance*, Tavistock, 1957.

more primitive sadistic urges, offers an easy way out – a kind of perversion of 'good' behaviour.

But it would be wrong to suppose that unfettered instinctual expression would mean an end to conflict, for our instincts themselves can drive us in opposing directions. And we can embrace contradictory values, and intentions. We are reflexive beings, capable of standing back from our own experience, from our own identity, and questioning it. We can even take our own lives. Our 'selves' are ineluctably divided. Attempting to reconcile all this imposes a requirement for mental work which has, over the years, been undertaken by philosophy, religion and mythology.

To say that we experience conflict is, of course, different from saying that the mind has 'underlying structures' which are at war with one another, and certainly different from supposing that those structures are instantiated in anatomical reality, although the split-brain experiments described in the following chapter do raise this intriguing possibility. Modern 'object-relations theory' in psychoanalysis, exemplified in the work of Melanie Klein and her followers, paints a picture of our unconscious life in terms of psychological structures, internal combatants and internal referees – quasi-autonomous good and bad 'internal objects' whose relations determine our conscious experience. But does it help to understand ourselves in such terms or are they just a currently more acceptable idiom for describing conflict, previously conceived in terms of incubi and succubi, devil-possession and God-given strength? How best to describe and categorize the different parts of the mind or soul (if such they be), and how to understand their dealings with one another is a question which has received various answers over the years, and which remains bothersome. Yet no picture of the human mind which ignores the experience of conflict can strike us as in any way complete. Even when we think we have a good take on the contending elements, there is a problem in conceptualizing the means by which they are overseen, nicely articulated by Aristotle, and still only partially answered by Gerald Edelman's theory of 'Neuro-Darwinism'.[3]

3 See Edelman, pp. 272–7.

Religion, at least theistic religion, traditionally highlighted the conflict between sin and sanctity to be reconciled through the action of faith. Philosophy and nontheistic religion looked to reason or 'right thinking' for salvation. More than 2,500 years ago, Siddharta Gautama founded Buddhism, which advocated the conquest and extinction of desire, in fact the relinquishment of 'self' altogether, as the only satisfactory resolution. A century or so later, Plato envisaged a three-way division in our soul with appetite, temper and reason forming the contending parts, and he classified people according to which element had the upper hand. For him, appetite was not all bad, there were necessary aspects such as hunger, and harmless tastes for luxuries. But there were also anarchic desires so awful that they could only be revealed in dreams. It was the task of education to bring reason to bear on these appetites and so release us from their demands. One might say that Plato's education performed a function directly opposite to that of modern advertising. Rather than stimulating disruptive desire, it aimed at subduing it, bringing it into line with wisdom's judgement. Clearly a sense of unity was not something taken for granted, but had to be earned through hard psychological work. An educated man was someone who had learned to live with himself.

Throughout the Middle Ages, reason, the regulating principle, signified human approximation to the image of God. Man's animal nature was a threat to this lordly status. An elaborate theory of the passions and of the perversity of the will, much influenced by St Augustine, was developed. But Enlightenment thinking shifted the focus. One powerful trend in this fissiparous movement was represented by the thought of Jean Jacques Rousseau. It laid the blame for our struggle less on the urgency of animal instincts (which were natural), than on the manmade social arrangements that suppressed them. We started out blindly questing for pleasure, and biological maturation (which Rousseau called 'the education of nature') increased our capacity for self-control, but it also stoked up desire. We therefore needed to learn from others how to handle ourselves, make best use of our faculties, which he called 'the education of men'. And reality showed us that our wishes could not always be fulfilled, a frustration which Rousseau called 'the

education of things' – thus 'we are each taught by three masters',
he said. If the conflicting teaching could not be harmonized, we
would never be at peace. Man might be born free, his animal
instincts might be perfectly acceptable, but if freedom meant lack
of internal dissonance, even for Rousseau, it did not come easily.
Two millennia of Western thought had done little to alter the classical tripartite view of forces shaping the human condition.

But how was harmony to be brought about? By what means
could incompatible strivings be resolved? Maybe, left to our own
devices, we were not as wild as we feared? One answer, the one
Rousseau advocated, was to create a less restrictive society. The
idea was appealing, and has continued to inform liberal-
democratic thinking over the years. But for many, the naive faith
in man's 'natural' goodness as embodied in Enlightenment philosophy, simply did not ring true. Another strand of Western
thinking, most obviously characterized in the writings of the
German philosopher Friedrich Nietzsche,[4] saw a reaction against
the attenuated picture of man's mind, stripped of its irrationality
and its 'badness'. Social change would not, of itself, produce
salvation. We really needed, as both the ancients and the medieval
scholastics had understood, to do work on ourselves.

The explosion of interest in 'the unconscious', culminating in
the development of psychoanalysis towards the end of the nineteenth century, can be understood in terms of this task – the quest
for a locus for repudiated parts of the human mind. The need
to integrate these parts into a plausible representation meant that
they had to be included in the overall model. If the conscious
mind, the executive conscious ego, was to be preserved as the
domain of goodness and rationality, then everything else characteristic of human experience must exist somewhere outside it,
there must be a dark underside. Just what this shady area
contained proved to be a controversial matter.

Sigmund Freud, at first, conceived it as a reservoir of unacceptable (incestuous) infantile libido, kept out of consciousness

4 See Ernest Gellner's readable *The Psychoanalytic Movement*, Paladin, 1985, and
   L.L. Whyte's equally accessible *The Unconscious before Freud*, Julian Friedman,
   1978.

by dynamic processes of repression. Mental conflict was thus
fought out across the boundary between the unconscious and
conscious domains. Where consciousness encountered a threat to
its harmony it 'defended itself' – simply relegated the offending
thoughts and feelings into the underworld, a place where contradictions and paralogisms could exist side by side, as they do in
dreams, without causing any apparent disturbance.

'Human kind', as T.S. Eliot has it in his poem 'Burnt Norton',
'Cannot bear very much reality', a judgement with which psychoanalysis concurred. Rather than denying conflict, this new
psychology concerned itself with the way in which we dealt with
it – unconsciously 'adjusted our minds' – changed our subjective
reality in order to make life bearable. It suggested that the mental
work required in order to achieve a semblance of civilized living
occurred largely outside our awareness. Our complex adult
habits, interests and passions had a history, and could be seen in
the light of basic drives which had been transformed so as to
render them socially innocuous. Early psychoanalysis concentrated on investigating the extraordinary nature of the unconscious mental gymnastics which allowed this to happen, so that
we came to love the order we had formerly hated, despise the
instinctual gratification we had once loved. Freud's 1908 paper,
'Character and Anal Erotism', in which he traces the transformation of infantile coprophilia (relegated to the unconscious) into
conscious adult cleanliness, is the most succinct expression of this
idea.[5]

However, just as the notion that conflict stemmed primarily
from social repression ran into difficulty, so the idea that
conscious repression of unconscious desires was the central
process, failed to correspond with experience. When Freud
thought he had discovered *unconscious guilt*, at the root of
neurotic punishment-seeking behaviour, he was forced to concede
that the unconscious mind was not, after all, a 'conflict-free' zone.
There could be conflict *within* the unconscious, inhibitions of
which we were unaware, between impulse and conscience,

5 S. Freud, SE. IX 169–73.

between what was desired and what was allowed or simply what was possible. Freud's later theorizing therefore reinstituted something like the old Platonic model, repositioning the theoretical conflict so that it now occurred between three mental agencies or psychic structures – id (instinct), ego (mediating the demands of external reality and having executive powers) and superego (conscience), all of which, he now thought, could exist in unconscious form.

The most controversial aspect of Freud's model of mental development was the role it allocated to infantile sexual impulses. Freud saw the origin of conscience and morality in the necessity for a small child to change the nature of its passionate attachment to parents, to learn that it could not possess them exclusively and instead must internalize them as objects of desire. In his theory they were to be incorporated into the child's mind in the form of its 'superego' – the 'heir to the Oedipus Complex'*. The arena of conflict was thus shifted from external to internal reality and the difficult task of resolving it allocated to the 'ego'. Failures in this regard were held to lie at the root of human neurosis.

In contrast to the Buddhist prescription for a total annihilation of desire, psychoanalysis offered to facilitate a metamorphosis of infantile libidinal attachment. Desire remained to be 'conquered' but would be subsumed into the structure of the ego under the motto 'Where id was, there ego shall be' – a change that was to be brought about not by the exercise of reason or education, but through the transformative experience of the psychoanalytic relationship.

But for Freud's erstwhile colleague, Carl Gustav Jung, the unconscious mind was less a cauldron of repressed sexuality than a container for complementary qualities, a kind of reciprocal of the consciously manifest mind. It was a treasure-house of inherited talent and hidden knowledge. If its potential could be unlocked, it was not just the ego that would be strengthened but the whole personality that would be expanded. And for Alfred Adler, the heir to Schopenhauer's thinking, it was primarily concerned with power relations, motivating a drive toward independence and attempting to compensate for weakness. Since the unconscious mind is by definition just that, *unconscious*, what goes on in it will always be a matter for inference and speculation.

THE ANCIENTS

Conflict Within the Soul: Are There Two or Three Warring Principles?

Plato[6] *is concerned to explain mental conflict in a person by analogy to social conflict in his model state. Just as there are three social classes, workers, soldiers and rulers, so there are three corresponding components of the soul: desire, spirit and reason. Social harmony is brought about in the state when each class does what it's supposed to do, sticks to its given role and doesn't interfere with the other. Similarly, mental harmony is achieved when a man learns how to balance the competing demands of desire and reason. Spirit, Plato argues here, once subordinated to reason, acts as an ally in overcoming unruly desire.*

In a dialogue between Socrates and his pupil Adeimantus, Plato suggests that under reason's hegemony, conflict between the two other components will be minimized. However, a well-known objection points to the existence of conflict within the component parts. Opposing desires may exist as may incompatible reasons. Plato's conflict-free model man seems as unachievable as his just state.

And might a man be thirsty, and yet unwilling to drink?

Yes, he said, that often happens.

And in such a case what is one to say? Would you not say that there is one principle in the soul bidding a man to drink, and a second forbidding him, which is other and stronger than that which bids him?

That is my view, he replied.

6 See biographical note on p. 72.

And the forbidding principle is derived from reason, and the bidding and attracting principles are the effects of passion and disorder?

Clearly.

Then we may fairly infer that they are two, and that they differ from one another; one of them we may call the rational principle of the soul, the other, which accompanies certain pleasures and satisfactions, is that with which a man loves and hungers and thirsts and feels the emotions of desire, and may be rightly termed irrational or appetitive?

Yes, he said, we shall not be far wrong in that.

Then let these be marked out as the two principles which there are existing in the soul. And what shall we say of passion, or spirit? Is that a third, or akin to one of the preceding?

I should be inclined to say – akin to desire.

Well, I said, there is a story which I remember to have heard, and on which I rely. The story is that Leontius, the son of Aglaion, was coming up from the Piraeus, under the north wall on the outside, and observed some dead bodies lying on the ground by the executioner. He felt a longing desire to see them; and also a disgust and abhorrence of them; for a time he turned away and averted his eyes, and then, suddenly overcome by the impulse, forced them open, and ran up, saying (to his eyes), Take your fill, ye wretches, of the fair sight.

I have heard the story myself, he said.

Now this seems to imply that anger differs from the desires, and is sometimes at war with them.

That is implied, he said.

And are there not many other cases in which we observe that, when a man's desires violently prevail over his reason, he reviles himself, and is angry at the violence within him, and that in this struggle, which is like the struggle of factions in a State, his spirit is on the side of his reason; – but that the passionate or spirited element should side with the desires when reason decides that she is not to be opposed, this sort of thing, I believe, you will say that you never observed occurring in yourself, nor, as I think, in any one else?

Certainly not, he said.

Suppose I said, that a man thinks he has done a wrong to another, the nobler he is the less able he is to get into a state of righteous indignation; his anger refuses to be excited at the hunger or cold or other suffering, which he deems that the injured person may justly inflict upon him?

True, he said.

But when he thinks that he is the sufferer of the wrong, then he boils and chafes, and is on the side of what he believes to be justice; and because he suffers hunger or cold or other pain he is only the more determined to persevere and conquer; he must do or die, and will not desist, until he hears the voice of the shepherd, that is, reason, bidding his dog bark no more.

That is a very good illustration, he replied; and in our State, as we were saying, the auxiliaries were to be dogs, and to hear the voice of the rulers, who are their shepherds.

I perceive, I said, that you quite understand me; there is, however, a further point which I would wish you to consider.

What may that be?

You remember that passion or spirit appeared at first sight to be a sort of desire, but now we would say the contrary; for in the conflict of the soul, spirit is arrayed on the side of the rational principle.

Most assuredly.

But a further question arises. *Is* the spirit different from reason also, or only a sort of reason; in which case, instead of three principles in the soul, there will be only two, the rational and the concupiscent; or rather, as the State was composed of three classes, traders, auxiliaries, counsellors, so may there not be in the individual soul a third element which is passion or spirit, and which is the auxiliary of reason when not corrupted by education?

Yes, he said, there must be a third.

Yes, I replied, if passion, which has already been shown to be different from desire, turn out also to be different from reason.

But that is obvious, he said, and is proved in the case of young children, who are full of spirit almost as soon as they are born, whereas some of them never seem to attain to the use of reason, and a good many only late in life.

Excellent, I said, and the same thing is seen in brute animals, which is a further proof of the truth of what you are saying. And Homer, whose words we have already quoted, may be again summoned as a witness, where he says,

He smote his breast, and thus rebuked his soul (*Od.* xx. 17)

for in those lines Homer has clearly supposed the power which reasons about the better and worse to be different from the unreasoning principle which is the subject of rebuke.

That is true, he said.

And now, after much tossing in the argument, we have reached land, and are fairly agreed that the principles which exist in the State, like those in the individual, are three in number, and the same with them.

Exactly.

And must we not infer that the individual is wise in the same way, and in virtue of the same quality which makes the State wise?

Certainly.

And the same quality which constitutes bravery in the State constitutes bravery in the individual, and the same is true of all the other virtues?

Assuredly.

And the individual will be acknowledged by us to be just in the same way that the State was just?

That will also follow of course.

And the justice of the State consisted, as we very well remember, in each of the three classes doing the work of that class?

We are not very likely to forget that, he said.

And we must also remember that the individual whose several principles do their own work will be just, and will do his own work?

Yes, he said, we must remember that.

And ought not the rational principle, which is wise, and has the care of the whole soul, to rule, and the passionate or spirited principle to be the subject and ally?

Quite true, he said.

And these two, thus nurtured and educated, and having learned truly to know their own functions, will set a rule over the concupiscent part of every man, which is the largest and most insatiable; over this they will set a guard, lest, waxing great with the fullness of bodily pleasures, as they are termed, and no longer confined to her own sphere, the concupiscent soul should attempt to enslave and rule those who are not her natural born subjects, and overturn the whole life of man?

Very true, he said.

The two will be the defenders of the whole soul and the whole body against attacks from without; the one counselling, and the other fighting under the command of their leader, and courageously executing his counsels.

True.

And he is deemed courageous who, having the element of passion working in him, preserves, in the midst of pain and pleasure, the notion of danger which reason prescribes?

Right, he replied.

And he is wise who has in him that little part which rules and gives orders; that part being supposed to have a knowledge of what is for the interest of each and all of the three other parts?

Assuredly.

And would you not say that he is temperate who has these three elements in friendly harmony, in whom the one ruling principle of reason, and the two subject ones of spirit and desire are equally agreed that reason ought to rule, and do not rebel?

Certainly, he said, that is the true account of temperance whether in the State or individual. [. . .]

Plato, *The Republic*, Book IV 438–42 (c.400BCE)

What Holds The Soul Together?

Aristotle puts his finger on the problem of the 'homunculus' (see p. 273). If, as Plato (and Freud) suggest, the soul can be divided into different component parts like desire and reason, and each of these parts acts as if it were an independent entity, an autonomous little man vying with his neighbour for resources

and attention, for dominance, we will always need to postulate
an extra part, another little man or 'big boss', who knows every-
thing and is in charge of it all. But he in turn will need to be
divided into parts, thus leading to an infinite regress.

Rather than dividing the mind into structural parts, Aristotle
concentrated on describing its functions. He saw these in a hier-
archy of dependence, so that reason, at the top, was dependent
on, but not necessarily in conflict with, the lower faculties such
as growth, locomotion, sensation, memory, imagination, emotion
and desire. If he thus avoided falling into Plato's errors, it was
more by side-stepping the problem of conflict, than by
contributing to our understanding of it.

Aristotle (384–322BCE), Greek philosopher, was the son of
the court physician to the king of Macedon. Born in the obscure
village of Stagira, he travelled to Athens at the age of seventeen
to join Plato's Academy, where he remained, first as a student
and then as a teacher, until Plato's death in the year 347BCE.
Twelve years later he returned to Athens to found his own school,
the Lyceum. Following the death of Alexander the Great in
323BCE, anti-Macedonian feeling forced him to flee the city and
return to his homeland, where not long afterwards he died.

Now some say that the soul can be divided into parts, one that
thinks, another that desires. If this is so, what holds the soul
together? Certainly not the body, on the contrary, it seems to be
held together by the soul; at any rate when the soul departs, the
body disintegrates and rots away. If, then, something else gives
unity to the soul, this other thing should, more properly speaking,
be called soul. We would then need to repeat the question: Is *it*
one or can it be divided? If it is one, why not attribute unity to
the soul itself in the first place? If, however, it turns out to consist
of different components, then again the question of what holds
them together must be asked, and so on ad infinitum? . . .

Aristotle, *On the Soul* (350BCE)

COMMON SENSE

The Inward Senses

Robert Burton (1577–1640), scholar, writer and clergyman, spent the whole of his adult life in Oxford. Educated at Brasenose College, he went on to become a Student of Christ Church and in 1616 was made vicar of St Thomas's Church. He understood melancholy to be both a physical and spiritual state, and therefore considered himself an appropriate anatomist.

His book, The Anatomy of Melancholy, *first published in 1621, is a compendium of information, anecdotes and literary references. In fact it is not restricted to the subject of sadness but ranges widely over diverse aspects of the human condition. The following passage reveals his notion of 'common sense' as the co-ordinating and perceiving faculty which he localizes in the forebrain.*

Common sense

Inner Senses are three in number, so called, because they be within the brain-pan, as *common sense, phantasie, memory.* Their objects are not only things present, but they perceive the sensible species of things *to come, past, absent,* such as were before in the sense. *This common sense* is the judge or moderator of the rest, by whom we discern all differences of objects; for by mine eye I do not know that I see, or by mine ear that I hear, but by my *common sense,* who judgeth of sounds and colours; they are but the organs to bring the species to be censured; so that all their objects are his, and all their offices are his. The forepart of the brain is his organ or seat.

Phantasie

Phantasie, or imagination, which some call *aestimative,* or *cogitative,* (confirmed, saith Fernalius, by frequent meditation) is an inner sense, which doth more fully examine the species perceived by *common sense,* of things present or absent, and keeps them longer, recalling them to mind again, or making new of his own.

In time of sleep, this faculty is free, and many times conceives strange, stupend, absurd shapes, as in sick men we commonly observe. His *organ* is the middle cell of the brain; his *objects*, all the species communicated to him by the *common sense*, by comparison of which, he feigns infinite other unto himself. In *melancholy* men, this faculty is most powerful and strong, and often hurts, producing many monstrous and prodigious things, especially if it be stirred up by some terrible object, presented to it from *common sense* or *memory*. In poets and painters, imagination forcibly works, as appears by their several fictions, anticks, images, as Ovid's house of Sleep, Psyche's palace in Apuleius, &c. In men it is subject and governed by *reason* or at least should be; but, in brutes, it hath no superiour, and is *ratio brutorum*, all the reason they have.

Memory
Memory layes up all the species which the senses have brought in, and records them as a good *register*, that they may be forthcoming when they are called for by *phantasie* and *reason*. His object is the same with *phantasie*; his seat and *organ*, the back part of the brain.

Affections of the senses, sleep and waking
The affections of these senses are *sleep* and *waking*, common to all sensible creatures. *Sleep is a rest or binding of the outward senses* [sight, smell, hearing, taste and touch, and possibly speech and titillation, ed.], *and of the common sense, for the preservation of body and soul* (as Scaliger defines it); for, when the common sense resteth, the outward senses rest also. The phantasie alone is free, and his commander reason; as appears by those imaginary dreams, which are of divers kinds, *natural, divine, daemonical*, & which vary according to humours, diet, actions, objects, &c. of which Artemidorus, Cardanus, and Sambucus, with their several interpretators, have written great volumes. This ligation of senses proceeds from an inhibition of spirits, the way being stopped by which they should come; this stopping is caused of vapours arising out of the stomach, filling the nerves, by which the spirits should be conveyed. When these

vapours are spent, the passage is open, and the spirits perform their accustomed duties; so that *waking is the action and motion of the senses, which the spirits, dispersed over all parts, cause.*

Robert Burton, *The Anatomy of Melancholy*: 'Anatomy of the Soul' (1651)

THE GALTONIAN UNCONSCIOUS

Catching the Mind at Work

Romantic psychology in the nineteenth century likened the human mind to a mansion. The mystery behind the genesis of ideas, passions, thoughts and mental imagery was hidden in an inaccessible room, with a one-way door into consciousness. But towards the end of the century, science seemed to offer a key to the unvisited phatasmagoric chambers of the mind. The metaphor began to change, losing its feminine mystique and taking on a mundane mechanistic character.

Francis Galton (1822–1911), Charles Darwin's cousin, pioneered the development of measurement and statistics in British psychology. He was a typical Victorian polymath, working outside the structure of a university and making contributions in a variety of fields. In 1854 he was elected a Fellow of the Royal Society for his exploration of Central South-West Africa. He experimented with electricity and was also one of the first to make a serious study of the weather, laying the foundation for the development of meteorology.

Galton antedated Freud in proposing a model of the mind in which unconscious thoughts were recognized and investigated by the observation of mental associations. However, where Galton tried to restrict his tendency toward reverie, Freud's method of 'free association' positively encouraged it. Galton concluded that a logical principle prevented unwanted or irrelevant mental contents from being summoned into consciousness. Freud held that the contents of the unconscious were unacceptable infantile sexual wishes, held back by a process of repression.

When we attempt to trace the first steps in each operation of our minds, we are usually baulked by the difficulty of keeping watch, without embarrassing the freedom of its action. The difficulty is much more than the common and well-known one of attending to two things at once. It is especially due to the fact that the elementary operations of the mind are exceedingly faint and evanescent, and that it requires the utmost painstaking to watch them properly. It would seem impossible to give the required attention to the processes of thought, and yet to think as freely as if the mind had been in no way preoccupied. The peculiarity of the experiments I am about to describe is that I have succeeded in evading this difficulty. My method consists in allowing the mind to play freely for a very brief period, until a couple or so of ideas have passed through it, and then, while the traces or echoes of those ideas are still lingering in the brain, to turn the attention upon them with a sudden and complete awakening; to arrest, to scrutinize them, and to record their exact appearance. Afterwards I collate the records at leisure, and discuss them, and draw conclusions. It must be understood that the second of the two ideas was never derived from the first, but always from the original object. This was ensured by absolutely withstanding all temptation to reverie. I do not mean that the first idea was of necessity a simple elementary thought; sometimes it was a glance down a familiar line of associations, sometimes it was a well-remembered mental attitude or mode of feeling, but I mean that it was never so far indulged in as to displace the object that had suggested it from being the primary topic of attention.

I must add, that I found the experiments to be extremely trying and irksome, and that it required much resolution to go through with them, using the scrupulous care they demanded. Nevertheless the results well repaid the trouble. They gave me an interesting and unexpected view of the number of the operations of the mind, and of the obscure depths in which they took place, of which I had been little conscious before. The general impression they have left upon me is like that which many of us have experienced when the basement of our house happens to be under thorough sanitary repairs, and we realize for the first time the complex system of drains and gas and water pipes, flues, bell-wires, and so forth, upon which our comfort depends, but which are usually hidden out of sight, and with whose existence, so long as they acted well, we had never troubled ourselves.

The Mind's Architecture

When I am engaged in trying to think anything out, the process of doing so appears to me to be this: the ideas that lie at any moment within my full consciousness seem to attract of their own accord the most appropriate out of a number of other ideas that are lying close at hand, but imperfectly within the range of my consciousness. There seems to be a presence-chamber in my mind where full consciousness holds court, and where two or three ideas are at the same time in audience, and an antechamber full of more or less allied ideas, which is situated just beyond the full ken of consciousness. Out of this antechamber the ideas most nearly allied to those in the presence-chamber appear to be summoned in a mechanically logical way, and to have their turn of audience.

The successful progress of thought appears to depend – first, on a large attendance in the antechamber; secondly, on the presence there of no ideas except such as are strictly germane to the topic under consideration; thirdly, on the justness of the logical mechanism that issues the summons. The thronging of the antechamber is, I am convinced, altogether beyond my control; if the ideas do not appear, I cannot create them, nor compel them to come. The exclusion of alien ideas is accompanied by a sense of mental effort and volition whenever the topic under consideration is unattractive, otherwise it proceeds automatically, for if an intruding idea finds nothing to cling to, it is unable to hold its place in the antechamber, and slides back again. An animal absorbed in a favourite occupation shows no sign of painful effort of attention; on the contrary, he resents interruption that solicits his attention elsewhere.

The consequence of all this is that the mind frequently does good work without the slightest exertion. In composition it will often produce a better effect than if it had acted with effort, because the essence of good composition is that the ideas should be connected by the easiest possible transitions. When a man has been thinking hard and long upon a subject, he becomes temporarily familiar with certain steps of thought, certain short cuts, and certain far-fetched associations, that do not commend themselves to the minds of other persons, nor indeed to his own at other times; therefore, it is better that his transitory familiarity with them should have come to an end before he begins to write or speak. When he returns to the work after a sufficient pause he is conscious that his ideas have settled; that is, they have lost their adventitious relations to one another, and stand in those to which they are likely to reside permanently in his own mind, and to exist in the minds of others.

Although the brain is able to do very fair work fluently in an automatic way, and though it will of its own accord strike out sudden and happy ideas, it is questionable if it is capable of working thoroughly and profoundly without past or present effort. The character of this effort seems to me chiefly to lie in bringing the contents of the antechamber more nearly within the ken of consciousness, which then takes comprehensive note of all its contents, and compels the logical faculty to test them *seriatum* before selecting the fittest for a summons to the presence-chamber.

Francis Galton, *Enquiries into Human Faculty and Its Development* (1883)

THE FREUDIAN UNCONSCIOUS

The Unkindest Blow to Man's Narcissism

Freud[7] *believed science (in which he included psychoanalysis) to have inflicted three severe blows on man's perception of himself. In the sixteenth century, Copernicus inflicted a cosmological blow by demonstrating that the earth moved around the sun, and was not the centre of the universe. In the nineteenth century, Darwin inflicted a biological blow by showing man's evolutionary continuity with other animals. And in the twentieth, his own emphasis on the unconscious determination of human behaviour dealt a*

7 See biographical note on p. 155.

drastic blow to man's sense of psychological freedom. Freud
thought neurotic symptoms reminded us of a fundamental truth,
our subordination to the unconscious mind. This implied an
absence of conscious choice, which we ignored in our 'normal'
day-to-day functioning.

Although thus humbled in its external relations, man feels himself
to be supreme within his own mind. Somewhere in the core of
his ego he has developed an organ of observation to keep a watch
on his impulses and actions and see whether they harmonize with
its demands. If they do not, they are ruthlessly inhibited and
withdrawn. His internal perception, consciousness, gives the ego
news of all the important occurrences in the mind's working, and
the will, directed by these reports, carries out what the ego orders
and modifies anything that seeks to accomplish itself spontaneously. For this mind is not a simple thing; on the contrary, it
is a hierarchy of superordinated and subordinated agencies, a
labyrinth of impulses striving independently of one another
towards action, corresponding with the multiplicity of instincts
and of relations with the external world, many of which are
antagonistic to one another and incompatible. For proper functioning it is necessary that the highest of these agencies should
have knowledge of all that is going forward and that its will
should penetrate everywhere, so as to exert its influence. And in
fact the ego feels secure both as to the completeness and trustworthiness of the reports it receives and as to the openness of
the channels through which it enforces its commands.

In certain diseases – including the very neuroses of which we
have made special study – things are different. The ego feels
uneasy; it comes up against limits to its power in its own house,
the mind. Thoughts emerge suddenly without one's knowing
where they come from, nor can one do anything to drive them
away. These alien guests even seem to be more powerful than
those which are at the ego's command. They resist all the proved
measures of enforcement used by the will, remain unmoved by
logical refutation, and are unaffected by the contradictory asser-
tions of reality. Or else impulses appear which seem like those

of a stranger, so that the ego disowns them; yet it has to fear
them and take precautions against them. The ego says to itself:
'This is an illness, a foreign invasion.' It increases its vigilance,
but cannot understand why it feels so strangely paralysed.

Psychiatry, it is true, denies that such things mean the intru-
sion into the mind of evil spirits from without; beyond this,
however, it can only say with a shrug: 'Degeneracy, hereditary
disposition, constitutional inferiority!' Psycho-analysis sets out to
explain these uncanny disorders; it engages in careful and labo-
rious investigations, devises hypotheses and scientific constructions, until at length it can speak thus to the ego: –

'Nothing has entered into you from without; a part of the
activity of your own mind has been withdrawn from your knowledge and from the command of your will. That, too, is why you
are so weak in your own defence; you are using one part of your
force to fight the other part and you cannot concentrate the whole
of your force as you would against an external enemy. And it is
not even the worst or least important part of your mental forces
that has become antagonistic to you and independent of you.
The blame, I am bound to say, lies with yourself. You over-
estimated your strength when you thought you could treat your
sexual instincts as you liked and could utterly ignore their intentions. The result is that they have rebelled and have taken their
own obscure paths to escape this suppression; they have
established their rights in a manner you cannot approve. How
they have achieved this, and the paths which they have taken,
have not come to your knowledge. All you have learned is the
outcome of their work – the symptom which you experience as
suffering. Thus you do not recognize it as a derivative of your
own rejected instincts and do not know that it is a substitutive
satisfaction of them.

'The whole process, however, only becomes possible through
the single circumstance that you are mistaken in another important point as well. You feel sure that you are informed of all
that goes on in your mind if it is of any importance at all,
because in that case, you believe, your consciousness gives you
news of it. And if you have had no information of something
in your mind you confidently assume that it does not exist there.

Indeed, you go so far as to regard what is "mental" as identical with what is "conscious" – that is, with what is known to you – in spite of the most obvious evidence that a great deal more must constantly be going on in your mind than can be known to your consciousness. Come, let yourself be taught something on this one point! What is in your mind does not coincide with what you are conscious of; whether something is going on in your mind and whether you hear of it, are two different things. In the ordinary way, I will admit, the intelligence which reaches your consciousness is enough for your needs; and you may cherish the illusion that you learn of all the more important things. But in some cases, as in that of an instinctual conflict such as I have described, your intelligence service breaks down and your will then extends no further than your knowledge. In every case, however, the news that reaches your consciousness is incomplete and often not to be relied on. Often enough, too, it happens that you get news of events only when they are over and when you can no longer do anything to change them. Even if you are not ill, who can tell all that is stirring in your mind of which you know nothing or are falsely informed? You behave like an absolute ruler who is content with the information supplied him by his highest officials and never goes among the people to hear their voice. Turn your eyes inward, look into your own depths, learn first to know yourself! Then you will understand why you were bound to fall ill; and perhaps, you will avoid falling ill in future.'

Sigmund Freud, *A Difficulty in the Path of Psycho-Analysis* (1917)

Unconscious Self-Punishment

It is well known that in the severer cases of psychoneurosis instances of self-injury are occasionally found as symptoms and that in such cases suicide can never be ruled out as a possible outcome of psychical conflict. I have now learnt and can prove from convincing examples that many apparently accidental injuries that happen to such patients are really instances of self-injury. What happens is that an impulse to self-punishment, which is constantly on the watch and which normally finds expression in self-reproach or contributes to the formation of symptoms, takes ingenious advantage of an external situation that chance happens to offer, or lends assistance to that situation until the desired injurious effect is brought about. Such occurrences are by no means uncommon in cases even of moderate severity, and they betray the part which the unconscious intention plays by a number of special features – e.g. by the striking composure that the patients retain in what is supposed to be an accident.

Instead of a number of cases I will give a detailed report of only a single example from my medical experience. A young married woman broke her leg below the knee in a carriage accident, so that she was bed-ridden for weeks; what was striking was the absence of any expressions of pain and the calmness with which she bore her misfortune. This accident introduced a long and severe neurotic illness of which she was finally cured by psycho-analysis. In treating her I learnt of the circumstances surrounding the accident and of certain events that had preceded it. The young woman was staying with her very jealous husband on the estate of a married sister, in company with her numerous other sisters and brothers with their husbands and wives. One evening in this intimate circle she showed off one of her accomplishments: she gave an accurate performance of the can-can, which was received with hearty applause by her relatives but with scanty satisfaction by her husband, who afterwards whispered to her: 'Carrying on like a tart again!' The remark struck home – we will not enquire whether it was only on account of the dancing display. She spent a restless night. Next morning she felt the desire to go for a drive. She selected the horses herself, refusing one pair and asking for another. Her youngest sister wanted her baby and its nurse to go in the carriage with her; my patient vigorously opposed this. During the drive she showed signs of nerves; she warned the coachman that the horses were growing skittish, and when the restless animals were really causing a moment's difficulty she jumped out in a fright and broke her leg, while the others who stayed in the carriage were unharmed. Although after learning these details we can hardly remain in doubt that this accident was really contrived, we cannot fail to admire the skill which forced chance to mete out a punishment that fitted the crime so well. For it had now been made impossible for her to dance the can-can for quite a long time.

Sigmund Freud, 'Bungled Actions', *The Psychopathology of Everyday Life* (1901)

Slips of the Tongue

Freud wanted to show that the realm of the 'psychical' included more than just conscious awareness. It was indisputable that brain activity regulating all sorts of bodily and mental functions occurred outside the arena of conscious awareness, yet many following Descartes* held that everything mental was conscious and everything that was not conscious had to be physical (see Hugo Munsterberg*). Freud's unconscious mental processes were in many ways analogous to the conscious ones. He wanted to prove that it made sense to speak of unconscious wishes, feelings, desires and so on, and that such unconscious entities played an overwhelming part in determining our behaviour. If slips of the tongue and pen, bungled actions and apparently meaningless gestures could be shown to reveal hidden motives, then a prima facie case for the existence of an unconscious mind could be made.

I shall pick a single instance to represent an immensely large class of phenomena. The President of a public body (the Lower House of the Austrian Parliament) on one occasion opened a sitting with the following words: 'I take notice that a full quorum of members is present and herewith declare the sitting *closed*.' It was a slip of the tongue – for there can be no doubt that what the President intended to say was 'opened'. Why, then, did he say the opposite? We shall expect to be told it was an accidental mistake, a failure in carrying out an intention such as may easily happen for various reasons: it had no meaning – and in any case contraries are particularly easily substituted for each other. If, however, we bear in mind the situation in which the slip of the tongue occurred, we shall be inclined to prefer another explanation. Many of the previous sittings of the House had been disagreeably stormy and had accomplished nothing, so that it would be only too natural for the President to think at the moment of making his opening statement: 'If only the sitting that's just beginning were finished! I would much rather be closing than opening it!' When he began to speak he was probably not aware of this wish – it was not conscious to him – but it was certainly present and it succeeded in making itself effective, against the speaker's will, in his apparent mistake. A single instance can scarcely enable us to decide between two such different explanations. But what if every other instance of a slip of the tongue could be explained in the same way, and similarly every slip of the pen, every case of mis-reading or mis-hearing, and every faulty action? What if in all those instances (one might actually say, without a single exception) it was possible to demonstrate the presence of a psychical act – a thought, a wish or an intention – which would account for the apparent mistake and which was unconscious at the moment at which it became effective, even though it may have been conscious previously? If that were so, it would really no longer be possible to dispute the fact that psychical acts which are unconscious do exist and that they are even sometimes active while they are unconscious and that in that case they can even sometimes get the better of conscious intentions. The person concerned in a mistake of this kind can react to it in various ways. He may overlook it completely or he may notice it himself and become embarrassed and ashamed. He cannot as a rule find the explanation of it himself without outside help; and he often refuses to accept the solution when it is put before him – for a time, at all events.

Sigmund Freud, 'Some Elementary Lessons in Psycho-Analysis', *Outline of Psychoanalysis* (1938)

The Ego's Dilemma

Our ideas about the ego are beginning to clear, and its various relationships are gaining distinctness. We now see the ego in its strength and in its weaknesses. It is entrusted with important functions. By virtue of its relation to the perceptual system it gives mental processes an order in time and submits them to 'reality-testing'. By interposing the processes of thinking, it secures a postponement of motor discharges and controls the access to motility. This last power is, to be sure, a question more of form than of fact; in the matter of action the ego's position is like that of a constitutional monarch, without whose sanction no law can be passed but who hesitates long before imposing his veto on any measure put forward by Parliament. All the experiences of life that originate from without enrich the ego; the id, however, is its second external world, which it strives to bring into subjection to itself. It withdraws libido from the id and transforms the object-cathexes of the id [libidinal attachments, e.g. infantile bonds with parents, ed.] into ego-structures. With the aid of the super-ego, in a manner that is still obscure to us, it draws upon the experience of past ages stored in the id.

There are two paths by which the contents of the id can penetrate into the ego. The one is direct, the other leads by way of the ego ideal; which of these two paths they take may, for some mental activities, be of decisive importance. The ego develops from perceiving instincts to controlling them, from obeying instincts to inhibiting them. In this achievement a large share is taken by the ego ideal, which indeed is partly a reaction-formation against the instinctual processes of the id. Psycho-analysis is an instrument to enable the ego to achieve a progressive conquest of the id.

From the other point of view, however, we see this same ego as a poor creature owing service to three masters and consequently menaced by three dangers: from the external world, from the libido of the id, and from the severity of the super-ego. Three kinds of anxiety correspond to these three dangers, since anxiety is the expression of a retreat from danger. As a frontier-creature, the ego tries to mediate between the world and the id, to make the id pliable to the world and, by means of its muscular activity, to make the world fall in with the wishes of the id. In point of fact it behaves like the physician during an analytic treatment: it offers itself, with the attention it pays to the real world, as a libidinal object to the id, and aims at attaching the id's libido to itself. It is not only a helper to the id; it is also a submissive slave who courts his master's love. Whenever possible, it tries to remain on good terms with the id; it clothes the id's *Ucs.* [system unconscious, ed.] commands with its *Pcs.* [system preconscious, ed.] rationalizations; it pretends that the id is showing obedience to the admonitions of reality, even when in fact it is remaining obstinate and unyielding; it disguises the id's conflicts with reality and, if possible, its conflicts with the super-ego too. In its position midway between the id and reality, it only too often yields to the temptation to become sycophantic, opportunist and lying, like a politician who sees the truth but wants to keep his place in popular favour.

Towards the two classes of instincts the ego's attitude is not impartial. Through its work of identification and sublimation it gives death instincts in the id assistance in gaining control over the libido, but in so doing it runs the risk of becoming the object of the death instincts and of itself perishing. In order to be able to help in this way it has had itself to become filled with libido; it thus itself becomes the representative of Eros and thenceforward desires to live and be loved.

But since the ego's work of sublimation results in a defusion of the instincts and a liberation of the aggressive instincts in the super-ego, its struggle against the libido exposes it to the danger of maltreatment and death. In suffering under the attacks of the super-ego or perhaps even succumbing to them, the ego is meeting with a fate like that of the protista which are destroyed by the products of decomposition that they themselves have created. From the economic point of view the morality that functions in the super-ego seems to be a similar product of decomposition.

Among the dependent relationships in which the ego stands, that to the super-ego is perhaps the most interesting.

The ego is the actual seat of anxiety. Threatened by dangers from three directions, it develops the flight reflex by withdrawing its own cathexis from the menacing perception or from the similarly regarded process in the id, and emitting it as anxiety. This primitive reaction is later replaced by the carrying-out of protective cathexes (the mechanism of the phobias). What it is that the ego fears from the external and from the libidinal danger cannot be specified; we know that the fear is of being overwhelmed or annihilated, but it cannot be grasped analytically. The ego is simply obeying the warning of the pleasure principle. On the other hand, we can tell what is hidden behind the ego's dread of the super-ego, the fear of the conscience. The superior being, which turned into the ego ideal, once threatened castration, and this dread of castration is probably the nucleus round which the subsequent fear of conscience has gathered; it is this dread that persists as the ear of conscience.

Sigmund Freud, *The Ego and the Id* (1923)

Transforming Fear into Fortitude

Early psychoanalysis devoted attention to uncovering the natural history of unconscious ('id') impulses in psychic life. However in 1936, the publication of Anna Freud's book The Ego and the Mechanisms of Defence *signalled a change in emphasis. Here she set out to investigate the ways and means by which a person warded off anxiety or unpleasure, dealt with instinctual urges, and exercised control over his or her behaviour. These concerns became the hallmark of 'Ego Psychology'.*

Anna Freud (1895–1982) was the only one of Freud's immediate offspring to take a professional interest in his work. He saw nothing to deter him from assuming the role of her training analyst. In 1922 she was admitted to membership of the Vienna Psychoanalytical Society. She and her parents fled Nazi Austria in 1938, taking refuge in England. Together with her contemporary, Melanie Klein, she pioneered the application of psychoanalysis to children.

August Aichorn relates that, when he was giving advice on a child guidance committee, he had to deal with the case of a boy at an elementary school, who was brought to him because of a habit of making faces. The master complained that the boy's behaviour, when he was blamed or reproved, was quite abnormal. On such occasions he made faces which caused the whole class to burst out laughing. The master's view was that either the boy was consciously making fun of him or else the twitching of his face must be due to some kind of tic. His report was at once corroborated, for the boy began to make faces during the consultation, but when master, pupil and psychologist were together, the situation was explained. Observing the two attentively, Aichorn saw that the boy's grimaces were simply a caricature of the angry expression of the teacher and that, when he had to face a scolding by the latter, he tried to master his anxiety by involuntarily imitating him. The boy identified himself with the teacher's anger and copied his expression as he spoke, though the imitation was not recognized. Through his grimaces he was assimilating himself with the dreaded external object.

My readers will remember the case of the little girl who [. . .] was afraid to cross the hall in the dark, because she was afraid of seeing ghosts. Suddenly, however, she hit on a device which enabled her to do it: she would run across the hall, making all sorts of peculiar gestures as she went. Before long, she triumphantly told her little brother the secret of how she had got over her anxiety. 'There's no need to be afraid in the hall,' she said, 'you just have to pretend that you're the ghost who might meet you.' This shows that her magic gestures represented the movements which she imagined ghosts would make.

We might be inclined to regard this kind of conduct as an idiosyncrasy in the two children whose cases I have quoted, but it is really one of the most natural and widespread modes of behaviour on the part of the primitive ego and has long been familiar to those who have made a study of primitive methods of invoking spirits and of primitive religious ceremonies. Moreover, there are many children's games in which through the metamorphosis of the subject into a dreaded object anxiety is converted into pleasurable security. Here is another angle from which to study the games of impersonation which children love to play.

Anna Freud, 'Identification with the Aggressor' (1936)

Foul into Fair

Few have been more sensitive to the conflict inherent in human nature than Friedrich Nietzsche. His poetic description of the dilemma faced by modern man in an age of scientific rationalism struck a chord with many. Acknowledging and championing the instincts against moralistic censure, Nietzsche famously proclaimed 'God is dead', and saw each man's task as a struggle to 'overcome' himself, to become a 'superman', to find meaning in the here and now of purely human existence.

Nietzsche (1844–1900) was born near Leipzig, Germany, into a strongly Lutheran family. Both grandfathers and his father, who died when Nietzsche was five years old, were clergymen. Brought up in a household of women, he became a male chauvinist and an atheist. He was a brilliant student of classical philology, appointed professor at the University of Basel in 1868. He was much influenced by the thought of Arthur Schopenhauer* and formed an intense friendship with Richard Wagner which lasted about four years.

Nietzsche's time at Basel came to an end after ten years, when a loss of interest in philology coincided with a decline in his health and withdrawal from everyday life. In the next decade he travelled much in Italy and Switzerland, and produced his most important contributions to philosophy, widely bowdlerized by ideologies as different as Nazism and Existentialism. In 1889 he became unequivocally insane, possibly as a long-term result of syphilitic infection, and died in Turin the following year.

My brother, if you have virtue and it is your own virtue, you have it in common with no one.

To be sure, you want to call it by a name and caress it; you want to pull its ears and amuse yourself with it.

And behold! Now you have its name in common with the people and have become of the people and the herd with your virtue!

You would do better to say: 'Unutterable and nameless is that which torments and delights my soul and is also the hunger of my belly.'

Let your virtue be too exalted for the familiarity of names: and if you have to speak of it, do not be ashamed to stammer.

Thus say and stammer: 'This is *my* good, this I love, just thus do I like it, only thus do I wish the good.

'I do not want it as a law of God, I do not want it as a human statute: let it be no signpost to superearths and paradises.

'It is an earthly virtue that I love: there is little prudence in it, and least of all common wisdom.

'But this bird has built its nest beneath my roof: therefore I love and cherish it – now it sits there upon its golden eggs.'

Thus should you stammer and praise your virtue.

Once you had passions and called them evil. But now you have only your virtues: they grew from out your passions.

You laid your highest aim in the heart of these passions: then they became your virtues and joys.

And though you came from the race of the hot-tempered or of the lustful or of the fanatical or of the vindictive:

At last all your passions have become virtues and all your devils angels.

Once you had fierce dogs in your cellar: but they changed at last into birds and sweet singers.

From your poison you brewed your balsam; you milked your cow, affliction, now you drink the sweet milk of her udder.

And henceforward nothing evil shall come out of you, except it be the evil that comes from the conflict of your virtues.

My brother, if you are lucky you will have one virtue and no more: thus you will go more easily over the bridge.

To have many virtues is to be distinguished, but it is a hard fate; and many a man has gone into the desert and killed himself because he was tired of being a battle and battleground of virtues.

My brother, are war and battle evil? But this evil is necessary, envy and mistrust and calumny among your virtues is necessary.

Behold how each of your virtues desires the highest place: it wants your entire spirit, that your spirit may be *its* herald, it wants your entire strength in anger, hate and love.

Every virtue is jealous of the others, and jealousy is a terrible thing. Even virtues can be destroyed through jealousy.

He whom the flames of jealousy surround at last turns his poisoned sting against himself, like the scorpion.

Ah my brother, have you never yet seen a virtue turn upon itself and stab itself?

Man is something that must be overcome: and for that reason you must love your virtues – for you will perish by them.

Thus spoke Zarathustra.

Friedrich Nietzsche, 'Of Joys and Passions', *Thus Spoke Zarathustra* (1883)

Is There a Subconscious Mind?

The following passage, taken from a review of Psychotherapy *by Hugo Munsterberg, Professor of Psychology, Harvard University, appeared in the* British Medical Journal. *It encapsulates the materialist argument against the subconscious mind. The same position was advanced by Ewald Hering, thirty years earlier (see* Where Memories Live, *p. 81). The anonymous reviewer asks how the author squares his conception with the phenomena of hypnotism, somnambulism, day-dreaming, etc., and leaves it to the reader to decide.*

'The story of the subconscious mind can be told in three words – there is none.' The whole question of the subconscious of course turns on the nature of memory. For Professor Munsterberg, memories are physical traces which become mental only when they are reflected in consciousness, after which and before which, they are purely physical facts, 'dispositions of brain cells'. 'To have psychical existence at all means to be the object of awareness for a consciousness. Something psychical which simply exists but is not an object of consciousness is therefore an inner contradiction. Consciousness is the presupposition for the existence of psychical objects. Psychical objects which enjoy their existence below consciousness are thus as impossible as a wooden piece of iron.'

Anonymous book review, *British Medical Journal* (1910)

INFLUENCE

The Power of Suggestion

Throughout history the production and exploration of altered states of consciousness has been an elemental human preoccupation. Among the means used to do this – drugs, music, dance, incense, religious ritual, etc. – hypnotism holds a special fascination. Not only are there changes in levels of awareness, but sensory and motor activity can be affected and memory enhanced or blotted out. The mind's autonomy is apparently relinquished, its power to affect the body transferred to the hypnotist's will.

Rather than invoke witchcraft or spirit possession as an explanation, Enlightenment thinking sought a naturalistic account of such phenomena. Franz Anton Mesmer's (1734–1815) misguided theory of 'animal magnetism' was an attempt to satisfy the needs of his time for a scientific underpinning of trance states. He postulated a universal fluid which could be attracted into the human body by someone with special powers, using magnets and other materials. The fluid was supposedly responsible for a range of unusual effects, including the ability to predict the future and to see without the use of eyes. It took nearly a century for the extravagant claims of the magnetists to be separated from the still startling but more plausible observations of the hypnotists, and for a purely psychological description of trance states to be proposed.

It was James Braid (1795–1860), an English doctor, who in 1843 coined the term 'hypnotism'. His experiments exploded the fluidic theory of the magnetists, and demonstrated beyond doubt the power of suggestion. The mind, Braid insisted, was quite capable of generating every variety of feeling and movement – heat or cold, pricking, creeping, tingling, spasmodic twitching of the muscles, hallucinations of smell, taste and sound, in the absence of any external cause. The expectation or belief that something was about to happen to them was, in many people, sufficient to make it occur.

When in London lately I had the pleasure of calling upon an eminent and excellent physician, who is in the habit of using mesmerism in his practice, in suitable cases, just as he uses any other remedy. He spoke of the extraordinary effects which he had experienced from the use of magnets applied *during the mesmeric state*, and kindly offered to illustrate the fact on a patient who had been asleep all the time I was in the room, and in that stage, during which I felt assured she could overhear every word of our conversation. He told me, that when he put the magnet into her hands, it would produce catalepsy of the hands and arms, and such was the result. He wafted the hands and the catalepsy ceased. He said that a mere touch of the magnet on a limb, would stiffen it, and such he proved to be the fact.

I now told him, that I had got a little instrument in my pocket, which although far less than his, I felt assured would prove quite as powerful, and I offered to prove this by operating on the same patient, whom I had never seen before, and who was in the mesmeric state when I entered the room. My instrument was about three inches long, the thickness of a quill, with a ring attached to the end of it . . . I told him that when put into her hands, he would find it catalepsize both hands and arms as his had done, and such was the result. Having reduced this by wafting, I took my instrument from her, and again returned it, *in another position*, and told him it would *now* have the very reverse effect – that she would not be able to hold it, and that although I closed her hands on it, they would open, and that it would drop out of them, and such was the case – to the great surprise of my worthy friend, who now desired to be informed *what I had done to the instrument to invest it with this new and apposite power*. This I declined doing for the present; but I promised to do so, when he had seen some further proofs of its remarkable powers. I now told him that a touch with it, on either extremity would cause the extremity to rise and become cataleptic, and such was the result; that a second touch on the same point would reduce the rigidity, and cause it to fall, and such again was proved to be the fact. After a variety of other experiments, every one of which proved precisely as I had predicted, she was aroused. I now applied the ring of my instrument on the third finger of the right hand, from which it was suspended, and told the doctor, that when it was so suspended, it would send her to sleep. To this he replied '*it never will*', but I again told him that I felt confident that it would send her to sleep. We then were silent, and very speedily she was once more asleep. Having aroused her, I put the instrument on the second finger of her left hand, and told the doctor that it would be found she could NOT go to sleep, when it was placed there. He said he thought she would, and he sat steadily gazing at her, but I said firmly and confidently that she would not. After a considerable time the doctor asked her if she did not feel sleepy, to which she replied 'not at all', could you rise and walk? when she told him she could. I then requested her to look at the point of the fore-finger of her right hand, which I told the doctor would send her to sleep, and such was the result; and, after being aroused, I desired her to keep a steady gaze at the nail of the thumb of the left hand which would send her to sleep in like manner, and such proved to be the fact.

Having repaired to another room, I explained to the doctor the real nature and powers of my little and apparently magical instrument – that it was nothing more than my *portmanteau-key and ring*, and that what had imparted to it such apparently varied powers was merely the predictions which the patient had overheard me make to him, acting upon her in the peculiar state of the nervous sleep, as irresistible impulses to be affected, according to the results she had heard me predict.

James Braid, *The Power of the Mind Over the Body* (1846)

Hippolyte Bernheim (1840–1919), held the Chair of Medicine in the newly founded University of Nancy from 1869. His interest in hypnotism was sparked in 1882 by news of a popular local doctor, Ambroise-Auguste Liebault, who enjoyed considerable therapeutic success. Liebault used hypnotism to cure a patient of sciatica whom Bernheim had failed to help. Together they founded a clinic in Nancy dedicated to the clinical application of the hypnotic method. Unlike his famous Parisian rival, Jean-Martin Charcot, who believed that susceptibility to hypnotism derived from brain pathology (in hysterics) and used it only as an inves-

tigative tool, Bernheim's experience led him to believe that most
'normal' people responded in some degree to hypnotic sugges-
tion. If Bernheim's emphasis on the power of hypnotism to
increase a person's suggestibility avoided the pitfalls of pseudo-
science, it left us little wiser as to the underlying means whereby
this was accomplished.

I proceed to hypnotize in the following manner.

I begin by saying to the patient that I believe benefit is to be
derived from the use of suggestive therapeutics, that it is possible
to cure or relieve him by hypnotism; that there is nothing either
hurtful or strange about it; that it is an *ordinary sleep* or torpor
which can be induced in everyone, and that this quiet, beneficial
condition restores the equilibrium of the nervous system, etc. If
necessary, I hypnotize one or two subjects in his presence, in
order to show him that there is nothing painful in this condition
and that it is not accompanied with any unusual sensation. When
I have thus banished from his mind the idea of magnetism and
the somewhat mysterious fear that attaches to that unknown
condition, above all when he has seen patients cured or bene-
fited by the means in question, he is no longer suspicious, but
gives himself up, then I say, 'Look at me and think of nothing
but sleep. Your eyelids begin to feel heavy, your eyes tired. They
begin to wink, they are getting moist, you cannot see distinctly.
They are closed.' Some patients close their eyes and are asleep
immediately. With others, I have to repeat, lay more stress on
what I say, and even make gestures. It makes little difference
what sort of gesture is made. I hold two fingers of my right hand
before the patient's eyes and ask him to look at them, or pass
both hands several times before his eyes, or persuade him to fix
his eyes upon mine, endeavouring, at the same time, to concentrate his attention upon the idea of sleep. I say, 'Your lids are
closing, you cannot open them again. Your arms feel heavy, so
do your legs. You cannot feel anything. Your hands are motionless. You see nothing, you are going to sleep.' And I add in a
commanding tone, 'Sleep.' This word often turns the balance.
The eyes close and the patient sleeps or is at least influenced.

I use the word sleep, in order to obtain as far as possible over the patients a suggestive influence which shall bring about sleep or a state closely approaching it; for sleep properly, so called, does not always occur. If the patients have no inclination to sleep and show no drowsiness, I take care to say that sleep is not essential; that the hypnotic influence, whence comes the benefit, may exist without sleep; that many patients are hypnotized although they do not sleep.

If the patient does not shut his eyes or keep them shut, I do not require them to be fixed on mine, or on my fingers, for any length of time, for it sometimes happens that they remain wide open indefinitely, and instead of the idea of sleep being conceived, only a rigid fixation of the eyes results. In this case, closure of the eyes by the operator succeeds better. After keeping them fixed one or two minutes, I push the eye-lids down, or, stretch them slowly over the eyes, gradually closing them more and more and so imitating the process of natural sleep. Finally I keep them closed, repeating the suggestion, 'Your lids are stuck together; you cannot open them. The need of sleep becomes greater and greater, you can no longer resist.' I lower my voice gradually, repeating the command, 'Sleep,' and it is very seldom that more than three minutes pass before sleep or some degree of hypnotic influence is obtained. It is sleep by suggestion – a type of sleep which I insinuate into the brain.

[. . .]

Hypnotism manifests itself in different subjects in different ways. There may simply be drowsiness, or other induced sensations such as heat, pricking, etc. This is the lightest influence. We have more marked effects when suggestion affects motility; develops the cataleptic condition, the inability to move, contraction and automatic movements. It is still more decided when it affects the will and causes automatic obedience. All these manifestations of motion, will and even sensibility can be affected by suggestion with or without sleep, and even when it is powerless to induce sleep. In a more intense degree, suggestion produces sleep or an illusion of sleep. The subject convinced that he is sleeping, does not remember anything upon waking. In general, the more advanced degrees of suggestion affect the sensorial and sensory spheres – memory and imagination. Illusions may be created and destroyed, and the imagination may call forth the most varied memory pictures.

[. . .]

To define hypnotism as induced sleep, is to give too narrow a meaning to the word – to overlook the many phenomena which suggestion can bring about independently of sleep. I define hypnotism as the induction of a peculiar psychical condition which increases the susceptibility to suggestion. Often, it is true, the sleep that may be induced facilitates suggestion, but it is not the necessary preliminary. It is suggestion that rules hypnotism.

[. . .]

In order to awake the subject immediately, I use verbal suggestion, in the same manner as when sleep is to be induced. I say, 'It is over; wake up,' and this suffices, even when uttered in a low voice, to awake subjects who have already been hypnotized several times, immediately.

In some cases it is necessary to add, 'Your eyes are opening; you are awake.' If that is not enough, blowing once or twice on the eyes causes the subject to wake. I have never had to resort to other methods, such as sprinkling cold water on the subjects. The awakening has always been easy.

At times there is nothing so strange as this awakening. The subject is in deep sleep. I question him and he answers. If he is naturally a good talker he will speak fluently. In the midst of his conversation I suddenly say, 'Wake up.' He opens his eyes, and has absolutely no remembrance of what has happened. He does not remember having spoken to me, though he was speaking, perhaps, but one tenth of a second, before waking. In order to make the phenomenon more striking, I sometimes wake a patient in the following way. 'Count up to ten. When you say ten aloud, you will be awake.' The moment he says ten, his eyes open; but he does not remember having counted. Again I say 'You are going to count up to ten. When you get to six you will wake up, but you will keep on counting aloud up to ten. When he utters the word six, he opens his eyes but keeps on counting. When he has finished I say 'Why are you counting?' He no longer remembers that he has been counting.

I have repeated this experiment many times with very intelligent people.

Hippolyte Bernheim, 'On Suggestion in the Hypnotic State and During Wakefulness', *Hypnosis and Suggestion in Psychotherapy* (1884)

Obedience

Conservative philosophers have regarded obedience to institutionalized authority as a bulwark against individualism, a desirable curb on the expression of man's darker instincts. Humanists, on the other hand, have emphasized the importance of individual conscience and its primacy over outside authority in regulating the self. In modern times the horrors of the Nazi concentration camps and the inhuman excesses of other totalitarian regimes have demonstrated the dangers involved in unquestioning obedience to authority. The imposition of tyranny on a people, through instruments of coercion such as the army or secret police, implies the existence of resistance. But the large numbers of ordinary 'decent people' complicit in the running of such states and the recorded institutional abuses of human rights occurring within the liberal democracies themselves point to other factors than fear of retribution in accounting for widespread compliance. The influence of social arrangements in releasing individuals from conflict with their own conscience, and thus altering the moral equilibrium in a person's mind, is apparent.

In a famous series of experiments conducted in the Department of Psychology at Yale University between 1960 and 1963, Professor Stanley Milgram set out to test the limits to which ordinary men and women would go when confronted with an instruction to hurt somebody else, issued from an apparently legitimate authority. He concluded that a substantial proportion of people were so influenced by authority that they would do what they were told to do, irrespective of the content of the act and without limitation of conscience.

In order to take a close look at the act of obeying, I set up a simple experiment at Yale University. Eventually, the experiment was to involve more than a thousand participants and would be repeated at several universities, but at the beginning, the conception was simple. A person comes into a laboratory and is told to carry out a series of acts that come increasingly into conflict with conscience. The main question is how far the participant will comply with the experimenter's instructions before refusing to carry out the actions required of him.

But the reader needs to know a little more detail about the experiment. Two people come to a psychology laboratory to take part in a study of memory and learning. One of them is designated as 'teacher' and the other a 'learner'. The experimenter explains that the study is concerned with the effects of punishment on learning. The learner is conducted into a room, seated in a chair, his arms strapped to prevent excessive movement, and an electrode attached to his wrist. He is told that he is to learn a list of word pairs; whenever he make an error, he will receive electric shocks of increasing intensity.

The real focus of the experiment is the teacher. After watching the learner being strapped into place, he is taken into the main experimental room and seated before an impressive shock generator. Its main feature is a horizontal line of thirty switches, ranging from 15 volts to 450 volts, in 15 volt increments. There are also verbal designations which range from SLIGHT SHOCK to DANGER – SEVERE SHOCK. The teacher is told that he is to administer the learning test to the man in the other room. When the learner responds correctly, the teacher moves on to the next item; when the other man gives an incorrect answer, the teacher is to give him an electric shock. He is to start at the lowest shock level (15 volts) and to increase the level each time the man makes an error, going through 30 volts, 45 volts, and so on.

The 'teacher' is a genuinely naive subject who has come to the laboratory to participate in the experiment. The learner, or victim, is an actor who actually receives no shock at all. The point of the experiment is to see how far a person will proceed in a concrete and measurable situation in which he is ordered to inflict increasing pain on a protesting victim. At what point will the subject refuse to obey the experimenter?

Conflict arises when the man receiving the shock begins to

indicate that he is experiencing discomfort. At 75 volts, the 'learner' grunts. At 120 volts he complains verbally; at 150 volts he demands to be released from the experiment. His protests continue as the shocks escalate, growing increasingly vehement and emotional. At 285 volts his response can only be described as an agonized scream.

Observers of the experiment agree that its gripping quality is somewhat obscured in print. For the subject, the situation is not a game; conflict is intense and obvious. On one hand, the manifest suffering of the learner presses him to quit. On the other, the experimenter, a legitimate authority to whom the subject feels some commitment, enjoins him to continue. Each time the subject hesitates to administer shock, the experimenter orders him to continue. To extricate himself from the situation, the subject must make a clear break with authority. The aim of this investigation was to find when and how people would defy authority in the face of a clear moral imperative.

There are, of course, enormous differences between carrying out the orders of a commanding officer during times of war and carrying out the orders of an experimenter. Yet the essence of certain relationships remain, for one may ask in a general way: How does a man behave when he is told by a legitimate authority to act against a third individual? If anything, we may expect the experimenter's power to be considerably less than that of the general, since he has no power to enforce his imperatives, and participation in a psychological experiment scarcely evokes the sense of urgency and dedication engendered by participation in war. Despite these limitations, I thought it worth while to start careful observation of obedience even in this modest situation, in the hope that it would stimulate insights and yield general propositions applicable to a variety of circumstances.

A reader's initial reaction to the experiment may be to wonder why anyone in his right mind would administer even the first shocks. Would he not simply refuse and walk out of the laboratory? But the fact is that no one ever does. Since the subject has come to the laboratory to aid the experimenter, he is quite willing to start off with the procedure. There is nothing very extraordinary in this, particularly since the person who is to receive the shocks seems initially co-operative, if somewhat appre-hensive. What is surprising is how far ordinary individuals will go in complying with the experimenter's instructions. Indeed, the results of the experiment are both surprising and dismaying. Despite the fact that many subjects experience stress, despite the fact that many protest to the experimenter, a substantial propor-tion continue to the last shock on the generator.

Many subjects will obey the experimenter no matter how vehe-ment the pleading of the person being shocked, no matter how painful the shocks seem to be, and no matter how much the victim pleads to be let out. This was seen time and again in our studies and has been observed in several universities where the experiment has been repeated. It is the extreme willingness of adults to go to almost any lengths on the command of an authority that constitutes the chief finding of the study and the fact most urgently demanding explanation.

Stanley Milgram, *Obedience to Authority: An Experimental View* (1974)

Not Me, My Hand Did It

Small children sometimes disclaim responsibility for their actions on the grounds that their hand acted independently, and we tend to smile. Nearly a hundred years ago, however, the German neurologist Kurt Goldstein described just such a situation in a fifty-seven-year-old woman whose left hand had on one occasion tried to strangle her. She had suffered multiple strokes involving various regions of the brain. Post mortem findings also revealed a lesion in the corpus callosum, the chief connecting pathway between left and right hemispheres.[8]

On one occasion the hand grabbed her own neck and tried to throttle her, and could only be pulled off by force. Similarly, it tore off the bed covers against the patient's will . . . she soon is complaining about her hand; that it is a law unto itself, an organ

8 See Michael Gazzaniga, pp. 358–60.

without will [*willenloses Werkzeug*]; when once it has got hold of something, it refuses to let go: 'I myself can do nothing with it; if I'm having a drink and it gets hold of the glass, it won't let go and spills [the drink] out. Then I hit it and say: "Behave yourself, hand" [literally, *mein Händchen*]' (Smiling.) 'I suppose there must be an evil spirit in it.'

Kurt Goldstein, *Journal of Psychology and Neurology* (1908)

THE KLEINIAN UNCONSCIOUS

Is Unconscious Phantasy Real . . .?

If unconscious mental activity is more than mere metabolism, if there is some kind of experience, some underlying psychological happening below the level of awareness, in what does it consist? One answer to this question is 'unconscious phantasy'. The child psychoanalyst, Melanie Klein, inferred the existence of an unconscious world of phantasy, made manifest in the imaginative play of children (and by extension the behaviour and conscious experience of adults). She conceived the inner world of phantasy as a small society populated by 'internal objects' and 'part-objects' that appeared to have a life of their own. They inhabited a world, a kind of dream world, that seemed to just 'happen' inside us. Thus a maternal breast or paternal penis might be unconsciously personified, and experienced as having a character and tendency to good or bad behaviour. The nature of the internal object-relationships that ensued – the phantasized relationships – Klein thought, informed our everyday adult life and determined our state of mind and sense of well-being.

Where Freud had been inconsistent in his use of the term 'instinct', sometimes speaking of it as a purely biological phenomenon, sometimes as a mental one, Klein and her followers made a conceptual clarification. Their observations in play-therapy led them to see the origin of 'unconscious phantasy' in the psychical component or mental representation of bodily happenings. Pain, for example, might be unconsciously experienced in the form of persecution by a phantasized attacking breast. In directing their investigations toward the way in which such happenings were symbolized, they elaborated a new vision of the unconscious mind.

Lancashire born and bred, Susan Isaacs (1885–1948), educationalist and psychoanalyst, was one of the most eloquent advocates of the 'Kleinian' position.

The first mental processes, the psychic representatives of libidinal and destructive instincts, are to be regarded as the earliest beginnings of phantasies. In the mental development of the infant, however, phantasy soon becomes also a means of defence against anxieties, a means of inhibiting and controlling instinctual urges and an expression of reparative wishes as well. The relation between phantasy and wish-fulfilment has always been emphasized; but our experience has shown, too, that most phantasies (like symptoms) also serve various other purposes as well as wish-fulfilment; e.g. denial, reassurance, omnipotent control, reparation, etc. It is, of course, true that, in a wider sense, all these mental processes which aim at diminishing instinctual tension, anxiety and guilt, also serve the aim of wish fulfilment; but it is useful to discriminate the specific modes of these different processes and their particular aims.

All impulses, all feelings, all modes of defence are experienced in phantasies which give them *mental* life and show their direction and purpose.

A phantasy represents the particular contents of the urges or feelings (for example, wishes, fears, anxieties, triumphs, love or sorrow) dominating the mind at the moment. In early life, there is indeed a wealth of unconscious phantasies which take specific form in conjunction with the cathexis [libidinal investment, ed.] of particular bodily zones. Moreover, they rise and fall in complicated patterns according to the rise and fall and modulation of the primary instinct-impulses which they express. The world of phantasy shows the same protean and kaleidoscopic changes as the contents of a dream. These changes occur partly in response to external stimulation and partly as a result of the interplay between the primary instinctual urges themselves.

[. . .]

We are able to conclude that when the child shows his desire for his mother's breast, he *experiences* this desire as a specific phantasy – 'I want to suck the nipple'. If desire is very intense (perhaps on account of anxiety), he is likely to feel: 'I want to eat her all up.' Perhaps to avert the repetition of loss of her, or for his pleasure, he may feel: 'I want to keep her inside me.' If he is feeling fond, he may have the phantasy: 'I want to stroke her face, to pat and cuddle her.' At other times, when he is frustrated or provoked, his impulses may be of an aggressive character; he will experience these as, e.g.: 'I want to bite the breast; I want to tear her to bits.' Or if, e.g.: urinary impulses are dominant, he may feel: 'I want to drown and burn her.' If anxiety is stirred by such aggressive wishes, he may phantasy: 'I myself shall be cut or bitten up by mother'; and when his anxiety refers to his internal object, the breast which has been eaten up and kept inside, he may want to eject her and feel: 'I want to throw her out of me.' When he feels loss and grief, he experiences, as Freud described: 'My mother has gone for ever.' He may feel: 'I want to bring her back, I must have her *now*', and then try to overcome his sense of loss and grief and helplessness by the phantasies expressed in auto-erotic satisfactions, such as thumb-sucking and genital play: 'If I suck my thumb, I feel she *is* back here as part of me, belonging to me and giving me pleasure.' If, after having in his phantasy attacked his mother and hurt and damaged her, libidinal wishes come up again, he may feel he wants to restore his mother and will then phantasy: 'I want to put the bits together again', 'I want to make her better', 'I want to feed her as she has fed me'; and so forth.

Not merely do these phantasies appear and disappear according to changes in the instinctual urges stirred up by outer circumstances, they also exist together, side by side in the mind, even though they be contradictory; just as in a dream, mutually exclusive wishes may exist and be expressed together.

Not only so: these early mental processes have an omnipotent character. Under the pressure of instinct tension, the child in his earliest days not only feels: 'I want to', but implicitly phantasies: 'I am doing' this and that to mother; 'I *have* her inside me', when he wants to. The wish and the impulse, whether it be love or hate, libidinal or destructive, tends to be felt as actually fulfilling itself, whether with an external or an internal object. This is partly because of the overwhelmingness of his desires and feelings. In his earliest days, his own wishes and impulses fill the whole world at the time when they are felt. It is only slowly that he learns to distinguish between the wish and the deed, between external facts and his feelings about them. The degree of differentiation partly depends upon the stage of development reached at the time, and partly upon the momentary intensity of the desire or emotion. This omnipotent character of early wishes and feelings links with Freud's views about hallucinatory satisfaction in the infant.

Susan Isaacs, 'The Nature and Function of Phantasy' (1952)

. . . Or Is It Just a Theoretical Artifact?

R.D. Laing (1927–89), psychiatrist and psychoanalyst, achieved fame in the 1960s for his critique of established psychiatric practice. His voice became synonymous with 'anti-psychiatry'. He suggested that psychiatric diagnoses, such as schizophrenia, were not objective descriptions of a patient's mental state but socially constructed categories produced by a depersonalized professional. The diagnosis, he thought, harmed the nominated patient and was a further attack on his or her identity. Psychiatrists were unwittingly cutting off their patients from the chance of renewing and reuniting their 'divided selves'.

In the following passage Laing points to the difficulties and confusions generated by the notion of 'unconscious phantasy'. Although we are inclined to say that our minds are 'in' our bodies, and to feel that our ideas are 'in' our minds, we are not justified in making this a basis for psychological theorizing, he says.

Is it a contradiction in terms to speak of 'unconscious experience'? A person's experience comprises anything that 'he' or 'any part of him' is aware of, whether 'he' or every part of him is aware of every level of his awareness or not. His experiences are inner or outer; of his own body or of other person's bodies; real or unreal; private or shared. The psychoanalytic contention is that our desires present themselves to us in our experience, but we may not recognize them. This is one sense in which we are unconscious of our experience. We misconstrue it.

But even if we can find a formula to avoid using 'unconscious' to qualify experience directly, there are issues in Isaac's paper that present what seem to be intractable difficulties. They run through the whole of Isaac's presentation, and through psychoanalytic theory in general. They are crystallized in the following passage:

When contrasted with external bodily realities, the phantasy, like other mental activities, is a figment, since it cannot be touched or handled or seen; yet it is real in the experience of the subject. It is a true mental function and it has real effects, not only in the inner world of the mind but also in the external world of the subject's bodily development and behaviour, and hence of other people's minds and bodies (p. 99) [in Isaacs' article, ed.].

Phantasy is 'real in the experience of the subject'. It is also 'a figment, *since* it cannot be touched or handled or seen'. The term denotes both 'real' experiences of which the subject is unconscious, and a mental function which has 'real' effects. These real *effects* are the real experiences. Phantasy appears now to be the *cause* of itself, as an effect, and the effect of itself, as a cause. It may be we are touching upon a critical insight that is obscured by a tangle into which we have been led by some of our theoretical distinctions.

One source of confusion is the particular dichotomous schema in which the whole theory is cast. This particular schema entails the distinction between 'the inner world of the mind', on the one hand, and 'the external world of the subject's bodily development and behaviour, and hence of other people's minds and bodies', on the other.

This contradistinction generates, in Isaacs's paper and in many psychoanalytic works, two opposed clusters of terms, namely:

inner	in contrast to	*outer*
mental	in contrast to	*physical*
mental activity	in contrast to	*external and bodily realities*
figment	in contrast to	*what can be touched, handled, seen*
psychical reality	in contrast to	*physical reality*
the inner world of the mind	in contrast to	*body*

In terms of this set of distinctions, we have to suppose that phantasy begins on the left as an inner mental activity, etc., and crosses over somehow to the right. Despite the peculiar position we are led to, we have to suppose it comes to be *experienced* only on the right, for we are told that it is experienced in terms of external and bodily reality, both as to one's own body and as to the bodies of others.

Terms like conversion, a shift from mind to body; projection, a shift from inner to outer, are caught and entangled by this theoretical split. Instead of describing facts of experience, they are used to explain artifacts of theory. The dual series, still less these transitions, does not belong to the series of facts Isaacs sets out to describe. A person may experience himself in terms of this set of distinctions. He 'feels' his 'mind' contains 'contents', he testifies that his 'body' is 'outside' his 'mind'. Strange though this may sound, we may suppose that he is not a liar and is choosing his words carefully. However, it is quite another matter to take such a form of self-division as one's theoretical starting point.

Phantasy can also be *imagined* to go on 'in' the 'mind'. One may ask why it should be so imagined, without undertaking to work out the imaginary problem itself.

If one does not adopt, or if one gives up, this particular dichotomy of inner-mental and external-physical, other problems come into view. These are not *the same* problems dressed in other words. The true problem at the moment is to allow the problems to arise. They can do so only when the phenomena are no longer masked by false problems.

R.D. Laing, 'Phantasy and Experience', *Self and Others* (1969)

THE JUNGIAN UNCONSCIOUS

Innate Knowledge and the Collective Unconscious

Carl Gustav Jung* (1875–1961) was the son of a pastor of the Swiss Reformed Church. When he was three years old, his mother was admitted to a mental hospital. Since his father suffered from depressive episodes, Jung was sent to live with an aunt. In 1879 his family moved to Klein-Hüningen, near Basel, where Jung spent most of his childhood. He qualified in medicine from the University of Basel and went on to specialize in psychiatry, working under Eugen Bleuler at the Burghölzli mental hospital in Zurich.

In addition to his medical studies Jung read widely in philosophy and comparative religion and, like his maternal grandparents, developed an interest in spiritualism and the occult. He first made contact with Sigmund Freud*, twenty years his senior, in 1906, sending him word-association data which supported psychoanalytic ideas. A friendship developed between the two men, and Freud elected Jung the 'Crown prince' of psychoanalysis, destined to ensure its future dissemination beyond the narrow confines of Vienna.

However, neither man was good at sustaining same-sex relations. In 1913 Jung struck out on his own, accusing Freud of intellectual intolerance. Freud felt betrayed. Jung's ideas concerning the unconscious mind were sufficiently different from Freud's to constitute a new school of thought, which he named Analytical Psychology. Following Plato, Jung laid great stress on the achievement of wholeness and unity through integration of the different parts of the personality. He saw the relations between conscious and unconscious aspects of the mind as essentially complementary. He saw the mind as a kind of homeostatic, self-regulating system. He laid less emphasis on the determining role of infantile experience in causing adult neurosis and was less concerned with the vicissitudes of infantile sexuality. Although Freud also subscribed to the view that certain mental contents could be inherited phylogenetically (as part of the common prehistory of our species), Jung gave it centre-stage in his psychological system.

Where Freud preferred to see himself as a supreme rationalist/

*atheist, and made expansion of the 'conscious ego' the hallmark
of psychoanalysis, Jung doubted the overwhelming value of
rationality. Although he rejected organized religion, the attraction of mystical thinking in his life was always very strong.*

A high regard for the unconscious psyche as a source of knowledge is by no means such a delusion as our Western rationalism
likes to suppose. We are inclined to assume that, in the last resort,
all knowledge comes from without. Yet today we know for certain
that the unconscious contains contents which would mean an
immeasurable increase in knowledge if they could only be made
conscious. Modern investigation of animal instinct, as for
example in insects, has brought together a rich fund of empirical findings which show that if man acted as certain insects do
he would possess a higher intelligence than at present. It cannot,
of course, be proved that insects possess conscious knowledge,
but common-sense cannot doubt that their unconscious action-
patterns are psychic functions. Man's unconscious likewise
contains all the patterns of life and behaviour inherited from his
ancestors, so that every human child, prior to consciousness, is
possessed of a potential system of adapted psychic functioning.
In the conscious life of the adult, as well, this unconscious, instinctive functioning is always present and active. In this activity all
the functions of the conscious psyche are prepared for. The unconscious perceives, has purposes and intuitions, feels and thinks as
does the conscious mind. We find sufficient evidence for this in
the field of psycho-pathology and the investigation of dream-
processes. Only in one respect is there an essential difference
between the conscious and the unconscious functioning of the
psyche. While consciousness is intensive and concentrated, it is
transient and is directed upon the immediate present and the
immediate field of attention; moreover, it has access only to
material that represents one individual's experience stretching
over a few decades. A wider range of 'memory' is artificially
acquired and consists mostly of printed paper. But matters stand
very differently with the unconscious. It is not concentrated and
intensive, but shades off into obscurity; it is highly extensive and

can juxtapose the most heterogeneous elements in the most paradoxical way. More than this, it contains, besides an indeter-
minable number of subliminal perceptions, an immense fund of
accumulated inheritance-factors left by one generation of men
after another, whose mere existence marks a step in the differentiation of the species. If it were permissible to personify the
unconscious, we might call it a collective human being combining
the characteristics of both sexes, transcending youth and age,
birth and death, and, from having at his command a human experience of one or two million years, almost immortal. If such a
being existed, he would be exalted above all temporal change;
the present would mean neither more nor less to him than any
year in the one hundredth century before Christ; he would be a
dreamer of age-old dreams and, owing to his immeasurable experience, he would be an incomparable prognosticator. He would
have lived countless times over the life of the individual, of the
family, tribe and people, and he would possess the living sense
of rhythm of growth, flowering and decay.

Unfortunately – or rather let us say, fortunately – this being
dreams. At least it seems to us as if the collective unconscious,
which appears to us in dreams, has no consciousness of its own
contents – though of course we cannot be sure of this, any more
than we are in the case of insects. The collective unconscious, moreover, seems not to be a person, but something like an unceasing
stream or perhaps ocean of images and figures which drift into
consciousness in our dreams or in abnormal states of mind.

It would be positively grotesque for us to call this immense
system of experience of the unconscious psyche an illusion, for
our visible and tangible body itself is such a system. It still carries
within it the discernible traces of primeval evolution, and it is
certainly a whole that functions purposively – for otherwise we
could not live. It would never occur to anyone to look upon
comparative anatomy or physiology as nonsense. And so we
cannot dismiss the collective unconscious as illusion, or refuse to
recognize and study it as a valuable source of knowledge.

Carl Gustav Jung, 'The Basic Postulates of Analytical Psychology', *Modern
Man in Search of a Soul* (1933)

The Anima and the Persona

The relation of the individual to the outer object must be sharply distinguished from the relation to the subject. By the subject I mean those vague, dim stirrings, feelings, thoughts, and sensations which have no demonstrable flow towards the object from the continuity of consciousness, but well up like a disturbing, inhibiting, or at times beneficent, influence from the dark inner depths, from the background and underground of consciousness which, in their totality, constitute one's perception of unconscious life. The subject, conceived as the 'inner' object, is the unconscious. There is a relation to the inner object, viz. an inner attitude, which is immediately perceived by everyone. Nevertheless, the task of making a concept of this inner attitude does not seem to be impossible. All those so-called accidental inhibitions, fancies, moods, vague feelings, and fragments of phantasy, which occasionally harass and disturb the accomplishment of concentrated work, not to mention the repose of the most normal of men, and which evoke rational explanations either in the form of physical causes or reasons of like nature, usually have their origin, not in the reasons ascribed to them by consciousness, but in the perceptions of unconscious processes, which, in fact, they are. Among such phenomena, dreams also naturally belong: these are admittedly liable to be accounted for by such external and superficial causes as indigestion, sleeping on one's back, and the like, in spite of the fact that such explanations never withstand a searching criticism. The attitude of individual men to these things is extremely variable. One man will not allow himself to be disturbed in the smallest degree by his inner processes – he can, as it were, ignore them entirely; while another is in the highest degree subject to them: at the first waking moment some phantasy or other, or a disagreeable feeling, spoils his temper for the whole day; a vague, unpleasant sensation suggests the idea of a secret malady or a dream leaves him with a gloomy foreboding, although in other ways he is by no means superstitious. To others, again, these unconscious stirrings have only a very episodic access, or only a certain category of them come to the surface. For one man, perhaps, they have never yet appeared to consciousness as anything worth thinking about, while for another they are a problem of daily brooding. The one values them physiologically, or ascribes them to the conduct of his neighbours; another finds in them a religious revelation.

These entirely different ways of dealing with the stirrings of the unconscious are just as habitual as the attitudes to the outer object. The inner attitude, therefore, corresponds with just as definite a function-complex as the outer attitude. Those cases in which the inner psychic processes appear to be entirely overlooked are lacking a typical inner attitude just as little as those who constantly overlook the outer object and the reality of facts lack a typical outer attitude. The persona of these latter, by no means infrequent cases, has the character of unrelatedness, or at times even a blind inconsiderateness, which frequently yields only to the harshest blows of fate. Not seldom, it is just those individuals whose persona is characterized by a rigid inconsiderateness and absence of relations who possess an attitude to the unconscious processes which suggests a character of extreme susceptibility. As they are inflexible and inaccessible outwardly, so they are weak, flaccid, and determinable in relation to their inner processes. In such cases, therefore, the inner attitude corresponds with an inner personality diametrically opposed and different from the outer. I know a man, for instance, who without pity blindly destroyed the happiness of those nearest to him, and yet he would interrupt his journey when travelling on important business just to enjoy the beauty of a forest scene glimpsed from the carriage window. Cases of this kind are doubtless familiar to everyone; it is needless therefore to enumerate further examples. With the same justification as daily experience furnishes us for speaking of an outer personality are we also justified in assuming the existence of an inner personality. The inner personality is the manner of one's behaviour towards the inner psychic processes; it is the inner attitude, the character that is turned towards the unconscious. I term the outer attitude, or outer character, the *persona*, the inner attitude I term the *anima*, or *soul*. In the same degree as an attitude is habitual, is it a more or less firmly welded function-complex, with which the ego may be more or less identified. This is plastically expressed in language: of a man who has a habitual attitude towards certain situations, we are accustomed to say: He is quite *another man* when doing this or that. This is a practical demonstration of the independence of the function-complex of an habitual attitude; it is as though another personality had taken possession of the individual, as 'though another spirit had entered into him'. The same autonomy as is so often granted to the outer attitude is also claimed by the soul or inner attitude. One of the most difficult of all educational achievements is this task of changing the outer attitude, or persona but to change the soul is just as difficult, since its structure tends to be just as firmly welded as is that of the persona. Just as the persona is an entity, which often appears to constitute the whole character of a man, even accompanying him practically without change throughout his entire life, so the soul is also a definitely circumscribed entity, with a character which may prove unalterably firm and independent. Hence, it frequently offers itself to characterization and description.

As regards the character of the soul, my experience confirms the validity of the general principle that it maintains, on the whole, a *complementary* relation to the outer character. Experience teaches us that the soul is wont to contain all those general human qualities the conscious attitude lacks. The tyrant tormented by bad dreams, gloomy forebodings, and inner fears, is a typical figure. Outwardly inconsiderate, harsh and unapproachable, he is inwardly susceptible to every shadow, and subject to every fancy, as though he were the least independent, and the most impressionable, of men. Thus his soul contains those general human qualities of suggestibiliy and weakness which are wholly lacking in his outer attitude, or persona. Where the persona is intellectual, the soul is quite certainly sentimental. That the complementary character of the soul is also concerned with the sex-character is a fact which can no longer seriously be doubted. A very feminine woman has a masculine soul, and a very manly man a feminine soul. This opposition is based upon the fact that a man, for instance, is not in all things wholly masculine, but has also certain feminine traits. The more manly his outer attitude, the more will his womanly traits be effaced; these then appear in the soul. This circumstance explains why it is that the very manly men are most subject to characteristic weaknesses; their attitude to the unconscious has a womanly weakness and impressionability and, vice versa, it is often just the most womanly women who, in respect of certain inner things, have an extreme intractableness, obstinacy, and wilfulness; which qualities are found in such intensity only in the outer attitude of men. These are manly traits, whose exclusion from the womanly outer attitude makes them qualities of the soul. If, therefore, we speak of the *anima* of a man, we must logically speak of the *animus* of a woman, if we are to give the soul of a woman its right name. Whereas logic and objective reality commonly prevail in the outer attitude of man, or are at least regarded as ideal, in the case of woman it is feeling. But in the soul the relations are reversed: inwardly it is the man who feels, and the woman who reflects. Hence man's greater liability to total despair, while a woman can always find comfort and hope; hence man is more liable to put an end to himself than woman. [. . .]

Carl Gustav Jung, 'Soul Anima', *Psychological Types* (1923)

THE ADLERIAN UNCONSCIOUS

The Hidden Goal Towards Which We Strive

If the Freudian 'unconscious' was ultimately concerned with biologically driven sexual and antisexual conflict, Alfred Adler (1870–1937) saw social striving as the hidden basis for character formation. Given the prolonged dependency of human children, Adler emphasized the universal need to reconcile individual autonomy with parental power, and ultimately the power of the social group. But some children were born more handicapped than others and different parents mediated their power in different ways. Thus neglect or pampering could make it more difficult for the young person to adjust. Miserable failure might then dominate the picture rather than 'compensation' for inferiority with constructive striving.

Adler's ideas are clearly rooted in his own experience. He was

*the second and favourite son of a Viennese grain merchant. He
suffered from rickets in childhood and felt himself to be ugly
and deformed. He almost died from a severe illness at the age
of five. His early years were also marred by envy of his older
brother who was an athletic 'model child', and his mother's
favourite.*

*After qualifying in medicine in 1895, Adler practised as a physi-
cian. In 1902 he was one of the founder members of the
Wednesday Psychological Society, convened by Freud, and later
to become the Vienna Psychoanalytic Society. By 1910, when
Freud resigned his Presidency in favour of Adler, their ideas already
deviated significantly, and the following year they parted company.
Adler went on to found the Society for Individual Psychology.
His fame led to lecture tours abroad and appointments as a lecturer
at Columbia University and professor of medical psychology at
Long Island College of Medicine. In 1934 he emigrated to the
United States, but three years later returned to Europe for a stren-
uous lecture tour which ended up in Scotland, where he died.*

We must remember that all children occupy an inferior and
dependent position in life. Without a certain amount of social
feeling on the part of their family they would be incapable of
existence. We realize that the beginning of every life is fraught
with a fairly deep-seated sense of inferiority when we see the
weakness and helplessness of all children. Sooner or later all children become conscious of their inability to cope alone with the
challenges of existence. This feeling of inferiority is the driving
force, the starting point from which every childish striving originates. It determines how individual children acquire peace and
security in life, it determines the very goal of their existence and
it prepares the path along which this goal may be approached.
    [. . .]
The tendency to push oneself into the limelight, to demand
parents' attention, makes itself apparent in the first days of life.
Here are found the first indications that the awakening desire
for recognition is developing alongside the sense of inferiority.

Its purpose is the attainment of a state in which individuals are seemingly superior to their environment.

The degree and quality of a person's social feeling helps to determine their goal of superiority. We cannot judge individuals, whether children or adults, without comparing their goal of personal superiority with the extent of their social feeling. Their goal is so constructed that its achievement promises the possibility either of a feeling of superiority or an elevation of the personality to a level that makes life seem worth living. It is this goal that gives value to our experiences. It links and co-ordinates our feelings, shapes our imagination, directs our creative powers and determines what we will remember and what we must forget. We can see how relative the values of sensations, sentiments, emotions and imagination are; these elements of our psychological activity are influenced by our striving for a definite goal. Our very perceptions are prejudiced by it and are chosen, so to speak, with a hidden reference to the final goal towards which the personality is striving.

Alfred Adler, 'The Inferiority Complex', *Understanding Human Nature* (1927)

THE PHYSIOLOGICAL UNCONSCIOUS

Stimulus-Response Psychology and the Reflex Arc

Early in the nineteenth century the British neurologist, Marshall Hall, drew attention to the automatic motor responses that could occur when a sensory nerve was stimulated. He called them reflexes. The most familiar reflex is the stretch reflex of muscles, for example the knee-jerk which occurs when the tendon just below the knee-cap is tapped with a patella hammer. Impulses are carried from the stretched muscle tendon to the spinal cord along a sensory, afferent nerve. They are then conducted towards the motor, efferent nerve cell, which in turn becomes excited and carries impulses back to the muscle, causing it to contract.

The neurophysiological understanding of this simple process led to the elaboration of a model of mental organization based upon it. Attempts to understand the functioning of the human mind are limited by the sophistication of our thinking in other areas of science, which provide examples of the way things work. We are always looking for the fundamental building blocks. If mental phenomena are, in essence, a product of bodily and brain processes, then they should ultimately be explicable in biological terms. The distinguished Victorian physician, Henry Maudsley (1835–1916), championed this view, regarding nervous disorder as the underlying cause of all mental disorder. In the following extract, he makes the case for regarding reason, arguably our highest mental activity, as being rooted in reflex behaviour. His thinking presages the later development of psychological behaviourism, which was to become the dominant paradigm for academic psychology in the twentieth century.[9]

What is the mental organization? The key of its structure and function is a simple reflex or excitomotor act. The type of its structure is, on the one side, a sensory or afferent nerve along which, in response to an impression made on its endings, an ingoing current passes to a central nerve-cell, and on the other side a motor or efferent nerve connected also with the nerve-cell, along which the resulting outgoing current passes to the muscles that react on the outer world. Such simple nervous structure by which a message is received from without and fit reaction made to it is practically the entire nervous system of the lowest creature which owns one, and it is the basis of the more complex structures that subserve the adjustments of the highest creatures to their external conditions; for it is by the multiplication of cells and fibres, and by complication of tracts and connections, that their nervous structures, however complex, are built up. In the complex plexuses formed by the multiplication and complication of cells, fibres and connections, there are the obvious means of

9 See J.B. Watson, (pp. 216–21) B.F. Skinner (pp. 214–16), also G. Ryle (pp. 246–51) and D. Dennett (pp. 285–6) for philosophical behaviourism.

associating several ingoing currents proceeding from different sensory endings and of making fit distributions of energy and different combinations of distributions along several tracks or lines of conduction. Moreover, in the ascending scale of animal organization from the more simple and general to the more complex and special structure there is a further complication of different levels of nerve-plexuses; and it is obvious that in the superposition of areas of higher level of reflex action with which areas of lower level are connected, and in the more abstract superordinate functions of which their lower functions are represented, there are the means by which pregnant impulses may descend from the higher areas of the nervous hierarchy to the several subordinate centres and be there suitably analysed, as it were, and distributed.

Considering that there are some hundreds of millions of nerve-cells and fibres in the cerebral cortex of man, that every cell which is not unattached has its own connection or connections, and that every one of the multitude of fibres goes separate to its destination, whatever that be, imagination may go some way to realize how exceedingly fine, numerous, intricate, and complex are the nervous networks which constitute the mental organization. There are abundant means of physical reflection to serve all the purposes of mental reflection, more perhaps than have ever yet been made full use of by minds of the largest capacity; indeed it is a specious surmise that there are multitudes of available cells in the cortex waiting to make their connections as fast as new observations and reflections shall require and use them to register newly discovered relations of things.

As the mechanism of the simple reflex act is the elemental type of the complex mental structure, so the simple reflex act is the elemental type of the complex mental function. To receive an impression and to make a fit reaction to it, either in order to embrace the stimulus when it is agreeable and useful, or to repel and evade it when it is painful and hurtful, that is the fundamental factor in all mental function; the most complex of which represents essentially, though in abstract representations, by cortical registrations – as it were by a system of algebraic symbols – the greatest number of the fittest movements in answer to the greatest number of fitting impressions. Many small creatures are admirable in the adaptation of their acts to their ends, being more perfect than man in that respect, but the range of their impressions is very limited and special compared with the wider and ever-widening range of experience which his senses open to him; they are perfect machines for their comparatively narrow ends, their more simple nervous system being wholly appropriated and, as it were, stereotyped to certain set uses; whereas his complex nervous system is a progressive and perfecting machine plastic to the new uses which his pains and gains through the ages gradually incorporate into it. What could be more clever than a bee along the tracks of its instincts, what more stupid than a bee outside them? Growing reason is the progressive gaining by experience of what, in elementary form, is innate or instinct in many of the lower animals.[†] Purposive reflex action without conscious design we call instinct, and the more complex the act the more wonderful the instinct, but purposive action consciously adapted is called reason, because it is desire guided to its end by experience. At bottom the latter is just as reflex as the former, and the former as essentially reason as the latter, instinct being formed reason and reason instinct in process of formation; or they are both alike acts of reason, if that description of them be preferred, the one of implicit the other of explicit reason – the actual processes of the same nature, however we choose to name them.

Henry Maudsley, *The Pathology of Mind, a Study of Its Distempers, Deformities and Disorders* (1895)

[†] Having found the powers to do a variety of acts instinct in different animal organizations, men have thereupon made *instinct* a substantive faculty and treated it as an explanation. It would be just as good an explanation to make of *innate* or of *implant* a substantive faculty and thereupon to ascribe them to it. That so much time and work have been given to tedious doubts and discussions whether such animals as dogs and horses possess reason is a proof how little psychology has been a science of observation, and how much its concern has been with words not things; since there was not an intelligent shepherd or groom who could not at any time, had the problem been intelligently put to him, have settled it offhand and was not daily solving by his daily management of these animals. The question. Are animals machines? might profitably be supplemented by the question, Is reason mechanical? That is to say, organic machinery in mechanical making.

Blindsight

Certain kinds of brain damage lead to alterations in our aware-
ness of both the mental and non-mental worlds. Studying their
effects casts light on the relation between different levels of
psychological functioning. The research of Professor Weiskrantz
demonstrates that many such patients retain intact capacities to
discriminate and remember of which they are unaware. This has
become known as 'covert processing'. In the following extract
the discovery of 'blindsight', the disconnection between the
capacity to see and the experience of seeing, is described.

Lawrence Weiskrantz is Emeritus Professor of Psychology at
Oxford University, a Fellow of the Royal Society and a member
of the US National Academy of Sciences. He was educated at
Oxford and Harvard Universities and subsequently worked at
Cambridge University for eleven years, before returning to
Oxford in 1967 to become Director of the Department of
Experimental Psychology, a post he held for twenty-six years.

One cannot ask a monkey whether it 'sees' a stimulus or not:
one requires it to make a forced-choice discrimination; e.g. if
stimulus A, do X, if B, do Y. Or, if and only if A is present, do
R. One of the surprising results to emerge recently from testing
patients with field defects caused by striate cortex damage is that
they, too, if required to respond by forced-choice to visual stimuli
projected into their 'blind' fields, can discriminate those stimuli,
even though they may fervently deny that they 'see' them. The
subject must be persuaded to play a kind of game, like 'if the
grating (that you cannot see) is vertical, say "vertical", and if it
is horizontal, say "horizontal". Even if you cannot *see* it, have
a guess.'

Using forced-choice methods, evidence has been produced
that patients can detect visual events in their 'blind' fields, can
locate them in space by pointing or moving their eyes (although
with reduced accuracy), can make discriminations between gratings of different orientations with quite good (if not quite
normal) accuracy, and can carry out some types of simple shape

discriminations. Indeed, as far as one can make direct comparisons, their capacities are of the same order as monkeys in which there is a striate cortex lesion. The first group to have persuaded patients to play the 'respond-by-moving-your-eyes-even-though-you-do-not-see' game was Pöppel et al. (1973), but we soon afterwards studied a patient (DB) in whom a similar but larger range of residual visual capacities was seen, and since then a number of reports, as well as a critique, have appeared.

Despite the demonstration of visual discriminative capacity, the subject characteristically will say that he does not 'see'. He is playing the experimenter's game, and making a forced-choice response such as 'horizontal' or 'vertical' (or 'yes' present, 'no' not present; or 'moving' or 'not moving', or 'X' or 'O', depending on the task). Indeed with the first patient whom we tested, we did not (and still do not) give knowledge of results during the test: when he was told of his impressive results afterwards he expressed open surprise – he thought he was just guessing. We called this phenomenon 'blindsight', which might have been unfortunate because the term has become much better known than the details of the findings. But at least in the sense of connoting a disconnection between a capacity and experience, the term is not entirely misplaced. Interestingly, a closely similar phenomenon has been reported in the somatosensory mode for localization of touch on the hand of a patient with hemi-anaesthesia caused by a cortical lesion in sensory-motor cortex. It has been called 'blind touch' by Paillard et al. (1983). That is, the patient could locate touch stimuli to her skin, but had no awareness of actually being touched.

[. . .]

The patients I have discussed seem to be disconnected from a monitoring system, one that is not part of the serial information-processing chain itself, but can monitor what is going on. This disconnection is not the only thing that has happened to such patients, or possibly even the most interesting thing – other issues such as multiple memory systems and 'two visual system' organization are also illuminated by them – but it is what concerns us here. But, at least in the case of blindsight, the first evidence came from animals; it was the fact that monkeys can still carry out

visual discriminations, and display control of their eye movements by visual events, that led to a re-examination of the human
cases. And so the question arises as to how we would know
whether or not the 'monitoring system' is functioning in a non-
verbal animal. Without such a general and abstract solution the
neuroscience of the matter will reach a stalemate.

No one, of course, has the answer as yet, but I speculate that
one approach is to put the 'monitoring' response itself under
separate control. One approach to this has been developed by
Beninger *et al.* (1974), who in effect asked laboratory rats if they
knew what they were doing. They allowed the rats to do any
one of four possible things that rats do quite frequently and naturally without training: to face-wash, to rear up, to walk, and to
remain immobile. But to get food reward, after they had
performed any one of these four acts they had to press one of
four different levers, so as to indicate what it was they had done.
The rats could do that. I have no doubt monkeys could do it.
But could a frog, or a pigeon? I doubt that a sea slug or a crab
could.

The 'monitoring' level is, in effect, a 'commentary' lever, and
one that runs in parallel with the levers involved in the discriminative capacities themselves. In the present connection, however,
it would relate not to reports of a subject's own acts, as in the
Beninger study, but to his discriminations or retention of stimuli
to which he is exposed. To take the case of blindsight, if *we* had
to discriminate between highly distinctive vertical and horizontal
gratings we could press one of two keys appropriately to indicate 'horizontal' or 'vertical', and we would also typically have
no difficulty in pressing a third key that indicated that we were
'seeing' and not 'guessing' (although it should not be assumed
that we would always be accurate under all conditions). This is
where we would differ from a blindsight patient, whose third-
key response would be 'guessing'.

Similarly, the amnesic patient [who denies remembering
although capable of doing tasks dependent on memory, ed.] would
press one of two keys to discriminate between items to which he
may have previously been exposed, but his third key would indicate 'guessing' and not 'remembering'. With more refinement, of

course, a confidence rating could be made, as is the practice in some psychophysical procedures. To take another example, a blindfolded paraplegic patient might well display intact spinal reflexes to aversive stimuli applied below the level of the spinal section, but his 'commentary' key responses would obviously and conspicuously not correlate with his reflex responses. But how one might go from the principle of the 'third key' to the actual practice of training a non-verbal or 'non-experiencing' subject makes a challenging 'thought experiment'.

There is a further feature of our adaptability that introduces both a difficulty and a further insight for analysis, namely that we tend to transform as much as we possibly can into automatic routines, even though at the outset they may involve much thought and reflection. Many quite skilled acts, such as are prac-tised by aircraft controllers or pilots, become routine without thought and might even be impeded by thought. Therefore, the status of responses on the 'commentary key' might actually change as acts change from a training phase to a skilled phase [. . .]

[. . .]

We do not yet know how to identify the neural equivalent of the 'third key', but the first stage in the nervous system at which it is likely to emerge, in the case of vision of *objects*, is not the striate cortex but the region where information from the whole of the visual field is united. In the monkey this is thought to be in the infero-temporal cortex (for information about objects; spatial mapping may follow a different anatomical route), which lies several synapses beyond the striate cortex of each hemisphere.

Lawrence Weiskrantz, 'Some Contributions of Neuropsychology of Vision and Memory to the Problem of Consciousness' (1988) [References omitted, ed.]

THE SELF

The Interpreter

Patients suffering from intractable epilepsy can be helped to control it by neurosurgery. Cerebral commisurotomy in which the corpus callosum (the main connecting pathway between right and left sides of the brain) and the anterior commisure (a smaller connecting pathway) are divided, is an operation which has been successfully carried out for more than forty years. Patients who have undergone this procedure have become known as 'split-brain' subjects, and show no obvious ill effects from the surgery. However, because there is no high-level communication between the left and right halves of their brains, it is possible to investigate the function of each side separately.

Visual information from the left field is normally processed in the right hemisphere of the brain and vice versa. Similarly motor activity on one side of the body is controlled by the opposite side of the brain. The input of visual information can be experimentally restricted to one hemisphere by using special contact lenses that blot out the opposite field. Another method involves using a machine called a tachistoscope, that can flash signals to only one peripheral field while the subject is looking straight ahead. The output of each hemisphere can be experimentally tested by asking the subject to perform tasks with either the right or left hand. When a light was flashed to his isolated right hemisphere, early split-brain subject W.J. said (with his left hemisphere) that he did not see anything, even though his left hand (controlled by his right hemisphere) pushed a Morse code key, to indicate that he had!

The experimenter's ability to communicate with each half of the brain separately, gave rise to the intriguing possibility that each might be shown to have its own centre of consciousness – thinking, feeling and behaving in different ways. Early work appeared to show that each hemisphere had its own 'cognitive style', the right one specializing in visuo-spacial tasks, the left in linguistic ability. But extensive investigation over the years has shown that there is diversity in the lateralization of brain function. In most people, however, it appears that the left hemisphere is considerably brighter than the right! The right hemisphere is usually dumb, it cannot speak, is unable to analyse data, calculate or make causal inferences.

Michael Gazzaniga, Professor of Neuroscience at the University of California, concludes that there is no generalized computational capacity spread across the whole of the brain's cortex, rather that there are specialized circuits for different cognitive activities, of which we may or may not be conscious. Unconscious activity is not necessarily restricted to subcortical levels of brain function. In the following passage he describes how the left brain, kept ignorant of the cause, attempts to make sense of the right brain's behaviour.

We first revealed the interpreter using a simultaneous concept test. The patient is shown two pictures, one exclusively to the left hemisphere and one exclusively to the right, and is asked to choose from an array of pictures placed in full view in front of him the ones associated with the pictures lateralized to the left and right brain. In one example of this kind of test, a picture of a chicken claw was flashed to the left hemisphere and a picture of a snow scene to the right hemisphere. Of the array of pictures placed in front of the subject, the obviously correct association is a chicken for the chicken claw and a shovel for the snow scene. Split-brain subject P.S. responded by choosing the shovel with the left hand and the chicken with the right. When asked why he chose these items, his left hemisphere replied, 'Oh, that's simple. The chicken claws go with the chicken, and you need a shovel to clean out the chicken shed.' Here, the left brain, observing the left hand's response, interprets that response according to a context consistent with its sphere of knowledge – one that does not include information about the left hemifield snow scene.

Another example of this phenomenon of the left brain interpreting actions produced by the disconnected right brain involves lateralizing a written command such as 'laugh', to the right hemisphere by tachistoscopically presenting it to the left visual field. After the stimulus is presented, the patient laughs, and when asked why, says, 'You guys come up and test us every month. What a way to make a living!' In still another example, if the command walk is flashed to the right hemisphere, the patient will typically stand up from the chair and begin to take leave from the testing van. When asked where he or she is going, the subject's left brain says, 'I'm going into the house to get a Coke.' However this type of test is manipulated, it always yields the same kind of result.

There are many ways to influence the left-brain interpreter. As already mentioned, we wanted to know whether or not the emotional response to stimuli presented to one half of the brain would have an effect on the affective tone of the other half of the brain. In this particular study, we showed under lateralized stimulus presentation procedures a series of film vignettes that included either violent or calm sequences. We showed that the emotional valence of the stimulus crossed over from the right to the left hemisphere. The left hemisphere remains unaware of the content that produced the emotional change, but it experiences and must deal with the emotion and give it an interpretation [. . .]

The modular organization of the human brain has now been well established. The functioning modules do have some kind of physical instantiation, but the brain sciences are not yet able to specify the nature of the actual neural networks involved. What is clear is that they operate largely outside the realm of awareness and announce their computational products to various executive systems that result in behaviour or cognitive states. Catching up with all this parallel and constant activity seems to be a function of the left hemisphere's interpreter module. The interpreter is the system of primary importance to the human brain. It is what allows for the formation of beliefs, which in turn are mental constructs that free us from simply responding to stimulus-response aspects of everyday life. In many ways it is the system that provides the story line or narrative of our lives. Yet, it would not appear to be the system that provides the heat, the stuff, the feelings about our thoughts.

Michael Gazzaniga, 'Consciousness and the Cerebral Hemispheres', *The Cognitive Neurosciences* (1995)

Conquering Self

According to Buddha, Siddharta Gautama (Sakyamuni 563–483BCE), son of Prince Suddhodana, life is characterized by pain, the root of which is desire. On this view, seeking satisfaction is counterproductive and leads to an increase in desire. Accordingly, release from pain may be effected only by conquering and extinguishing desire – Nirvana. This process involves disinvesting the 'self', the individual, with significance.

'The loss of virtue and of merit which we mourn proceeds from "pride of self", throughout; and as I am a conqueror (*Gina*) amid conquerors* so he who (they who) conquers self, is one with me. 1811

'He who little cares to conquer self, is but a foolish master; beauty (or, earthly things), family renown (and such things), all are utterly inconstant, and what is changeable can give no rest of interval.† 1812

'If in the end the law of entire destruction (is exacted) what use is there in indolence and pride? Covetous desire (lust) is the greatest (source of) sorrow, appearing as a friend in secret 'tis our enemy. 1813

'As a fierce fire excited from within (a house), so is the fire of covetous desire: the burning flame of covetous desire is fiercer far than the fire which burns the world (world fire). 1814

'For fire may be put out by water in excess, but what can overpower the fire of lust? The fire which fiercely burns the desert grass (dies out), and then the grass will grow again; 1815

---

* Here there is allusion to Buddha's name 'Deva among Devas'. The construction of these sentences is obscure on account of the varied use of the word 'I' 'ngo'); this symbol is used sometimes, as in the line under present consideration, as a pronoun, but in the next line it means the evil principle of 'self'. I have found it difficult to avoid comparing this use of the word 'I', meaning the 'evil self', with the phrase the 'carnal mind'. The question, in fact, is an open one, whether the Buddhist teaching respecting the non-existence of 'I', i.e. a personal self or soul, may not justly be explained as consisting in the denial of the reality of the 'carnal self'.

† I should like to translate it no 'interval of rest', but it seems to mean the only rest given is momentary, no rest from interval, i.e. constant change.

'But when the fire of lust burns upon the heart, then how hard for true religion there to dwell! for lust seeks worldly pleasures, these pleasures add to an impure karman;* 1816

'By this evil karman a man falls into perdition (evil way), and so there is no greater enemy to man than lust. Lusting, man gives way to amorous indulgence (lit. lust, then it brings forth love'), by this he is led to practise (indulge in) every kind of lustful longing; 1817

'Indulging thus, he gathers frequent sorrow (all sorrow, or accumulated sorrow, referring to the second of the 'four truths' [that the cause of pain is desire or attachment to life, ed.]. No greater evil (excessive evil) is there than lust. Lust is a dire disease, and the foolish master stops (i.e. neglects) the medicine of wisdom. 1818

'(The study of) heretical books not leading to right thought, causes the lustful heart to increase and grow, for these books are not correct (pure) on the points of impermanency, the non-existence of self, and any object (ground) for 'self'.† 1819

'But a true and right apprehension through the power of wisdom, is effectual to destroy that false desire (heretical longing), and therefore our object (aim or purpose) should be to practise this true apprehension. 1820

'Right apprehension (views) once produced then there is deliverance from covetous desire, for a false estimate of excellency produces a covetous desire to excel, whilst a false view of demerit produces anger (and regret); 1821

'But the idea of excelling and also of inferiority (in the sense of demerit) both destroyed, the desire to excel and also anger (on account of inferiority) are destroyed. Anger! how it changes

---

* The impure karman is, of course, the power of evil (in the character) to bring about suffering by an evil birth.

† The meaning is that heretical books, i.e. books of the Brahmans and so on, teach no sound doctrine as to the unreality of the world, the non-existence of a 'personal self', and the impropriety of any personal selfish aim, and therefore not teaching these, men who follow them are taken up with the idea that there is reality in worldly pleasures, that there is a personal self capable of enjoying them, and that the aim after such enjoyment is a right aim. All this Buddha and his doctrine exclude.

the comely face, how it destroys the loveliness of beauty! 1822

Asuaghosa Bodhisattua, *The Fo-Sho-Hing-Tsan-King* (c.420)

Being Oneself

Philip Roth, a leading American writer, was born in 1933. His career has spanned more than forty years. Among his best-known novels are the controversial bestseller Portnoy's Complaint *(1969) and* The Human Stain *(2000).*

Being Zuckerman is one long performance and the very opposite of what is thought of as *being oneself*. In fact, those who most seem to be themselves appear to me people impersonating what they think they might like to be, believe they ought to be, or wish to be taken to be by whoever is setting standards. So in earnest are they that they don't even recognize that being in earnest *is the act*. For certain self-aware people, however, this is not possible: to imagine themselves, living their own real, authentic, or genuine life, has for them all the aspects of a hallucination.

I realize that what I am describing, people divided in themselves, is said to characterize mental illness and is the absolute opposite of our idea of emotional integration. The whole Western idea of mental health runs in precisely the opposite direction: what is desirable is congruity between your self-consciousness and your natural being. But there are those whose sanity flows from the conscious *separation* of those two things. If there even *is* a natural being, an irreducible self, it is rather small, I think, and may even be the root of all impersonation – the natural being may be the skill itself, the innate capacity to impersonate. I'm talking about recognizing that one is acutely a performer, rather than swallowing whole the guise of naturalness and pretending that it isn't a performance but you.

There is no you, Maria, any more than there's a me. There is only this way that we have established over the months of performing together, and what it is congruent with isn't 'ourselves' but past performances – we're has-beens at heart, routinely trotting out the old, old act . . .

Philip Roth, *The Counterlife* (1986)

The Idea of a Unique Self

In his novel Thinks, *the novelist David Lodge (1935–) has one of his characters, Helen Reed (also a novelist), reflect on the following stanzas taken from 'The Garden', a poem by the seventeenth-century English poet, Andrew Marvell, during a presentation at a conference.*

> 'Mean while the Mind, from pleasure less,
> Withdraws into its happiness:
> The Mind, that Ocean where each kind
> Does streight its own resemblance find;
> Yet it creates, transcending these,
> Far other Worlds, and other Seas;
> Annihilating all that's made
> To a green Thought in a green Shade.
> [. . .]
> Here at the Fountains sliding foot,
> Or at some Fruit-trees mossy root,
> Casting the Bodies Vest aside
> My Soul into the boughs does glide:
> There like a Bird it sits, and sings,
> Then whets, and combs its silver Wings;
> And, till prepar'd for longer flight,
> Waves in its Plumes the various Light.

'Descartes, I have been told, believed in the immortality of the soul because he could imagine his mind existing apart from his body. Marvell expresses that idea in the very beautiful image of the bird. He imagines his soul leaving his body temporarily to perch on the branch of a tree, where it preens and grooms itself in anticipation of its final flight to heaven. I don't expect to carry you with him there. Such an idea of the soul would seem fanciful today even to believing Christians. But the Christian idea of the soul is continuous with the humanist idea of the self, that is to say, the sense of the personal identity, the sense of one's mental and emotional life having a unity and an extension in time and an ethical responsibility, sometimes called conscience.

'This idea of the self is under attack today, not only in much scientific discussion of consciousness, but in the humanities too. We are told that it is a fiction, a construction, an illusion, a myth. That each of us is "just a pack of neurons", or just a junction for converging discourses, or just a parallel processing computer running by itself without an operator. As a human being and as a writer, I find that view of consciousness abhorrent – and intuitively unconvincing. I want to hold on to the traditional idea of the autonomous individual self. A lot that we value in civilization seems to depend on it – law, for instance, and human rights – including copyright. Marvell wrote 'The Garden' before the concept of copyright existed, but the fact remains that nobody else could have written it, and nobody else will ever write it again – except in the trivial sense of copying it out word for word.

'The poem is a celebratory one, so it focuses on consciousness as a state of happiness. It is about bliss. But there is a tragic dimension to consciousness, which has also been hardly touched on in this conference. There is madness, depression, guilt, and dread. There is the fear of death – and strangest of all, the fear of life. If human beings are the only living creatures that really know they are going to die, they are also the only ones who knowingly take their own lives. For some people, in some circumstances, consciousness becomes so unbearable that they commit suicide to bring it to an end. "To be or not to be?" is a peculiarly human question. Literature can help us to understand the dark side of consciousness too. Thank you.'

David Lodge, *Thinks* (2001)

ACKNOWLEDGEMENTS

The editor and publishers are grateful to the following authors, their representatives and publishers for permission to reproduce copyright material in this anthology as follows:

ALFRED ADLER, *Understanding Human Nature* (1927), Oneworld Publications, translated by Colin Brett, 1992. SALVATORE AGLIOTI, FELICIANA CORTESE and CRISTINA FRANCHINI, 'Rapid sensory remapping in the adult human brain as inferred from phantom breast perception' in *Neuroreport 5*, 473–6. ANONYMOUS, *Hindu Scriptures*, ed. Dominic Goodall, J.M. Dent. SAMUEL BECKETT, *Murphy* (1938), by permission of Calder Publications. WILFRED BION, *Second Thoughts* (1967), first published by William Heinemann Medical Books Ltd. Reprinted by permission of Francesca Bion on behalf of the Estate of Wilfred R. Bion and Karnac Books. DANIEL DENNET, *Consciousness Explained* copyright © 1991 by Daniel C Dennett 1991. Reprinted by permission of Penguin Books Ltd, 1993 and Little, Brown and Company, (Inc.) FYODOR DOSTOYEVSKY, *The Idiot* (1878) Translated by David Magarshack, Penguin Classics, 1955, copyright © David Magarshack, 1955. Reproduced by permission of Penguin Books Ltd. JOHN ECCLES, *The Self and Its Brain*, 1977. Reprinted by permission of Springer-Verlag on behalf of the Estate of John Eccles. GERALD EDELMAN, *Bright Air, Brilliant Fire*, Allen Lane, The Penguin Press, 1992, copyright © Gerald Edelman, 1992 and copyright © 1992 by Basic Books, Inc. Reprinted by permission of Penguin Books Ltd and Basic Books, a member of Perseus Books, L.L.C. PAUL EMMERSON, 'Effects of Environmental Context on Recognition Memory in an Unusual Environment', *Perceptual and Motor Skills*, 1986, 63, 1047–1050. © Perceptual and Motor Skills 1986. ANNA FREUD and SIGMUND FREUD, all works reprinted by permission of the Estate of Sigmund Freud. ERICH FROMM, *The*

Anatomy of Human Destructiveness © 1973 by Erich Fromm. Reprinted by permission of Henry Holt and Company, LLC and Jonathan Cape. GALEN, *Selected Works* copyright © P.N. Singer 1997, translated with an introduction and notes by PN Singer (World's Classics, 1997). Reprinted by permission of Oxford University Press. MICHAEL GAZZANIGA, 'Consciousness and the Cerebral Hemispheres' in *The Cognitive Neurosciences*, MIT Press, 1995. DANIEL GOLEMAN, *Emotional Intelligence* copyright © 1995 by Daniel Goleman. Used by permission of Bantam Books, a division of Random House, Inc and Bloomsbury Publishing Plc. HALLIGAN ET AL, 'Three arms: a case study of supernumerary phantom limb after right hemisphere stroke', *Journal of Neurology, Neurosurgery, and Psychiatry*, 56 (1993), 159–166. Reprinted by permission of the BMJ Publishing Group. ALDOUS HUXLEY, *Heaven and Hell*, copyright 1955, © 1956 by Aldous Huxley. Copyright renewed 1983, 1984 by Laura Huxley. Reprinted by permission of HarperCollins Publishers, Inc. Originally published by Chatto & Windus. Reprinted by permission of The Random House Group Limited © the Estate of Mrs Laura Huxley. SUSAN ISAACS, 'The Nature and Function of Phantasy' in *Developments in Psychoanalysis*, edited by Joan Rivière, Hogarth Press, 1952. KAY REDFIELD JAMISON, *An Unquiet Mind* copyright © 1995 by Kay Redfield Jamison. Reprinted by permission of Alfred A. Knopf, Inc. JULIAN JAYNES, *The Origins of Consciousness in the Breakdown of the Bicameral Mind*, Allen Lane, 1979, second edition 1993, copyright © 1976, 1990 by Julian Jaynes. Reprinted by permission of Houghton Mifflin Company and Penguin Books Ltd. All rights reserved. CARL GUSTAV JUNG, *Modern Man in Search of a Soul*, Routledge, 1961 and *Psychological Types*, Routledge, 1989. FRANZ KAFKA, *Diaries 1910–1923*, edited by Max Brod. Copyright © 1949, copyright renewed 1977 by Schocken Books, Inc. Reprinted by permission of Schocken Books, a division of Random House, Inc and Secker and Warburg. SERGEI KORSAKOFF, 'Psychic Disorder in Conjunction with Multiple Neuritis' trans. Maurice Victor and Paul Yakovlev in *Neurology 5*. SØREN KIERKEGAARD, *Either/Or* © 1971 Princeton University Press MELANIE KLEIN, *Love, Guilt and Reparation and Other Works*, published by The Hogarth Press.

Random House Group Limited and the Estate of Marcel Proust. MARCEL PROUST, *Remembrance of Things Past*, Vol Three © 1981 by Random House, Inc. and Chatto & Windus. M. ROSSOR, E. WARRINGTON and L CIPOLOTTI PHILIP ROTH, *The Counterlife* © 1986 by Philip Roth. Reprinted by permission of Farrar, Straus and Giroux, LLC and Jonathan Cape. JEAN JACQUES ROUSSEAU, *Emile* (1792), translated by Barbara Foxley, Everyman, JM Dent, 1911. BERTRAND RUSSELL, *The Analysis of Mind* (1921), Routledge, 1997. GILBERT RYLE, *The Concept of Mind*. Reprinted by permission of Routledge, 1949 and the Principal, Fellows and Scholars of Hertford College, in the University of Oxford. OLIVER SACKS, *Inaugural Lecture, Opening Centre for the Mind, Australian National University*, 10 January 1998 © 1998 by Oliver Sacks. JEAN-PAUL SARTRE, *The Psychology of the Imagination* (1948), Rider, London 1950. Reprinted by permission of Sanford J. Greenburger, New York, on behalf of The Philosophical Library. BERNHARD SCHLINK, *The Reader*, translated by Carol Brown Janeway, Phoenix House, London and Random House, Inc., New York. WILLIAM SCOVILLE and BRENDA MILNER, 'Loss of Recent Memory After Bilateral Hippocampal Lesions' *Journal of Neurology, Neurosurgery, and Psychiatry* 1993, 56, originally in *Journal of Neurology, Neurosurgery and Psychiatry* 1957, 20. HANNA SEGAL, *The Work of Hanna Segal: A Kleinian Approach to Clinical Practice* copyright © 1981 by Jason Aronson Inc. Reprinted by permission of the publisher, Jason Aronson Inc. B.F. SKINNER, *Beyond Freedom and Dignity* © 1971 by B. F. Skinner. Reprinted by permission of Jonathan Cape and Alfred A Knopf, a Division of Random House. K. SMITH, C. FAIRBURN and P. COWEN, 'Relapse of depression after rapid depletion of tryptophan', *Lancet*, 349, 29 March 1997, 915–919. Reprinted with permission from Elsevier Science. ADRIAN STOKES, *A Game that Must Be Lost: Collected Papers*, Carcanet Press Ltd., 1973. Reprinted by permission of Carcanet Press Ltd. on behalf of The Estate of Adrian Stokes. ANTHONY STORR, *Music and the Mind* copyright © 1992 by Anthony Storr. Reprinted with the permission of The Free Press, a Division of Simon & Schuster Adult Publishing Group and HarperCollins Publishers Ltd. GALEN STRAWSON, 'Esprit De Core', *TLS*, 7 October 2000. VICTOR TAUSK,

'On the Origin of the "Influencing Machine" in Schizophrenia', *The Psychoanalytic Quarterly*, II, 1933, 519, translated by Dorian Feigenbaum, Otherpress. LEO TOLSTOY, *Childhood, Boyhood and Youth*, translated by Rosemary Edmonds, Penguin Classics, 1964, copyright © Rosemary Edmonds, 1964. LAWRENCE WEISKRANTZ, 'Some Contributions of Neuropsychology of Vision and Memory to the Problem of Consciousness' in *Consciousness in Contemporary Science*, edited by A. J. Marcel and E. Bisiach, 1988. Reprinted by permission of Oxford University Press. DONALD WINNICOTT, *Collected Papers: Through Paediatrics to Psychoanalysis*, published by Hogarth Press. Used by permission of the Random House Group Limited. LUDWIG WITTGENSTEIN, *Philosophical Investigations*, translated by G. Anscombe, Blackwell Publishers, 1953. DANAH ZOHAR and IAN MARSHALL, *Spiritual Intelligence*. Reprinted by permission of Bloomsbury Publishing Plc.

Thanks are also due to the members of my family and friends who have helped by reading various sections and making comments, giving me valuable suggestions (not all of which made it into the final draft) and much support. I am grateful to Robin and Daphne Briggs, Bo Korting, Phil Cowen, Roland Fleming, Rochelle Hausman, Mathew Hollis, Dan Isaacson, David Kennard, Jean Knox, Jenny Lewis, Mandy Little, Jamie Mackendrick, Douglas and Tamsin Palmer, Anne Ridgeway, Anna and Dan Shrimpton, Shawn 'the-cat', Clive Sinclair, Peter and Galen Strawson, Derek Summers, my editor Bill Swainson, Katherine Greenwood, Joanna Tucker, Connie Webber, Bernard Williams, Ben Wilson, Stijn Broecke for help in all sorts of ways and teaching me tricks on the computer, Lara Wilson especially for help with Greek and Latin translations, Jonathan Wilson and Kate Wilson. I am also grateful to staff at the Bodleian, Radcliffe Science and Regent's Park College Libraries, Neal Thurley at the Cairns Library, Radcliffe Infirmary and Father Richard at Blackfriars Library.

BIBLIOGRAPHY

In this bibliography the date of first publication, or in the case of older texts, the date of composition (where known), is given in brackets after the title of the work, followed by the publication details of the edition used for this book. In the case of Sigmund Freud, I have followed the usual practice and cited SE (Standard Edition, The Hogarth Press, London, under the General Editorship of James Strachey), followed by the volume number.

Adler, Alfred, *Understanding Human Nature* (1927), trans. Colin Brett, Oneworld, Oxford, 1992.

Aglioti, Salvatore, Cortese, Feliciana and Franchini, Cristina, 'Rapid Sensory Remapping in the Adult Human Brain as Inferred from Phantom Breast Perception', *NeuroReport* 5, Oxford, 1994.

Anon., review of *Psychotherapy* by Hugo Munsterberg, *British Medical Journal*, London, 1910.

Aristotle, *On the Soul* (350 BCE), trans. Robert Drew, Cambridge University Press, Cambridge, 1907. (Transposed into Modern English by the editor of this volume, 2000.)

Augustine, Saint, *Confessions* (397–8), trans. Sir Tobie Matthew, 1620. (Transposed into Modern English by the editor of this volume, 2000.)

Bacon, Francis, *Essays* (1596), ed. W. Aldis Wright, Macmillan, London, 1903.

Beckett, Samuel, *Murphy* (1938), John Calder (Publishers) Ltd., London, 1977.

Berkeley, George, *Three Dialogues between Hylas and Philonus* (1713), in *The Works of George Berkeley*, 2 vols, Thomas Tegg, London, 1843.

Bernheim, Hippolyte, *Hypnosis and Suggestion in Psychotherapy:*

A Treatise on the Nature and Uses of Hypnotism (1844), trans. Christain Herter (1889),: University Books, Inc., New Hyde Park, NY, 1964.

Bion, Wilfred R., 'A Theory of Thinking', *Second Thoughts* (1962), Jason Aronson, New York, 1967.

Blake, William, *A Vision of the Last Judgment* (1810), ed. Geoffrey Keynes, *Blake: Complete Writings*, Oxford University Press, Oxford, 1972.

Bodhisattua, Asuaghosa, *The Fo-Sho-Hing-Tsan-King: A Life Of Buddha* (420), trans. from Sanskrit into Chinese by Dharmaraksha and from Chinese into English by Samuel Beal, Clarendon Press, Oxford, 1883.

Braid, James, *The Power of the Mind Over the Body* (1846), John Churchill, London and Edinburgh, 1846.

Bunyan, John, *The Pilgrim's Progress* (1678), ed. Roger Sharrock, Oxford University Press, Oxford, 1966.

Burton, Robert, *The Anatomy of Melancholy* (1651), Thornton's of Oxford, Oxford, 1993.

Clare, John, 'I Am' (1865), in *Beyond Bedlam*, ed. Ken Smith and Mathew Sweeney, Anvil Press, London 1997.

Coleridge, Samuel Taylor, *Biographia Literaria* (1815–1817), ed. H. Jackson, Oxford University Press, Oxford, 1985.

Coleridge, Samuel Taylor, *Notebooks* (1815–1817), ed. I.A. Richards, *The Portable Coleridge*, Viking, New York, 1950.

Darwin, Charles 'Reasons for Noting Adverse Observations' in *The Life and Letters of Charles Darwin*, John Murray, London, 1887.

Darwin,Charles, *The Expression of the Emotions In Man And Animals* (1872), University of Chicago, Chicago, 1965.

Delitzsch, Franz Julius, *A System of Biblical Psychology* (1867), T. and T. Clark, Edinburgh, 1867.

Dennett, Daniel, *Consciousness Explained* (1991), London, Viking Penguin, 1991.

Descartes, René, *Meditation on the First Philosophy* (1641), trans. John Veitch (1853), Blackwood, Edinburgh and London, 1879.

Dostoyevsky, Fyodor, *The Idiot* (1878), trans. David Magarshack, Penguin, Harmondsworth, 1955.

Eccles, John, in *The Self and Its Brain* (co-authored with Karl Popper) (1977), Springer-Verlag, Berlin, 1977.

Edelman, Gerald, *Bright Air, Brilliant Fire: On the Matter of the Mind* (1992), Basic Books, New York, 1992.

Eliot, George, *Middlemarch* (1871), Penguin, Harmondsworth, 1965.

Emerson, Ralph Waldo, *Essays* (1841), Macmillan, London, 1910.

Emmerson, Paul, 'Effects of Environmental Context on Recognition Memory in an Unusual Environment' (1986), *Perceptual and Motor Skills,* 63, Missoula, MT, 1986.

Epicurus, *Morals* (c.300 BCE), trans. Walter Charleton (1655), ed. F. Manning, *Morals,* Peter Davies, London, 1926.

Freud, Anna, 'Identification and the Aggressor', *The Ego and the Mechanisms of Defence* (1936), trans. Cecil Baines, Hogarth Press, London, 1937.

Freud, Sigmund, 'Letter to William Fliess' (1897), trans. and ed. Jeffrey Masson, *The Complete Letters of Sigmund Freud to Wilhelm Fliess*, Harvard University Press, Harvard, MA, 1985.

Freud, Sigmund, *The Psychopathology of Everyday Life* (1901), SE VI (paragraph added 1917).

Freud, Sigmund, *A Difficulty in the Path of Psycho-Analysis,* (1917), SE XVII.

Freud, Sigmund, 'General Theory of the Neuroses', *Introductory Lectures On Psycho-Analysis* (1917), SE XVI.

Freud, Sigmund, *The Ego and the Id* (1923), SE XIX, 55–57.

Freud, Sigmund, *Some Elementary Lessons in Psycho-Analysis* (1938), SE XXIII.

Fromm, Erich *The Anatomy of Human Destructiveness* (1973), Holt, Rinehart and Winston, New York, 1973.

Galen, 'The Affections and Errors of the Soul' (193–c.210), trans. P.N. Singer, *Galen: Selected Works*, Oxford University Press, Oxford, 1997.

Galton, Francis, *Inquiries into Human Faculty and its Development* (1883), J.M. Dent, London, 1883.

Gazzaniga, Michael S., 'Consciousness and the Cerebral Hemispheres', *The Cognitive Neurosciences* (1995), MIT Press, Cambridge, MA, and London, 1995.

Goldstein, Kurt, *Journal of Psychology and Neurology,* 11 (1908), cited by A. Harrington, *Medicine, Mind and the Double*

Brain: A Study in Ninetenth-Century Thought, Princeton University Press, Princeton, MA, 1987.

Goleman, Daniel, *Emotional Intelligence* (1995), Bloomsbury, London, 1995.

Granville, George, 'Love' (18th-century), ed. Jon Stallworthy, *The Penguin Book of Love Poetry*, Penguin, London, 1973.

Halligan, P., Marshall, J. and Wade, D., 'Three Arms: a Case Study of Supernumerary Phantom Limb after Right Hemisphere Stroke' (1993), *Journal of Neurology, Neurosurgery, and Psychiatry*, 56, 1993.

Harlow, John M., *Recovery from the Passage of an Iron Bar Through the Head* (1868), read before the Massachusetts Medical Society, 3 June 1868, David Clapp and Son, Boston, 1869. Reprinted in *History of Psychiatry*, iv, 1993.

Hazlitt, William, 'The Letter Bell', *Sketches and Essays* (1839), Grant Richards, London, 1902.

Helmholtz, Hermann von, 'Concerning the Perceptions in General', *Physiological Optics* (1866), trans. J.P.C. Southall, Optical Society of America, city, 1925.

Hering, Eweld, *On Memory* (1880), trans. Samuel Butler, *Unconscious Memory*, David Bogue, London, 1880.

Holmes, Oliver Wendell, *The Autocrat of the Breakfast-Table*, 62–67 (1858), Croome and Co., London.

Hopkins, Gerard Manley, *Poems* (1918), Oxford University Press, Oxford, 1918.

Hume, David, *A Treatise of Human Nature* (1739), J.M. Dent, London, 1911.

Hunter, John, *A Treatise on the Venereal Disease* (1786) [publisher not known], London, 1786.

Huxley, Aldous, *Heaven and Hell* (1956), Chatto and Windus, London, 1956.

Huxley, Thomas Henry, 'On the Hypothesis that Animals Are Automata', *Fortnightly Review* (1874), London, 1874.

Isaacs, Susan, 'The Nature and Function of Phantasy', *Developments in Psychoanalysis*, Hogarth Press, London, 1952.

Jackson, John Hughlings, *Selected Writings of John Hughlings Jackson* (1873), ed. J. Taylor, Basic Books, New York, 1958 and Staples Press, London, 1958.

James, William, *Principles of Psychology*, Vol. 2 (1890), Macmillan, London, 1890.

Jamison, Kay Redfield, *An Unquiet Mind* (1995), Picador, London, 1996.

Jaynes, Julian, *The Origins of Consciousness in the Breakdown of the Bicameral Mind* (1977), Penguin, London, 1979.

Johnson, Samuel, 'Means of Regulating Sorrow', *The Rambler* (1750–52), J.M. Dent, London, 1953.

Jones, Ernest, The Theory of Symbolism in *Papers on Psychoanalysis* (1916), Bailliere, Tindall & Cox, 1948.

Jung, Carl Gustav, *Psychological Types* (1923), trans. H. Godwin Baynes, Kegan Paul, London and Harcourt Brace, New York, 1923.

Jung, Carl Gustav, *Modern Man in Search of a Soul* (1933), trans. W.S. Dell and C. F. Baynes, Routledge, London, 1961.

Kafka, Franz, *Diaries* (1910–23), Secker and Warburg, London, 1949.

Kant, Immanuel, *Critique of Pure Reason* (1781), trans. Norman Kemp Smith, Macmillan, London, 1933.

Keats, John, 'On Melancholy' (1820), *Poems of John Keats*, J.M. Dent, London, 1906.

Kierkegaard, Søren, *Either /Or* (1843), trans. Walter Lowrie and Howard A. Johnson, Doubleday, New York, 1959.

Klein, Melanie, *Love, Guilt and Reparation and Other Works* (1937) Hogarth Press, London, 1975.

Korsakoff, Sergei, 'Psychic Disorder in Conjunction with Multiple Neuritis' (1889), trans. Maurice Victor and Paul Yakovlev, *Neurology* 5, 1955, Lancet Publications Inc., Minneapolis, Minnesota, 1955.

Kosslyn, Stephen and Sussman, Amy, 'Roles of Imagery in Perception: Or, There Is No Such Thing as Immaculate Perception', *The Cognitive Neurosciences* (1995), ed. Michael Gazzaniga, MIT Press, Cambridge, Mass. and London, 1995.

Laing, R.D., *Self and Others* (1961), Tavistock Publications, London, 1961.

Langer, Susan, *Philosophy In A New Key* (1942), Harvard University Press, Harvard, 1942.

LeDoux, Joseph, *The Emotional Brain* (1998), Weidenfeld and Nicolson, London, 1998.

Lewes, George Henry, *The Principles of Success in Literature* (1865), Gregg International Publishers, Farnborough, Hants., 1969.

Locke, John, *An Essay Concerning Human Understanding* (1690), J.M. Dent, London, 1961.

Lodge, David, *Thinks* (2001), Penguin, London, 2002.

Lorenz, Konrad, *On Aggression* (1963), trans. Marjorie Latzke, Methuen, London, 1966.

Mandukya Upanishad (c.500 BCE) in *Hindu Scriptures*, ed. Dominic Goodall, J.M. Dent, London, 1996.

Maudsley, Henry, *The Pathology of Mind, a Study of Its Distempers, Deformities and Disorders* (1895), Macmillan, London, 1895.

Melville, Herman, 'Letter to Evert A. Duyckinck, 3 March' (1849), *The Oxford Book of Letters*, ed. Frank Kermode and Anita Kermode, Oxford University Press, Oxford, 1995.

Milgram, Stanley, *Obedience To Authority: An Experimental View* (1974), Harper and Row, New York, 1974.

Mill, John Stuart, *Autobiography* (1873), Columbia University Press, New York, 1924.

Milton, John, *Paradise Lost* (1667), ed. A. Fowler, Longman, London, 1968.

Montaigne, Michel de, *Essays* (1587), trans. the editor of this volume, 2000.

Nagel, Thomas, *Mortal Questions* (1979), Cambridge University Press, Cambridge, 1979.

Nietzsche, Friedrich, *Thus Spoke Zarathustra* (1883), trans. R.J. Hollingdale, Penguin, Harmondsworth, 1961.

Nijinsky, Vaslav, 'On life', *The Diary of Vaslav Nijinsky* (1919), trans. Kyril Fitzlyon, Penguin, London, 2000.

Pavlov, Ivan Petrovitch, *Lectures on Conditioned Reflexes*, 2 vols (1940), trans. W.H. Gantt, Lawrence and Wishart, London, 1941.

Pearson, Samuel Burton, 'Brain-fever', *Medical and Physical Journal, IX* (1801), reprinted in *Edinburgh Medical and Surgical Journal* (1813).

Piaget, Jean, *The Child's Conception of the World* (1929), trans. Joan and Andrew Tomlinson, Routledge and Kegan Paul, London, 1973.

Plato, *Theaetetus* (c.340 BCE) and *The Republic* (c.400 BCE), trans. Jowett, B., *Dialogues of Plato*, Clarendon Press, Oxford, 1871.

Pratt, A, *Wild Flowers* (1853), Society for Promoting Christian Knowledge, London, 1853.

Priestley, Joseph, *Disquisitions Relating to Matter and Spirit* (1777), J. Johnson, London, 1777.

Prince, Morton, 'Association Neuroses', *Journal of Nervous and Mental Disease*, 16 (1891), in *Classics of American Psychiatry*, ed. John Brady, Warren Green, Inc., St Louis, 1975.

Proust, Marcel, *Time Regained* (1927), trans. Andreas Mayor, C., Random House, London, 1981.

Reynolds, J. Russel, 'Remarks on Paralysis, and other Disorders of Motion and Sensation Dependent on Idea' (1869), *British Medical Journal*, 6 November 1869.

Romanes, G.J., 'Mind and Motion' (1885), in *Body And Mind*, ed. G.Vesey, Unwin, London,1964.

Rossor, M.N., Warrington, E.K. and Cipolotti, L., 'The Isolation of Calculation Skills', *Journal of Neurology*, Springer-Verlag, Berlin, 1995.

Roth, Philip, *The Counterlife* (1986), Jonathan Cape, London, 1987.

Rousseau, Jean Jacques, *Emile* (1792), trans. Barbara Foxley, J.M. Dent, London, 1911.

Rush, Benjamin, 'Medical Inquiries and Observations upon the Diseases of the Mind' (1812), extracted in Richard Hunter and Ida Macalpine, *Three Hundred Years of Psychiatry 1535–1860*, Oxford University Press, Oxford, 1963.

Russell, Bertrand, *The Analysis of Mind* (1921), Routledge, London, 1997.

Ryle, Gilbert, *The Concept of Mind* (1949), Penguin Books, London, 1963.

Sacks, Oliver, 'Creativity, Imagination and Perception', Inaugural Lecture, Centre For The Mind, Australian National University (1998), 10 January 1998. Personal communication with the editor of the volume.

Sartre, Jean-Paul, *The Psychology of the Imagination* (1948), Rider, London, 1950.

Schlink, Bernhard, *The Reader* (1997), trans. Carol Brown Janeway, Phoenix House, London, 1997.

Schopenhauer, Arthur, *Supplementary Volume: The World As Will And Idea* (1844), trans. R.B. Haldane and J. Kemp, Kegan Paul, Trench, Trübner, London, 1893.

Scoville, William and Milner, Brenda, 'Loss of Recent Memory after Bilateral Hippocampal Lesions', *Journal of Neurology, Neurosurgery and Psychiatry*, 20(1957), BMJ Publishing Group, London, 1957.

Segal, Hanna, *Psychoanalysis and Freedom of Thought* (1977), Inaugural Lecture, Freud Memorial Visiting Professor of Psychoanalysis, University College, London in *The Work of Hanna Segal*, Jason Aronson, Inc., New York, 1981.

Shakespeare, William, *A Midsummer Night's Dream* (1594), Act 5, Scene 1.

Skinner, B.F., *Beyond Freedom and Dignity* (1971), Jonathan Cape, London, 1971.

Smith, K., Fairburn and C., Cowen, P., 'Relapse of depression after Rapid Depletion of Tryptophan', *Lancet*, 349 (1997), London, 29 March 1997.

Spinoza, Baruch, 'Ethics' (1662–1675, ed. Arnold Zweig, *The Living Thoughts of Spinoza*, Premier, New York 1959.

Stevenson, Robert Louis, 'On Falling In Love', *Virginibus Puerisque* (1881), J.M. Dent, London, 1963.

Stevenson, Robert Louis, 'A Chapter on Dreams', *Across the Plains* (1892), Chatto and Windus, London, 1920.

Stokes, Adrian, *A Game that Must Be Lost* (1973), Carcanet Press, Manchester, 1973.

Storr, Anthony, *Music And The Mind* (1992), HarperCollins, London, 1992.

Strawson, Galen, 'Esprit De Core' (2000), *Times Literary Supplement*, London, 27 October 2000.

Tausk, Victor, 'On the Origin of the "Influencing Machine" in Schizophrenia' (1919), trans., Dorian Feigenbaum in *The Psychoanalytic Quarterly*, II, 1933.

Teichman, Jenny, *The Mind and the Soul* (1974), Routledge and Kegan Paul, London, 1974.

Tolstoy, Leo, *Childhood, Boyhood and Youth* (1854), trans. Rosemary Edmonds, Penguin, Harmondsworth, 1964.

Watson, John Broadus, *Psychology from the Standpoint of a Behaviourist* (1919), Routledge, London, 1994.

Weiskrantz, Lawrence, 'Some Contributions of Neuropsychology of Vision and Memory to the Problem of Consciousness' (1988), eds. Marcel, A. and Bisiach, E., *Consciousness in Contemporary Science*, Oxford University Press, Oxford, 1988.

Wilde, Oscar, 'The Ballad of Reading Gaol' (1898) in *Modern Verse 1900–1950*, Oxford University Press, Oxford, 1940.

Willis, Thomas, *Two Discourses Concerning the Soul of Brutes, Which is the Vital and Sensitive of Man* (1672), trans. S. Pordage (1683), Scholar's Facsimiles and Reprints, Gainesville, FA, 1971.

Winnicott, D.W., 'Hate in the Counter-Transference'(1949), *International Journal of Psycho-Analysis*, XXX, London, 1949.

Wittgenstein, Ludwig, *Philosophical Investigations* (1953), trans. G. Anscombe, Blackwell, Oxford, 1953.

Woolf, Virginia, *The Common Reader* (1925), Hogarth Press, London, 1925.

Wordsworth, William, *The Prelude* (1799), ed. J. Wordsworth, M. H. Abrams and S. Gill, *The Prelude 1799, 1805, 1850: William Wordsworth*, W.W. Norton and Co, New York, 1979.

Zohar, Danah and Ian Marshall, *Spiritual Intelligence* (2000), Bloomsbury, London, 2000.

INDEX

Adler, Alfred: 348–50, and depth
  psychology xvi; and
  Schopenhauer, 300; and the
  unconscious, 300; and Vienna
  Psychoanalytic Society, 349;
  and Society for Individual
  Psychology, 349; and inferiority complex, 348–50
Aggression: and babies' emotions,
  159; and Melanie Klein, 159;
  and Joan Riviere, 159 fn; and
  Konrad Lorenz, 178
Aglioti, Salvatore, 45
Alcohol: and Delirium Tremens,
  36; and memory 79, 85; and
  Korsakoff's Psychosis, 85; its
  effect on conscience 295
Amnesia, 83–4, 85–8
Amygdala, xviii,134–6
Anal erotism, 299
Anger: evoking the power of
  speech, 47; a deadly sin 95; as
  interpretation of bodily function, 98; a sickness of the
  soul, 132; 129–34; lack of
  when own hatred known,
  141; overcoming through
  reflection, 169; effect on the
  body, 186; not a desire, 302;
  boy's identification with
  teacher's, 322; as a virtue,
  324; produced by false view

of inferiority, 362; destroys
  beauty, 362
Anima/Animus, 345–8
Anxiety: in Brain-fever, 37–8;
  imaginary, 46; Proust's disap-
  pears after eating madeleine,
  67; relieved by psycho-surgery,
  163; and copulation, 262;
  corresponding to three
  dangers, 319–21; defence
  against 321, 337–8
Archetype, 56,
Aristotle, 296, 305–6
Augustine, Saint, 78–9, 297
Authority: institutionalised,
  231, 332; of scripture, 243;
  scholastic and of the church,
  244; and conscience, 295,
  332–6

Bacon, Francis, 115–16
Bad: imagination, 5; luck of bridegrooms, 48; faith, 52; smell,
  145, 149; internal 'no-breast',
  188; name of introspection,
  240; internal objects, 188, 296,
  336; thoughts, 197, 218;
  appetite, 297; dreams, 347;
Beckett, Samuel, 258–60
Behaviourism, 211–22;
  manifesto, 217; discredited,
  237–8

A NOTE ON THE AUTHOR

Stephen Wilson is a Fellow of the Royal College of Psychiatrists and was honorary Senior Clinical Lecturer at the University of Oxford. He is a practising psychotherapist, both privately and as a consultant in the NHS. His other publications include *The Cradle of Violence: Essays on Psychiatry, Psychoanalysis and Literature* (1995), a brief biography of *Sigmund Freud* (1997) and *Introducing The Freud Wars* (2002). He has contributed reviews and articles to many papers including the *Times Literary Supplement*, the *Independent*, the *London Review of Books* and the *New York Times*.

A NOTE ON THE TYPE

The text of this book is set in Linotype Sabon, named after the type founder, Jacques Sabon. It was designed by Jan Tschichold and jointly developed by Linotype, Monotype and Stempel, in response to a need for a typeface available in identical form for mechanical hot metal composition and hand composition using foundry type.

Tschichold based his design for Sabon roman on a fount engraved by Garamond, and Sabon italic in a fount by Granjon. It was first used in 1966 and has proved an enduring modern classic.

11, 13
81-2
88-91
109
183-4+2
212-3
151-5
214-6
227-30
243
244-251
272-7-293
312-22
325-332
339-41
347-53
358-765